A
METHOD FOR PRAYER

WITH

SCRIPTURE EXPRESSIONS
PROPER TO BE USED UNDER EACH HEAD
1710 EDITION

A
METHOD FOR PRAYER

WITH

SCRIPTURE EXPRESSIONS
PROPER TO BE USED UNDER EACH HEAD
1710 EDITION

I am in the midst of the paradise of God

BY

REV. MATTHEW HENRY,

Minister of the gospel in Chester

LONDON
1710.

Paperback ISBN 978-1-304-44702-9
Hardcover ISBN 978-1-304-63556-3

Book description

This Prayerbook is the Puritan writer Matthew Henry's world renowned Christian
classic 'A Method for Prayer' -the 1710 edition. Professionally typeset in a classic prayerbook format with modernized spelling, and with all the cross references from Matthew
Henry's original prayerbook. With added devotional prayers and Bible study aids from
the publisher/author of this new blue expanded edition. –Featuring a collection of
devotional prayers to the Godhead of Jesus Christ called 'My Affection' –A poetic setting
of Psalm 119. –A Glossary containing 2400 words of the King James Bible. –And a daily
Bible reading plan.

TO THE READER

RELIGION is so much the business of our lives, and the worship of God so much the business of our religion, that what hath a sincere intention, and probable tendency, to promote and assist the acts of religious worship (I think) cannot be unacceptable to any that heartily wish well to the interests of God's kingdom among men: For if we have spiritual senses exercised, true devotion, that aspiring flame of pious affections to God, as far as in a judgment of charity we discern it in others (though in different shapes and dresses, which may seem uncouth to one another) cannot but appear beautiful and amiable, and as far as we feel it in our own breasts, cannot but be found very pleasant and comfortable.

Prayer is a principal branch of religious worship, which we are moved to by the very light of nature, and obliged to by some of its fundamental laws. *Pythagoras's* golden verses begin with this precept; Whatever men made a god of they prayed to, Deliver me, for thou art my god, *Isaiah 44:17*. Nay, whatever they prayed to, they made a god of—*Deos qui rogat ille facit*. It is a piece of respect and homage so exactly consonant to the natural ideas which all men have of God, that it is certain those that live without prayer live without God in the world.

Prayer is the solemn and religious offering up of devout acknowledgments and desires to God, or a sincere representation of holy affections, with a design to give unto God the glory due unto his name thereby, and to obtain from him promised favours, and both through the mediator. Our English word prayer is too strait, for that properly signifies petition, or request; whereas humble adorations of God, and thanksgivings to him, are as necessary in prayer, as any other part of it. The Greek word *Proseuche* from *Euche* is a vow directed to God. The Latin word *Votum* is used for prayer: Jonah's mariners with their sacrifices made vows; for prayer is to move and oblige ourselves, not to move or oblige God. *Clemens Alexandrinus, Strom 7. p. 722. Edit. Colon.* calls prayer (with an excuse for the boldness of the expression)

Homilia pros ton Theon, it is conversing with God: And it is the scope of a long discourse of his there to shew that his *ho gosnoticos, i.e.* his believer (for faith is called knowledge, and p. *719*. he makes his companions to be *hoi homoioos pepis teucotes*, those that have in like manner believed) lives a life of communion with God, and so is praying always; that he studies by his prayers continually to converse with God. Some (saith he) have their stated hours of prayer, but he *para holon euchatai ton bion*, prays all his life long. The scripture describes prayer to be our drawing near to God, lifting up our souls to him, pouring out our hearts before him.

This is the life and soul of prayer; but this soul in the present state must have a body, and that body must be such as becomes the soul, and is suited and adapted to it. Some words there must be, of the mind at least, in which, as in the smoke, this incense must ascend; not that God may understand us, for our thoughts afar off are known to him, but that we may the better understand ourselves.

A golden thread of heart-prayer must run through the web of the whole Christian life; we must be frequently addressing ourselves to God in short and sudden ejaculations, by which we must keep up our communion with God in providences and common actions, as well as in ordinances and religious services. Thus prayer must be *sparsim* (a sprinkling of it) in every duty, and our eyes must be ever towards the Lord.

In mental prayer thoughts are words, and they are the first-born of the soul, which are to be consecrated to God. But if when we pray alone we see cause for the better fixing of our minds, and exciting of our devotions, to clothe our conceptions with words; if the conceptions be the genuine products of the new nature, one would think words should not be far to seek: *Verbaque proevisam rem non invita sequuntur.* Nay if the groanings be such as cannot be uttered, he that searcheth the heart knows them to be the mind of the Spirit, and will accept of them, *Romans 8:26, 27.* and answer the voice of our breathing, *Lamentations 3:56.* Yet through the infirmity of the flesh, and the aptness of our hearts to wander and trifle, it is often necessary that words should go first, and be kept in mind for the directing and exciting of devout affections, and in order thereunto the assistance here offered I hope will be of some use.

When we join with others in prayer, who are our mouth to God, our minds must attend them, by an intelligent believing concurrence with that which is the sense and scope and substance of what they say, and affections working in us suitable thereunto: And this the scripture directs us to signify, by saying Amen, mentally if not vocally, at their giving of thanks, 1 *Corinthians 14:16*. And as far as our joining with them will permit, we may intermix pious ejaculations of our own, with their addresses, provided they be pertinent, that not the least fragment of praying time may be lost.

But he that is the mouth of others in prayer, whether in publick or private, and therein useth that *parrosia*, that freedom of speech, that holy liberty of prayer which is allowed us (and which we are sure many good Christians have found by experience to be very comfortable and advantageous in this duty) ought not only to consult the workings of his own heart (though them principally, as putting most life and spirit into the performance) but the edification also of those that join with him; and both in matter and words should have an eye to that; and for service in that case I principally design this endeavour.

That bright ornament of the church, the learned Dr. Wilkins, bishop of Chester, hath left us an excellent performance much of the same nature with this, in his discourse concerning the gift of prayer; which, some may think, makes this of mine unnecessary: But the multiplying of books of devotion is what few serious Christians will complain of: And as on the one hand I am sure those that have this poor essay of mine will still find great advantage by that: so on the other hand I think those who have *that* may yet find some further assistance by *this*.

It is desirable that our prayers should be copious and full: Our burdens, cares, and wants are many, so are our sins and mercies. The promises are numerous and very rich, our God gives liberally, and hath bid us open our mouths wide, and he will fill them, will satisfy them with good things. We are not straitened in him, why then should we be stinted and straitened in our own bosoms? Christ had taught his disciples the Lord's prayer, and yet tells them *(John 16:24)* that hitherto they had asked nothing, *i.e.* nothing in comparison with what they should ask when the Spirit should be poured out, to abide with the church for ever; and they should see greater things than these. Then ask, and ye shall receive, that your joy may be full. We are encouraged to be particular in prayer, and in every thing to make our requests known to God, as we ought also to be particular in the adoration of the divine perfections, in the confession of our sins, and our thankful acknowledgments of God's mercies.

But since at the same time we cannot go over the tenth part of the particulars which are fit to be the matter of prayer, without making the duty burdensome to the flesh which is weak, even where the spirit is willing (an extreme which ought carefully to be avoided) and without danger of intrenching upon other religious exercises, it will be requisite that what is but briefly touched upon at one time, should be enlarged upon at another time: And herein this storehouse of materials for prayer may be of use to put us in remembrance of our several errands at the throne of grace, that none may be quite forgotten.

And it is requisite to the decent performance of the duty, that some proper method be observed, not only that what is said be good, but that it be said in its proper place and time; and that we offer not any thing to the glorious majesty of heaven and earth, which is confused, impertinent, and indigested. Care must be taken then more than ever, that we be not rash with our mouth, nor hasty to utter any thing before God; that we say not what comes uppermost, nor use such repetitions as evidence not the fervency, but the barrenness and slightness of our spirits; but that the matters we are dealing with God about being of such vast importance, we observe a decorum in our words, that they be well chosen, well weighed, and well placed.

And as it is good to be methodical in prayer, so it is to be sententious: The Lord's prayer is remarkably so; and David's psalms, and many of St. Paul's prayers which we have in his epistles: We must consider that the greatest part of those that join with us in prayer will be in danger of losing or mistaking the sense, if the period be long, and the parentheses many, and in this as in other things, they that are strong ought to bear the infirmities of the weak: Jacob must lead as the children and flocks can follow.

As to the words and expressions we use in prayer, though I have here in my enlargements upon the several heads of prayer confined myself almost wholly to scripture language, because I would give an instance of the sufficiency of the scripture to furnish us for every good work, yet I am far from thinking but that it is convenient and often necessary to use other expressions in prayer besides those that are purely scriptural; only I would advise that the sacred dialect be most used, and made familiar to us and others in our dealing about sacred things; that language Christian people are most accustomed to, most affected with, and will most readily agree to; and where the scriptures are opened and explained to the people in the ministry of the word, scripture language will be most intelligible, and the sense of it best apprehended. This is sound speech that cannot be condemned. And those that are able to do it may do well to enlarge by way of descant or paraphrase upon the scriptures they make use of; still speaking according to that rule, and comparing spiritual things with spiritual, that they may illustrate each other.

And it is not to be reckoned a perverting of scripture, but is agreeable to the usage of many divines, especially the fathers, and I think is warranted by divers quotations in the new testament out of the old, to allude to a scripture phrase, and to make use of it by way of accommodation to another sense than what was the first intendment of it, provided it agree with the analogy of faith. As for instance, those words, *Psalm 87:7. All my springs are in thee,* may very fitly be applied to God, though there it appears by the feminine article in the original, to be meant of *Sion*: Nor has it ever been thought any wrong to the scripture phrase to pray for the blessings of the upper *springs* and the nether *springs,* though the expression from whence it is borrowed, *Judges 1:15.* hath no reference at all to what we mean; but by common use every one knows the signification, and many are pleased with the significancy of it.

Divers heads of prayer may no doubt be added to those which I have here put together, and many scripture expressions too, under each head (for I have only set down such as first occurred to my thoughts) and many other expressions too, not in scripture words, which may be very comprehensive and emphatical, and apt to excite devotion. And perhaps those who covet earnestly this excellent gift, and covet to excel in it, may find it of use to them to have such a book as this interleaved, in which to insert such other heads and expressions as they think will be most agreeable to them, and are wanting here. And though I have here recommended a good method for prayer, and that which has been generally approved, yet I am far from thinking we should always tie ourselves to it; that may be varied as well as the expression: Thanksgiving may very aptly be put sometimes before confession or petition, or our intercessions for others before our petitions for ourselves, as in the Lord's prayer. Sometimes one of these parts of prayer may be enlarged upon much more than another; or they may be decently interwoven in some other method: *Ars est celare artem.*

There are those (I doubt not) who at some times have their hearts so wonderfully elevated and enlarged in prayer, above themselves at other times; such a fixedness and fulness of thought, such a fervour of pious and devout affections, the product of which is such a fluency and variety of pertinent and moving expressions, and in such a just and natural method, that then to have an eye to such a scheme as this would be a hindrance to them, and would be in danger to cramp and straiten them: If the heart be full of its good matter, it may make the tongue as the pen of a ready writer. But this is a case that rarely happens, and ordinarily there is need of proposing to ourselves a certain method to go by in prayer, that the service may be performed decently and in order; in which yet one would avoid that which looks too formal. A man may write straight without having his paper ruled.

Some few forms of prayer I have added in the last chapter, for the use of those who need such helps, and that know not how to do as well or better without them; and therefore I have calculated them for families. If any think them too long, let them observe that they are divided into many paragraphs, and those mostly independent, so that when brevity is necessary some paragraphs may be omitted.

But after all, the intention and close application of the mind, the lively exercises of faith and love, and the outgoings of holy desire towards God, are so essentially necessary to prayer, that without these in sincerity, the best and most proper language is but a lifeless image. If we had the tongue of men and angels, and have not the heart of humble serious Christians in prayer, we are but as a sounding brass and a tinkling cymbal. It is only the effectual fervent prayer, the *Deesis energumene*, the in-wrought, in-laid prayer that avails much. Thus therefore we ought to approve ourselves to God in the integrity of our hearts, whether we pray by, or without a precomposed form.

When I had finished the third volume of expositions of the Bible, which is now in the press; before I proceed, as I intend, in an humble dependance on the divine providence and grace, to the fourth volume, I was willing to take a little time from that work to this poor performance, in hopes it might be of some service to the generation of them that seek God, that seek the face of the God of Jacob: And if any good Christians receive assistance from it in their devotions, I hope they will not deny me one request, which is, that they will pray for me, that I may obtain mercy of the Lord to be found among the faithful watchmen on Jerusalem's walls, who never hold their peace day or night, but give themselves to the word and prayer, that at length I may finish my course with joy.

Matth. Henry.

CHESTER, Mar. 25.
        1710.

CONTENTS

xiv

1

Adoration

Adoration

Our spirits being composed into a very reverent serious frame, our thoughts gathered in, and all that is within us charged in the name of the great God carefully to attend the solemn and awful service that lies before us, and to keep close to it, we must with a fixed intention and application of mind, and an active lively faith, set the Lord before us, see His eye upon us, and set ourselves in His special presence, presenting ourselves to Him, as living sacrifices, which we desire may be holy and acceptable, and a reasonable service; and then bind these sacrifices with cords to the horns of the altar, in such thoughts as these: Romans 12:1. Psalm 118:27.

LET us now lift up our hearts with our eyes and our hands unto God in the heavens. *Lamentations 3:41. John 17:1.*

Let us stir up ourselves to take hold on God, to seek his face, and to give him the glory due unto his name. *Isaiah 64:7. Psalm 27:8. Psalm 29:2.*

Unto thee, O Lord, do we lift up our souls. *Psalm 25:1.*

Let us now, with humble boldness, enter into the Holiest by the blood of Jesus, in the new and living way, which he hath consecrated for us through the vail. *Hebrews 10:19, 20.*

Let us now attend upon the Lord without distraction, and let not our hearts be far from him when we draw nigh to him with our mouths, and honour him with our lips. *1 Corinthians 7:35. Matthew 15:8.*

Let us now worship God who is a Spirit, in the spirit and in truth; for such the Father seeks to worship him. *John 4:24, 23.*

Having thus engaged our hearts to approach unto God, *Jeremiah 30:21.*

WE MUST SOLEMNLY ADDRESS OURSELVES TO THAT INFINITELY GREAT AND GLORIOUS BEING WITH WHOM WE HAVE TO DO, AS THOSE THAT ARE POSSESSED WITH A FULL BELIEF OF HIS PRESENCE, AND A HOLY AWE AND REVERENCE OF HIS MAJESTY, WHICH WE MAY DO IN SUCH EXPRESSIONS AS THESE

oly, holy, holy, Lord God Almighty, which art and wast, and art to come. *Revelation 4:8.*

O thou whose name alone is JEHOVAH, and who art the most high over all the earth. *Psalm 83:18.*

O God, thou art our God, early will we seek thee; Our God, and we will praise thee; our fathers God, and we will exalt thee. *Psalm 63:1. Exodus 15:2.*

O thou who art the true God, the living God, the one only living and true God, and the everlasting king. THE LORD OUR GOD WHO IS ONE LORD. *Jeremiah 10:10. 1 Thessalonians 1:9. Deuteronomy 6:4.*

— And we may thus distinguish ourselves from the worshippers of false gods.

The idols of the heathen are silver and gold, they are vanity and a lie, the work of mens hands; they that make them are like unto them, and so is every one that trusteth in them. But the portion of Jacob is not like them, for he is the former of all things, and Israel is the rod of his inheritance, the Lord of hosts is his name; God over all, blessed for evermore. *Psalm 115:4, 8. Jeremiah 10:15, 16. Romans 9:5.*

Their rock is not our Rock, even the enemies themselves being judges, for he is the Rock of ages, THE LORD JEHOVAH, with whom is everlasting strength. Whose name shall endure for ever, and his memorial unto all generations, when the gods that have not made the heavens and the earth, shall perish from off the earth, and from under those heavens. *Deuteronomy 32:31. Isaiah 26:4. Psalm 135:13. Jeremiah 10:11.*

WE MUST REVERENTLY ADORE GOD AS A BEING TRANSCENDENTLY BRIGHT AND BLESSED, SELF-EXISTENT AND SELF-SUFFICIENT, AN INFINITE AND ETERNAL SPIRIT, THAT HAS ALL PERFECTIONS IN HIMSELF, AND GIVE HIM THE GLORY OF HIS TITLES AND ATTRIBUTES

Lord our God, thou art very great, thou art clothed with honour and majesty, thou coverest thyself with light as with a garment, and yet as to us makest darkness thy pavilion, for we cannot order our speech by reason of darkness. *Psalm 104:1, 2. Psalm 18:11. Job 37:19.*

This is the message which we have heard of thee, and we set to our seal that it is true, that God is light, and in him is no darkness at all: And that God is love, and they that dwell in love, dwell in God, and God in them. *1 John 1:5. John 3:33. 1 John 4:16.*

Thou art the Father of lights, with whom is no variableness or shadow of turning, and from whom proceedeth every good and perfect gift. *James 1:17.*

Thou art the blessed and only Potentate; the King of kings, and Lord of lords, who only hast immortality, dwelling in the light which no man can approach unto, whom no man hath seen nor can see. *1 Timothy 6:15, 16.*

— *We must acknowledge His being to be unquestionable and past dispute.*

The heavens declare thy glory, O God, and the firmament sheweth thy handy work, and by the things that are made is clearly seen and understood thine eternal power and GODHEAD. So that they are fools without excuse, who say there is no God; for verily there is a reward for the righteous, verily there is a God that judgeth in the earth, and in heaven too. *Psalm 19:1. Romans 1:20. Psalm 14:1. Psalm 58:11.*

We therefore come to thee, believing that thou art, and that thou art the powerful and bountiful rewarder of them that diligently seek thee. *Hebrews 11:6.*

— Yet we must own His nature to be incomprehensible.

We cannot by searching find out God, we cannot find out the Almighty unto perfection. *Job 11:7.*

Great is the Lord, and greatly to be praised, and his greatness is unsearchable. *Psalm 145:3.*

Who can utter the mighty acts of the Lord, who can shew forth all his praise? *Psalm 106:2.*

— And His perfections to be matchless and without compare.

Who is a God like unto thee, glorious in holiness, fearful in praises, doing wonders? *Exodus 15:11.*

Who in the heaven can be compared unto the Lord? who among the sons of the mighty can be likened unto the Lord? O Lord God of hosts, who is a strong Lord like unto thee, or to thy faithfulness round about thee? *Psalm 89:6, 8.*

Among the gods there is none like unto thee, O Lord, neither are there any works like unto thy works: For thou art great, and dost wondrous things; thou art God alone. *Psalm 86:8, 10.*

There is not any creature that has an arm like God, or can thunder with a voice like him. *Job 40:9.*

— And that He is infinitely above us and all other beings.

Thou art God and not man; hast not eyes of flesh, nor seest thou as man seeth: Thy days are not as the days of man, nor thy years as man's days. *Hosea 11:9. Job 10:4, 5.*

As heaven is high above the earth, so are thy thoughts above our thoughts, and thy ways above our ways. *Isaiah 55:9.*

All nations before thee are as a drop of the bucket, or the small dust of the balance, and thou takest up the isles as a very little thing: They are as nothing, and are counted to thee less than nothing, and vanity. *Isaiah 40:15, 17.*

— Particularly in our adorations we must acknowledge,

1.   *That He is an eternal immutable God, without beginning of days, or end of life, or change of time.*

Thou art the King eternal, immortal, invisible. *1 Timothy 1:17.*

Before the mountains were brought forth, or ever thou hadst formed the earth and the world, from everlasting to everlasting thou art God; the same yesterday, to day, and for ever. *Psalm 90:2. Hebrews 13:8.*

Of old hast thou laid the foundation of the earth, and the heavens are the works of thy hands: They shall perish, but thou shalt endure; yea all of them shall wax old like a garment, as a vesture shalt thou change them, and they shall be changed; but thou art the same, and thy years shall have no end. *Psalm 102:25, 26, 27.*

Thou art God, and changest not; therefore is it that we are not consumed. *Malachi 3:6.*

Art thou not from everlasting, O Lord our God, our Holy One? The everlasting God, even the Lord, the Creator of the ends of the earth, who faintest not, neither art weary; there is no searching out of thine understanding. *Habakkuk 1:12. Isaiah 40:28.*

2. *That He is present in all places, and there is no place in which He is included, or out of which He is excluded.*

Thou art a God at hand, and a God afar off; None can hide himself in secret places that thou canst not see him, for thou fillest heaven and earth. *Jeremiah 23:23, 24.*

Thou art not far from every one of us. *Acts 17:27.*

We cannot go any whither from thy presence, or flee from thy spirit: If we ascend into heaven, thou art there; if we make our bed in hell, in the depths of the earth, behold thou art there; if we take the wings of the morning, and dwell in the uttermost parts of the sea, even there shall thy hand lead us, and thy right hand shall hold us, that we cannot out-run thee. *Psalm 139:7-10.*

3. *That He hath a perfect knowledge of all persons and things, and sees them all, even that which is most secret, at one clear, certain, and unerring view.*

All things are naked and open before the eyes of him with whom we have to do; even the thoughts and intents of the heart. *Hebrews 4:13, 12.*

Thine eyes are in every place beholding the evil and the good; they run to and fro through the earth, that thou mayest shew thyself strong on the behalf of those whose hearts are upright with thee. *Proverbs 15:3. 2 Chronicles 16:9.*

Thou searchest the heart, and triest the reins, that thou mayest give to every man according to his ways, and according to the fruit of his doings. *Jeremiah 17:10.*

O God, thou hast searched us and known us, thou knowest our down-sitting and our up-rising, and understandest our thoughts afar off: Thou compassest our path and our lying down, and art acquainted with all our ways: There is not a word in our tongue, but lo, O Lord, thou knowest it altogether. Such knowledge is too wonderful for us, it is high, we cannot attain unto it. *Psalm 139:1-4, 6.*

Darkness and light are both alike to thee. *Psalm 139:12.*

4.   *That His wisdom is unsearchable, and the counsels and designs of it cannot be fathomed.*

Thine understanding, O Lord, is infinite, for thou tellest the number of the stars, and callest them all by their names. *Psalm 147:5, 4.*

Thou art wonderful in counsel, and excellent in working. Wise in heart, and mighty in strength. *Isaiah 28:29. Job 9:4.*

O Lord, how manifold are thy works, in wisdom hast thou made them all; all according to the counsel of thine own will. *Psalm 104:24. Ephesians 1:11.*

O the depth of the wisdom and knowledge of God! how unsearchable are his judgments, and his ways past finding out. *Romans 11:33.*

5.   *That His sovereignty is uncontestable, and He is the owner and absolute Lord of all.*

The heavens, even the heavens are thine, and all the hosts of them: The earth is thine, and the fulness thereof, the world and they that dwell therein. In thy hand are the deep places of the earth, and the strength of the hills is thine also: The sea is thine, for thou madest it, and thy hands formed the dry land: All the beasts of the forest are thine, and the cattle upon a thousand hills: Thou art therefore a great God, and a great King above all gods. *Psalm 115:16. Psalm 24:1. Psalm 95:4, 5. Psalm 50:10, 11. Psalm 95:3.*

In thy hand is the soul of every living thing, and the breath of all mankind. *Job 12:10.*

Thy dominion is an everlasting dominion, and thy kingdom is from generation to generation: Thou dost according to thy will in the armies of heaven, and among the inhabitants of the earth, and none can stay thy hand, or say unto thee, What doest thou, or Why doest thou so? *Daniel 4:34, 35.*

6.   *That His power is irresistible, and the operations of it cannot be controlled.*

We know, O God, that thou canst do every thing, and that no thought can be with-holden from thee: Power belongs to thee; And with thee nothing is impossible. *Job 42:2. Psalm 62:11. Luke 1:37.*

All power is thine both in heaven and in earth. *Matthew 28:18.*

Thou killest and thou makest alive, thou woundest and thou healest, neither is there any that can deliver out of thy hand. *Deuteronomy 32:39.*

What thou hast promised thou art able also to perform. *Romans 4:21.*

7. *That He is a God of unspotted purity and perfect rectitude.*

Thou art holy, O thou that inhabitest the praises of Israel: Holy and reverend is thy name; and we give thanks at the remembrance of thy holiness. *Psalm 22:3. Psalm 111:9. Psalm 30:4.*

Thou art of purer eyes than to behold iniquity, neither shall evil dwell with thee. *Habakkuk 1:13. Psalm 5:4.*

Thou art the Rock, thy work is perfect, all thy ways are truth and judgment; a God of truth, and in whom there is no iniquity. Thou art our rock, and there is no unrighteousness in thee. *Deuteronomy 32:4. Psalm 92:15.*

Thou art holy in all thy works, and holiness becomes thy house, O Lord, for ever. *Psalm 145:17. Psalm 93:5.*

8. *That He is just in the administration of His government, and never did, nor ever will do wrong to any of His creatures.*

Righteous art thou, O God, when we plead with thee, and wilt be justified when thou speakest, and clear when thou judgest. *Jeremiah 12:1. Psalm 51:4.*

Far be it from God that he should do wickedness, and from the Almighty that he should commit iniquity; for the work of a man shall he render unto him. *Job 34:10, 11.*

Thy righteousness is as the great mountains, even then when thy judgments are a great deep! And though clouds and darkness are round about thee, yet judgment and justice are the habitation of thy throne. *Psalm 36:6. Psalm 97:2.*

9. *That His truth is inviolable, and the treasures of His goodness inexhaustible.*

Thou art good, and thy mercy endures for ever. Thy loving-kindness is great towards us, and thy truth endureth to all generations. *Psalm 136:1. Psalm 117:2. Psalm 100:5.*

Thou hast proclaimed thy name: The Lord, The Lord God, merciful and gracious, slow to anger, abundant in goodness and truth, keeping mercy for thousands, forgiving iniquity, transgression and sin. And this name of thine is our strong tower. *Exodus 34:6, 7. Proverbs 18:10.*

Thou art good and dost good; good to all, and thy tender mercy is over all thy works. But truly God is in a special manner good to Israel, even to them that are of a clean heart. *Psalm 119:68. Psalm 145:9. Psalm 73:1.*

O that thou wouldst cause thy goodness to pass before us; that we may taste and see that the Lord is good; and his loving kindness may be always before our eyes. *Exodus 33:19. Psalm 34:8. Psalm 26:3.*

10.   *Lastly, that when we have said all we can of the glorious perfections of the divine nature, we fall infinitely short of the merit of the subject.*

Lo these are but parts of thy ways, and how little a portion is heard of God! But the thunder of his power who can understand? *Job 26:14.*

Touching the Almighty we cannot find him out, he is excellent in power and in judgment, and in plenty of justice; and he is exalted far above all blessing and praise. *Job 37:23. Nehemiah 9:5.*

WE MUST GIVE TO GOD THE PRAISE OF THAT SPLENDOR AND GLORY WHEREIN HE IS PLEASED TO MANIFEST HIMSELF IN THE UPPER WORLD

THOU hast prepared thy throne in the heavens, and it is a throne of glory, high and lifted up, and before thee the seraphims cover their faces. And it is in compassion to us that thou holdest back the face of that throne, and spreadest a cloud upon it. *Psalm 103:19. Isaiah 6:1, 2. Job 26:9.*

Thou makest thine angels spirits, and thy ministers a flame of fire. Thousand thousands of them minister unto thee, and ten thousand times ten thousand stand before thee, to do thy pleasure: They excel in strength, and hearken to the voice of thy word. And we are come by faith and hope and holy love into a spiritual communion with that innumerable company of angels, and the spirits of just men made perfect, even to the general assembly and church of the first-born, in the heavenly Jerusalem. *Psalm 104:4. Daniel 7:10. Psalm 103:21, 20. Hebrews 12:22, 23.*

WE MUST GIVE GLORY TO HIM AS THE CREATOR OF THE WORLD, AND THE GREAT PROTECTOR, BENEFACTOR AND RULER OF THE WHOLE CREATION

THOU art worthy, O Lord, to receive blessing, and honour, and glory, and power; for thou hast created all things, and for thy pleasure, and for thy praise they are and were created. *Revelation 4:11.*

We worship him that made the heaven and the earth, the sea and the fountains of waters; who spake and it was done, who commanded and it stood fast; who said, Let there be light, and there was light; Let there be a firmament, and he made the firmament; and he made all very good; and they continue this day according to his ordinance; for all are his servants. *Revelation 14:7. Psalm 33:9. Genesis 1:3, 6, 7, 31. Psalm 119:91.*

The day is thine, the night also is thine; thou hast prepared the light and the sun: Thou hast set all the borders of the earth, thou hast made summer and winter. *Psalm 74:16, 17.*

Thou upholdest all things by the word of thy power, and by thee all things consist. *Hebrews 1:3. Colossians 1:17.*

The earth is full of thy riches; so is the great and wide sea also. The eyes of all wait upon thee, and thou givest them their meat in due season: Thou openest thy hand, and satisfiest the desire of every living thing. Thou preservest man and beast, and givest food to all flesh. *Psalm 104:24, 25. Psalm 145:15, 16. Psalm 36:6. Psalm 136:25.*

Thou, even thou art Lord alone; thou hast made heaven, the heaven of heavens, with all their host, the earth and all things that are therein, the seas and all that is therein, and thou preservest them all: And the host of heaven worshippeth thee, whose kingdom ruleth over all. *Nehemiah 9:6. Psalm 103:19.*

A sparrow falls not to the ground without thee. *Matthew 10:29.*

Thou madest man at first of the dust of the ground, and breathedst into him the breath of life, and so he became a living soul. *Genesis 2:7.*

And thou hast made of that one blood, all nations of men, to dwell on all the face of the earth, and hast determined the times before appointed, and the bounds of their habitation. *Acts 17:26.*

Thou art the most High, who rulest in the kingdom of men, and givest it to whomsoever thou wilt; for from thee every man's judgment proceeds. *Daniel 4:25. Proverbs 29:26.*

Hallelujah, the Lord God omnipotent reigns, and doth all according to the counsel of his own will, to the praise of his own glory. *Revelation 19:6. Ephesians 1:11, 12.*

WE MUST GIVE HONOUR TO THE THREE PERSONS IN THE GODHEAD DISTINCTLY, TO THE FATHER, THE SON, AND THE HOLY GHOST, THAT GREAT AND SACRED NAME INTO WHICH WE WERE BAPTIZED, AND IN WHICH WE ASSEMBLE FOR RELIGIOUS WORSHIP, IN COMMUNION WITH THE UNIVERSAL CHURCH

E pay our homage to the three that bear record in heaven, the Father, the Word, and the Holy Ghost; for these three are one. *1 John 5:7.*

We adore thee, O Father, Lord of heaven and earth; and the eternal Word, who was in the beginning with God, and was God, by whom all things were made, and without whom was not any thing made that was made, and who in the fulness of time was made flesh, and dwelt among us, and shewed his glory, the glory as of the only begotten of the Father, full of grace and truth. *Matthew 11:25. John 1:1, 2, 3. Galatians 4:4. John 1:14.*

And since it is the will of God that all men should honour the Son as they honour the Father, we adore him as the brightness of his Father's glory, and the express image of his person; herein joining with the angels of God, who were all bid to worship him. *John 5:23. Hebrews 1:3, 6.*

We pay our homage to the exalted Redeemer, who is the faithful witness, the first begotten from the dead, and the prince of the kings of the earth, confessing that Jesus Christ is Lord, to the glory of God the Father. *Revelation 1:5. Philippians 2:11.*

We also worship the Holy Ghost the Comforter, whom the Son hath sent from the Father, even the Spirit of truth who proceedeth from the Father, and who is sent to teach us all things, and to bring all things to our remembrance; who indited the scriptures, holy men of God writing them as they were moved by the Holy Ghost. *John 15:26. John 14:26. 2 Peter 1:21.*

WE MUST ACKNOWLEDGE OUR DEPENDANCE UPON GOD, AND OUR OBLIGATIONS TO HIM, AS OUR CREATOR, PRESERVER, AND BENEFACTOR

THOU, O God, madest us, and not we ourselves, and therefore we are not our own, but thine, thy people and the sheep of thy pasture; Let us therefore worship, and fall down and kneel before the Lord our maker. *Psalm 100:3. 1 Corinthians 6:19. Psalm 95:6.*

Thou, Lord, art the former of our bodies, and they are fearfully and wonderfully made, and curiously wrought. Thine eye did see our substance yet being imperfect, and in thy book all our members were written, which in continuance were fashioned, when as yet there was none of them. *Psalm 139:14, 15, 16.*

Thou hast clothed us with skin and flesh, thou hast fenced us with bones and sinews; Thou hast granted us life and favour, and thy visitation preserves our spirits. *Job 10:11, 12.*

Thou art the Father of our spirits; for thou formest the spirit of man with him, and madest us these souls. The Spirit of God hath made us, and the breath of the Almighty hath given us life. Thou puttest wisdom in the inward part, and givest understanding to the heart. *Hebrews 12:9. Zechariah 12:1. Jeremiah 38:16. Job 33:4. Job 38:36.*

Thou art God our maker, who teachest us more than the beasts of the earth, and makest us wiser than the fowls of heaven. *Job 35:10, 11.*

We are the clay, and thou our potter, we are the work of thy hand. *Isaiah 64:8.*

Thou art he that tookest us out of the womb, and keepest us in safety when we were at our mother's breasts; We have been cast upon thee from the womb, and holden up by thee, thou art our God from our mother's bowels, and therefore our praise shall be continually of thee. *Psalm 22:9, 10. Psalm 71:6.*

In thee, O God, we live and move, and have our being; for we are thine offspring. *Acts 17:28.*

In thy hand our breath is, and thine are all our ways; for the way of man is not in himself, neither is it in man that walketh to direct his steps; but our times are in thy hand. *Daniel 5:23. Jeremiah 10:23. Psalm 31:15.*

Thou art the God that hast fed us all our life long unto this day, and redeemed us from all evil. *Genesis 48:15, 16.*

It is of thy mercies that we are not consumed, even because thy compassions fail not, they are new every morning, great is thy faithfulness. *Lamentations 3:22, 23.*

If thou take away our breath we die, and return to the dust out of which we were taken. *Psalm 104:29, 30.*

Who is he that saith and it cometh to pass, if thou commandest it not? Out of thy mouth, O most High, both evil and good proceed. *Lamentations 3:37, 38.*

WE MUST AVOUCH THIS GOD TO BE OUR GOD, AND OWN OUR RELATION TO HIM, HIS DOMINION OVER US, AND PROPRIETY IN US

UR souls have said unto the Lord, Thou art our Lord, though our goodness extendeth not unto thee, neither if we are righteous art thou the better. *Psalm 16:2. Job 35:7.*

Thou art our King, O God: Other lords besides thee have had dominion over us, but from henceforth by thee only will we make mention of thy name. *Psalm 44:4. Isaiah 26:13.*

We avouch the Lord this day to be our God, to walk in his ways, and to keep his statutes, and his commandments, and his judgments, and to hearken to his voice, and give ourselves unto him to be his peculiar people as he hath promised, that we may be a holy people unto the Lord our God; and may be unto him for a name, and for a praise, and for a glory. *Deuteronomy 26:17, 18, 19. Jeremiah 13:11.*

O Lord, truly we are thy servants, we are thy servants born in thy house, and thou hast loosed our bonds; we are bought with a price, and therefore we are not our own; but yield ourselves unto the Lord, and join ourselves to him in an everlasting covenant that shall never be forgotten. *Psalm 116:16. 1 Corinthians 6:20, 19. 2 Chronicles 30:8. Jeremiah 50:5.*

We are thine, save us; for we seek thy precepts: It is thine own, Lord, that we give thee, and that which cometh of thine hand. *Psalm 119:94. 1 Chronicles 29:16.*

WE MUST ACKNOWLEDGE IT AN UNSPEAKABLE FAVOUR, AND AN INESTIMABLE PRIVILEGE, THAT WE ARE NOT ONLY ADMITTED, BUT INVITED AND ENCOURAGED TO DRAW NIGH TO GOD IN PRAYER

THOU hast commanded us to pray always, with all prayer and supplication, with thanksgiving, and to watch thereunto with all perseverance and supplication for all saints; to continue in prayer; and in every thing with prayer and supplication to make our requests known to God. *Ephesians 6:18. Colossians 4:2. Philippians 4:6.*

Thou hast directed us to ask and seek and knock, and hast promised that we shall receive, we shall find, and it shall be opened to us. *Matthew 7:7, 8.*

Thou hast appointed us a great high priest, in whose name we may come boldly to the throne of grace, that we may find mercy and grace to help in time of need. *Hebrews 4:14-16.*

Thou hast assured us that while the sacrifice of the wicked is an abomination to the Lord, the prayer of the upright is his delight; and that he that offers praise glorifies thee, and the sacrifice of thanksgiving shall please the Lord better than that of an ox or bullock that has horns and hoofs. *Proverbs 15:8. Psalm 50:23. Psalm 69:30, 31.*

Thou art he that hearest prayer, and therefore unto thee shall all flesh come. *Psalm 65:2.*

Thou sayest, Seek ye my face, and our hearts answer, Thy face, Lord, will we seek. For should not a people seek unto their God? Whither shall we go but to thee? Thou hast the words of eternal life. *Psalm 27:8. Isaiah 8:19. John 6:68.*

WE MUST EXPRESS THE SENSE WE HAVE OF OUR OWN MEANNESS AND UNWORTHINESS TO DRAW NEAR TO GOD, AND SPEAK TO HIM

BUT will God in very deed dwell with man upon the earth? that God whom the heaven of heavens cannot contain, with man that is a worm, and the son of man that is a worm. *2 Chronicles 6:18. Job 25:6.*

Who are we, O Lord God, and what is our father's house, that thou hast brought us hitherto, to present ourselves before the Lord; that we have through Christ an access by one Spirit unto the Father: And yet as if this had been a small thing in thy sight, thou hast spoken concerning thy servants for a great while to come, and is this the manner of men, O Lord God? *2 Samuel 7:18. Ephesians 2:18. 2 Samuel 7:19.*

What is man that thou art thus mindful of him, and the son of man that thou visitest him? and dost thus magnify him. *Psalm 8:4. Job 7:17.*

O let not the Lord be angry, if we that are but dust and ashes take upon us to speak unto the Lord of glory. *Genesis 18:30, 27.*

We are not worthy of the least of all the mercies, and of all the truth which thou hast shewed unto thy servants; nor is it meet to take the childrens bread, and cast it to such as we are; yet the dogs eat of the crumbs which fall from their master's table: And thou art rich in mercy to all that call upon thee. *Genesis 32:10. Matthew 15:26, 27. Romans 10:12.*

WE MUST HUMBLY PROFESS THE DESIRE OF OUR HEARTS TOWARDS GOD AS OUR FELICITY AND PORTION, AND THE FOUNTAIN OF LIFE AND ALL GOOD TO US

WHOM have we in heaven but thee; and there is none upon earth that we desire besides thee, or in comparison of thee: When our flesh and our heart fail, be thou the strength of our heart, and our portion for ever; the portion of our inheritance in the other world, and of our cup in this, and then we will say that the lines are fallen to us in pleasant places, and that we have a goodly heritage. *Psalm 73:25, 26. Psalm 16:5, 6.*

The desire of our souls is to thy name, and to the remembrance of thee; with our souls have we desired thee in the night, and with our spirits within us will we seek thee early. *Isaiah 26:8, 9.*

As the hart panteth after the water brooks, so panteth our soul after thee, O God; our soul thirsteth for God, for the living God; who will command his loving-kindness in the day-time, and in the night his song shall be with us, and our prayer to the God of our life. *Psalm 42:1, 2, 8.*

O that we may come hungering and thirsting after righteousness; for thou fillest the hungry with good things, but the rich thou sendest empty away. *Matthew 5:6. Luke 1:53.*

O that our souls may thirst for thee, and our flesh long for thee in a dry and thirsty land, where no water is, that we may see thy power and thy glory, as we have seen thee in the sanctuary. Thy loving-kindness is better than life; our souls shall be satisfied with that as with marrow and fatness, and then our mouths shall praise thee with joyful lips. *Psalm 63:1, 2, 3, 5.*

WE MUST LIKEWISE PROFESS OUR BELIEVING HOPE AND CONFIDENCE IN GOD, AND HIS ALL-SUFFICIENCY, IN HIS POWER, PROVIDENCE, AND PROMISE

N thee, O God, do we put our trust, let us never be ashamed; yea let none that wait on thee be ashamed. *Psalm 31:1. Psalm 25:3.*

Truly our souls wait upon God; from him cometh our salvation; he only is our rock and our salvation: In him is our glory, our strength, and our refuge, and from him is our expectation. *Psalm 62:1, 2, 7, 5.*

When refuge fails us, and none cares for our souls, we cry unto thee, O Lord; Thou art our refuge and our portion in the land of the living. *Psalm 142:4, 5.*

Some trust in chariots, and some in horses, but we will remember the name of the Lord our God. We will trust in thy mercy, O God, for ever and ever, and will wait on thy name, for it is good before thy saints. *Psalm 20:7. Psalm 52:8, 9.*

We have hoped in thy word; O remember thy word unto thy servants, upon which thou hast caused us to hope. *Psalm 119:74, 49.*

WE MUST INTREAT GOD'S FAVOURABLE ACCEPTANCE OF US AND OUR POOR PERFORMANCES

HERE be many that say, Who will shew us any good? But this we say, Lord, lift up the light of thy countenance upon us, and that shall put gladness into our hearts more than they have whose corn and wine increaseth. *Psalm 4:6, 7.*

We intreat thy favour with our whole hearts; for in this we labour, that whether present or absent we may be accepted of the Lord. *Psalm 119:58. 2 Corinthians 5:9.*

Hear our prayers, O Lord, give ear to our supplications; in thy faithfulness answer us. And be nigh unto us in all that which we call upon thee for; for thou never saidst to the seed of Jacob, Seek ye me in vain. *Psalm 143:1. Deuteronomy 4:7. Isaiah 45:19.*

Thou that hearest the young ravens which cry, Be not silent to us, lest if thou be silent to us, we be like them that go down to the pit. *Psalm 147:9. Psalm 28:1.*

Let our prayer be set forth before thee as incense, and the lifting up of our hands be acceptable in thy sight as the evening sacrifice. *Psalm 141:2.*

WE MUST BEG FOR THE POWERFUL ASSISTANCE AND INFLUENCE OF THE BLESSED SPIRIT OF GRACE IN OUR PRAYERS

ORD, we know not what to pray for as we ought, but let thy Spirit help our infirmities, and make intercession in us. *Romans 8:26.*

O pour upon us the spirit of grace and supplication; the Spirit of adoption teaching us to cry, Abba Father; that we may find in our hearts to pray this prayer: *Zechariah 12:10. Romans 8:15. 2 Samuel 7:27.*

O send out thy light and thy truth, let them lead us, let them guide us to thy holy hill, and thy tabernacles; to God our exceeding joy. *Psalm 43:3, 4.*

O Lord, open thou our lips, and our mouth shall shew forth thy praise. *Psalm 51:15.*

WE MUST MAKE THE GLORY OF GOD OUR HIGHEST END IN ALL OUR PRAYERS

THIS is that which thou, O Lord, hast said, that thou wilt be sanctified in them that come nigh unto thee, and before all the people thou wilt be glorified; we therefore worship before thee, O Lord, that we may glorify thy name; and therefore we call upon thee, that thou mayest deliver us, and we may glorify thee. *Leviticus 10:3. Psalm 86:9. Psalm 50:15.*

For of thee, and through thee, and to thee, are all things. *Romans 11:36.*

WE MUST PROFESS OUR ENTIRE RELIANCE ON THE LORD JESUS CHRIST ALONE FOR ACCEPTANCE WITH GOD, AND COME IN HIS NAME

E do not present our supplication before thee for our own righteousness; for we are before thee in our trespasses, and cannot stand before thee because of them: But we make mention of Christ's righteousness, even of his only, who is THE LORD OUR RIGHTEOUSNESS. *Daniel 9:18. Ezra 9:15. Psalm 71:16. Jeremiah 23:6.*

We know that even spiritual sacrifices are acceptable to God only through Christ Jesus, nor can we hope to receive any thing but what we ask of thee in his name, and therefore make us accepted in the beloved; that other angel, who puts much incense to the prayers of saints, and offers them up upon the golden altar before the throne. *1 Peter 2:5. John 16:23. Ephesians 1:6. Revelation 8:3.*

We come in the name of the great high priest, who is passed into the heavens, Jesus the Son of God, who was touched with the feeling of our infirmities, and is therefore able to save to the uttermost all those that come to God by him, because he ever lives making intercession. *Hebrews 4:14, 15. Hebrews 7:25.*

Behold, O God our shield, and look upon the face of thine anointed, in whom thou hast by a voice from heaven declared thyself to be well pleased; Lord, be well pleased with us in him. *Psalm 84:9. Matthew 3:17.*

2

Confession of Sin

Confession of Sin

OF THE SECOND PART OF PRAYER, WHICH IS, CONFESSION OF SIN, COMPLAINTS OF OURSELVES, AND HUMBLE PROFESSIONS OF REPENTANCE

Having given glory to God, which is his due, we must next take shame to ourselves, which is our due, and humble ourselves before him in the sense of our own sinfulness and vileness; and herein also we must give glory to him, as our judge, by whom we deserve to be condemned, and yet hope, through Christ, to be acquitted and absolved. Joshua 7:19.

In this part of our work,

We must acknowledge the great reason we have to lie very low before God, and to be ashamed of ourselves when we come into His presence, and to be afraid of His wrath, having made ourselves both odious to His holiness, and obnoxious to His justice.

Our God, we are ashamed and blush to lift up our faces before thee, our God; for our iniquities are increased over our head, and our trespass is grown up unto the heavens. *Ezra 9:6.*

To us belongs shame and confusion of face, because we have sinned against thee. *Daniel 9:8.*

Behold we are vile, what shall we answer thee? we will lay our hand upon our mouth, and put our mouth in the dust, if so be there may be hope; crying with the convicted leper under the law, Unclean, unclean. *Job 40:4. Lamentations 3:29. Leviticus 13:45.*

Thou puttest no trust in thy saints, and the heavens are not clean in thy sight: How much more abominable and filthy is man, who drinketh iniquity like waters! *Job 15:15, 16.*

When our eyes have seen the King, the Lord of hosts, we have reason to cry out, Woe unto us, for we are undone. *Isaiah 6:5.*

Dominion and fear are with thee, thou makest peace in thy high places: There is not any number of thine armies, and upon whom doth not thy light arise? How then can man be justified with God, or how can he be clean that is born of a woman? *Job 25:2, 3, 4.*

Thou, even thou art to be feared, and who may stand in thy sight, when once thou art angry? Even thou, our God, art a consuming fire, and who knows the power of thine anger? *Psalm 76:7. Hebrews 12:29. Psalm 90:11.*

If we justify ourselves, our own mouths shall condemn us, if we say we are perfect, that also shall prove us perverse; for if thou contend with us, we are not able to answer thee for one of a thousand. *Job 9:20, 3.*

If we knew nothing by ourselves, yet were we not thereby justified, for he that judgeth us is the Lord; who is greater than our hearts, and knows all things. But we ourselves know that we have sinned, Father, against heaven, and before thee, and are no more worthy to be called thy children. *1 Corinthians 4:4. 1 John 3:20. Luke 15:21.*

WE MUST TAKE HOLD OF THE GREAT ENCOURAGEMENT GOD HATH GIVEN US TO HUMBLE OURSELVES BEFORE HIM WITH SORROW AND SHAME, AND TO CONFESS OUR SINS

IF thou, Lord, shouldest mark iniquities, O Lord, who should stand? But there is forgiveness with thee that thou mayest be feared; with thee there is mercy, yea with our God there is plenteous redemption, and he shall redeem Israel from all his iniquities. *Psalm 130:3, 4, 7, 8.*

Thy sacrifices, O God, are a broken spirit; a broken and a contrite heart, O God, thou wilt not despise: Nay, though thou art the high and lofty One that inhabitest eternity, whose name is Holy; though the heaven be thy throne, and the earth thy footstool, yet to this man wilt thou look, that is poor and humble, of a broken and a contrite spirit, and that trembleth at thy word, to revive the spirit of the humble, and to revive the heart of the contrite ones. *Psalm 51:17. Isaiah 57:15. Isaiah 66:1, 2. Isaiah 57:15.*

Thou hast graciously assured us, that though they that cover their sins shall not prosper, yet those that confess and forsake them shall find mercy. And when a poor penitent said, I will confess my transgression unto the Lord, thou forgavest the iniquity of his sin, and for this shall every one that is godly in like manner pray unto thee, in a time when thou mayest be found. *Proverbs 28:13. Psalm 32:5, 6.*

We know that if we say, We have no sin, we deceive ourselves, and the truth is not in us; but thou hast said that if we confess our sins, thou art faithful and just to forgive us our sins, and to cleanse us from all unrighteousness. *1 John 1:8, 9.*

WE MUST THEREFORE CONFESS AND BEWAIL OUR ORIGINAL CORRUPTION IN THE FIRST PLACE, THAT WE ARE THE CHILDREN OF APOSTATE AND REBELLIOUS PARENTS, AND THE NATURE OF MAN IS DEPRAVED, AND WRETCHEDLY DEGENERATED FROM ITS PRIMITIVE PURITY AND RECTITUDE, AND OUR NATURE IS SO

ORD, thou madest man upright, but they have sought out many inventions; And being in honour did not understand, and therefore abode not, but became like the beasts that perish. *Ecclesiastes 7:29. Psalm 49:12, 20.*

By one man sin entered into the world, and death by sin, and so death passed upon all men, for that all have sinned; By that one man's disobedience many were made sinners, and we among the rest. *Romans 5:12, 19.*

We are a seed of evil doers; our father was an Amorite, and our mother a Hittite, and we ourselves were called (and not miscalled) transgressors from the womb, and thou knewest we would deal very treacherously. *Isaiah 1:4. Ezekiel 16:3. Isaiah 48:8.*

The nature of man was planted a choice and noble vine, wholly a right seed, but it is become the degenerate plant of a strange vine; producing the grapes of Sodom, and the clusters of Gomorrah. How is the gold become dim, and the most fine gold changed! *Jeremiah 2:21. Deuteronomy 32:32. Lamentations 4:1.*

Behold we were shapen in iniquity, and in sin did our mothers conceive us. For who can bring a clean thing out of an unclean? Not one. We are by nature children of wrath, because children of disobedience, even as others. *Psalm 51:5. Job 14:4. Ephesians 2:3, 2.*

All flesh hath corrupted their way, we are all gone aside, we are all together become filthy, there is none that doth good, no, no not one. *Genesis 6:12. Psalm 14:3.*

WE MUST LAMENT OUR PRESENT CORRUPT DISPOSITIONS TO THAT WHICH IS EVIL, AND OUR INDISPOSEDNESS TO AND IMPOTENCY IN THAT WHICH IS GOOD. WE MUST LOOK INTO OUR OWN HEARTS, AND CONFESS WITH HOLY BLUSHING

1.   *The blindness of our understandings, and their unaptness to admit the rays of the divine light.*

Y nature our understandings are darkened, being alienated from the life of God through the ignorance that is in us, because of the blindness of our hearts. *Ephesians 4:18.*

The things of the Spirit of God are foolishness, to the natural man, neither can he know them, because they are spiritually discerned. *1 Corinthians 2:14.*

We are wise to do evil, but to do good we have no knowledge. We know not, neither do we understand, we walk on in darkness. *Jeremiah 4:22. Psalm 82:5.*

God speaketh once, yea twice, but we perceive it not; but hearing we hear, and do not understand, and we see men as trees walking. *Job 33:14. Matthew 13:14. Mark 8:24.*

2.   *The stubbornness of our wills, and their unaptness to submit to the rules of the divine law.*

We have within us a carnal mind, which is enmity against God, and is not in subjection to the law of God, neither indeed can be. *Romans 8:7.*

Thou hast written to us the great things of thy law, but they have been accounted by us as a strange thing, and our corrupt hearts have been sometimes ready to say, What is the Almighty that we should serve him? And that we would certainly do whatsoever thing goes forth out of our own mouth. For we have walked in the way of our own heart, and in the sight of our eyes, fulfilling the desires of the flesh and of the mind. *Hosea 8:12. Job 21:15. Jeremiah 44:17. Ecclesiastes 11:9. Ephesians 2:3.*

Our neck hath been an iron sinew, and we have made our heart as an adamant; we have refused to hearken, have pulled away the shoulder, and stopped our ears, like the deaf adder, that will not hearken to the voice of the charmer, charm he never so wisely. *Isaiah 48:4. Zechariah 7:12, 11. Psalm 58:4, 5.*

How have we hated instruction, and our heart despised reproof, and have not obeyed the voice of our teachers, nor inclined our ear to them that instructed us? *Proverbs 5:12, 13.*

3. *The vanity of our thoughts, their neglect of those things which they ought to be conversant with, and dwelling upon those things that are unworthy of them, and tend to corrupt our minds.*

Every imagination of the thought of our heart is evil, only evil, and that continually, and it has been so from our youth. *Genesis 6:5. Genesis 8:21.*

O how long have those vain thoughts lodged within us! those thoughts of foolishness which are sin. From within out of the heart proceed evil thoughts; which devise mischief upon the bed, and carry the heart with the fool's eyes into the ends of the earth. *Jeremiah 4:14. Proverbs 24:9. Matthew 15:19. Micah 2:1. Proverbs 17:24.*

But God is not in all our thoughts, it is well if he be in any: Of the Rock that begat us we have been unmindful, and have forgotten the God that formed us: We have forgotten him days without number, and our hearts have walked after vanity, and become vain. Their inward thought having been that our houses should continue for ever; this our way is our folly. *Psalm 10:4. Deuteronomy 32:18. Jeremiah 2:32, 5. Psalm 49:11, 13.*

4. *The carnality of our affections, their being placed upon wrong objects, and carried beyond due bounds.*

We have set those affections on things beneath, which should have been set on things above, where our treasure is, and where Christ sits on the right hand of God, the things which we should seek. *Colossians 3:2, 1. Matthew 6:21.*

We have followed after lying vanities, and forsaken our own mercies; have forsaken the fountain of living waters, for cisterns, broken cisterns that can hold no water. *Jonah 2:8. Jeremiah 2:13.*

We have panted after the dust of the earth, and have been full of care what we shall eat, and what we shall drink, and wherewithal we shall be clothed, the things after which the Gentiles seek, but have neglected the kingdom of God and the righteousness thereof. *Amos 2:7. Matthew 6:31, 32, 33.*

We have lifted up our souls unto vanity, and set our eyes upon that which is not, have looked at the things that are seen which are temporal, but the things that are not seen that are eternal, have been forgotten and postponed. *Psalm 24:4. Proverbs 23:5. 2 Corinthians 4:18.*

5.   *The corruption of the whole man: irregular appetites towards those things that are pleasing to sense, and inordinate passions against those things that are displeasing, and an alienation of the mind from the principles, powers and pleasures of the spiritual and divine life.*

We are born of the flesh, and we are flesh: Dust we are: We have borne the image of the earthly; and in us, that is, in our flesh, there dwells no good thing: For if to will is present to us, yet how to perform that which is good we find not; for the good that we would do we do it not, and the evil which we would not do that we do. *John 3:6. Genesis 3:19. 1 Corinthians 15:49. Romans 7:18, 19.*

We have a law in our members warring against the law of our mind, and bringing us into captivity to the law of sin that is in our members: So that when we would do good, evil is present with us, and most easily besets us. *Romans 7:23, 21. Hebrews 12:1.*

The whole head is sick, the whole heart faint, from the sole of the foot even unto the head there is no soundness in us, but wounds and bruises, and putrifying sores. *Isaiah 1:5, 6.*

There is in us a bent to backslide from the living God: Our hearts are deceitful above all things, and desperately wicked; who can know them? They start aside like a broken bow. *Hosea 11:7. Jeremiah 17:9. Hosea 7:16.*

WE MUST LAMENT AND CONFESS OUR OMISSIONS OF OUR DUTY, OUR NEGLECT OF IT, AND TRIFLINGS IN IT, AND THAT WE HAVE DONE SO LITTLE SINCE WE CAME INTO THE WORLD OF THE GREAT WORK WE WERE SENT INTO THE WORLD ABOUT, SO VERY LITTLE TO ANSWER THE END EITHER OF OUR CREATION OR OF OUR REDEMPTION, OF OUR BIRTH OR OF OUR BAPTISM, AND THAT WE HAVE PROFITED NO MORE BY THE MEANS OF GRACE

E have been as fig-trees planted in the vineyard, and thou hast come many years seeking fruit from us, but hast found none; and therefore we might justly have been cut down and cast into the fire for cumbering the ground: Thou hast come looking for grapes, but behold wild grapes; or we have been empty vines, bringing forth fruit unto ourselves. *Luke 13:6, 7. Matthew 3:10. Isaiah 5:4. Hosea 10:1.*

We have known to do good, but have not done it: We have hid our Lord's money, and therefore deserve the doom of the wicked and slothful servant. *James 4:17. Matthew 25:18, 26.*

We have been unfaithful stewards, that have wasted our Lord's goods; for one sinner destroys much good. *Luke 16:1. Ecclesiastes 9:18.*

Many a price hath been put into our hand to get wisdom, which we have had no heart to; or our heart has been at our left hand. *Proverbs 17:16. Ecclesiastes 10:2.*

Our childhood and youth was vanity, and we have brought our years to an end, as a tale that is told. *Ecclesiastes 11:10. Psalm 90:9.*

We have not known, or improved, the day of our visitation, have not provided meat in summer, nor gathered food in harvest, though we have had guides, overseers and rulers. *Luke 19:44. Proverbs 6:8, 7.*

We are slow of heart to understand and believe, and whereas for the time we might have been teachers of others, we are yet to learn the first principles of the oracles of God, have need of milk, and cannot bear strong meat. *Luke 24:25. Hebrews 5:12.*

We have cast off fear, and restrained prayer before God; have not called upon thy name, nor stirred up ourselves to take hold on thee. *Job 15:4. Isaiah 64:7.*

We have come before thee as thy people come, and have sat before thee as thy people sit, and have heard thy words, when our hearts at the same time have been going after our covetousness. And thus have we brought the torn, and the lame, and the sick for sacrifice, have offered that to our God, which we would not have offered to our governor; and have vowed and sacrificed to the Lord a corrupt thing, when we had in our flock a male. *Ezekiel 33:31. Malachi 1:8, 14.*

WE MUST LIKEWISE BEWAIL OUR MANY ACTUAL TRANSGRESSIONS, IN THOUGHT, WORD, AND DEED

E have sinned, Father, against heaven and before thee; we have all sinned, and have come short of the glory of God; for the God in whose hand our breath is, and whose are all our ways, have we not glorified. *Luke 15:18. Romans 3:23. Daniel 5:23.*

Against thee, thee only have we sinned, and have done much evil in thy sight; neither have we obeyed the voice of the Lord our God, to walk in his laws which he hath set before us; though they are all holy, just, and good. *Psalm 51:4. Daniel 9:10. Romans 7:12.*

Who can understand his errors? Cleanse thou us from secret faults. *Psalm 19:12.*

In many things we all offend; and our iniquities are more than the hairs of our head. *James 3:2. Psalm 40:12.*

As a fountain casteth out her waters, so do our hearts cast out wickedness; and this hath been our manner from our youth up, that we have not obeyed thy voice. *Jeremiah 6:7. Jeremiah 22:21.*

Out of the evil treasure of our hearts we have brought forth many evil things. *Matthew 12:35.*

1.   *We must confess and bewail the workings of pride in us.*

We have all reason to be humbled for the pride of our hearts, that we have thought of ourselves above what hath been meet, and have not thought soberly, nor walked humbly with our God. *2 Chronicles 32:26. Romans 12:3. Micah 6:8.*

We have leaned to our own understanding; and trusted in our own hearts; and have sacrificed to our own net. *Proverbs 3:5. Proverbs 28:26. Habakkuk 1:16.*

We have sought our own glory more than the glory of him that sent us; and have been puffed up for that for which we should have mourned. *John 7:18. 1 Corinthians 5:2.*

2. *The breaking out of passion and rash anger.*

We have not had the rule which we ought to have had over our own spirits, which have therefore been as a city that is broken down, and has no walls. *Proverbs 25:28.*

We have been soon angry, and anger hath rested in our bosoms. And when our spirits have been provoked, we have spoken unadvisedly with our lips; and have been guilty of that clamour and bitterness which should have been put far from us. *Proverbs 14:17. Ecclesiastes 7:9. Psalm 106:33. Ephesians 4:31.*

3. *Our covetousness and love of the world.*

Our conversation has not been without covetousness, nor have we learned in every state to be content with such things as we have. *Hebrews 13:5. Philippians 4:11.*

Who can say he is clean from that love of money, which is the root of all evil, that covetousness which is idolatry. *1 Timothy 6:10. Colossians 3:5.*

We have sought great things to ourselves, when thou hast said, Seek them not. *Jeremiah 45:5.*

4. *Our sensuality and flesh-pleasing.*

We have minded the things of the flesh more than the things of the Spirit, and have lived in pleasure on the earth, and been wanton, and have nourished our hearts as in a day of slaughter. *Romans 8:5. James 5:5.*

We have made provision for the flesh to fulfil the lusts of it; even those lusts which war against our souls: and in many instances have acted as if we had been lovers of pleasure more than lovers of God. *Romans 13:14. 1 Peter 2:11. 2 Timothy 3:4.*

When we did eat, and when we did drink, did we not eat to ourselves, and drink to ourselves? *Zechariah 7:6.*

5. *Our security and unmindfulness of the changes we are liable to in this world.*

We have put far from us the evil day, and in our prosperity have said we should never be moved, as if to morrow must needs be as this day, and much more abundant. *Amos 6:3. Psalm 30:6. Isaiah 56:12.*

We have encouraged our souls to take their ease, to eat and drink and be merry, as if we had goods laid up for many years, when perhaps this night our souls may be required of us. *Luke 12:19, 20.*

We have been ready to trust in uncertain riches more than in the living God; to say to the gold thou art our hope, and to the fine gold thou art our confidence. *1 Timothy 6:17. Job 31:24.*

6. *Our fretfulness and impatience and murmuring under our afflictions, our inordinate dejection, and distrust of God and His providence.*

When thou hast chastised us and we were chastised, we have been as a bullock unaccustomed to the yoke; and though our own foolishness hath perverted our way, yet our heart hath fretted against the Lord; and thus in our distress we have trespassed yet more against the Lord. *Jeremiah 31:18. Proverbs 19:3. 2 Chronicles 28:22.*

We have either despised the chastening of the Lord, or fainted when we have been rebuked of him; and if we faint in the day of adversity, our strength is small. *Proverbs 3:11. Proverbs 24:10.*

We have said in our haste we are cut off from before thine eyes, and that the Lord hath forsaken us, our God hath forgotten us, as if God would be favourable no more; as if he had forgotten to be gracious, and had in anger shut up his tender mercies. This has been our infirmity. *Psalm 31:22. Isaiah 49:14. Psalm 77:7, 9, 10.*

7. *Our uncharitableness towards our brethren, and unpeaceableness with our relations, neighbours and friends, and perhaps injustice towards them.*

We have been verily guilty concerning our brother; for we have not studied the things that make for peace, nor things wherewith we might edify one another. *Genesis 42:21. Romans 14:19.*

We have been ready to judge our brother, and to set at nought our brother, forgetting that we must all shortly stand before the judgment seat of Christ. *Romans 14:10.*

Contrary to the royal law of charity, we have vaunted ourselves, and been puffed up, have behaved ourselves unseemly, and sought our own, have been easily provoked, have rejoiced in iniquity, and been secretly glad at calamities. *1 Corinthians 13:4, 5, 6. Proverbs 17:5.*

We have been desirous of vain-glory, provoking one another, envying one another; when we should have considered one another to provoke to love and to good works. *Galatians 5:26. Hebrews 10:24.*

The bowels of our compassion have been shut up from those that are in need; and we have hidden ourselves from our own flesh. Nay, perhaps our eye has been evil against our poor brother, and we have despised the poor. *1 John 3:17. Isaiah 58:7. Deuteronomy 15:9. James 2:6.*

And if in any thing we have gone beyond and defrauded our brother, if we have walked with vanity, and our foot hath hasted to deceit, and any blot hath cleaved to our hands, Lord, discover it to us, that if we have done iniquity, we may do so no more. *1 Thessalonians 4:6. Job 31:5, 7. Job 34:32.*

8.   *Our tongue-sins.*

In the multitude of our words there wanteth not sin, nor can a man full of talk be justified. *Proverbs 10:19. Job 11:2.*

While the lips of the righteous feed many, our lips have poured out foolishness, and spoken frowardness. *Proverbs 10:21. Proverbs 15:2. Proverbs 10:32.*

Much corrupt communication hath proceeded out of our mouths; that foolish talking and jesting which is not convenient; and little of that which is good, and to the use of edifying, and which might minister grace unto the hearers. *Ephesians 4:29. Ephesians 5:4.*

If for every idle word that men speak they must give an account, and by our words we must be justified, and by our words we must be condemned, Woe unto us, for we are undone! for we are of unclean lips, and dwell in the midst of a people of unclean lips. *Matthew 12:36, 37. Isaiah 6:5.*

What would become of us, if God should make our own tongues to fall upon us. *Psalm 64:8.*

9.   *Our spiritual slothfulness and decay.*

We have been slothful in the business of religion, and not fervent in spirit, serving the Lord. *Romans 12:11.*

The things which remain are ready to die, and our works have not been found perfect before God. *Revelation 3:2.*

We have observed the winds, and therefore have not sown, have regarded the clouds, and therefore have not reaped; and with the sluggard have frightened ourselves with the fancy of a lion in the way, a lion in the streets, and have turned on our bed as the door on the hinges; still crying, Yet a little sleep, a little slumber. *Ecclesiastes 11:4. Proverbs 26:13, 14. Proverbs 6:10.*

We have lost our first love, and where is now the blessedness we sometimes spake of? *Revelation 2:4. Galatians 4:15.*

Our goodness hath been as the morning cloud and the early dew which passeth away. *Hosea 6:4.*

And that which is at the bottom of all, is the evil heart of unbelief in us, which inclines us to depart from the living God. *Hebrews 3:12.*

WE MUST ACKNOWLEDGE THE GREAT EVIL THAT THERE IS IN SIN, IN OUR SIN; THE MALIGNITY OF ITS NATURE, AND ITS MISCHIEVOUSNESS TO US

1. *The sinfulness of sin.*

That sin may appear sin to us, may appear in its own colours, and that by the commandment we may see it to be exceeding sinful; because it is the transgression of the law. *Romans 7:13. 1 John 3:4.*

By every wilful sin we have in effect said, We will not have this man to reign over us; And who is the Lord, that we should obey his voice? And thus have we reproached the Lord, and cast his law behind our backs. *Luke 19:14. Exodus 5:2. Numbers 15:30. Nehemiah 9:26.*

2. *The foolishness of sin.*

O God, thou knowest our foolishness, and our sins are not hid from thee: We were foolish in being disobedient; and our lusts are foolish and hurtful. *Psalm 69:5. Titus 3:3. 1 Timothy 6:9.*

Foolishness was bound up in our hearts when we were children; for though vain man would be wise, he is born like the wild ass's colt. *Proverbs 22:15. Job 11:12.*

Our way hath been our folly, and in many instances we have done foolishly, very foolishly. *Psalm 49:13. 2 Samuel 24:10.*

So foolish have we been and ignorant, and even as beasts before God. *Psalm 73:22.*

3. *The unprofitableness of sin.*

We have sinned and perverted that which was right, and it profited us not. *Job 33:27.*

What fruit have we now in those things whereof we have cause to be ashamed; seeing the end of those things is death? And what are we profited, if we should gain the whole world, and lose our own souls? *Romans 6:21. Matthew 16:26.*

4. *The deceitfulness of sin.*

Sin hath deceived us, and by it slain us; for our hearts have been hardened through the deceitfulness of sin; and we have been drawn away of our own lust, and enticed. *Romans 7:11. Hebrews 3:13. James 1:14.*

It hath promised us liberty, but has made us the servants of corruption; hath promised that we shall not surely die, and that we shall be as gods; but it has flattered us, and spread a net for our feet. *2 Peter 2:19. Genesis 3:4, 5. Proverbs 29:5.*

The pride of our heart particularly has deceived us. *Obadiah 3.*

5. *The offence which by sin we have given to the Holy God.*

By breaking the law we have dishonoured God, and have provoked the Holy One of Israel to anger most bitterly. And many a thing that we have done hath displeased the Lord. *Romans 2:23. Isaiah 1:4. Hosea 12:14. 2 Samuel 11 (v. 27).*

God has been broken by our whorish heart, and our eyes that have gone a whoring after our idols. *Ezekiel 6:9.*

We have tempted him, and proved him, and grieved him in the wilderness; have rebelled and vexed his holy Spirit, and pressed him with our iniquities, as a cart is pressed that is full of sheaves. *Psalm 95:9, 10, 8. Isaiah 63:10. Amos 2:13.*

We have grieved the holy Spirit of God, by whom we are sealed to the day of redemption. *Ephesians 4:30.*

6. *The damage which by sin we have done to our own souls, and their great interests.*

By our iniquities we have sold ourselves, and in sinning against thee have wronged our own souls. *Isaiah 50:1. Proverbs 8:36.*

Our sins have separated between us and God, and have kept good things from us; and by them our minds and consciences have been defiled. *Isaiah 59:2. Jeremiah 5:25. Titus 1:15.*

Our own wickedness hath corrected us, and our backslidings have reproved us, and we cannot but know and see, that it is an evil thing, and bitter, that we have forsaken the Lord our God, and that his fear hath not been in us. *Jeremiah 2:19.*

O what fools are they that make a mock at sin! *Proverbs 14:9.*

WE MUST AGGRAVATE OUR SINS, AND TAKE NOTICE OF THOSE THINGS WHICH MAKE THEM MORE HEINOUS IN THE SIGHT OF GOD, AND MORE DANGEROUS TO OURSELVES

 E bewail before thee all our sins, and all our transgressions in all our sins. *Leviticus 16:21.*

1. *The more knowledge we have of good and evil, the greater is our sin.*

We have known our Master's will, but have not done it, and therefore deserve to be beaten with many stripes. *Luke 12:47.*

We have known the way of the Lord, and the judgments of our God, and yet have altogether broken the yoke, and burst the bonds. *Jeremiah 5:4, 5.*

We have known the judgment of God, that they which do such things are worthy of death, and yet have done them, and have had pleasure in them that do them. *Romans 1:32.*

We have taught others, and yet have not taught ourselves; and while we profess to know God, we have in works denied him. *Romans 2:21. Titus 1:16.*

2. *The greater profession we have made of religion, the greater hath been our sin.*

We call ourselves of the holy city, and stay ourselves upon the God of Israel, and make mention of his name, but not in truth and righteousness. For we have dishonoured that worthy name by which we are called, and given great occasion to the enemies of the Lord to blaspheme. *Isaiah 48:2, 1. James 2:7, 23. 2 Samuel 12:14.*

We have named the name of Christ, and yet have not departed from iniquity. *2 Timothy 2:19.*

3. *The more mercies we have received from God, the greater hath been our sin.*

Thou hast nourished and brought us up as children, but we have rebelled against thee. *Isaiah 1:2.*

We have ill requited thee, O Lord, as foolish people and unwise: Though thou art our Father that hast made us, and bought us, and established us, yet our spot has not been the spot of thy children. *Deuteronomy 32:6, 5.*

We have not rendered again according to the benefit done unto us. *2 Chronicles 32:25.*

4. *The fairer warning we have had from the word of God, and from our own consciences, concerning our danger of sin, and danger by sin, the greater is the sin if we go on in it.*

We have been often reproved, and yet have hardened our neck; and have gone on frowardly in the way of our heart. *Proverbs 29:1. Isaiah 57:17.*

Thou hast sent to us, saying, O do not this abominable thing which I hate; but we have not hearkened, nor inclined our ear. *Jeremiah 44:4, 5.*

The word of God hath been to us, precept upon precept, and line upon line; and though we have beheld our natural faces in the glass of it, yet we have gone away, and straitway forgot what manner of men we were. *Isaiah 28:13. James 1:23, 24.*

5. *The greater afflictions we have been under for sin, the greater is the sin if we go on in it.*

Thou hast stricken us, but we have not grieved, we have refused to receive correction, and have made our faces harder than a rock; and the rod hath not driven the foolishness out of our hearts. *Jeremiah 5:3. Proverbs 22:15.*

Thou hast chastened us with the rod of men, and with the stripes of the children of men, yet we have not turned to him that smiteth us, nor have we sought the Lord of hosts. *2 Samuel 7:14. Isaiah 9:13.*

When some have been overthrown as Sodom and Gomorrah were, we have been as brands plucked out of the fire, yet have we not returned unto thee, O Lord. And when thy hand has been lifted up, we have not seen it. *Amos 4:11. Isaiah 26:11.*

6. *The more vows and promises we have made of better obedience, the greater has our sin been.*

We have not performed the words of the covenant which we made before thee, but as treacherous dealers we have dealt treacherously. *Jeremiah 34:18. Isaiah 24:16.*

Did we not say we would not transgress, we would not offend any more? We did, and yet we have returned with the dog to his vomit; have returned to folly after God hath spoken peace. *Jeremiah 2:20. Job 34:31. 2 Peter 2:22. Psalm 85:8.*

WE MUST JUDGE AND CONDEMN OURSELVES FOR OUR SINS, AND OWN OURSELVES LIABLE TO PUNISHMENT

AND now, O our God, what shall we say after this, for we have forsaken thy commandments? We have sinned, what shall we do unto thee, O thou preserver of men? *Ezra 9:10. Job 7:20.*

We know that the law curseth every one that continues not in all things that are written in the book of the law to do them; that the wages of every sin is death; and that for these things sake cometh the wrath of God upon the children of disobedience. *Galatians 3:10. Romans 6:23. Ephesians 5:6.*

And we are all guilty before God; the scripture hath concluded us all under sin; and therefore thou mightest justly be angry with us till thou hadst consumed us; so that there should be no remnant, nor escaping. *Romans 3:19. Galatians 3:22. Ezra 9:14.*

If thou shouldest lay righteousness to the line and judgment to the plummet, thou mightest justly separate us unto all evil, according to all the curses of the covenant, and blot out our names from under heaven. *Isaiah 28:17. Deuteronomy 29:21, 20.*

Thou mightest justly swear in thy wrath, that we should never enter into thy rest; mightest justly set us naked and bare, and take away our corn in the season thereof, and our wine in the season thereof, and put into our hands the cup of trembling, and make us drink even the dregs of that cup. *Psalm 95 (v. 11). Hosea 2:3, 9. Isaiah 51:22.*

Thou art just in whatever thou art pleased to lay upon us; for thou hast done right, but we have done wickedly: Nay, thou our God hast punished us less than our iniquities have deserved. *Nehemiah 9:33. Ezra 9:13.*

Thou therefore shalt be justified when thou speakest, and clear when thou judgest; and we will accept of the punishment of our iniquity, and humble ourselves under thy mighty hand, and say the Lord is righteous. *Psalm 51:4. Leviticus 26:43. 1 Peter 5:6. 2 Chronicles 12:6.*

Wherefore should a living man complain, a man for the punishment of his sins? No, we will bear the indignation of the Lord, because we have sinned against him. *Lamentations 3:39. Micah 7:9.*

We must give to God the glory of His patience and long-suffering towards us, and His willingness to be reconciled

The riches of the patience and forbearance of God! how long-suffering is he to us ward, not willing that any should perish, but that all should come to repentance. *Romans 2:4. 2 Peter 3:9.*

Thou hast not dealt with us according to our sins, nor rewarded us after our iniquities; but thou waitest to be gracious to us. *Psalm 103:10. Isaiah 30:18.*

Sentence against our evil works has not been executed speedily; but thou hast given us space to repent, and make our peace with thee; and callest even backsliding children to return to thee, and hast promised to heal their backslidings; And therefore, behold we come unto thee, for thou art THE LORD OUR GOD. *Ecclesiastes 8:11. Revelation 2:21. Jeremiah 3:22, 23.*

Surely the long-suffering of our Lord, is salvation; and if the Lord had been pleased to kill us, he would not as at this time have shewed us such things as these. *2 Peter 3:15. Judges 13:23.*

And O that this goodness of God might lead us to repentance! for though we have trespassed against our God, yet now there is hope in Israel concerning this thing. *Romans 2:4. Ezra 10:2.*

Thou hast said it, and hast confirmed it with an oath, that thou hast no pleasure in the death of sinners, but rather that they should turn and live: Therefore will we rent our hearts and not our garments, and turn to the Lord our God; for he is gracious and merciful, slow to anger, and of great kindness, who knows if he will return and repent, and leave a blessing behind him. *Ezekiel 33:11. Joel 2:13, 14.*

WE MUST HUMBLY PROFESS OUR SORROW AND SHAME FOR SIN, AND HUMBLY ENGAGE OURSELVES IN THE STRENGTH OF DIVINE GRACE, THAT WE WILL BE BETTER AND DO BETTER FOR THE FUTURE

LORD, we repent, for the kingdom of heaven is at hand; to which thou hast exalted thy Son Christ Jesus to give repentance and remission of sins. *Matthew 3:2. Acts 5:31.*

We have heard of thee by the hearing of the ear, but now our eye sees thee; wherefore we abhor ourselves, and repent in dust and ashes. Therefore will we be like the doves of the valleys, every one mourning for his iniquities. *Job 42:5, 6. Ezekiel 7:16.*

O that our heads were waters, and our eyes fountains of tears, that we might weep day and night for our transgressions, and might in such a manner sow in those tears, as that at last we may reap in joy; may now go forth weeping, bearing precious seed, and may in due time come again with rejoicing, bringing our sheaves with us. *Jeremiah 9:1. Psalm 126:5, 6.*

Our iniquities are gone over our heads as a heavy burden, they are too heavy for us; but weary and heavy laden under this burden we come to Christ, who has promised that in him we shall find rest for our souls. *Psalm 38:4. Matthew 11:28, 29.*

O that knowing every man the plague of his own heart, we may look unto him whom we have pierced, and may mourn, and be in bitterness for him as one that is in bitterness for a first-born. That we may sorrow after a godly sort, with that sorrow which worketh repentance unto salvation, not to be repented of; and that we may remember and be confounded, and never open our mouth any more, because of our shame when thou art pacified towards us. *1 Kings 8:38. Zechariah 12:10. 2 Corinthians 7:10. Ezekiel 16:63.*

And, O that we may bring forth fruits meet for repentance! and may never return again to folly! for what have we to do any more with idols? Sin shall not have dominion over us, for we are not under the law, but under grace. *Matthew 3:8. Psalm 85:8. Hosea 14:8. Romans 6:14.*

We have gone astray like lost sheep; seek thy servants, for we do not forget thy commandments. *Psalm 119 (v. 176).*

3

Petitions and Requests

Petitions and Requests

OF THE THIRD PART OF PRAYER, WHICH IS PETITION AND SUPPLICATION FOR THE GOOD THINGS WHICH WE STAND IN NEED OF

Having opened the wounds of sin, both the guilt of it, and the power of it, and its remainders in us, we must next seek unto God for the remedy, for healing and help, for from Him alone it is to be expected, and He will for this be enquired of by us. And now we must affect our hearts with a deep sense of the need we have of those mercies which we pray for, that we are undone, for ever undone, without them; and with a high esteem and value for them, that we are happy, we are made for ever, if we obtain them; that we may like Jacob wrestle with Him in prayer as for our lives, and the lives of our souls. But we must not think in our prayers to prescribe to Him, or by our importunity to move Him. He knows us better than we know ourselves, and knows what He will do. But thus we open our wants and our desires, and then refer ourselves to His wisdom and goodness: And hereby we give honour to Him as our protector and benefactor, and take the way which He Himself hath appointed of fetching in mercy from Him, and by faith plead His promise with Him; and if we are sincere herein, we are through His grace qualified according to the tenor of the new covenant to receive His favours, and are to be assured, that we do and shall receive them. Ezekiel 36:37. John 6:6. Mark 11:24.

AND now, Lord, what wait we for? Truly our hope is even in thee: Deliver us from all our transgressions, that we may not be the reproach of the foolish. *Psalm 39:7, 8.*

Lord, all our desire is before thee, and our groaning is not hid from thee; even the groanings which cannot be uttered: For he that searcheth the heart, knows what is the mind of the Spirit. *Psalm 38:9. Romans 8:26, 27.*

We do not think that we shall be heard for our much speaking; for our Father knows what things we have need of before we ask him; but our Master hath told us, that whatsoever we ask the Father in his name he will give it us. And he hath said, Ask and ye shall receive, that your joy may be full. *Matthew 6:7, 8. John 16:23, 24.*

And this is the confidence that we have in him, that if we ask any thing according to his will, he heareth us: And if we know that he hear us, whatsoever we ask, we know that we have the petitions that we desired of him. *1 John 5:14, 15.*

We must earnestly pray for the pardon and forgiveness of all our sins.

Lord, we come to thee, as the poor publican, that stood afar off, and would not so much as lift up his eyes to heaven, but smote upon his breast; and we pray his prayer, God be merciful to us sinners. The God of infinite mercy be merciful to us. *Luke 18:13.*

O wash us throughly from our iniquity, and cleanse us from our sin, for we acknowledge our transgressions, and our sin is ever before us. O purge us with hyssop and we shall be clean, wash us and we shall be whiter than snow: Hide thy face from our sins, and blot out all our iniquities. *Psalm 51:2, 3, 7, 9.*

Be thou merciful to our unrighteousness, and our sins and our iniquities do thou remember no more. O forgive us that great debt. *Hebrews 8:12. Matthew 18:32.*

Let us be justified freely by thy grace through the redemption that is in Jesus, from all those things from which we could not be justified by the law of Moses. *Romans 3:24. Acts 13:39.*

O let not our iniquity be our ruin; but let the Lord take away our sin that we may not die, not die eternally: that we may not be hurt of the second death. *Ezekiel 18:30. 2 Samuel 12:13. Revelation 2:11.*

Blot out as a cloud our transgressions, and as a thick cloud our sins; for we return unto thee because thou hast redeemed us. *Isaiah 44:22.*

Enter not into judgment with thy servants, O Lord, for in thy sight shall no flesh living be justified. *Psalm 143:2.*

Take away all iniquity, and receive us graciously; Heal our backslidings, and love us freely, and let thine anger be turned away from us; for in thee the fatherless findeth mercy. *Hosea 14:2, 4, 3.*

Though our sins have been as scarlet, let them be as white as snow, and though they have been red like crimson, let them be as wool, that being willing and obedient, we may eat the good of the land. *Isaiah 1:18, 19.*

We will say unto God, Do not condemn us, but deliver us from going down to the pit, for thou hast found the ransom. *Job 10:2. Job 33:24.*

For the encouraging of our faith, and the exciting of our fervency in this petition for the pardon of sin, we may plead with God,

1. *The infinite goodness of His nature, His readiness to forgive sin, and His glorying in it.*

Thou, Lord, art good, and ready to forgive; and rich in mercy to all them that call upon thee. Thou art a God full of compassion and gracious, long-suffering and plenteous in mercy and truth. *Psalm 86:5, 15.*

Thou art a God of pardons, merciful, slow to anger, and of great kindness; that dost not always chide, nor keep thine anger for ever. *Nehemiah 9:17. Psalm 103:9.*

Thou, even thou art he that blottest out our transgressions for thine own sake, and wilt not remember our sins; which we are here to put thee in remembrance of, to plead with thee and to declare that we may be justified. *Isaiah 43:25, 26.*

And now we beseech thee, let the power of our Lord be great, according as thou hast spoken, saying, The Lord is long-suffering and of great mercy, forgiving iniquity and transgression. Pardon, we beseech thee, the iniquity of thy people, according unto the greatness of thy mercy; and as thou hast forgiven, even until now. *Numbers 14:17, 18, 19.*

For who is a God like unto thee, that pardonest iniquity, and passeth by the transgression of the remnant of thine heritage; who retainest not thine anger for ever, because thou delightest in mercy. O that thou wouldest have compassion upon us, and subdue our iniquities, and cast all our sins into the depths of the sea. *Micah 7:18, 19.*

2. *The merit and righteousness of our Lord Jesus Christ, which we rely upon as our main plea in our petition for the pardon of sin.*

We know that as thou art gracious and merciful, so thou art the righteous God that loveth righteousness, and wilt by no means clear the guilty. We cannot say, Have patience with us, and we will pay thee all; for we are all as an unclean thing, and all our righteousnesses are as filthy rags. But Jesus Christ is made of God to us righteousness; being made sin for us, though he knew no sin, that we might be made the righteousness of God in him. *Psalm 11:7. Exodus 34:7. Matthew 18:26. Isaiah 64:6. 1 Corinthians 1:30. 2 Corinthians 5:21.*

We have sinned, but we have an advocate with the Father, JESUS CHRIST THE RIGHTEOUS, who is the propitiation for our sins, and not for ours only, but for the sins of the whole world. *1 John 2:1, 2.*

It is God that justifieth, who is he that shall condemn? It is Christ that died, yea rather that is risen again, and now is even at the right hand of God; who also maketh intercession for us, and whose blood speaks better things than that of Abel. *Romans 8:33, 34. Hebrews 12:24.*

We desire to count every thing loss for Christ; and dung that we may win Christ, and be found in him, not having any righteousness of our own, but that which is through the faith of Christ. *Philippians 3:7, 8, 9.*

This is the name whereby we will call him, THE LORD OUR RIGHTEOUSNESS. In him, Lord, we believe, help thou our unbelief. *Jeremiah 23:6. Mark 9:24.*

Lord, remember David and all his troubles; the Son of David. Remember all his offerings, and accept his burnt sacrifice; and turn not away the face of thine anointed; who by his own blood is entered into heaven itself, now to appear in the presence of God for us. *Psalm 132:1. Psalm 20:3. Psalm 132:10. Hebrews 13:12. Hebrews 9:24.*

Hast not thou thyself set forth thy Son Christ Jesus to be a propitiation for sin through faith in his blood, to declare thy righteousness for the remission of sins, to declare at this time thy righteousness, that thou mayest be just, and the justifier of him which believeth in Jesus; And we now receive the atonement. *Romans 3:25, 26. Romans 5:11.*

3. *The promises God hath made in His word to pardon and absolve all them that truly repent, and unfeignedly believe His holy gospel.*

Lord, is not this the word which thou hast spoken, that if the wicked forsake his way, and the unrighteous man his thoughts, and return unto the Lord, even to our God, that thou wilt abundantly pardon, wilt multiply to pardon? *Isaiah 55:7.*

To thee the Lord our God belong mercies and forgivenesses, though we have rebelled against thee. *Daniel 9:9.*

Is not this the covenant which thou hast made with the house of Israel, that thou wilt take away their sins; that thou wilt forgive their iniquity, and remember their sin no more; that the iniquity of

Israel shall be sought for, and there shall be none; and the sins of Judah, and they shall not be found? *Romans 11:27. Jeremiah 31:34. Jeremiah 50:20.*

Hast thou not said, that if the wicked will turn from all his sins which he hath committed, and keep thy statutes, he shall live, he shall not die, all his transgressions shall not be mentioned unto him? *Ezekiel 18:21, 22.*

Hast thou not appointed that repentance and remission of sins should be preached in Christ's name unto all nations? *Luke 24:47.*

Didst thou not promise, that when the sins of Israel were put upon the head of the scapegoat, they should be sent away into the wilderness, into a land not inhabited? And as far as the east is from the west, so far dost thou remove our transgressions from us. *Leviticus 16:21, 22. Psalm 103:12.*

O remember these words unto thy servants, upon which thou hast caused us to hope. *Psalm 119:49.*

4.   *Our own misery and danger because of sin.*

For thy name's sake, O Lord, pardon our iniquity, for it is great; for innumerable evils have compassed us about, our iniquities have taken hold upon us, so that we are not able to look up. Be pleased, O Lord, to deliver us; O Lord, make haste to help us. *Psalm 25:11. Psalm 40:12, 13.*

O remember not against us former iniquities, let thy tender mercies speedily prevent us, for we are brought very low. Help us, O God of our salvation, for the glory of thy name; deliver us, and purge away our sins for thy name's sake. *Psalm 79:8, 9.*

Remember not the sins of our youth, nor our transgressions; according to thy mercy remember thou us, for thy goodness sake, O Lord. *Psalm 25:7.*

5.   *The blessed condition which they are in whose sins are pardoned.*

O let us have the blessedness of those whose transgression is forgiven, and whose sin is covered; of that man unto whom the Lord imputeth not iniquity, and in whose spirit there is no guile. *Psalm 32:1, 2.*

O let us have redemption through Christ's blood, even the forgiveness of sins, according to the riches of thy grace; wherein thou hast abounded towards us in all wisdom and prudence. That being in Christ Jesus, there may be no condemnation to us. *Ephesians 1:7, 8. Romans 8:1.*

That our sins, which are many, being forgiven us, we may go in peace: And the inhabitant shall not say, I am sick, if the people that dwell therein be forgiven their iniquity. *Luke 7:47, 50. Isaiah 33 (v. 24).*

WE MUST LIKEWISE PRAY THAT GOD WILL BE RECONCILED TO US, THAT WE MAY OBTAIN HIS FAVOUR AND BLESSING, AND GRACIOUS ACCEPTANCE

1.   *That we may be at peace with God; and His anger may be turned away from us.*

BEING justified by faith, let us have peace with God through our Lord Jesus Christ, and through him let us have access into that grace wherein believers stand, and rejoice in hope of the glory of God. *Romans 5:1, 2.*

Be not thou a terror to us, for thou art our hope in the day of evil. *Jeremiah 17:17.*

In Christ Jesus let us, who sometimes were afar off, be made nigh by the blood of Christ; For he is our peace, who hath broken down the middle wall of partition between us, and that he might reconcile us to God by his cross, hath slain the enmity thereby, so making peace. Through him therefore let us who had made ourselves strangers and foreigners, become fellow citizens with the saints, and of the household of God. *Ephesians 2:13-16, 19.*

Fury is not in thee, who would set the briers and thorns against thee in battle, thou wouldest go through them, yea thou wouldst burn them together; but thou hast encouraged us to take hold on thy strength that we may make peace, and hast promised that we shall make peace; O let us therefore acquaint ourselves with thee, and be at peace, that thereby good may come unto us. *Isaiah 27:4, 5. Job 22:21.*

Heal us and we shall be healed, save us, and we shall be saved, for thou art our praise. Be not angry with us for ever, but revive us again, that thy people may rejoice in thee. Shew us thy mercy, O Lord, and grant us thy salvation. *Jeremiah 17:14. Psalm 85:5-7.*

2.   *That we may be taken into covenant with God, and admitted into relation to Him.*

Be thou to us a God, and take us to be to thee a people; and make us a willing people in the day of thy power. *Hebrews 8:10. Psalm 110:3.*

Though we are no more worthy to be called thy children; for how shouldest thou put us that have been rebellious among the children, and give us the pleasant land? But thou hast said that we shall call thee our Father, and not turn away from thee. Shall we not therefore from this time cry unto thee, Our Father, thou art the guide of our youth. *Luke 15:19. Jeremiah 3:19, 4.*

Lord, we take hold of thy covenant, to thee we join ourselves in a perpetual covenant; O that thou wouldest cause us to pass under the rod, and bring us into the bond of the covenant, that we may become thine. *Isaiah 56:4. Jeremiah 50:5. Ezekiel 20:37. Ezekiel 16:8.*

Make with us an everlasting covenant, even the sure mercies of David. *Isaiah 55:3.*

3.   *That we may have the favour of God, and an interest in His special love.*

We intreat thy favour, O God, with our whole hearts; be merciful to us according to thy word, for in thy favour is life, yea thy loving kindness is better than life itself. *Psalm 119:58. Psalm 30:5. Psalm 63:3.*

Lord, make thy face to shine upon us, and be gracious unto us; Lord, lift up the light of thy countenance upon us, and give us peace. *Numbers 6:25, 26.*

Remember us, O Lord, with the favour that thou bearest unto thy people, O visit us with thy salvation, that we may see the good of thy chosen, and may rejoice in the gladness of thy nation, and may glory with thine inheritance. *Psalm 106:4, 5.*

4.   *That we may have the blessing of God.*

O God, be merciful to us and bless us, and cause thy face to shine upon us; yea let God, even our own God, give us his blessing. *Psalm 67:1, 6.*

The Lord that made heaven and earth, bless us out of Zion; bless us with all spiritual blessings in heavenly things by Christ Jesus. *Psalm 134:3. Ephesians 1:3.*

O that thou wouldest bless us indeed! Command the blessing upon us, even life for ever more; For thou blessest, O Lord, and it shall be blessed. *1 Chronicles 4:10. Psalm 133:3. 1 Chronicles 17:27.*

Let us receive the blessing from the Lord, even righteousness from the God of our salvation. *Psalm 24:5.*

Hast thou but one blessing? Yea, thou hast many blessings: Bless us, even us also, O our Father; yea, let the blessing of Abraham come upon us, which comes upon the Gentiles through faith. And the blessing of Jacob, for we would not let thee go, except thou bless us. *Genesis 27:38. Galatians 3:14. Genesis 32:26.*

5.   *That we may have the presence of God with us.*

If thy presence go not up with us, carry us not up hence; never leave us nor forsake us. *Exodus 33:15. Hebrews 13:5.*

O cast us not away from thy presence, nor ever take thy holy spirit away from us; but let us always dwell with the upright in thy presence. *Psalm 51:11. Psalm 140:13.*

WE MUST PRAY FOR THE COMFORTABLE SENSE OF OUR RECONCILIATION TO GOD, AND OUR ACCEPTANCE WITH HIM

1. *That we may have some evidence of the pardon of our sins, and of our adoption.*

     Make us to hear joy and gladness, that the bones which sin hath broken may rejoice. *Psalm 51:8.*
    Say unto each of us, Son, Daughter, be of good cheer, thy sins are forgiven thee. *Matthew 9:2.*
    Let the blood of Christ, who through the eternal Spirit offered himself without spot to God, purge our conscience from dead works to serve thee the living God. *Hebrews 9:14.*
    Let thy Spirit witness with our spirits that we are the children of God, and if children, then heirs, heirs of God, and joint-heirs with Christ. *Romans 8:16, 17.*
    Say unto our souls, that thou art our salvation. *Psalm 35:3.*

2. *That we may have a well-grounded peace of conscience; a holy security and serenity of mind arising from a sense of our justification before God, and a good work wrought in us.*

    The Lord of peace himself give us peace, all peace, always, by all means; that peace which Jesus Christ hath left with us, which he gives to us, such a peace as the world can neither give nor take away; such a peace as that our hearts may not be troubled or afraid. *2 Thessalonians 3:16. John 14:27.*
    Let the work of righteousness in our souls be peace, and the effect of righteousness quietness and assurance for ever. *Isaiah 32:17.*
    Speak peace unto thy people and to thy saints, and let not them turn again to folly. *Psalm 85:8.*
    O create the fruit of the lips, Peace, peace to them that are afar off and to them that are nigh, and restore comfort to thy mourners. *Isaiah 57:19, 18.*
    Where the sons of peace are, let thy peace find them out, and rest upon them. *Luke 10:6.*

Cause us to hear thy loving kindness, and to taste that thou art gracious, for in thee do we trust. *Psalm 143:8. 1 Peter 2:3.*

Let the peace of God which passeth all understanding, keep our hearts and minds through Christ Jesus; and let that peace rule in our hearts, unto which we are called. *Philippians 4:7. Colossians 3:15.*

Now the God of hope fill us with all joy and peace in believing, that we may abound in hope through the power of the Holy Ghost. *Romans 15:13.*

WE MUST PRAY FOR THE GRACE OF GOD, AND ALL THE KIND AND POWERFUL INFLUENCES AND OPERATIONS OF THAT GRACE

E come to the throne of grace, that we may obtain not only mercy to pardon, but grace to help in every time of need; grace for seasonable help. *Hebrews 4:16.*

From the fulness that is in Jesus Christ (in whom it pleased the Father that all fulness should dwell) let every one of us receive, and grace for grace. *John 1:16. Colossians 1:19.*

1.   *We must pray for grace to fortify us against every evil thought, word and work. Having been earnest for the removing of the guilt of sin, that we may not die for it as a crime; we must be no less earnest for the breaking of the power of sin, that we may not die by it as a disease; but that it may be mortified in us.*

O let no iniquity have dominion over us, because we are not under the law, but under grace. *Romans 6:14.*

Let the flesh be crucified in us with its affections and lusts; that walking in the Spirit we may not fulfil the lusts of the flesh. *Galatians 5:24, 16.*

Let our old man be crucified with Christ, that the body of sin may be destroyed, that henceforth we may not serve sin; and let not sin reign in our mortal bodies (in our immortal souls) that we should obey it in the lusts thereof. But being made free from sin, let us become the servants of righteousness. *Romans 6:6, 12, 18.*

Let the law of the Spirit of life, which is in Christ Jesus, make us free from the law of sin and death. *Romans 8:2.*

Give us grace to put off the old man, which is corrupt according to the deceitful lusts, that we may put on the new man, which after God is created in righteousness and true holiness. *Ephesians 4:22, 24.*

That the world may be crucified to us, and we to the world, by the cross of Christ. *Galatians 6:14.*

— *And that the temptations of Satan may not overcome us.*

We pray that we may not enter into temptation: Or however, that no temptation may take us but such as is common to men, and let the faithful God never suffer us to be tempted above what we are able, but with the temptation make way for us to escape. *Matthew 26:41. 1 Corinthians 10:13.*

Put upon us the whole armour of God, that we may be able to stand against the wiles of the devil, to withstand in the evil day, and having done all to stand; Let our loins be girt about with truth: put on us the breast-plate of righteousness, and let our feet be shod with the preparation of the gospel of peace. Give us the shield of faith, wherewith we may quench all the fiery darts of the wicked, and the helmet of salvation; and let the sword of the Spirit, which is the word of God, be always ready to us. *Ephesians 6:11-17.*

Enable us so to resist the devil, as that he may flee from us; to resist him stedfast in the faith. And the God of peace tread Satan under our feet, and do it shortly. *James 4:7. 1 Peter 5:9. Romans 16:20.*

2. *We must pray for grace to furnish us for every good thought, word, and work; that we may not only be kept from sin, but may be in every thing as we should be, and do as we should do.*

Let Christ be made of God to us not only righteousness, but wisdom, sanctification and redemption. *1 Corinthians 1:30.*

Let us be planted together in the likeness of Christ's death and resurrection, that as he was raised from the dead by the glory of the Father, so we also may walk in newness of life. *Romans 6:5, 4.*

(a) *That the work of grace may be wrought there where it is not yet begun.*

Lord, teach transgressors thy ways, and let sinners be converted unto thee; and let the disobedient be turned to the wisdom of the just; and made ready, a people prepared for the Lord. *Psalm 51:13. Luke 1:17.*

Let those be quickened that are yet dead in trespasses and sins: Say unto them, Live; yea, say unto them, Live; and the time shall be a time of love. *Ephesians 2:1. Ezekiel 16:6, 8.*

Open their eyes, and turn them from darkness to light, and from the power of Satan unto God, that they may receive forgiveness of sins, and an inheritance among them which are sanctified. *Acts 26:18.*

By the blood of the covenant send forth the prisoners out of the pit in which is no water, that they may turn to the strong hold, as prisoners of hope. *Zechariah 9:11, 12.*

Let the word of God prevail to the pulling down of strong holds, and the casting down of imaginations, and every high thing that exalteth itself against the knowledge of God, and let every thought be brought into obedience to Christ. *2 Corinthians 10:4, 5.*

(b) That where it is begun it may be carried on, and at length perfected, and the foundation that is well laid may be happily built upon.

Fulfil in us all the good pleasure of thy goodness, and the work of faith with power. *2 Thessalonians 1:11.*

Let the God that has begun a good work in us, perform it unto the day of Christ. *Philippians 1:6.*

Perfect, O God, that which concerns us: Thy mercy, O Lord, endures for ever; forsake not the work of thine own hands. *Psalm 138:8.*

Lord, let thy grace be sufficient for us, and let thy strength be made perfect in weakness; that where we are weak there we may be strong; strong in the Lord and the power of his might. *2 Corinthians 12:9, 10. Ephesians 6:10.*

3.   *More particularly we must pray for grace.*

(a) To teach and instruct us, and make us knowing and intelligent in the things of God.

Give us so to cry after knowledge, and lift up our voice for understanding, to seek for it as silver, and to search for it as for hid treasure, that we may understand the fear of the Lord, and find the knowledge of God. *Proverbs 2:3, 4, 5.*

Give us all to know thee, from the least even to the greatest, and to follow on to know thee; and so to know thee the only true God, and Jesus Christ whom thou hast sent, as may be life eternal to us. *Hebrews 8:11. Hosea 6:3. John 17:3.*

Give us the spirit of wisdom and revelation in the knowledge of Christ, that the eyes of our understanding being enlightened, we may know what is the hope of his calling, and what the riches of the glory of his inheritance in the saints, and may experience what is the exceeding greatness of his power to us ward who believe; according to the working of his mighty power. *Ephesians 1:17, 18, 19.*

Open thou our eyes, that we may see the wondrous things of thy law and gospel. *Psalm 119:18.*

Give us to know the certainty of those things wherein we have been instructed; and let our knowledge grow up to all riches of the full assurance of understanding, to the acknowledgment of the mystery of God, even of the Father and of Christ. *Luke 1:4. Colossians 2:2.*

Deal with thy servants according to thy mercy, and teach us thy statutes; we are thy servants, give us understanding that we may know thy testimonies. Let our cry come before thee, O Lord, give us understanding according to thy word; that good understanding which have they that do thy commandments; whose praise endureth for ever. *Psalm 119:124, 125, 169. Psalm 111:10.*

(b) To lead us into, and keep us in the way of truth, and if in any thing we be in an error, to rectify our mistake.

Let the Spirit of truth guide us into all truth, and cause us to understand wherein we have erred. *John 16:13. Job 6:24.*

That which we see not teach thou us, and enable us so to prove all things, as to hold fast that which is good. *Job 34:32. 1 Thessalonians 5:21.*

Lord, grant that we may not be as children, tossed to and fro, and carried about with every wind of doctrine, by the slight of men, but speaking the truth in love, may grow up into Christ in all things, who is the head. *Ephesians 4:14, 15.*

Lord, give us so to do thy will, as that we may know of the doctrine whether it be of God; and so to know the truth, as that the truth may make us free, may make us free indeed. *John 7:17. John 8:32, 36.*

Enable us, we pray thee, to hold fast the form of sound words, which we have heard, in faith and love which is in Christ Jesus, and to continue in the things which we have learned and been assured of. *2 Timothy 1:13. 2 Timothy 3:14.*

(c) To help our memories, that the truths of God may be ready to us, whenever we have occasion to use them.

Lord, let thy Spirit teach us all things, and bring all things to our remembrance, whatsoever thou hast said unto us; that the word of Christ may dwell richly in us in all wisdom and spiritual understanding. *John 14:26. Colossians 3:16. Colossians 1:9.*

Lord, grant that we may give a more earnest heed to the things which we have heard, lest at any time we let them slip, and may keep in memory what hath been preached to us, and may not believe in vain. *Hebrews 2:1. 1 Corinthians 15:2.*

Lord, make us ready and mighty in the scriptures, that we may be perfect, throughly furnished unto all good works; and being well instructed unto the kingdom of heaven, may as the good householder, bring out of our treasure things new and old. *Acts 18:24. 2 Timothy 3:17. Matthew 13:52.*

(d) *To direct our consciences, to shew us the way of our duty, and to make us wise, knowing, judicious Christians.*

Lord, give us a wise and an understanding heart, that wisdom which in all cases is profitable to direct; that wisdom of the prudent which is to understand his way. *1 Kings 3:9, 12. Ecclesiastes 10:10. Proverbs 14:8.*

This we pray, that our love may abound yet more and more in knowledge, and in all judgment, that we may discern things that differ, and may approve things that are excellent; That we may be sincere and without offence unto the day of Christ, and may be filled with the fruits of righteousness, which are by Jesus Christ unto the glory and praise of God. *Philippians 1:9, 10, 11.*

O that we may be filled with the knowledge of thy will in all wisdom and spiritual understanding; That we may walk worthy of the Lord unto all pleasing, being fruitful in every good work, and increasing in the knowledge of God. *Colossians 1:9, 10.*

Teach us thy way, O God, and lead us in a plain path, because of our observers. *Psalm 27:11.*

When we know not what to do, our eyes are up unto thee; Then let us hear the word behind us, saying, This is the way, walk in it, that we turn not to the right hand, or to the left. *2 Chronicles 20:12. Isaiah 30:21.*

Order our steps in thy word, and let no iniquity have dominion over us. *Psalm 119:133.*

(e) *To sanctify our natures, to plant in us all holy principles and dispositions, and to increase every grace in us.*

The very God of peace sanctify us wholly, and we pray God our whole spirit, and soul and body, may be preserved blameless unto the coming of our Lord Jesus Christ; for faithful is he that calleth us, who also will do it. *1 Thessalonians 5:23, 24.*

Create in us a clean heart, O God, and renew a right spirit within us; Cast us not away from thy presence, and take not thy holy spirit away from us; Restore unto us the joy of thy salvation, and uphold us with thy free spirit. *Psalm 51:10, 11, 12.*

Write thy law in our hearts, and put it in our inward part, that we may be the epistles of Christ written by the Spirit of the living God, not in tables of stone, but in fleshy tables of the heart, that the law of our God being in our heart, none of our steps may slide, and we may delight to do thy will, O God, may delight in the law of God after the inward man. *Hebrews 8:10. 2 Corinthians 3:3. Psalm 37:31. Psalm 40:8. Romans 7:22.*

O that we may obey from the heart that form of doctrine into which we desire to be delivered, as into a mould, that our whole souls may be leavened by it; and that we may not be conformed to this world, but transformed by the renewing of our mind; may not fashion ourselves after our former lusts in our ignorance, but as obedient children may be holy in all manner of conversation, as he which hath called us is holy. *Romans 6:17. Matthew 13:33. Romans 12:2. 1 Peter 1:14, 15.*

1)   *We must pray for faith.*

Unto us (Lord) let it be given to believe; for the faith by which we are saved is not of ourselves, it is the gift of God. *Philippians 1:29. Ephesians 2:8.*

Lord, increase our faith; and perfect what is lacking in it, that we may be strong in faith, giving glory to God. *Luke 17:5. 1 Thessalonians 3:10. Romans 4:20.*

Lord, give us so to be crucified with Christ, as that the life we now live in the flesh we may live by the faith of the Son of God, who loved us, and gave himself for us; And so to bear about with us continually the dying of the Lord Jesus, as that the life also of Jesus may be manifested in our mortal bodies. *Galatians 2:20. 2 Corinthians 4:10.*

As we have received Christ Jesus the Lord, enable us so to walk in him, rooted and built up in him, and stablished in the faith as we have been taught, abounding therein with thanksgiving. *Colossians 2:6, 7.*

Let every word of thine profit us, being mixed with faith, by which we receive thy testimony, and set to our seal that God is true. *Hebrews 4:2. John 3:33.*

We beseech thee work in us that faith which is the substance of things hoped for, and the evidence of things not seen, by which we may look above the things that are seen that are temporal, and may look at the things that are not seen that are eternal. *Hebrews 11:1. 2 Corinthians 4:18.*

Enable us by faith to set the Lord always before us, and to have our eyes ever towards him; that we may act in every thing as seeing him that is invisible, and having a respect to the recompence of reward. *Psalm 16:8. Psalm 25:15. Hebrews 11:27, 26.*

Let our hearts be purified by faith, and let it be our victory overcoming the world. And let us be kept from fainting by believing that we shall see the goodness of the Lord in the land of the living. *Acts 15:9. 1 John 5:4. Psalm 27:13.*

2)   *We must pray for the fear of God.*

Lord, work in us that fear of thee, which is the beginning of wisdom, which is the instruction of wisdom, and which is a fountain of life to depart from the snares of death. *Proverbs 1:7. Proverbs 15:33. Proverbs 14:27.*

Unite our hearts to fear thy name, that we may keep thy commandments, which is the whole of man. *Psalm 86:11. Ecclesiastes 12:13.*

O put thy fear into our hearts, that we may never depart from thee. Let us all be devoted to thy fear; And let us be in the fear of the Lord every day, and all the day long. *Jeremiah 32:40. Psalm 119:38. Proverbs 23:17.*

3)   *We must pray that the love of God and Christ may be rooted in us, and in order thereunto, that the love of the world may be rooted out of us.*

Give us grace (we beseech thee) to love thee the Lord our God with all our heart and soul, and mind and might, which is the first and great commandment, to set our love upon thee, and to delight ourselves always in thee, and therein we shall have the desire of our heart. *Matthew 22:37, 38. Psalm 91:14. Psalm 37:4.*

Circumcise our hearts to love thee the Lord our God with all our heart, and with all our soul, that we may live. *Deuteronomy 30:6.*

O that the love of God may be shed abroad in our hearts by the Holy Ghost. *Romans 5:5.*

O that Jesus Christ may be very precious to us, as he is to all that believe, that he may be in our account the chiefest of ten thousands, and altogether lovely; and that he may be our beloved and our friend: That though we have not seen him, yet we may love him, and though now we see him not, yet believing we may rejoice with joy unspeakable and full of glory. *1 Peter 2:7. Canticle (Song of Solomon) 5:10, 16. 1 Peter 1:8.*

Let the love of Christ to us constrain us to live, not to ourselves, but to him that died for us and rose again. *2 Corinthians 5:14, 15.*

And, Lord, grant that we may not love the world, nor the things that are in the world, because if any man love the world, the love of the Father is not in him; that we may set our affections on things above, and not on things that are on the earth. *1 John 2:15. Colossians 3:1, 2.*

4) *We must pray that our consciences may be always tender, and that we may live a life of repentance.*

Lord, take away the stony heart out of our flesh, and give us a heart of flesh. *Ezekiel 11:19.*

Make us afraid of all appearances of evil, and careful not to give Satan advantage against us, as being not ignorant of his devices. *1 Thessalonians 5:22. 2 Corinthians 2:11.*

Lord, give us the happiness which they have that fear always; that when we think we stand, we may take heed lest we fall. *Proverbs 28:14. 1 Corinthians 10:12.*

5) *We must pray to God to work in us charity and brotherly love.*

Lord, put upon us that charity which is the bond of perfectness, that we may keep the unity of the Spirit in the bond of peace, and may live in love and peace, that the God of love and peace may be with us. *Colossians 3:14. Ephesians 4:3. 2 Corinthians 13:11.*

Lord, give us to love our neighbour as ourselves, with that love which is the fulfilling of the law; to love one another with a pure heart fervently, that hereby all men may know that we are Christ's disciples. *Romans 13:9, 10. 1 Peter 1:22. John 13:35.*

And as we are taught of God to love one another, give us to abound therein more and more, and as we have opportunity to do good to all men, and as much as in us lies to live peaceably with all men; always following after the things that make for peace, and things wherewith one may edify another. *1 Thessalonians 4:9, 10. Galatians 6:10. Romans 12:18. Romans 14:19.*

Lord, make us able to love our enemies, to bless them that curse us, and to pray for them that despitefully use us, and to do good to them that hate us, forbearing one another, and forgiving one another in love, as Christ forgave us. *Matthew 5:44. Colossians 3:13.*

6)   *We must pray for the grace of self-denial.*

Lord, give us grace to deny ourselves, to take up our cross daily, and to follow Christ, to keep under the body, and bring it into subjection. *Matthew 16:24. 1 Corinthians 9:27.*

Lord, keep us from being lovers of our own selves, from being wise in our own conceit, and leaning to our own understanding. *2 Timothy 3:2. Proverbs 3:7, 5.*

Lord, give us to seek not our own only, but every one his brother's welfare. *1 Corinthians 10:24.*

And grant that none of us may live to ourselves, or die to ourselves, but whether we live or die we may be the Lord's, and may live and die to him. *Romans 14:7, 8.*

7)   *We must pray for humility and meekness.*

Lord, give us all to learn of Christ to be meek and lowly in heart, that we may find rest to our souls; and that herein the same mind may be in us that was also in Christ Jesus. *Matthew 11:29. Philippians 2:5.*

Lord, hide pride from us, and clothe us with humility, and put upon us the ornament of a meek and quiet spirit, which in thy sight is of great price. *Job 33:17. 1 Peter 5:5. 1 Peter 3:4.*

Lord, give us grace to walk worthy of the vocation wherewith we are called, with all lowliness and meekness, with long-suffering forbearing one another in love. *Ephesians 4:1, 2.*

Let anger never rest in our bosoms, nor the sun ever go down upon our wrath; but enable us to shew all meekness towards all men, because we ourselves also were sometimes foolish and disobedient. *Ecclesiastes 7:9. Ephesians 4:26. Titus 3:2, 3.*

Let us be clothed as becomes the elect of God, holy and beloved, with bowels of mercies, kindness, humbleness of mind, meekness, and long-suffering; that being merciful as our Father which is in heaven is merciful, we may be perfect as he is perfect. *Colossians 3:12. Luke 6:36. Matthew 5 (v. 48).*

8)   *We must pray for the grace of contentment and patience, and a holy indifferency to all the things of sense and time.*

Lord, teach us whatsoever state we are in therewith to be content; let us know both how to be abased, and how to abound, every where and in all things let us be instructed both to be full and to be hungry, both to abound and to suffer need; And let godliness with contentment be great gain to us; and a little with the fear of the Lord and quietness, is better than great treasure and trouble therewith. *Philippians 4:11, 12. 1 Timothy 6:6. Proverbs 15:16. Proverbs 17:1.*

Lord, grant that our conversation may be without covetousness, and we may always be content with such things as we have; still saying, The will of the Lord be done. *Hebrews 13:5. Acts 21:14.*

Enable us in our patience to possess our own souls; and let patience always have its perfect work, that we may be perfect and entire, wanting nothing. *Luke 21:19. James 1:4.*

Lord, give us grace to weep as though we wept not, and to rejoice as though we rejoiced not, and to buy as though we possessed not, and to use this world as not abusing it, because the time is short, and the fashion of this world passeth away. *1 Corinthians 7:29, 30, 31.*

9)   *We must pray for the grace of hope; a hope in God and Christ, and a hope of eternal life.*

Let patience work experience in us, and experience hope, such a hope as maketh not ashamed. Through patience and comfort of the scriptures let us have hope, and be saved by hope. *Romans 5:4, 5. Romans 15:4. Romans 8:24.*

Let the God of Jacob be our help, and our hope always be in the Lord our God. *Psalm 146:5.*

Let us be begotten again to a lively hope by the resurrection of Jesus Christ, and let that hope be to us as an anchor of the soul, sure and stedfast, entering into that within the vail, whither the forerunner is for us entered. *1 Peter 1:3. Hebrews 6:19, 20.*

Let us have Christ in us the hope of glory, and never be moved away from that hope of the gospel; but enable us to give diligence unto the full assurance of hope unto the end. *Colossians 1:27, 23. Hebrews 6:11.*

10) *We must pray for grace to preserve us from sin, and all appearances of it and approaches towards it.*

Now we pray to God that we may do no evil, but may be blameless and harmless as the children of God, without rebuke, in the midst of a crooked and perverse generation. *2 Corinthians 13:7. Philippians 2:15.*

Turn away our eyes from beholding vanity, and quicken thou us in thy way; Remove from us the way of lying, and grant us thy law graciously. *Psalm 119:37, 29.*

Incline not our hearts to any evil thing, to practise wicked works with them that work iniquity, and let us not eat of their dainties. *Psalm 141:4.*

O cleanse us from our secret faults, keep back thy servants also from presumptuous sins; let not them have dominion over us, but let us be upright and innocent from the great transgressions, and grant that hereby we may prove ourselves upright before thee, by keeping ourselves from our own iniquity. *Psalm 19:12, 13. Psalm 18:23.*

Let thy word be hid in our hearts, that we may not sin against thee, and thy grace be at all times sufficient for us, ready to us, and mighty in us, and never give us up to our own hearts lusts, to walk in our own counsels. *Psalm 119:11. 2 Corinthians 12:9. Psalm 81:12.*

Enable us to walk circumspectly, not as fools, but as wise, so circumspectly, that we may cut off occasion from them which desire occasion to blaspheme that worthy name by which we are called, and with well-doing may put to silence the ignorance of foolish men, and may adorn the doctrine of God our Saviour, in all things. *Ephesians 5:15. 2 Corinthians 11:12. James 2:7. 1 Peter 2:15. Titus 2:10.*

4. *We must pray for grace to enable us, both to govern our tongues well, and to use them well.*

Lord, enable us to take heed to our ways, that we offend not with our tongue, and to keep our mouth as it were with a bridle, that it may not be hasty to utter any thing. *Psalm 39:1. Ecclesiastes 5:2.*

Set a watch, O Lord, before our mouth, keep the door of our lips, that we may not offend in word. *Psalm 141:3. James 3:2.*

Let our speech be always with grace seasoned with salt, and enable us always out of the good treasure of our heart to bring forth good things. Let our mouth speak wisdom, and our tongue talk of judgment; and let not thy words depart out of our mouth, nor out of the mouth of our seed, or our seed's seed, from henceforth and for ever. *Colossians 4:6. Matthew 12:35. Psalm 37:30. Isaiah 59:21.*

Enable us always to open our mouth with wisdom, and let the law of kindness be in our tongue: Give us to know what is acceptable, that our tongue may be as choice silver, and our lips may feed many. *Proverbs 31:26. Proverbs 10:32, 20, 21.*

5. *We must pray for grace to direct and quicken us to, and to strengthen and assist us in our duty in the whole course of our conversation.*

Let the grace of God, which hath appeared to us, and to all men, bringing salvation, effectually teach us to deny all ungodliness and worldly fleshly lusts, and to live soberly, righteously and godly in this present world, looking for the blessed hope, and the glorious appearing of the great God and our Saviour Jesus Christ, who gave himself for us, that he might redeem us from all iniquity, and purify unto himself a peculiar people zealous of good works. *Titus 2:11-14.*

(a) That we may be prudent and discreet in our duty.

Thou hast said, If any man lack wisdom, he must ask it of God, who gives to all men liberally, and upbraideth not, and it shall be given him. Lord, we want wisdom, make us wise as serpents, and harmless as doves, that wisdom may make our face to shine, and may be better to us than weapons of war. *James 1:5. Matthew 10:16. Ecclesiastes 8:1. Ecclesiastes 9:18.*

Enable us to walk in wisdom towards them that are without, redeeming the time. *Colossians 4:5.*

Give us to order all our affairs with discretion; and to behave ourselves wisely in a perfect way, with a perfect heart. *Psalm 112:5. Psalm 101:2.*

(b) That we may be honest and sincere in our duty.

Let our wisdom be not that from beneath, which is earthly, sensual, devilish, but wisdom from above, which is first pure, then peaceable, gentle, and easy to be intreated, full of mercy and good fruits, without partiality, and without hypocrisy. *James 3:15, 17.*

O that we may always have our conversation in the world in simplicity and godly sincerity, not with fleshly wisdom, but by the grace of God. *2 Corinthians 1:12.*

Lord, uphold us in our integrity, and set us before thy face for ever, and let integrity and uprightness preserve us, for we wait on thee. *Psalm 41:12. Psalm 25:21.*

Let our hearts be sound in thy statutes, that we be not ashamed; and let our eye be single, that our whole body may be full of light. *Psalm 119:80. Matthew 6:22.*

(c) That we may be active and diligent in our duty.

Lord, quicken us to work the works of him that was sent us, while it is day, because the night comes wherein no man can work; and what good our hand finds to do, to do it with all our might, because there is no work or knowledge in the grave, whither we are going. *John 9:4. Ecclesiastes 9:10.*

Lord, grant that we may never be slothful in any good business, but fervent in spirit serving the Lord; stedfast and unmoveable, always abounding in the work of the Lord, forasmuch as we know that our labour is not in vain in the Lord. *Romans 12:11. 1 Corinthians 15:58.*

Lord, make us zealously affected in every good work; and what we do enable us to do it heartily as unto the Lord, and not unto men. *Galatians 4:18. Colossians 3:23.*

Lord, enable us to do the work of every day in its day, according as the duty of the day requires, redeeming the time, because the days are evil; that when our Lord comes he may find us doing. *Ezra 3:4. Ephesians 5:16. Luke 12:43.*

(d) That we may be resolute and courageous in our duty, as those that know that though we may be losers for Christ, we shall not be losers by Him in the end.

Lord, teach us to endure hardness as good soldiers of Jesus Christ; that we may not fear the reproach of men, or their revilings, nor be ashamed of Christ or of his words, knowing whom we have believed, even one who is able to keep what we have committed to him against that day. *2 Timothy 2:3. Isaiah 51:7. Mark 8:38. 2 Timothy 1:12.*

Though bonds and afflictions should abide us, Lord, grant that none of these things may move us, and that we may not count life itself dear to us, so we may finish our course with joy. *Acts 20:23, 24.*

Enable us in all things to approve ourselves to God, and then to pass by honour and dishonour, by evil report and good report, clad with the armour of righteousness on the right hand and on the left, as those that account it a very small thing to be judged of man's judgment, for he that judgeth us is the Lord. *2 Corinthians 6:4, 8, 7. 1 Corinthians 4:3, 4.*

(e) That we may be pleasant and cheerful in our duty.

Lord, enable us to rejoice evermore; to rejoice in the Lord always, because he hath again said unto us, Rejoice; that we may go on our way rejoicing, may eat our bread with joy, and drink our wine with a merry heart, as we shall have reason to do if God now accepteth our works. *1 Thessalonians 5:16. Philippians 4:4. Acts 8:39. Ecclesiastes 9:7.*

Give us grace to serve thee the Lord our God with joyfulness and gladness of heart in the abundance of all things; And to sing in the ways of the Lord, because great is the glory of our God. *Deuteronomy 28:47. Psalm 138:5.*

Let us have that cheerfulness of heart which doth good like a medicine, and deliver us from that heaviness which maketh the heart stoop, and that sorrow of the world which worketh death. *Proverbs 17:22. Proverbs 12:25. 2 Corinthians 7:10.*

(f) That we may do the duty of every condition of life, every event of providence, and every relation wherein we stand.

Lord, enable us, in a day of prosperity to be joyful, and in a day of adversity, to consider, because God hath set the one over against the other; to add to our knowledge temperance, and to temperance patience. *Ecclesiastes 7:14. 2 Peter 1:6.*

Give us grace to abide with thee in the calling wherein we are called; and in all our ways to acknowledge thee, and be thou pleased to direct our steps. *1 Corinthians 7:24. Proverbs 3:6.*

Let those that are called, being servants, be the Lord's freemen, and those that are called, being free, be Christ's servants. *1 Corinthians 7:22.*

Let all in every relation dwell together in unity, that it may be as the dew of Hermon, and as the dew that descended upon the mountains of Zion. O that we may dwell together as joint-heirs of the grace of life, that our prayers may not be hindered. *Psalm 133:1, 3. 1 Peter 3:7.*

Give us grace to honour all men, to love the brotherhood, to fear God, and to be subject to the higher powers, not only for wrath, but also for conscience sake. *1 Peter 2:17. Romans 13:1, 5.*

(g) That we may be universally conscientious.

O that we may stand perfect and complete in all the will of God. *Colossians 4:12.*

O that our ways were directed to keep thy commandments! And then shall we not be ashamed, when we have a respect to them all. *Psalm 119:5, 6.*

Teach us, O Lord, the way of thy statutes, and we shall keep it unto the end: Give us understanding, and we shall keep thy law, yea we shall observe it with our whole heart: Make us to go in the path of thy commandments, for therein do we delight. Incline our hearts unto thy testimonies, and not to covetousness. *Psalm 119:33-36.*

Grant us, we pray thee, according to the riches of thy glory, that we may be strengthened with all might by thy Spirit in the inner man: That Christ may dwell in our hearts by faith, and that we being rooted and grounded in love, may be able to comprehend with all saints what is the breadth, and length, and depth, and height, and may know the love of Christ which passeth knowledge; and be filled with a divine fulness, and may partake of a divine nature. *Ephesians 3:16-19. 2 Peter 1:4.*

And let the love of Christ constrain us to live not to ourselves, but to him that died for us, and rose again. *2 Corinthians 5:14, 15.*

6.   *We must pray for grace to make us wiser and better every day than other.*

Lord, give us to increase with the increases of God; to grow in grace, and in the knowledge of our Lord and Saviour Jesus Christ; to hold on our way, and having clean hands to grow stronger and stronger. *Colossians 2:19. 2 Peter 3:18. Job 17:9.*

Let our path be as the shining light, which shines more and more to the perfect day. *Proverbs 4:18.*

We have not yet attained, nor are we already perfect; Lord, grant that therefore forgetting the things that are behind, we may reach forth to those things that are before, for the prize of the high calling of God in Christ Jesus. *Philippians 3:12, 13, 14.*

Be thou as the dew unto us, that we may grow as the lily, and cast forth our roots as Lebanon; that our branches may spread, and our beauty be as the olive-tree. And let the Sun of righteousness arise upon us with healing under his wings, that we may go forth and grow up as calves of the stall. *Hosea 14:5, 6. Malachi 4:2.*

7.   *We must pray for effectual support and comfort under all the crosses and afflictions that we meet with in this world.*

We know that we are born to trouble as the sparks fly upward; but in six troubles, be thou pleased to deliver us, and in seven let no evil touch us. *Job 5:7, 19.*

Let the eternal God be our refuge, and underneath be the everlasting arms; that the spirit thou hast made may not fail before thee, nor the soul that thou hast redeemed. *Deuteronomy 33:27. Isaiah 57:16. Psalm 71:23.*

Let us be strengthened with all might according to thy glorious power, unto all patience and long-suffering with joyfulness. *Colossians 1:11.*

Let thy statutes be our songs in the house of our pilgrimage; and let thy testimonies, which we have taken as a heritage for ever, be always the rejoicing of our hearts. *Psalm 119:54, 111.*

When we are troubled on every side, yet let us not be distressed, and when we are perplexed, yet let us not be in despair; but as sorrowful, and yet always rejoicing, as having nothing, and yet possessing all things. *2 Corinthians 4:8. 2 Corinthians 6:10.*

8.   *We must pray for grace to preserve us to the end, and to fit us for whatever lies before us betwixt and the grave.*

Lord, deliver us from every evil work, and preserve us to thy heavenly kingdom, being kept from falling, that we may be presented faultless at the coming of thy glory with exceeding joy. *2 Timothy 4:18. Jude 24.*

Lord, make us to increase and abound in love one towards another, and towards all men, that our hearts may be established unblameable in holiness, before God even our Father, at the coming of our Lord Jesus Christ with all his saints. *1 Thessalonians 3:12, 13.*

If Satan desire to have us that he may sift us as wheat, yet let Christ's intercession prevail for us, that our faith fail not. *Luke 22:31, 32.*

Till we are taken out of the world, let us be kept from the evil, and sanctified through thy truth; thy word is truth. *John 17:15, 17.*

Build us up, we pray thee, in our most holy faith, and keep us in the love of God, looking for the mercy of our Lord Jesus Christ unto eternal life. *Jude 20, 21.*

Grant that we may continue to call upon thee as long as we live, and till we die may never remove our integrity from us; and that our righteousness we may hold fast, and never let it go, and our hearts may not reproach us so long as we live. *Psalm 116:2. Job 27:5, 6.*

9.   *We must pray for grace to prepare us for death, and to carry us well through our dying moments.*

Lord, make us to know our end, and the measure of our days what it is, that we may know and consider how frail we are; and that our days are as a hand breadth, and that every man at his best state is altogether vanity, and our days upon earth are as a shadow, and there is no abiding. *Psalm 39:4, 5. 1 Chronicles 29:15.*

Lord, teach us so to number our days, that we may apply our hearts unto wisdom, and make us to consider our latter end. *Psalm 90:12. Deuteronomy 32:29.*

Lord, make us always ready, with our loins girded about, and our lights burning, because the Son of man comes at an hour that we think not. *Luke 12:35, 40.*

Keep us all the days of our appointed time, waiting till our change comes; and then shalt thou call, and we will answer. *Job 14:14, 15.*

Bring us to our grave as a shock of corn in its season; satisfy us with life, whether it be longer or shorter, and shew us thy salvation. *Job 5:26. Psalm 91 (v. 16).*

And when we walk through the valley of the shadow of death, be thou with us, that we may fear no evil, let thy rod and thy staff comfort us. *Psalm 23:4.*

Let goodness and mercy follow us all the days of our life, and let us dwell in the house of the Lord for ever. Mercy and truth be with us. *Psalm 23:6. 2 Samuel 15:20.*

Redeem our souls from the power of the grave, and receive us; Guide us by thy counsel, and afterwards receive us to glory. *Psalm 49:15. Psalm 73:24.*

10.   *We must pray for grace to fit us for heaven, and that we may at length be put in possession of eternal life.*

Lord, make us meet to partake of the inheritance of the saints in light; let God himself work us to the self-same thing, and give us the earnest of the Spirit in our hearts. *Colossians 1:12. 2 Corinthians 5:5.*

O that we may now have our conversation in heaven, that we may from thence with comfort look for the Saviour the Lord Jesus, who shall change our vile bodies, that they may be fashioned like unto his glorious body. *Philippians 3:20, 21.*

O that now we may set our affections on things above, and that our life may be hid with Christ in God, that when Christ who is our life shall appear, we may also appear with him in glory; that when he shall appear we may be like him, and may see him as he is, may behold his face in righteousness, and when we awake may be satisfied with his likeness. *Colossians 3:2, 3, 4. 1 John 3:2. Psalm 17:15.*

When we fail, let us be received into everlasting habitations, in the city that hath foundation, whose builder and maker is God, that we may be together for ever with the Lord, to see as we are seen, and know as we are known. *Luke 16:9. Hebrews 11:10. 1 Thessalonians 4:17. 1 Corinthians 13:12.*

And in the mean time help us to comfort ourselves and one another with these words; and having this hope in us to purify ourselves even as Christ is pure. *1 Thessalonians 4:18. 1 John 3:3.*

Now our Lord Jesus Christ himself, and God, even our Father, who hath loved us, and hath given us everlasting consolation and good hope through grace, comfort our hearts, and stablish us in every good word and work. *2 Thessalonians 2:16, 17.*

11.   *We must pray for the good things of this life, with an humble submission to the will of God.*

Lord, thou hast told us, that godliness hath the promise of the life that now is, as well as of that which is to come; And that if we seek first the kingdom of God and the righteousness thereof, other things shall be added to us; and therefore we cast all our care about these things upon thee, who carest for us, for our heavenly Father knows that we have need of all these things. *1 Timothy 4:8. Matthew 6:33. 1 Peter 5:7. Matthew 6:32.*

(a) We must pray to be preserved from the calamities to which we are exposed.

Thou, Lord, art our refuge and our fortress, and under thy wings will we trust, thy truth shall be our shield and buckler; Let us therefore not be afraid for the terror by night, nor for the arrow that flieth by day. Having made the Lord our refuge, and the most High our habitation, let no evil befall us, nor any plague come nigh our dwelling. *Psalm 91:2, 4, 5, 9, 10.*

Let the Lord be our keeper, even he that keepeth Israel, and neither slumbers nor sleeps. Let the Lord be our shade on our right hand; That the sun may not smite us by day, nor the moon by night; Let the Lord preserve us from all evil, the Lord preserve our souls; The Lord preserve our going out and coming in, from this time forth, and even for ever more. *Psalm 121:4-8.*

Lord, make a hedge about us, about our houses, and about all that we have round about; and take sickness away from the midst of us. *Job 1:10. Exodus 23:25.*

(b) We must pray to be supplied with the comforts and supports we daily stand in need of.

O that the beauty of the Lord our God may be upon us, prosper thou the work of our hands upon us, yea the work of our hands establish thou it; Save now, we beseech thee, O Lord; O Lord, we beseech thee send now prosperity. *Psalm 90:17. Psalm 118:25.*

Let our sons be as plants grown up in their youth, and our daughters as corner stones polished after the similitude of a palace: Let our garners be full, affording all manner of store; And let there be no breaking in or going out; no complaining within our streets: Happy is the people that is in such a case, yea rather happy is the people whose God is the Lord. *Psalm 144:12-15.*

Let us be blessed in the city, and blessed in the field, let our basket and store be blessed, let us be blessed when we come in, and when we go out. *Deuteronomy 28:3, 5, 6.*

Let thy good providence so order all events concerning us, as that they may be made to work for good to us, as thou hast promised they shall to all that love thee and are called according to thy purpose. *Romans 8:28.*

Give us to trust in the Lord and do good, and then we shall dwell in the land, and verily we shall be fed; and be thou pleased to bring forth our righteousness as the light, and our judgment as the noonday. *Psalm 37:3, 6.*

Let us be hid from the scourge of the tongue, and not be afraid of destruction when it cometh; let us be in league with the stones of the field, and let the beasts of the field be at peace with us; let us know that our tabernacle is in peace, and let us visit our habitation and not sin. *Job 5:21, 23, 24.*

And if God will be with us, and will keep us in the way that we go, during our pilgrimage in this world, and will give us bread to eat, and raiment to put on, so that we may come to our heavenly Father's house in peace, then the Lord shall be our God. *Genesis 28:20, 21.*

12. *We must plead the promises of God for the enforcing of all our petitions, put these promises in suit, and refer ourselves to them.*

Lord, thou hast given us many exceeding great and precious promises, which are all yea and Amen in Christ. Now be it unto thy servants according to the word which thou hast spoken. *2 Peter 1:4. 2 Corinthians 1:20. Luke 1:38. 2 Samuel 7:25.*

Give us to draw water with joy out of those wells of salvation, to suck and be satisfied from those breasts of consolation; And now, O Lord God, let the word which thou hast spoken concerning thy servants be established for ever, and do as thou hast said. *Isaiah 12:3. Isaiah 66:11. 2 Samuel 7:25. 1 Chronicles 17:23.*

Deal with us according to the tenor of the everlasting covenant, which is well ordered in all things and sure, and which is all our salvation, and all our desire. *2 Samuel 23:5.*

Look upon us and be merciful to us, as thou usest to do unto those that love thy name, and do more for us than we are able to ask or think, and supply all our needs according to thy riches in glory by Christ Jesus. *Psalm 119:132. Ephesians 3:20. Philippians 4:19.*

4

Thanksgiving

Thanksgiving

OF THE FOURTH PART OF PRAYER, WHICH IS THANKSGIVING FOR THE MERCIES WE HAVE RECEIVED FROM GOD, AND THE MANY FAVOURS OF HIS WE ARE INTERESTED IN, AND HAVE AND HOPE FOR BENEFIT BY

Our errand at the throne of grace is not only to seek the favour of God, but to give unto Him the glory due unto His name, and that not only by an awful adoration of His infinite perfections, but by a grateful acknowledgment of His goodness to us, which cannot indeed add any thing to His glory, but He is pleased to accept of it, and to reckon Himself glorified by it, if it come from a heart that's humbly sensible of its own unworthiness to receive any favour from God, that values the gifts, and loves the giver of them.

We must stir up ourselves to praise God, with the consideration both of the reason and of the encouragement we have to praise Him.

NTO thee, O God, do we give thanks, unto thee do we give thanks, for that thy name is near thy wondrous works declare. *Psalm 75:1.*

Let our souls bless the Lord, and let all that is within us bless his holy name; yea, let our souls bless the Lord, and not forget any of his benefits. *Psalm 103:1, 2.*

We will praise the Lord, for it is good, it is pleasant, and praise is comely for the upright, yea it is a good thing to give thanks unto the Lord, and to sing praises unto thy name, O most High, to shew forth thy loving-kindness in the morning, and thy faithfulness every night. *Psalm 147:1. Psalm 92:1, 2.*

We will extol thee our God, O king, and will bless thy name for ever and ever; Every day will we bless thee, and will praise thy name for ever and ever; we will abundantly utter the memory of thy great goodness, and sing of thy righteousness. *Psalm 145:1, 2, 7.*

We will sing unto the Lord a new song, and his praise in the congregation of saints; O let Israel rejoice in him that made him, let the children of Zion be joyful in their King; Let the saints be joyful in glory, and let the high praises of God be in their hearts, and in their mouths. *Psalm 149:1, 2, 5, 6.*

While we live we will bless the Lord, and will sing praises unto our God while we have any being; and when we have no being on earth, we hope to have a being in heaven to be doing it better. *Psalm 146:2.*

We are here through Jesus Christ to offer the sacrifice of praise to thee, which we desire to do continually, that is the fruit of our lips, giving thanks to thy name. And thou hast said that he that offers praise glorifies thee, and that this also shall please the Lord better than an ox or bullock that hath horns and hoofs. *Hebrews 13:15. Psalm 50 (v. 23). Psalm 69:31.*

We will mention the loving-kindnesses of the Lord, and the praises of the Lord, according to all that the Lord hath bestowed on us, and the great goodness towards the house of Israel which he hath bestowed on them, according to his mercies, and according to the multitude of his loving kindnesses. *Isaiah 63:7.*

WE MUST BE PARTICULAR IN OUR THANKSGIVINGS TO GOD

1.   *For the discoveries which He has made to us in His word of the goodness of His nature.*

E give thanks unto the God of gods, unto the Lord of lords, for his mercy endures for ever. *Psalm 136:2, 3.*

Thy goodness is thy glory, and it is that for which all thy works do praise thee, and thy saints do bless thee. *Exodus 33:19. Psalm 145:10.*

Thou art gracious and full of compassion, slow to anger, and of great mercy, and hast told us that thou dost not afflict willingly, or grieve the children of men, but though thou cause grief, yet thou wilt have compassion, according to the multitude of thy mercies. *Psalm 145:8. Lamentations 3:33, 32.*

Thou takest pleasure in them that fear thee, in them that hope in thy mercy. *Psalm 147:11.*

2.   *For the many instances of His goodness.*

A) *The goodness of His providence relating to our bodies, and the life that now is; and this,*

1)   *First, with reference to all the creatures, and the world of mankind, in general.*

Thou hast stretched out the heavens like a curtain, and in them hast thou set a tabernacle for the sun, which is as a bridegroom coming out of his chamber, and rejoiceth as a strong man to run a race. And thou causest thy sun to shine on the evil and on the good, and sendest rain on the just and on the unjust. *Psalm 104:2. Psalm 19:4, 5. Matthew 5:45.*

When we consider the heavens the work of thy fingers, the sun, the moon, and the stars which thou hast ordained, Lord, what is man that thou thus visitest him? For truly the light is sweet, and a pleasant thing it is for the eyes to behold the sun: All the glory be to the Father of lights, who commandeth the morning, and causeth the day-spring to know his place. *Psalm 8:3, 4. Ecclesiastes 11:7. James 1:17. Job 38:12.*

Thou didst not leave thyself without witness among the heathen, in that thou didst good, and gavest them rain from heaven, and fruitful seasons, filling their hearts with food and gladness. *Acts 14:17.*

Thou coverest the heavens with clouds, and preparest rain for the earth, and makest grass to grow upon the mountains: Thou givest to the beast his food, and to the young ravens which cry. *Psalm 147:8, 9.*

Thou causest it to rain on the wilderness where there is no man, to satisfy the desolate and waste ground. *Job 38:26, 27.*

Thou visitest the earth, and waterest it, thou greatly enrichest it with the river of God, which is full of water; thou preparest them corn when thou hast so provided for it: Thou waterest the ridges thereof abundantly, thou settlest the furrows thereof, thou makest it soft with showers, thou blessest the springing thereof; Thou crownest the year with thy goodness, and thy paths drop fatness. *Psalm 65:9, 10, 11.*

Thou sendest the springs into the valleys which run among the hills; and they give drink to every beast of the field; and by them the fowls of the heaven have their habitation, which sing among the branches. *Psalm 104:10, 11, 12.*

Thou hast laid the foundations of the earth, that it should not be removed for ever, and settest bounds to the waters of the sea, that they turn not again to cover the earth; Thou hast shut up the sea with doors, and broken up for it thy decreed place, saying, Hitherto shalt thou come but no further, here shall thy proud waves be stayed. And thou hast made good what thou hast sworn, that the waters of Noah should no more go over the earth. *Psalm 104:5, 9. Job 38:8, 10, 11. Isaiah 54:9.*

Thy covenant of the day and of the night is not broken, but still thou givest the sun for a light by day, and the ordinances of the moon and of the stars for a light by night; and art faithful to that covenant of providence, that while the earth remains, seed-time and harvest, cold and heat, summer and winter, day and night shall not cease. *Jeremiah 33:20. Jeremiah 31:35. Genesis 8:22.*

The heaven, even the heavens are thine, but the earth thou hast given to the children of men; and thou hast put all things under their feet, and made them to have dominion over the works of thy hands; so that the fear of man and the dread of man is upon every beast of the earth, and upon the fowl of the air, and into his hand they are delivered, because thou hadst a favour to him, and thy delights were with the sons of men. *Psalm 115:16. Psalm 8:6. Genesis 9:2. Proverbs 8:31.*

Thou causest the grass to grow for the cattle, and herb for the service of man, that thou mayest bring forth food out of the earth; Wine that makes glad the heart of man, and oil to make his face to shine, and bread which strengthens man's heart. *Psalm 104:14, 15.*

Thou givest to all life and breath and all things, and the earth, O Lord, is full of thy mercy. *Acts 17:25. Psalm 119:64.*

All the creatures wait upon thee, that thou mayest give them their meat in due season; That thou givest them they gather, thou openest thy hand, they are filled with good: Thou sendest forth thy spirit they are created, thou renewest the face of the earth. This thy glory shall endure for ever, and thou rejoicest in these works. *Psalm 104:27, 28, 30, 31.*

It is through thy goodness, O Lord, that as one generation of mankind passeth away, another generation comes, and that thou hast not blotted out the name of that corrupt and guilty race from under heaven. *Ecclesiastes 1:4. Deuteronomy 29:20.*

2)   *Secondly, with reference to us in particular.*

(a) We must give thanks that He hath made us reasonable creatures, capable of knowing, loving, serving and enjoying Him, and that He hath not made us as the beasts that perish.

We will praise thee, for we are fearfully and wonderfully made, and that our souls, our nobler part, know right well; for what man knows the things of a man, save the spirit of man which is in him? *Psalm 139:14. 1 Corinthians 2:11.*

Thou hast made us of that rank of beings which is little lower than the angels, and is crowned with glory and honour; For there is a spirit in man, and the inspiration of the Almighty giveth them understanding. And the spirit of a man is the candle of the Lord. *Psalm 8:5. Job 32:8. Proverbs 20:27.*

Our bodies are capable of being the temples of the Holy Ghost, and our souls of having the Spirit of God dwell in them; we therefore glorify thee with our bodies, and with our spirits, which are thine. *1 Corinthians 6:19. 1 Corinthians 3:16. 1 Corinthians 6:20.*

Thou, Lord, hast formed us for thyself, that we might shew forth thy praise. *Isaiah 43:21.*

(b) We must give thanks for our preservation, that our lives are prolonged, and that the use of our reason and understanding, our limbs and senses, is continued to us.

It was owing to thy good providence that we died not from the womb, and did not give up the ghost when we came out of the belly, that the knees prevented us, and the breasts that we should suck. *Job 3:11, 12.*

Though we were called transgressors from the womb, yet by thy power we have been borne from the belly, and carried from the womb; and thou holdest our souls in life, and sufferest not our foot to be moved. *Isaiah 48:8. Isaiah 46:3. Psalm 66:9.*

All our bones shall say, Lord, who is like unto thee, for thou keepest all our bones, not one of them is broken. *Psalm 35:10. Psalm 34:20.*

We lay us down and sleep, for thou, Lord, makest us to dwell in safety. *Psalm 3:5. Psalm 4:8.*

Thou hast given thine angels a charge concerning us, to keep us in all our ways, to bear us up in their hands, lest we dash our foot against a stone. And they are all ministering spirits sent forth to minister for the good of them that shall be heirs of salvation. *Psalm 91:11, 12. Hebrews 1:14.*

(c) For signal recoveries from danger by sickness, or otherwise.

When perhaps there has been but a step between us and death, and we have received a sentence of death within ourselves, and have been ready to say in the cutting off of our days we should go to the gates of the grave, and were deprived of the residue of our years, yet thou hast in love to our souls delivered them from the pit of corruption, and cast all our sins behind thy back. *1 Samuel 20:3. 2 Corinthians 1:9. Isaiah 38:10, 17.*

When the sorrows of death have compassed us, and the pains of hell have got hold upon us, we have called upon the name of the Lord, and have found that gracious is the Lord and righteous, yea, our God is merciful; we have been brought low and he hath helped us, and hath delivered our souls from death, our eyes from tears, and our feet from falling. We will therefore walk before the Lord in the land of the living. *Psalm 116:3-6, 8, 9.*

(d) For the supports and comforts of this life, which have hitherto made the land of our pilgrimage easy and pleasant to us.

Blessed be the Lord, who daily loads us with his benefits, even the God of our salvation. *Psalm 68:19.*

Thou makest us to lie down in green pastures, thou feedest us beside the still waters: Thou preparest a table for us in the presence of our enemies, thou anointest our head, and our cup runs over. *Psalm 23:2, 5.*

It may be we were sent forth without purse or scrip, but lacked we any thing? Nothing, Lord. *Luke 22:35.*

The candle of God hath shined upon our head, and by his light we have walked through darkness, and the secret of God has been in our tabernacle. *Job 29:3, 4.*

Thou hast given us all things richly to enjoy, and into our hands hast brought plentifully. *1 Timothy 6:17. Job 12:6.*

Many a time we have eaten and been filled, and have delighted ourselves in thy great goodness. *Nehemiah 9:25.*

When we remember all the way which the Lord our God hath led us for so many years in this wilderness, we must here set up a stone and call it Eben-ezer, for hitherto the Lord hath helped us. *Deuteronomy 8:2. 1 Samuel 7:12.*

(e) For success in our callings and affairs, comfort in relations, and comfortable places of abode.

It is God that girdeth us with strength, and maketh our way perfect; that hath blessed the work of our hands, and it may be so as that though our beginning was small, yet our latter end hath greatly increased. *Psalm 18:32. Job 1:10. Job 8:7.*

Our houses have been safe from fear, and there hath been no rod of God upon us; so that the voice of rejoicing and salvation hath been in our tabernacle from day to day. *Job 21:9. Psalm 118:15.*

With our staff it may be we have passed over this Jordan, and now we are become two bands; and it is God that setteth the solitary in families. *Genesis 32:10. Psalm 68:6.*

If we have lived joyfully with our relations, and they have been to us as the loving hind and as the pleasant roe, we must give thee thanks for it; for every creature is that to us, and no more, that thou makest it to be. *Ecclesiastes 9:9. Proverbs 5:19.*

(f) For our share in the publick plenty, peace, and tranquillity.

When we have eaten and are full, we have reason to bless thee for the good land which thou hast given us: A land which the eyes of the Lord our God are always upon, from the beginning of the year even to the end of the year. *Deuteronomy 8:10. Deuteronomy 11:12.*

Thou makest peace in our borders, and fillest us with the finest of the wheat: We are delivered from the noise of archers at the places of drawing water; there therefore will we rehearse the righteous acts of the Lord, even his righteous acts towards the inhabitants of his villages. *Psalm 147:14. Judges 5:11.*

We thank thee that the powers that are set over us are ministers of God to us for good, that they seek the welfare of our people, speaking peace to all their seed. *Romans 13:4. Esther 10:3.*

B) The goodness of His grace relating to our souls, and the life that is to come.

But especially blessed be the God and Father of our Lord Jesus Christ, who hath blessed us with all spiritual blessings in heavenly things in Christ. *Ephesians 1:3.*

1) First, we must give God thanks for His kindness to the children of men relating to their better part and their future state, and His favours to the church in general.

(a) We must give thanks for the gracious design and contrivance of man's redemption and salvation, when he was lost and undone by sin.

O how wonderfully did the kindness and love of God our Saviour towards man appear, not by any works of righteousness, which he had done, but according to his mercy he saved us: We had destroyed ourselves, but in thee, and thee only was our help. *Titus 3:4, 5. Hosea 13:9.*

When we were cast out in the open field, and no eye pitied us, thou sawest us polluted in our own blood, and thou saidst unto us, Live; yea, thou saidst unto us, Live; and the time was a time of love. *Ezekiel 16:5, 6, 8.*

When the redemption of the soul was so precious, as that it must have ceased for ever, and no man could by any means redeem his brother, or give to God a ransom for him, then thou wast pleased to find a ransom, that we might be delivered from going down to the pit. *Psalm 49:8, 7. Job 33:24.*

When we must needs die, and were as water spilt upon the ground, which cannot be gathered up again, then didst thou devise means that the banished might not be for ever expelled from thee. *2 Samuel 14:14.*

When thou sparedst not the angels that sinned, but didst cast them down to hell, thou saidest concerning the race of mankind, Destroy it not for a blessing is in it. *2 Peter 2:4. Isaiah 65:8.*

Herein appears the wisdom of God in a mystery, even the hidden wisdom which God ordained before the world for our glory. *1 Corinthians 2:7.*

(b) For the eternal purposes and counsels of God concerning man's redemption.

We are bound to give thanks always to thee, O God, because thou hast from the beginning chosen some to salvation through sanctification of the Spirit: That there is a remnant according to the election of grace, whom God hath chosen in Christ before the foundation of the world, that they should be holy and without blame before thee in love, having predestinated them to the adoption of children, by Jesus Christ unto thyself, according to the good pleasure of thy will, to the praise of the glory of thy grace. *2 Thessalonians 2:13. Romans 11:5. Ephesians 1:4, 5, 6.*

Thine they were, and thou gavest them to Christ, and this is thy will, that of all that thou hast given him he should lose nothing, but should raise it up at the last day. *John 17:6. John 6:39.*

(c) For the appointing of the Redeemer, and God's gracious condescension to deal with man upon new terms, receding from the demands of the broken covenant of innocency.

We bless thee that when sacrifice and offering thou wouldest not, and in it hadst no pleasure, that then the eternal Son of God said, Lo I come to do thy will, O God, and a body hast thou prepared me: And that as in the volume of the book it was written of him, he did delight to do thy will, O God, yea, thy law was within his heart. *Hebrews 10:5, 6, 7. Psalm 40:7, 8.*

Thou hast laid help upon one that is mighty, one chosen out of thy people: Thou hast found David thy servant with thy holy oil, thou hast anointed him, even with the oil of gladness above his fellows, and didst promise that with him thy hand should be established, and thy arm should strengthen him, and that thou wouldest make him thy first-born, higher than the kings of the earth. *Psalm 89:19, 20. Psalm 45:7. Psalm 89:21, 27.*

We bless thee that the Father now judgeth no man, but hath committed all judgment to the Son: That as he has life in himself, so he hath given to the Son to have life in himself, and hath given him authority to execute judgment also, because he is the Son of man: That the Father loveth the Son, and hath given all things into his hand. And that the counsel of peace is between them both. *John 5:22, 26, 27. John 3:35. Zechariah 6:13.*

That he is thy servant whom thou dost uphold, thine elect in whom thy soul delighteth: Thy beloved Son in whom thou art well pleased: That thou hast given him for a covenant of the people, and that through him we are not under the law, but under grace. *Isaiah 42:1. Matthew 17:5. Isaiah 49:8. Romans 6:14.*

That God so loved the world, as to give his only begotten Son, that whosoever believes in him should not perish, but have everlasting life. *John 3:16.*

(d) For the early and ancient indications of this gracious design concerning fallen man.

We bless thee, that as soon as ever man had sinned, it was graciously promised that the seed of the woman should break the serpent's head; and that in the old testament sacrifices Jesus Christ was the Lamb slain from the foundation of the world. *Genesis 3:15. Revelation 13:8.*

And that by faith the elders, though they received not the promise, yet obtained a good report, for they obtained witness that they were righteous. *Hebrews 11:39, 2, 4.*

We bless thee for the promise made to Abraham, that in his seed all the families of the earth should be blessed, and to Jacob that the Shiloh should come, and to him should the gathering of the people be: And that the patriarchs rejoiced to see Christ's day, and they saw it and were glad. *Genesis 12:3. Genesis 49:10. John 8:56.*

(e) For the many glorious instances of God's favour to the old testament church.

We adore that wisdom, power and goodness with which thou broughtest the vine out of Egypt, didst cast out the heathen and plant it; thou preparedst room before it, and didst cause it to take deep root, and it filled the land. *Psalm 80:8, 9.*

And they got not the land in possession by their own sword, neither did their own arm save them, but thy right hand, and thine arm, and the light of thy countenance, because thou hadst a favour to them. *Psalm 44:3. Psalm 136:10. & others.*

We bless thee that to the Jews were committed the oracles of God; that they had the adoption, and the glory, and the covenants, the giving of the law, and the service of God, and the promises: And that there did not fail one word of all thy good promise, which thou promisedst by the hand of Moses thy servant. *Romans 3:2. Romans 9:4. 1 Kings 8:56.*

We bless thee for all that which thou didst at sundry times and in divers manners speak in time past unto the fathers by the prophets, those holy men of God, who spake as they were moved by the Holy Ghost, and prophesied of the grace that should come unto us, testifying beforehand the sufferings of Christ, and the glory that should follow, and that not to themselves only, but to us they ministered those great things, things which the angels themselves desire to look into. *Hebrews 1:1. 2 Peter 1:21. 1 Peter 1:10, 11, 12.*

And especially we bless thee that thou hast provided some better thing for us, that they without us should not be made perfect. *Hebrews 11:40.*

(f) For the wonderful and mysterious incarnation of the Son of God, and His coming into the world.

We bless thee that when the fulness of time was come, thou didst send forth thy Son made of a woman, made under the law, to redeem them that were under the law, that we might receive the adoption of sons. *Galatians 4:4, 5.*

That the eternal Word was made flesh, and dwelt among us, and there were those who saw his glory, the glory as of the only begotten of the Father, full of grace and truth. And without controversy great is the mystery of godliness, that God was manifested in the flesh. *John 1:14. 1 Timothy 3:16.*

We bless thee that to this end he was born, and for this cause he came into the world, that he might bear witness of the truth, and we believe and are sure, that he is that Christ, the Son of the living God; that it is he that should come, and we are to look for no other. *John 18:37. John 6:69. Matthew 11:3.*

We bless thee that the Son of man is come to seek and to save that which was lost; that he is come that we might have life, and that we might have it more abundantly, and that for this purpose the Son of God was manifested, that he might destroy the works of the devil. *Luke 19:10. John 10:10. 1 John 3:8.*

Lord, we receive it as a faithful saying, and well worthy of all acceptation, that Christ Jesus came into the world to save sinners, even the chief. *1 Timothy 1:15.*

We bless thee that forasmuch as the children are partakers of flesh and blood, he also himself likewise took part of the same: That he took not on him the nature of angels, but our nature, and was in all things made like unto his brethren, that he might be a merciful and faithful high priest, in things pertaining to God, to make reconciliation for the sins of the people; and that he is not ashamed to call them brethren. *Hebrews 2:14, 16, 17, 11.*

And that the first begotten was brought into the world with a charge given to all the angels of God to worship him. *Hebrews 1:6.*

(g) For God's gracious owning of Him in His undertaking, and in the carrying of it on.

We bless thee that thou wast in Christ reconciling the world to thyself, not imputing their trespasses unto them, and that thou hast committed unto us the word of reconciliation. *2 Corinthians 5:19.*

That thou hast thyself given him for a witness to the people, a leader and commander to the people. That he was sanctified and sealed and sent into the world, and that the Father which sent him did not leave him alone, for he always did those things that pleased him. *Isaiah 55:4. John 10:36. John 6:27. John 8:29.*

Glory be to God in the highest, for in and through Jesus Christ there is on earth peace, and good-will towards men. *Luke 2:14.*

In this was manifested the love of God towards us, because that God sent his only begotten Son into the world, that we might live through him. *1 John 4:9.*

We thank thee for the power thou hast given him over all flesh, that he should give eternal life to as many as were given him. *John 17:2.*

(h) For His Holy life, His excellent doctrine, and the glorious miracles He wrought to confirm His doctrine.

We bless thee for the assurance we have that he is a teacher come from God, since no man could do those miracles which he did, except God were with him. *John 3:2.*

That thou hast in these last days spoken unto us by thy Son, whose doctrine was not his, but his that sent him, and he spake as one having authority, and that we are encouraged to come and learn of him, because he is meek and lowly in heart, and in learning of him we shall find rest to our souls. *Hebrews 1:2. John 7:16. Matthew 7 (v. 29). Matthew 11:29.*

We bless thee that he hath left us an example, that we should follow his steps, in that he did no sin, neither was guile found in his mouth, and when he was reviled, he reviled not again; and his meat and drink was to do the will of his Father; in that he was holy, harmless, undefiled, separate from sinners. O that we may be armed with the same mind, and that as he was so we may be in this world; and that we may so walk even as he walked. *1 Peter 2:21, 22, 23. John 4:34. Hebrews 7:26. 1 Peter 4:1. 1 John 4:17. 1 John 2:6.*

We bless thee that the works which he did, the same bore witness of him that the Father had sent him, that by his power the blind received their sight, the lame walked, the lepers were cleansed, the deaf heard, the dead were raised up, and the poor had the gospel preached to them; and even the winds and the sea obeyed him; for which we glorify the God of Israel. Doubtless this was the Son of God. *John 5:36. Matthew 11:5. Matthew 8:27. Matthew 15:31. Matthew 27:54.*

(i) For the great encouragements Christ gave to poor sinners to come to Him.

We bless thee that Jesus Christ came to call, not the righteous, but sinners (such as we are) to repentance, and had power on earth to forgive sin; that he came to save his people from their sins; and is the Lamb of God that takes away the sin of the world, and that he is (to his honour, not to his reproach) a friend to publicans and sinners. *Matthew 9:13, 6. Matthew 1:21. John 1:29. Matthew 11:19.*

We thank thee for the gracious invitation he gave to those who are weary and heavy laden, to come to him for rest: And for the assurance he hath given that whosoever comes unto him he will in no wise cast out. *Matthew 11:28. John 6:37.*

That he made a gracious offer, that whosoever thirsts might come unto him and drink. *John 7:37.*

(j) For the full satisfaction which He made to the justice of God for the sin of man by the blood of His cross, for the purchases, victories, and triumphs of the cross, and for all the precious benefits which flow to us from the dying of the Lord Jesus.

Herein indeed God commendeth his love to us, in that while we were yet sinners Christ died for us, that we might be reconciled to him by the death of his Son. Herein is love, not that we loved God, but that he loved us, and sent his Son to be the propitiation for our sins, and not for ours only, but for the sins of the whole world; that he tasted death for every man, that through death he might destroy him that had the power of death, that is, the devil. *Romans 5:8, 10. 1 John 4:10. 1 John 2:2. Hebrews 2:9, 14.*

We bless thee, that by one offering he hath perfected for ever them that are sanctified, that he hath finished transgression, made an end of sin, made reconciliation for iniquity, and hath brought in an everlasting righteousness. *Hebrews 10:14. Daniel 9:24.*

That he hath redeemed us from the curse of the law, by being made a curse for us. *Galatians 3:13.*

That what the law could not do, in that it was weak through the flesh, God hath done by sending his own Son in the likeness of sinful flesh, who by a sacrifice for sin condemned sin in the flesh. *Romans 8:3.*

That he was wounded for our transgressions, and bruised for our iniquities, and that the chastisement of our peace was upon him, and by his stripes we are healed; and that the Lord having laid upon him the iniquity of us all, it pleased the Lord to bruise him, and put him to grief. *Isaiah 53:5, 6, 10.*

That appearing to put away sin by the sacrifice of himself, he did by the eternal Spirit offer himself without spot unto God, and by his own blood entered in once into the holy place, having obtained eternal redemption for us. *Hebrews 9:26, 14, 12.*

That he hath spoiled principalities and powers, and made a shew of them openly, triumphing over them in his cross, and hath blotted out the hand-writing of ordinances which was against us, which was contrary to us, taking it out of the way by nailing it to his cross. *Colossians 2:15, 14.*

That he is our peace, who having broken down the middle wall of partition between Jew and Gentile, hath made himself of twain one new man, hath reconciled both unto God, in one body by the cross, having slain the enmity thereby. *Ephesians 2:14, 15, 16.*

That he hath loved us, and washed us from our sins in his own blood, and hath made us unto our God kings and priests. *Revelation 1:5, 6.*

O the height, and depth, and length, and breadth of that love of Christ which passeth knowledge; that great love wherewith he loved us. *Ephesians 3:18, 19. Ephesians 2:4.*

Worthy is the Lamb that was slain to receive power, and riches, and wisdom, and strength, and honour, and glory, and blessing; for he was slain, and hath redeemed us to God by his blood. *Revelation 5:12, 9.*

(k) For His resurrection from the dead on the third day.

We thank thee that as he was delivered for our offences, so he rose again for our justification, and was declared to be the Son of God with power by the resurrection from the dead. *Romans 4 (v. 25). Romans 1:4.*

That though he was dead, yet he is alive, and lives for evermore, and hath the keys of hell and death, and being raised from the dead, he dies no more, death has no more dominion over him. *Revelation 1:18. Romans 6:9.*

That now is Christ risen from the dead, and is become the first fruits of them that slept, that as in Adam all died, so in Christ all might be made alive, and every one in his own order. *1 Corinthians 15:20, 22, 23.*

That God suffered not his Holy One to see corruption, but loosed the pains of death, because it was impossible he should be holden of them, and so declared to all the house of Israel, that that same Jesus whom they crucified, is both Lord and Christ. *Acts 2:27, 31, 24, 36.*

And that for this end Christ both died and rose and revived, that he might be Lord both of the dead and living, and that whether we wake or sleep, we might live together with him. *Romans 14:9. 1 Thessalonians 5:10.*

(l) For His ascension into heaven, and His sitting at God's right hand there.

We bless thee that our Lord Jesus is ascended to his Father and our Father, to his God and our God; is ascended up on high, having led captivity captive, and hath received gifts for men, yea, even for the rebellious also, that the Lord God might dwell among them. *John 20:17. Psalm 68:18.*

That as the fore-runner he is for us entered; entered into heaven itself now to appear in the presence of God for us, a Lamb as it had been slain standing in the midst of the throne. *Hebrews 6:20. Hebrews 9:24. Revelation 5:6.*

That he is set on the right hand of the throne of the Majesty in the heavens, angels, and authorities, and powers being made subject to him. *Hebrews 8:1. 1 Peter 3:22.*

That he is gone before to prepare a place for us in his Father's house, where there are many mansions; and though whether he is gone we cannot follow him now, yet we hope to follow him hereafter, when he shall come again to receive us to himself, that where he is there we may be also. *John 14:2. John 13:36. John 14:3.*

(m) For the intercession which He ever lives to make in the virtue of His satisfaction.

We thank thee that having borne the sins of many, he makes intercession for transgressors; and prays not for those only that were given him when he was upon earth, but for all that shall believe on him through their word; That they all may be one. *Isaiah 53:12. John 17:20, 21.*

That we have an advocate with the Father, even JESUS CHRIST THE RIGHTEOUS, who is therefore able to save to the uttermost all those that come to God as a Father by him as mediator, seeing he ever lives making intercession. *1 John 2:1. Hebrews 7:25.*

That we have a high priest taken from among men, and ordained for men in things pertaining to God, that he may offer both gifts and sacrifice for sin, who can have compassion on the ignorant, and on them that are out of the way, and that he is become the author of eternal salvation to all them that obey him. *Hebrews 5:1, 2, 9.*

(n) For the dominion and sovereignty to which the Redeemer is exalted.

We thank thee that because our Lord Jesus humbled himself, and became obedient unto death, even the death of the cross, therefore God hath highly exalted him, and given him a name above every name, that in the name of JESUS every knee might bow, and every tongue confess (as we do at this time) that Jesus Christ is Lord to the glory of God the Father. *Philippians 2:8-11.*

That all power is given unto him both in heaven and in earth, that thou hast set him over the works of thy hands, and hast put all things in subjection under his feet, and so hast crowned him with glory and honour. *Matthew 28:18. Hebrews 2:7, 8, 9.*

That he is KING OF KINGS AND LORD OF LORDS; that the Ancient of days hath given him dominion and glory and a kingdom, an everlasting dominion, and a kingdom which shall not be destroyed. *Revelation 19:16. Daniel 7:13, 14.*

That the government is upon his shoulders, and that his name is called Wonderful, Counsellor, The mighty God, The everlasting Father, and The Prince of Peace; And of the increase of his government and peace there shall be no end. *Isaiah 9:6, 7.*

That thou hast set him as king upon thy holy hill of Zion, and that he shall reign over the house of Jacob for ever, shall reign till he has put down all opposing rule, principality and power, till all his enemies are made his footstool, and then he shall deliver up the kingdom to God, even the Father, that God may be all in all. *Psalm 2:6. Luke 1:33. 1 Corinthians 15:24, 25. Ephesians 6:12. Hebrews 10:13. 1 Corinthians 15:24, 28.*

(o) For the assurance we have of His second coming to judge the world.

We bless thee that thou hast appointed a day in which thou wilt judge the world in righteousness, by that man whom thou hast ordained, whereof thou hast given assurance unto all men, in that thou hast raised him from the dead. *Acts 17:31.*

That in that day the Lord Jesus shall be revealed from heaven with his mighty angels in flaming fire, taking vengeance on them that know not God, and that obey not the gospel of our Lord Jesus Christ: And shall come to be glorified in his saints, and admired in all them that believe; for them that sleep in Jesus he will bring with him. *2 Thessalonians 1:7, 8, 10. 1 Thessalonians 4:14.*

That he shall then send forth his angels to gather out of his kingdom all things that offend, and them which do iniquity, and to gather together his elect from the four winds, and then shall the righteous shine forth as the sun in the kingdom of their Father. *Matthew 13:41. Matthew 24:31. Matthew 13:43.*

And we then, according to thy promise, look for new heavens, and a new earth, wherein dwells righteousness: Lord, grant that seeing we look for such things, we may give diligence to be found of him in peace without spot and blameless: And then come, Lord Jesus, come quickly. *2 Peter 3:13, 14. Revelation 22:20.*

(p) For the sending of the Holy Spirit to supply the want of Christ's bodily presence, to carry on His undertaking, and to prepare things for His second coming.

We bless thee that when our Lord Jesus went away he sent us another Comforter to abide with us for ever, even the Spirit of truth, who shall glorify the Son, for he shall take of his, and shall shew it unto us. *John 14:16, 17. John 16:14.*

That being by the right hand of God exalted, and having received of the Father the promise of the Holy Ghost, he poured it forth as rivers of living water. *Acts 2:33. John 7:38.*

Blessed be God for the signs and wonders, and divers miracles, and gifts of the Holy Ghost, with which God bare witness to the great salvation. *Hebrews 2:4, 3.*

And blessed be God for the promise, that as earthly parents, though evil, know how to give good gifts to their children, so our heavenly Father will give the Holy Spirit to them that ask him, that holy Spirit of promise, which is the earnest of our inheritance until the redemption of the purchased possession. *Luke 11:13. Ephesians 1:13, 14.*

(q) For the covenant of grace made with us in Jesus Christ, and all the exceeding great and precious privileges of that covenant, and for the seals of it.

We thank thee that in Jesus Christ thou hast made an everlasting covenant with us, even the sure mercies of David, and that though the mountains may depart, and the hills be removed, yet this covenant of thy peace shall never be removed. *Isaiah 55:3. Isaiah 54:10.*

That thou hast given unto us exceeding great and precious promises, that by these we might be partakers of a divine nature: and that Jesus Christ is the mediator of this better covenant, which is established upon better promises. *2 Peter 1:4. Hebrews 8:6.*

That though thou chasten our transgression with the rod, and our iniquity with stripes, yet thy loving kindness thou wilt not utterly take away, nor cause thy faithfulness to fail, thy covenant thou wilt not break, nor alter the thing that is gone out of thy lips. *Psalm 89:32, 33, 34.*

That being willing more abundantly to shew to the heirs of promise the immutability of thy counsel, thou hast confirmed it by an oath, That by two immutable things in which it was impossible for God to lie, we might have strong consolation, who have fled for refuge to lay hold on the hope set before us. *Hebrews 6:17, 18.*

That baptism is appointed to be a seal of the righteousness which is by faith, as circumcision was: That it assures us of the remission of sins and the gift of the Holy Ghost; and that this promise is to us and our children. And that the cup in the Lord's supper is the blood of the new testament, which was shed for many for the remission of sins. *Romans 4:11. Acts 2:38, 39. Matthew 26:28.*

(r) For the writing of the scriptures, and the preserving of them pure and entire to our day.

We thank thee that we have the scriptures to search, and that in them we have eternal life, and that they testify of Christ, and that all scripture is given by inspiration of God, and is profitable for doctrine, for reproof, for correction, and for instruction in righteousness. *John 5:39. 2 Timothy 3:16.*

That whatsoever things were written aforetime, were written for our learning, that we through patience and comfort of the scripture might have hope: And that we have this most sure word of prophecy as a light shining in a dark place. *Romans 15:4. 2 Peter 1:19.*

That the vision is not become to us as the words of a book that is sealed, but that we hear in our own tongue the wonderful works of God. *Isaiah 29:11. Acts 2:11.*

We thank thee, Father, Lord of heaven and earth, that the things which were hid from the wise and prudent, and which many prophets and kings desired to see and might not, are revealed unto us babes; Even so, Father, for so it seemed good in thy sight. *Luke 10:21, 24.*

(s) For the institution of ordinances, and particularly that of the ministry.

We thank thee that thou hast not only shewed thy word unto Jacob, but thy statutes and judgments unto Israel, unto us: Thou hast not dealt so with other nations, and as for thy judgments, they have not known them. *Psalm 147:19, 20.*

That the tabernacle of God is with men, and he will dwell with them, and that he hath set his sanctuary in the midst of them for evermore, and there will meet with the children of Israel. *Revelation 21:3. Ezekiel 37:26. Exodus 29:43.*

We thank thee that thou hast made known unto us thy holy sabbaths; and that still there remains the keeping of a sabbath to the people of God. *Nehemiah 9:14. Hebrews 4:9.*

And that when the Lord Jesus ascended up on high, he gave gifts unto men, not only prophets, apostles, evangelists, but pastors and teachers, for the perfecting of the saints, for the work of the ministry, for the edifying of the body of Christ, till we all come in the unity of the faith, and of the knowledge of the Son of God, unto a perfect man, unto the measure of the stature of the fulness of Christ! And that while they teach us to observe all things which Christ hath commanded, he hath promised to be with them always even unto the end of the world. *Ephesians 4:8, 11, 12, 13. Matthew 28:20.*

(t) For the planting of the Christian religion in the world, and the setting up of the gospel church, in despite of all the oppositions of the powers of darkness.

We thank thee that the preaching of Jesus Christ according to the commandment of the everlasting God, and the gospel which was made known to all nations for the obedience of faith, was mighty through God to the pulling down of strong holds. That the Lord wrought with it, and confirmed the word by signs following; so that Satan fell as lightning from heaven. *Romans 16:25, 26. 2 Corinthians 10:4. Mark 16:20. Luke 10:18.*

That though the gospel was preached in much contention, yet it grew and prevailed mightily, and multitudes turned to God from idols, to serve the living and true God, and to wait for his Son from heaven. *1 Thessalonians 2:2. Acts 19:20. 1 Thessalonians 1:9, 10.*

Now came salvation and strength, and the kingdom of our God, and the power of his Christ: And the exalted Redeemer rode forth with his bow, and with his crown conquering, and to conquer; and nations were born at once. *Revelation 12:10. Revelation 6:2. Isaiah 66:8.*

(u) For the preservation of Christianity in the world unto this day.

We bless thee that though the enemies of Israel have afflicted them from their youth up, have many a time afflicted them, yet they have not prevailed against them, though the plowers have plowed on their back, yet the righteous Lord has cut asunder the cords of the wicked. *Psalm 129:1-4.*

That Jesus Christ hath built his church upon a rock, which the gates of hell cannot prevail against, but his seed shall endure for ever, and his throne as the days of heaven. *Matthew 16:18. Psalm 89:29.*

(v) For the martyrs and confessors, the lights of the church, and the good examples of those that are gone before us to heaven.

We bless thee for all those who have been enabled to approve themselves to God in much patience in afflictions, in necessities, in distresses, who when they have been brought before governors and kings for Christ's sake, it has turned to them for a testimony, and God has given them a mouth and wisdom, which all their adversaries were not able to gainsay or resist. *2 Corinthians 6:4. Luke 21:12, 13, 15.*

That those who for Christ's sake were killed all the day long, and accounted as sheep for the slaughter, yet in all these things were more than conquerors through him that loved us. *Romans 8:36, 37.*

That they overcame the accuser of the brethren by the blood of the Lamb, and by the word of their testimony, and by not loving their lives unto the death. *Revelation 12:10, 11.*

We bless thee for the cloud of witnesses with which we are compassed about, for the footsteps of the flock, for the elders that have obtained a good report, and are now through faith and patience inheriting the promises. Lord, give us to follow them as they followed Christ. *Hebrews 12:1. Canticle (Song of Solomon) 1:8. Hebrews 11:2. Hebrews 6:12. 1 Corinthians 11:1.*

(w) For the communion of saints, that spiritual communion which we have in faith and hope and holy love, and in prayers and praises with all good Christians.

We bless thee that if we walk in the light, we have fellowship one with another, even with all that in every place call on the name of Jesus Christ our Lord, both theirs and ours. *1 John 1:7. 1 Corinthians 1:2.*

That we being many are one bread and one body, and that though there are diversities of gifts and administrations, and operations, yet there is the same Spirit, the same Lord, and the same God, which worketh all in all. *1 Corinthians 10:17. 1 Corinthians 12:4, 5, 6.*

We thank thee that all the children of God, which were scattered abroad, are united in him, who is the head of the body the church; so that they are all our brethren and companions in tribulation, and in the kingdom and patience of Jesus Christ. *John 11:52. Colossians 1:18. Revelation 1:9.*

(x) For the prospect and hope of eternal life, when time and days shall be no more.

We thank thee for the crown of life which the Lord hath promised to them that love him; the inheritance incorruptible, undefiled, and that fadeth not away, reserved in heaven for us. *James 1:12. 1 Peter 1:4.*

That having here no continuing city, we are encouraged to seek the better country, that is, the heavenly, the city that hath foundations, whose builder and maker is God. *Hebrews 13:14. Hebrews 11:16, 10.*

That we are in hope of eternal life, which God that cannot lie hath promised; And that all true believers through grace have eternal life abiding in them. *Titus 1:2. Acts 18:27. 1 John 5:13.*

2)   *Secondly, we must give God thanks for the spiritual mercies bestowed upon us in particular, especially if we are called with an effectual call, and have a good work of grace begun in us.*

(a) *We must bless God for the strivings of His spirit with us, and the admonitions and checks of our own consciences.*

We bless thee that thou hast not given us over to a reprobate mind, that our consciences are not seared, that thou hast not said concerning us, They are joined to idols, let them alone, but that thy spirit is yet striving with us. *Romans 1:28. 1 Timothy 4:2. Hosea 4:17. Genesis 6:3.*

We thank thee for the work of the law written in our hearts, our own consciences also bearing witness, and our own thoughts between themselves accusing or excusing one another. *Romans 2:15.*

(b) *We must bless God if there be a saving change wrought in us by His blessed Spirit.*

And hath God by his grace translated us out of the kingdom of darkness into the kingdom of his dear Son? Hath he called us into the fellowship of Jesus Christ, and made us nigh by his blood, who by nature were afar off. Not unto us, O Lord, not unto us, but unto thy name give glory. *Colossians 1:13. 1 Corinthians 1:9. Ephesians 2:13. Psalm 115:1.*

We give thanks to God always for those to whom the gospel is come, not in word only, but in power, and in the Holy Ghost, and in much assurance. *1 Thessalonians 1:2, 5.*

Thou hast loved us with an everlasting love, and therefore with loving kindness thou hast drawn us, drawn us with the cords of a man, and the bands of love. *Jeremiah 31:3. Hosea 11:4.*

When the strong man armed kept his palace in our hearts, and his goods were in peace, it was a stronger than he that came upon him, and took from him all his armour, wherein he trusted, and divided the spoil. *Luke 11:21, 22.*

(c) We must give thanks for the remission of our sins, and the peace of our consciences.

We bless thee for the redemption we have through Christ's blood, even the forgiveness of sins according to the riches of thy grace, wherein thou hast abounded towards us. *Ephesians 1:7, 8.*

That thou hast forgiven all our iniquities, and healed all our diseases; and hast in love to our souls delivered them from the pit of corruption; for thou hast cast all our sins behind thy back. *Psalm 103:3. Isaiah 38:17.*

When thou broughtest us into the wilderness, yet there thou spakest comfortably to us, and gavest us our vineyards from thence; and the valley of Achor for a door of hope. *Hosea 2:14, 15.*

(d) For the powerful influences of the divine grace, to sanctify and preserve us, to prevent our falling into sin, and to strengthen us in doing our duty.

Thou hast not quenched the smoking flax, nor broke the bruised reed, nor despised the day of small things, but having obtained help of God, we continue hitherto. *Matthew 12:20. Zechariah 4:10. Acts 26:22.*

In the day when we cried, thou hast answered us, and hast strengthened us with strength in our souls. *Psalm 138:3.*

We have been continually with thee, thou hast holden us by thy right hand, when our feet were almost gone, and our steps had well nigh slipped. *Psalm 73:23, 2.*

We have reason never to forget thy precepts; for by them thou hast quickened us; And unless thy law had been our delight, we should many a time have perished in our affliction; for thy statutes have been our songs in the house of our pilgrimage. *Psalm 119:93, 92, 54.*

Unless the Lord had been our help, our souls had almost dwelt in silence: But when we said, Our foot slippeth, thy mercy, O Lord, held us up: And in the multitude of our thoughts within us, thy comforts have been the delight of our souls. *Psalm 94:17, 18, 19.*

(e) *For sweet communion with God in holy ordinances, and the communications of His favour.*

We have been abundantly satisfied with the fatness of thy house, and thou hast made us drink of the river of thy pleasures. For with thee is the fountain of life, in thy light shall we see light. *Psalm 36:8, 9.*

Thou hast brought us to thy holy mountain, and made us joyful in thy house of prayer, and we have found it good for us to draw near to God. *Isaiah 56:7. Psalm 73:28.*

We have had reason to say, That a day in thy courts is better than a thousand, and that it is better to be door-keepers in the house of our God, than to dwell in the tents of wickedness; For the Lord God is a sun and shield, he will give grace and glory, and no good thing will he with-hold from them that walk uprightly: O Lord of hosts, blessed is the man that trusteth in thee. *Psalm 84:10, 11, 12.*

We have sitten down under thy shadow with delight, and thy fruit hath been sweet unto our taste; Thou hast brought us into the banqueting house, and thy banner over us has been love. *Canticle (Song of Solomon) 2:3, 4.*

(f) *For gracious answers to our prayers.*

We have reason to love thee, O Lord, because thou hast heard the voice of our supplications, and because thou hast inclined thine ear unto us, we will therefore call upon thee as long as we live. *Psalm 116:1, 2.*

Out of the depths have we cried unto thee, O Lord, and thou hast heard our vows, and given us the heritage of those that fear thy name. *Psalm 130:1. Psalm 61:5.*

Nay, before we have called thou hast answered, and while we have been yet speaking thou hast heard, and hast said, Here I am, and hast been nigh unto us in all that which we call upon thee for. *Isaiah 65:24. Isaiah 58:9. Deuteronomy 4:7.*

Lord, thou hast heard the desire of the humble, thou wilt prepare their heart, and cause thine ear to hear. *Psalm 10:17.*

Blessed be God, who hath not turned away our prayer, or his mercy from us, for we have prayed, and have gone away, and our countenance has been no more sad. *Psalm 66:20. 1 Samuel 1:18.*

(g) *For support under our afflictions and spiritual benefit and advantage by them.*

Thou hast comforted us in all our tribulation, hast considered our trouble, and known our souls in adversity, and shewed us thy marvellous kindness as in a strong city. *2 Corinthians 1:4. Psalm 31:7, 21.*

When afflictions have abounded, consolations have much more abounded. *2 Corinthians 1:5.*

Though no affliction for the present hath been joyous, but grievous, nevertheless afterward it hath yielded the peaceable fruit of righteousness; and hath proved to be for our profit, that we might be partakers of thy holiness. *Hebrews 12:11, 10.*

We have had reason to say that it was good for us we were afflicted, that we might learn thy commandments; for before we were afflicted we went astray, but afterwards have kept thy word. *Psalm 119:71, 67.*

It has been but for a season, and when there was need that we were in heaviness, through manifold temptations: And we beg that all the trials of our faith may be found unto praise, and honour, and glory, at the appearing of Jesus Christ, whom having not seen we love, in whom though now we see him not, yet believing we rejoice with joy unspeakable and full of glory; are longing to receive the end of our faith, even the salvation of our souls. *1 Peter 1:6-9.*

(h) For the performance of God's promises.

Thou hast dealt well with thy servants, O Lord, according to thy word, and thou hast been ever mindful of thy covenant, the word which thou hast commanded to a thousand generations. *Psalm 119:65. Psalm 105:8.*

There hath not failed one word of all the good promise which thou hast promised, to David thy servant, and Israel thy people. *1 Kings 8:56, 66.*

And now what shall we render unto the Lord for all his benefits towards us. Let our souls return to him, and repose in him as their rest, because he hath dealt bountifully with us, we will take the cup of salvation, and call upon the name of the Lord; For the Lord is good, his mercy is everlasting, and his truth endureth to all generations. *Psalm 116:12, 7, 13. Psalm 100:5.*

We will bless the Lord at all times, yea his praise shall continually be in our mouths; we will sing unto the Lord as long as we live; and we hope to be shortly with those blessed ones, who dwell in his house above, and are still praising him, and who rest not day or night from saying, Holy, holy, holy, Lord God Almighty. *Psalm 34:1. Psalm 104:33. Revelation 4:8.*

5

Intercession

Intercession

OF THE FIFTH PART OF PRAYER, WHICH IS INTERCESSION, OR ADDRESS AND SUPPLICATION TO GOD FOR OTHERS

Our Lord Jesus hath taught us to pray, not only with, but for others: And the apostle hath appointed us to make supplication for all saints; and many of his prayers in his epistles are for his friends: And we must not think that when we are in this part of prayer, we may let fall our fervency, and be more indifferent, because we ourselves are not immediately concerned in it, but rather let a holy fire of love both to God and man here, make our devotions yet more warm and lively. Ephesians 6:18.

We must pray for the whole world of mankind, the lost world; and thus we must honour all men, and according to our capacity do good to all men. 1 Peter 2:17. Galatians 6:10.

E pray, as we are taught, for all men, believing that this is good and acceptable in the sight of God our Saviour, who will have all men to be saved, and to come unto the knowledge of the truth, and of Jesus Christ, who gave himself a ransom for all. *1 Timothy 2:1, 3, 4, 6.*

O look with compassion upon the world that lies in wickedness, and let the prince of this world be cast out, that has blinded their minds. *1 John 5:19. John 12:31. 2 Corinthians 4:4.*

O let thy way be known upon earth, that barbarous nations may be civilized, and those that live without God in the world may be brought to the service of the living God; and thus let thy saving health be known unto all nations: Let the people praise thee, O God, yea let all the people praise thee: O let the nations be glad, and sing for joy, for thou shalt judge the people righteously, and govern the nations upon earth. *Psalm 67:2. Ephesians 2:12. Psalm 67:3, 4.*

O let thy salvation and thy righteousness be openly shewed in the sight of the heathen, and let all the ends of the earth see the salvation of our God. *Psalm 98:2, 3.*

O give thy Son the heathen for his inheritance, and the uttermost parts of the earth for his possession! For thou hast said, It is a light thing for him to raise up the tribes of Jacob, and to restore the preserved of Israel, but thou wilt give him for a light to the Gentiles. *Psalm 2:8. Isaiah 49:6.*

Let all the kingdoms of this world become the kingdoms of the Lord and of his Christ. *Revelation 11:15.*

FOR THE PROPAGATING OF THE GOSPEL IN FOREIGN PARTS, AND THE ENLARGEMENT OF THE CHURCH BY THE BRINGING IN OF MANY TO IT

Let the gospel be preached unto every creature; for how shall men believe in him, of whom they have not heard? and how shall they hear without preachers? and how shall they preach, except they be sent? and who shall send forth labourers, but the Lord of the harvest? *Mark 16:15. Romans 10:14, 15. Matthew 9:38.*

Let the people which sit in darkness see a great light, and to them which sit in the region and shadow of death, let light spring up. *Matthew 4:16.*

Add unto thy church daily such as shall be saved; Enlarge the place of its tent, lengthen its cords, and strengthen its stakes. *Acts 2 (v. 47). Isaiah 54:2.*

Bring thy seed from the east, and gather them from the west; say to the north, Give up, and to the south, Keep not back: Bring thy sons from far, and thy daughters from the ends of the earth. Let them come with acceptance to thine altar, and glorify the house of thy glory; Let them fly as a cloud, and as the doves to their windows. *Isaiah 43:5, 6. Isaiah 60:7, 8.*

In every place let incense be offered to thy name, and pure offerings; And from the rising of the sun to the going down of the same, let thy name be great among the Gentiles; and let the offering up of the Gentiles be acceptable, being sanctified by the Holy Ghost. *Malachi 1:11. Romans 15:16.*

O let the earth be full of the knowledge of the Lord, as the waters cover the sea. *Isaiah 11:9.*

FOR THE CONVERSION OF THE JEWS

ET the branches which are broken off not abide still in unbelief, but be graffed in again into their own olive-tree. And though blindness is in part happened to Israel, yet let the fulness of the Gentiles come in, and let all Israel be saved. *Romans 11:17, 23-26.*

Let them be made to look unto him whom they have pierced, and that they may turn to the Lord, let the veil which is upon their hearts be taken away. *Zechariah 12:10. 2 Corinthians 3:15, 16.*

FOR THE EASTERN CHURCHES THAT ARE GROANING UNDER THE YOKE OF MAHOMETAN TYRANNY

ET the churches of Asia, that were golden candlesticks, which the Lord Jesus delighted to walk in the midst of, be again made so. *Revelation 1:11, 12. Revelation 2:1.*

Restore unto them their liberties as at the first, and their privileges as at the beginning; purely purge away their dross, and take away all their tin, and turn again their captivity as the streams in the south. *Isaiah 1:26, 25. Psalm 126:4.*

FOR THE CHURCHES IN THE PLANTATIONS

B E thou the confidence of all the ends of the earth, and of those that are afar off beyond the sea; And let them have the blessing which came upon the head of Joseph, and upon the crown of the head of him that was separated from his brethren, even to the utmost bound of the everlasting hills. *Psalm 65:5. Genesis 49:26.*

Create peace to those that are afar off, as well as to those that are nigh. *Isaiah 57:19.*

And let those that suck of the abundance of the seas, and of treasures hid in the sand, call the people to the mountain, that they may offer sacrifices of righteousness. *Deuteronomy 33:19.*

FOR THE UNIVERSAL CHURCH WHERE-EVER DISPERSED, AND FOR ALL THE INTERESTS OF IT

 UR heart's desire and prayer to God for the gospel Israel, is that it may be saved. *Romans 10:1.* Do good in thy good pleasure unto Zion, build thou the walls of Jerusalem. Peace be within her walls, and prosperity within her palaces; For our brethren and companions sake we will now say, Peace be within her. *Psalm 51:18. Psalm 122:7, 8.*

O that we may see the good of the gospel Jerusalem, all the days of our life, and peace upon Israel. And that thus we may have reason to answer the messengers of the nations, that the Lord hath founded Zion, and the poor of his people shall trust to that. *Psalm 128:5, 6. Isaiah 14:32.*

Save thy people, O Lord, and bless thine heritage: Feed them also, and lift them up for ever. Give strength unto thy people, and bless thy people with peace; with thy favour do thou compass them as with a shield. *Psalm 28 (v. 9). Psalm 29 (v. 11). Psalm 5 (v. 12).*

Grace be with all them that love the Lord Jesus Christ in sincerity; for thou knowest them that are thine; and give to all that name the name of Christ to depart from iniquity. *Ephesians 6:24. 2 Timothy 2:19.*

We pray for all that believe in Christ, that they all may be one; And since there is one body, and one Spirit, and one hope of our calling, one Lord, one faith, one baptism, and one God and Father of all, give to all Christians to be of one heart, and one way. *John 17:20, 21. Ephesians 4:4, 5, 6. Jeremiah 32:39.*

Let the word of the Lord in all places, have a free course, and let it be glorified. *2 Thessalonians 3:1.*

FOR THE CONVICTION AND CONVERSION OF ATHEISTS, DEISTS, AND INFIDELS, AND OF ALL THAT ARE OUT OF THE WAY OF TRUTH, AND OF PROFANE SCOFFERS, AND THOSE THAT DISGRACE CHRISTIANITY BY THEIR VICIOUS AND IMMORAL LIVES

Teach transgressors thy ways, and let sinners be converted unto thee. *Psalm 51:13.*

O give them repentance to the acknowledging of the truth, the truth as it is in Jesus, the truth which is according to godliness, that they may recover themselves out of the snare of the devil. *2 Timothy 2:25. Ephesians 4:21. Titus 1:1. 2 Timothy 2:26.*

Let those that are as sheep going astray return to Jesus Christ, the Shepherd and Bishop of our souls. *1 Peter 2:25.*

Shew those fools their folly and misery, that have said in their hearts there is no God, and that are corrupt, and have done abominable work. *Psalm 14:1.*

Lord, maintain the honour of the scripture, the law and the testimony, and convince those who speak not according to that word, that it is because there is no light in them; magnify that word above all thy name; magnify the law, magnify the gospel, and make both honourable. *Isaiah 8:20. Psalm 138:2. Isaiah 42:21.*

Let those that will not be won by the word, be won by the conversation of Christians, which we beg may be such in every thing, that they who believe not may be convinced of all, and judged of all, and may be brought to worship God, and to report that God is with them of a truth. *1 Peter 3:1. 1 Corinthians 14:24, 25.*

FOR THE AMENDING OF EVERY THING THAT IS AMISS IN THE CHURCH, THE REVIVING OF PRIMITIVE CHRISTIANITY, AND THE POWER OF GODLINESS, AND IN ORDER THEREUNTO, THE POURING OUT OF THE SPIRIT

LORD, let thy spirit be poured out upon thy churches from on high, and then the wilderness shall become a fruitful field, then judgment shall return unto righteousness, and all the upright in heart shall follow it. *Isaiah 32:15. Psalm 94:15.*

Let what is wanting be set in order, and let every plant that is not of our heavenly Father's planting, be plucked up. *Titus 1:5. Matthew 15:13.*

Let the Lord whom we seek come to his temple like a refiner's fire, and fuller's soap, and let him purify the sons of Levi, and all the seed of Israel, and purge them as gold and silver, that they may offer unto the Lord an offering in righteousness, pleasant to the Lord, as in the days of old, as in former years. *Malachi 3:1-4.*

Let pure religion and undefiled before God and the Father, flourish and prevail every where, that kingdom of God among men, which is not meat and drink, but righteousness, and peace, and joy in the Holy Ghost. O revive this work in the midst of the years, in the midst of the years make known, and let our times be times of reformation. *James 1 (v. 27). Romans 14:17. Habakkuk 3:2. Hebrews 9:10.*

FOR THE BREAKING OF THE POWER OF ALL THE ENEMIES OF THE CHURCH, AND THE DEFEATING OF ALL THEIR DESIGNS AGAINST HER

LET all that set themselves, and take counsel together against the Lord, and against his anointed, that would break their bands asunder, and cast away their cords from them, imagine a vain thing. Let him that sits in heaven laugh at them, and have them in derision; speak unto them in thy wrath, and vex them in thy sore displeasure. Give them, O Lord: what wilt thou give them? give them a miscarrying womb, and dry breasts. *Psalm 2:1-5. Hosea 9:14.*

O our God, make them like a wheel, and as stubble before the wind; Fill their faces with shame, that they may seek thy name, O Lord, and that men may know, that thou whose name is JEHOVAH, art the most high over all the earth. *Psalm 83:13, 16, 18.*

Put them in fear, O Lord, that the nations may know themselves to be but men, and wherein the proud enemies of thy church deal proudly, make it to appear that thou art above them. *Psalm 9:20. Exodus 18:11.*

Let them be confounded and turned back that hate Zion, and be as the grass upon the house-tops, which withereth before it groweth up. *Psalm 129:5, 6.*

Let no weapon formed against thy church prosper, and let every tongue that riseth against it in judgment be condemned. *Isaiah 54:17.*

Make Jerusalem a burdensome stone for all people, and let all that burden themselves with it be cut in pieces, though all the people of the earth should be gathered together against it; so let all thine enemies perish, O Lord, but let them that love thee be as the sun when he goes forth in his strength. *Zechariah 12:3. Judges 5 (v. 31).*

Lord, let the man of sin be consumed with the spirit of thy mouth, and destroyed with the brightness of thy coming: And let those be undeceived that have been long under the power of strong delusions to believe a lie, and let them receive the truth in the love of it. *2 Thessalonians 2:3, 8, 11, 10.*

Let Babylon fall, and sink like a mill-stone into the sea; And let the kings of the earth, that have given their power and honour to the beast, be wrought upon at length to bring it into the new Jerusalem. *Revelation 18:2, 21. Revelation 17:17. Revelation 21:24.*

FOR THE RELIEF OF SUFFERING CHURCHES, AND THE SUPPORT, COMFORT AND DELIVERANCE OF ALL THAT ARE PERSECUTED FOR RIGHTEOUSNESS SAKE

E desire in our prayers to remember them that are in bonds for the testimony of Jesus, as bound with them, and them which suffer adversity, as being ourselves also in the body. O send from above, and deliver them from those that hate them, and bring them forth into a large place. *Hebrews 13:3. Psalm 18:16, 17, 19.*

O let not the rod of the wicked rest upon the lot of the righteous, lest the righteous put forth their hands unto iniquity. *Psalm 125:3.*

Awake, awake, put on strength, O arm of the Lord; awake as in the ancient days, as in the generations of old, and make the depths of the sea a way for the ransomed of the Lord to pass over. *Isaiah 51:9, 10.*

For the oppression of the poor and the sighing of the needy, now do thou arise, O Lord, and set them in safety from them that puff at them. *Psalm 12:5.*

O strengthen the patience and faith of thy suffering saints, that they may hope and quietly wait for the salvation of the Lord. *Revelation 13:10. Lamentations 3:26.*

O let the year of thy redeemed come, and the year of recompences for the controversy of Zion. *Isaiah 63:4. Isaiah 34:8.*

O that the salvation of Israel were come out of Zion; and when the Lord bringeth back the captivity of his people, Jacob shall rejoice, and Israel shall be glad. *Psalm 14:7.*

O let not the oppressed return ashamed, but let the poor and needy praise thy name. *Psalm 74:21.*

Lord, arise, and have mercy upon Zion, and let the time to favour her, yea the set time come; yea let the Lord build up Zion, and appear in his glory. Lord, regard the prayer of the destitute, and do not despise their prayer. *Psalm 102:13, 16, 17.*

O Lord God, cease we beseech thee, by whom shall Jacob arise, for he is small! O cause thy face to shine upon that part of thy sanctuary that is desolate, for the Lord's sake. *Amos 7:5. Daniel 9:17.*

Let the sorrowful sighing of thy prisoners come before thee, and according to the greatness of thy power preserve thou those that for thy name's sake are appointed to die. *Psalm 79:11.*

Let those whose teachers are removed into corners, again see their teachers, though they have the bread of adversity, and the water of affliction. *Isaiah 30:20.*

FOR THE NATIONS OF EUROPE, AND THE COUNTRIES ABOUT US

HOU, Lord, art the governor among the nations: Who shall not fear thee, O King of nations? Thou sittest in the throne judging right; judge the world therefore in righteousness, and minister judgment to the people in uprightness. *Psalm 22:28. Jeremiah 10:7. Psalm 9:4, 8.*

Lord, hasten the time when thou wilt make wars to cease to the ends of the earth; when nation shall no more lift up sword against nation, nor kingdom against kingdom, but swords shall be beaten into plow-shares, and spears into pruning-hooks, and they shall not learn war any more. *Psalm 46:9. Isaiah 2:4.*

Make kings nursing fathers, and their queens nursing mothers to the Israel of God. *Isaiah 49:23.*

And in the days of these kings let the God of heaven set up a kingdom which shall never be destroyed, even the kingdom of the Redeemer. And whatever counsels there are in mens hearts, Lord, let thy counsel stand, and do thou fulfil the thoughts of thy heart unto all generations. *Daniel 2:44. Proverbs 19:21. Psalm 33:11.*

FOR OUR OWN LAND AND NATION, THE HAPPY ISLANDS OF GREAT BRITAIN AND IRELAND, WHICH WE OUGHT IN A SPECIAL MANNER TO SEEK THE WELFARE OF, THAT IN THE PEACE THEREOF WE MAY HAVE PEACE

1.   *We must be thankful to God for His mercies to our land.*

E bless thee that thou hast planted us in a very fruitful hill, and hast not made the wilderness our habitation, or the barren land our dwelling, but our land yields her increase. *Isaiah 5:1. Job 39:6. Psalm 85:12.*

Lord, thou hast dealt favourably with our land; We have heard with our ears, and our fathers have told us what work thou didst for us in their days, and in the times of old: And as we have heard, so have we seen; for we have thought of thy loving-kindness, O God, in the midst of thy temple. *Psalm 85:1. Psalm 44:1. Psalm 48:8, 9.*

Thou hast given us a pleasant land, it is Immanuel's land, it is a valley of vision, thou hast set up thy tabernacle among us, and thy sanctuary is in the midst of us. *Jeremiah 3:19. Isaiah 8:8. Isaiah 22:1. Ezekiel 37:27, 26.*

We dwell safely, under our own vines and fig-trees, and there is peace to him that goeth out, and to him that comes in. *1 Kings 4:25. 2 Chronicles 15:5.*

And because the Lord loved our people, therefore he hath set a good government over us to do judgment and justice; to be a terror to evil doers, and a protection and praise to them that do well. *1 Kings 10:9. Romans 13:3.*

2.   *We must be humbled before God for our national sins and provocations.*

But we are a sinful people, a people laden with iniquity, a seed of evil doers; And a great deal of reason we have to sigh and cry for the abominations that are committed among us. *Isaiah 1:4. Ezekiel 9:4.*

Iniquity abounds among us, and the love of many is waxen cold. *Matthew 24:12.*

We have not been forsaken nor forgotten of our God, though our land be full of sin against the Holy One of Israel. *Jeremiah 51:5.*

3. *We must pray earnestly for national mercies.*

(a) For the favour of God to us, and the tokens of His presence among us, as that in which the happiness of our nation is bound up.

O the hope of Israel, the saviour thereof in time of trouble, be not thou as a stranger in our land, or a way-faring man that turns aside to tarry but for a night; but be thou always in the midst of us, we are called by thy name, O leave us not: Though our iniquities testify against us, yet do thou it for thy name's sake; though our backslidings are many, and we have sinned against thee. *Jeremiah 14:8, 9, 7.*

Turn us to thee, O Lord God of hosts, and then cause thy face to shine, and we shall be saved. O stir up thy strength, and come and save us. *Psalm 80:3, 2.*

Shew us thy mercy, O Lord, and grant us thy salvation, yea let that salvation be nigh them that fear thee, that glory may dwell in our land: Let mercy and truth meet together, righteousness and peace kiss each other: Let truth spring out of the earth, and righteousness look down from heaven; yea let the Lord give that which is good: Let righteousness go before him, and set us in the way of his steps. *Psalm 85:7, 9-13.*

(b) For the continuance of the gospel among us, and the means of grace, and a national profession of Christ's holy religion.

O let the throne of Christ endure for ever, among us, even the place of thy sanctuary, that glorious high throne from the beginning. *Psalm 45:6. Jeremiah 17:12.*

Let our candlestick never be removed out of his place, though we have deserved it should, because we have left our first love. Never do to us as thou didst to thy place which was in Shiloh, where thou didst set thy name at the first. *Revelation 2:4, 5. Jeremiah 7:12.*

Let us never know what a famine of the word means; nor ever be put to wander from sea to sea, and from the river to the ends of the earth, to seek the word of God. *Amos 8:11, 12.*

Let wisdom and knowledge be the stability of our times and strength of salvation, and let the fear of the Lord be our treasure: Let the righteous flourish among us, and let there be those that shall fear thee in our land as long as the sun and moon endure throughout all generations, that there may be abundance of peace, and the children which shall be created may praise the Lord. *Isaiah 33:6. Psalm 72:5, 7. Psalm 102:18.*

(c) For the continuance of our outward peace and tranquillity, our liberty and plenty, for the prosperity of our trade, and a blessing upon the fruits of the earth.

Let God himself be a wall of fire round about us, and the glory in the midst of us, yea let his gospel be our glory, and upon all that glory let there be a defence; and create upon every dwelling-place of mount Zion, and upon her assemblies a cloud and smoke by day, and the shining of a flaming fire by night. *Zechariah 2:5. Isaiah 4:5.*

Peace be within our borders, and prosperity within our palaces, the prosperity both of merchandize and husbandry, that Zebulun may rejoice in his going out, and Issachar in his tents. *Psalm 122:7. Deuteronomy 33:18.*

Appoint salvation to us for walls and bulwarks, and in order to that let the gates be opened, that the righteous nation which keepeth the truth may enter in. *Isaiah 26:1, 2.*

Make our officers peace, and our exactors righteousness, let violence never be heard in our gates, wasting or destruction within our borders, but let our walls be called Salvation, and our gates Praise: Never let our land be termed Forsaken and Desolate, but let the Lord delight in us, and let our land be married to him. *Isaiah 60:17, 18. Isaiah 62:4.*

Let our peace be as a river, and in order to that, our righteousness as the waves of the sea: Let that righteousness abound among us which exalteth a nation, and deliver us from sin, which is a reproach to any people. *Isaiah 48:18. Proverbs 14:34.*

Never make our heavens as brass, and our earth as iron; nor take away thy corn in the season thereof, and thy wine in the season thereof, but give us rain moderately, the former and the later rain in due season, and reserve unto us the appointed works of harvest, giving us fair weather also in its season: Let our land yield her increase, and the trees their fruit; that we may eat bread to the full, and dwell in our land safely. *Deuteronomy 28:23. Hosea 2:9. Joel 2:23. Jeremiah 5:24. Leviticus 26:4, 5.*

Abundantly bless our provision, and satisfy our poor with bread, that they which have gathered it may eat and praise the Lord. Blow not thou upon it, for then when we look for much it will come to little, but bless our blessings, that all nations may call us blessed, and a delightsome land. *Psalm 132:15. Isaiah 62:9. Haggai 1:9. Malachi 3:10, 12.*

(d) For the success of all endeavours for the reformation of manners, the suppression of vice and profaneness, and the support of religion and virtue, and the bringing of them into reputation.

O let the wickedness of the wicked come to an end, but establish the just, O thou righteous God that triest the hearts and reins. Spirit many to rise up for thee against the evil doers, and to stand up for thee against the workers of iniquity. *Psalm 7:9. Psalm 94:16.*

Let the Redeemer come to Zion, and turn away ungodliness from Jacob; And let the filth of Jerusalem be purged from the midst thereof by the spirit of judgment, and the spirit of burning. *Romans 11:26. Isaiah 4:4.*

Let all iniquity stop her mouth, and let the infection of that plague be stayed, by executing judgment. *Psalm 107:42. Psalm 106:30.*

Let those that are striving against sin never be weary or faint in their minds. *Hebrews 12:4, 3.*

Cause the unclean spirit to pass out of the land, and turn to the people a pure language, that they may call on the name of the Lord. *Zechariah 13:2. Zephaniah 3:9.*

Make us high above all nations in praise and in name and in honour, by making us a holy people unto the Lord our God. *Deuteronomy 26:19.*

(e) For the healing of our unhappy divisions, and the making up of our breaches.

For the divisions that are among us, there are great searchings of heart; for there are three against two, and two against three in a house. But is the breach wide as the sea, which cannot be healed! Is there no balm in Gilead? Is there no physician there? Why then is not the health of the daughter of our people recovered? Lord, heal the breaches of our land, for because of them it shaketh. *Judges 5:16. Luke 12:52. Lamentations 2:13. Jeremiah 8 (v. 22). Psalm 60:2.*

We beg in the name of our Lord Jesus Christ, that there may be no divisions among us, but that we may be perfectly joined together in the same mind and in the same judgment. *1 Corinthians 1:10.*

Now the God of patience and consolation grant us to be likeminded one towards another, according to Christ Jesus, that we may with one mind and one mouth glorify God, even the Father of our Lord Jesus Christ, and promote the common salvation. *Romans 15:5, 6. Jude 3.*

Lord, keep us from judging one another, and despising one another, and give us to follow after the things which make for peace, and things wherewith one may edify another; that living in love and peace, the God of love and peace may be with us. *Romans 14:3, 19. 2 Corinthians 13:11.*

Let nothing be done through strife or vainglory, but every thing in lowliness of mind, and grant that our moderation may be known unto all men, because the Lord is at hand. *Philippians 2:3. Philippians 4:5.*

(f) For victory and success against our enemies abroad, that seek our ruin.

Rise, Lord, and let thine enemies be scattered, and let those that hate thee flee before thee, but return, O Lord, to the many thousands of thine Israel. *Numbers 10:35, 36.*

Give us help from trouble, for vain is the help of man; Through God let our forces do valiantly, yea let God himself tread down our enemies, and give them as dust to our sword, and as driven stubble to our bow. *Psalm 60:11, 12. Isaiah 41:2.*

Let us be a people saved by the Lord, as the shield of our help and the sword of our excellency; and make our enemies sensible that the Lord fighteth for us against them. *Deuteronomy 33 (v. 29). Exodus 14:25.*

Those who jeopard their lives for us in the high places of the field, teach their hands to war, and their fingers to fight, give them the shield of thy salvation, and let thy right hand hold them up, and cover their heads in the day of battle. *Judges 5:18. Psalm 144:1. Psalm 18:35. Psalm 140:7.*

(g) For all orders and degrees of men among us, and all we stand in any relation to.

1)   *For our sovereign lady the Queen, that God will protect her person, preserve her health, and continue her life and government long a publick blessing.*

Give the queen thy judgments, O God, and thy righteousness, that she may judge the poor of the people, may save the children of the needy, and may break in pieces the oppressor. *Psalm 72:1, 4.*

Let her throne be established with righteousness, and upheld with mercy: Give her long life and length of days for ever and ever, and let her glory be great in thy salvation, and make her exceeding glad with thy countenance: Through the mercy of the most High let her not be moved. *Proverbs 25:5. Proverbs 20:28. Psalm 21:4-7.*

Clothe her enemies with shame, but upon herself let the crown flourish, and continue her long, very long a nursing mother to thine Israel. *Psalm 132:18. Isaiah 49:23.*

2)   *For the succession in the Protestant line, that a blessing may attend it, that the entail of the crown may prove a successful expedient for the establishing of peace and truth in our days, the securing of them to posterity, and the extinguishing the hopes of our popish adversaries, and all their aiders and abettors.*

Lord, preserve to us the lamp which thou hast ordained for thine anointed, that the generation to come may know thee, even the children which shall be born, that they may set their hope in God, and keep his commandments. *Psalm 132:17. Psalm 78:6, 7.*

Let the Protestant succession abide before God for ever: O prepare mercy and truth which may preserve it, so will we sing praise unto thy name for ever. Thus let the Lord save Sion, and build the cities of Judah, and the seed of thy servants shall inherit it, and they that love thy name shall dwell therein. *Psalm 61:7, 8. Psalm 69:35, 36.*

Let their design who would make a captain to return into Egypt, be again defeated, and let not the deadly wound that hath been given to the beast be healed any more. *Numbers 14:4. Revelation 13:11, 12.*

Let our eyes see Jerusalem, the city of our solemnities, a quiet habitation, a tabernacle that shall not be taken down: Let none of the stakes thereof be removed, nor any of the cords thereof broken, but let the glorious Lord be unto us a place of broad waters and streams; for the Lord is our judge, the Lord is our lawgiver, the Lord is our king, he will save us. *Isaiah 33:20, 21, 22.*

3)   *For the privy counsellors, the ministers of state, the members of parliament, the embassadors and envoys abroad, and all that are employed in the conduct of publick affairs.*

Counsel our counsellors, and teach our senators wisdom: O give them a spirit of wisdom and understanding, a spirit of counsel and might, a spirit of knowledge and of the fear of the Lord, to make them of quick understanding in the fear of the Lord. *Psalm 105:22. Isaiah 11:2, 3.*

O remove not the speech of the trusty, nor take away the understanding of the aged, nor ever let the things that belong to the nation's peace be hid from the eyes of those that are intrusted with the nation's counsels. *Job 12:20. Luke 19:42.*

Make it to appear that thou standest in the congregation of the mighty, and judgest among the gods, and that when the princes of the people are gathered together, even the people of the God of Abraham, the God of Abraham himself is among them; And let the shields of the earth belong unto the Lord, that he may be greatly exalted. *Psalm 82:1. Psalm 47:9.*

Let those that be of us build the old waste places, and raise up the foundations of many generations, that they may be called the repairers of the breaches, and restorers of paths to dwell in. *Isaiah 58:12.*

4)   *For the magistrates, the judges and justices of peace in the several counties and corporations.*

Make those that rule over us just, ruling in the fear of God; and let those that judge remember that they judge not for man, but for the Lord, who is with them in the judgment, that therefore the fear of the Lord may be upon them. *2 Samuel 23:3. 2 Chronicles 19:6, 7.*

Make them able men, and men of truth, fearing God, and hating covetousness, that judgment may run down like a river, and righteousness as a mighty stream. *Exodus 18:21. Amos 5:24.*

Enable our magistrates to defend the poor and fatherless, to do justice for the afflicted and needy, to deliver the poor and needy, and to rid them out of the hand of the wicked; and let rulers never be a terror to good works, but to the evil. *Psalm 82:3, 4. Romans 13:3. 1 Peter 2:14.*

5)   *For all the ministers of God's holy word and sacraments, the masters of assemblies.*

Teach thy ministers how they ought to behave themselves in the house of God, which is the church of the living God, that they may not preach themselves, but Christ Jesus the Lord, and may study to shew themselves approved to God, workmen that need not to be ashamed, rightly dividing the word of truth. *1 Timothy 3:15. 2 Corinthians 4:5. 2 Timothy 2:15.*

Make them mighty in the scriptures, that from thence they may be thoroughly furnished for every good work, in doctrine shewing uncorruptness, gravity, and sincerity, and sound speech, which cannot be condemned. *Acts 18:24. 2 Timothy 3:17. Titus 2:7, 8.*

Enable them to give attendance to reading, to exhortation, to doctrine, to meditate upon these things, to give themselves to prayer and to the ministry of the word, to give themselves wholly to them; and to continue in them that they may both save themselves, and those that hear them. *1 Timothy 4:13, 15. Acts 6:4. 1 Timothy 4:15, 16.*

Let utterance be given to them, that they may open their mouths boldly to make known the mystery of the gospel, that thereof they may speak as they ought to speak, as able ministers of the new testament, not of the letter, but of the spirit, and let them obtain mercy of the Lord to be faithful. *Ephesians 6:19, 20. 2 Corinthians 3:6. 1 Corinthians 7:25.*

Let the arms of their hands be made strong by the hands of the mighty God of Jacob; and let them be full of power by the spirit of the Lord of hosts, to shew thy people their transgressions, and the house of Jacob their sins. *Genesis 49:24. Micah 3:8. Isaiah 58:1.*

Make them sound in the faith, and enable them always to speak the things which become sound doctrine, with meekness instructing those that oppose themselves; and let not the servants of the Lord strive, but be gentle to all men, apt to teach. *Titus 1:13. Titus 2:1. 2 Timothy 2:25, 24.*

Make them good examples to the believers in word, in conversation, in charity, in spirit, in faith, in purity; and let them be clean, that bear the vessels of the Lord, and let HOLINESS TO THE LORD be written upon their foreheads. *1 Timothy 4:12. Isaiah 52:11. Exodus 28:36.*

Lord, grant that they may not labour in vain, or spend their strength for nought, and in vain, but let the hand of the Lord be with them, that many may believe, and turn to the Lord. *Isaiah 49:4. Acts 11:21.*

6)   *For all the universities, schools, and nurseries of learning.*

Let the schools of the prophets be replenished with every good gift and every perfect gift from above from the Father of lights. *James 1:17.*

Cast salt into those fountains, and heal the waters thereof, that from thence may issue streams which shall make glad the city of our God, the holy place of the tabernacles of the most High. *2 Kings 2:21. Psalm 46:4.*

7) *For the common people of the land.*

Give grace to all the subjects of this land, that they may under the government God hath set over us, live quiet and peaceable lives in all godliness and honesty, dwelling together in unity, that the Lord may command a blessing upon us, even life for evermore. *1 Timothy 2:2. Psalm 133:1, 3.*

Let all of every denomination that fear God and work righteousness be accepted of him; yea let such as love thy salvation say continually, The Lord be magnified that hath pleasure in the prosperity of his servants. *Acts 10:35. Psalm 35:27.*

8) *For the several ages and conditions of men, as they stand in need of mercy and grace.*

(a) *For those that are young, and setting out in the world.*

Lord, give to those that are young to remember their Creator in the days of their youth, that thereby they may be kept from the vanity which childhood and youth are subject to, and may be restrained from walking in the way of their heart, and in the sight of their eyes, by considering that for all these things God will bring them into judgment. *Ecclesiastes 12:1. Ecclesiastes 11:10, 9.*

Lord, make young people sober-minded, and let the word of God abide in them, that they may be strong, and may overcome the wicked one. *Titus 2:6. 1 John 2:14.*

From the womb of the morning let Christ have the dew of the youth, and let him be formed in the hearts of those that are young. *Psalm 110:3. Galatians 4:19.*

Keep those that are setting out in the world from the corruption that is in the world through lust; and give to those that have been well educated to hold fast the form of sound words, and to continue in the things which they have learned. *2 Peter 1:4. 2 Timothy 1:13. 2 Timothy 3:14.*

(b) *For those that are old, and are of long standing in profession.*

There are some that are old disciples of Jesus Christ, Lord, give them still to bring forth fruit in old age, to shew that the Lord is upright, that he is their rock, and there is no unrighteousness in him. Now the evil days are come, and the years of which they say there is no pleasure in them, let thy comforts delight their souls. *Acts 21:16. Psalm 92:14, 15. Ecclesiastes 12:1. Psalm 94:19.*

Even to their old age be thou he, and to the hoary hairs do thou carry them, thou hast made, we beseech thee bear, yea do thou carry and deliver them. *Isaiah 46:4.*

Those whom thou hast taught from their youth up, and who have hitherto declared all thy wondrous works, now also when they are old and grey-headed leave them not, cast them not off in their old age, fail them not when their strength fails. *Psalm 71:17, 18, 9.*

Let every hoary head be a crown of glory to those that have it, being found in the way of righteousness, and give them to know whom they have believed. *Proverbs 16:31. 2 Timothy 1:12.*

(c) For those that are rich and prosperous in the world, some of whom perhaps need prayers as much as those that request them.

Lord keep those that are rich in the world from being high-minded, and trusting in uncertain riches, and give them to trust in the living God, who giveth us richly all things to enjoy: That they may do good, and be rich in good works, ready to distribute, willing to communicate, that they may lay up in store for themselves a good security for the time to come. *1 Timothy 6:17, 18, 19.*

Though it is hard for those that are rich to enter into the kingdom of heaven, yet with thee this is possible. *Matthew 19:23, 26.*

(d) For those that are poor and in affliction, for such we have always with us.

Lord, make those that are poor in the world rich in faith, and heirs of the kingdom, and give to them to receive the gospel. *James 2:5. Matthew 11:5.*

O that the poor of the flock may wait upon thee, and may know the word of the Lord. *Zechariah 11:11.*

Many are the troubles of the righteous, good Lord, deliver them out of them all, and though no affliction for the present seems to be joyous, but grievous, nevertheless afterward let it yield the peaceable fruit of righteousness to them that are exercised thereby. *Psalm 34:19. Hebrews 12:11.*

(e) For our enemies, and those that hate us.

Lord, give us to love our enemies, to bless them that curse us, and to pray for them that despitefully use us and persecute us. *Matthew 5:44.*

Father, forgive them, for they know not what they do; and lay not their malice against us to their charge, and work in us a disposition to forbear and forgive in love, as thou requirest we should when we pray. *Luke 23:34. Acts 7:60. Colossians 3:13. Mark 11:25.*

And grant that our ways may so please the Lord, that even our enemies may be at peace with us. Let the wolf and the lamb lie down together, and let there be none to hurt or destroy in all the holy mountain; let not Ephraim envy Judah, nor Judah vex Ephraim. *Proverbs 16:7. Isaiah 11:6, 9, 13.*

(f) For our friends, and those that love us.

And we wish for all those whom we love in the truth, that they may prosper, and be in health, especially that their souls may prosper. *3 John 1, 2.*

The grace of the Lord Jesus Christ be with their spirits. *Philemon (v. 25).*

6

Addresses to God upon particular occasions

Addresses to God upon particular occasions

OF ADDRESSES TO GOD UPON PARTICULAR OCCASIONS, WHETHER DOMESTICK OR PUBLICK

I T is made our duty, and prescribed as a remedy against disquieting care, that in every thing by prayer and supplication with thanksgiving we should make our requests known to God. And it is part of the parrhesia, the boldness, the liberty of speech (so the word signifies) which is allowed us in our access to God, that we may be particular in opening our case, and seeking to Him for relief; that according as the sore and the grief is, accordingly the prayer and the supplication may be by any man, or by the people of Israel. Not that God needs to be particularly informed of our condition, He knows it better than we ourselves do, and our souls too in our adversity, but it is His will that we should thus acknowledge Him in all our ways, and wait upon Him for the direction of every step, not prescribing, but subscribing to infinite wisdom, humbly shewing Him our wants, burdens, and desires, and then referring ourselves to Him, to do for us as He thinks fit. Philippians 4:6. Hebrews 10:19. 2 Chronicles 6:29. Proverbs 3:6. Psalm 37:23.

We shall instance in some of the occasions of particular address to God, more or less usual, which may either be the principal matter of a whole prayer, or inserted in our other prayers, and in some cases that are more peculiar to ministers, or others, in common to them with masters of families and private Christians. As there may be something particular.

IN OUR MORNING PRAYERS

OUR voice shalt thou now hear in the morning, in the morning will we direct our prayer unto thee, and will look up; for our souls wait for thee, O Lord, more than they that watch for the morning, yea more than they that watch for the morning; and we will sing aloud of thy mercy in the morning; for thou hast been our defence. *Psalm 5:3. Psalm 130:6. Psalm 59:16.*

It is thou (O God) that hast commanded the morning, and caused the day-spring to know its place, that it might take hold of the ends of the earth, and it is turned as clay to the seal. *Job 38:12, 13, 14.*

The day is thine, the night also is thine, thou hast prepared the light and the sun. *Psalm 74:16.*

With the light of the morning let the day-spring from on high visit us, to give us the knowledge of salvation, through the tender mercy of our God; And let the Sun of righteousness arise upon our souls with healing under his wings; and our path be as the shining light, which shines more and more to the perfect day. *Luke 1:78, 77. Malachi 4:2. Proverbs 4:18.*

It is of thy mercy, O Lord, that we are not consumed, even because thy compassions fail not, they are new every morning, great is thy faithfulness: And if weeping sometimes endures for a night, joy comes in the morning. *Lamentations 3:22, 23. Psalm 30:5.*

We thank thee that we have laid us down, have had where to lay our head, and have not been wandering in deserts and mountains, in dens, and caves of the earth: And that we have slept, and have not been full of tossings to and fro till the dawning of the day, that wearisome nights are not appointed to us, and we are not saying at our lying down, When shall we arise, and the night be gone? But our bed comforts us, and our couch easeth our complaint: Thou givest us sleep as thou givest it to thy beloved. And that having laid us down and slept, we have waked again; Thou hast lightened our eyes, so that we have not slept the sleep of death. *Matthew 8:20. Hebrews 11:38. Job 7:4, 3, 13. Psalm 127:2. Psalm 3:5. Psalm 13:3.*

Thou hast preserved us from the pestilence that walketh in darkness, and from the malice of the rulers of the darkness of this world, the roaring lion that goes about seeking to devour: He that keepeth Israel, and neither slumbers nor sleeps, has kept us, and so we have been safe. *Psalm 91:6. Ephesians 6:12. 1 Peter 5:8. Psalm 121:4.*

But we cannot say with thy servant David, that when we awake we are still with thee, or that our eyes have prevented the night watches, that we might meditate in thy word; but vain thoughts still lodge within us. O pardon our sins, and cause us to hear thy loving-kindness this morning, for in thee do we trust; cause us to know the way wherein we should walk, for we lift up our souls unto thee: Teach us to do thy will, for thou art our God, thy spirit is good, lead us into the way and land of uprightness. *Psalm 139:18. Psalm 119:148. Jeremiah 4:14. Psalm 143:8, 10.*

And now let the Lord preserve and keep us from all evil this day, yea let the Lord preserve our souls: Lord, preserve our going out, and coming in; Give thine angels charge concerning us, to bear us up in their hands, and keep us in all our ways. And give us grace to do the work of the day in its day, as the duty of the day requires. *Psalm 121:7, 8. Psalm 91:11, 12. Ezra 3:4.*

IN OUR EVENING PRAYERS

THOU, O God, makest the outgoings of the evening, as well as of the morning, to rejoice; for thereby thou callest us from our work and our labour, and biddest us rest a while. And now let our souls return to thee, and repose in thee as our rest, because thou hast dealt bountifully with us; so shall our sleep be sweet to us. *Psalm 65:8. Psalm 104:23. Mark 6:31. Psalm 116:7. Jeremiah 31:26.*

Blessed be the Lord, who daily loads us with his benefits, who hath this day preserved our going out and coming in: And now we have received from thee our daily bread, we pray, Father, forgive us our trespasses. *Psalm 68:19. Psalm 121:8. Matthew 6:11, 12.*

And we will lie us down and sleep; for thou, Lord, makest us to dwell in safety: Make a hedge of protection (we pray thee) about us and about our house, and about all that we have round about. Let the angels of God encamp round about us to deliver us; that we may lie down, and none may make us afraid. *Psalm 4:8. Job 1:10. Psalm 34:7. Job 11:19.*

Into thy hands we commit our spirits; that in slumberings upon the bed, our ears may be opened, and instruction sealed; And let the Lord give us counsel, and let our reins instruct us in the night season: Visit us in the night and try us, and enable us to commune with our own hearts upon our bed. *Psalm 31:5. Job 33:15, 16. Psalm 16:7. Psalm 17:3. Psalm 4:4.*

Give us to remember thee upon our bed, and to meditate upon thee in the night watches, with the saints that are joyful in glory, and that sing aloud upon their beds. *Psalm 63:6. Psalm 149:5.*

IN CRAVING A BLESSING BEFORE MEAT

THOU, O Lord, givest food to all flesh, for thy mercy endures for ever. The eyes of all wait on thee; but especially thou givest meat to them that fear thee, being ever mindful of thy covenant. *Psalm 136:25. Psalm 145:15. Psalm 111:5.*

Thou art our life, and the length of our days, the God that hast fed us all our life long unto this day: Thou givest us all things richly to enjoy, though we serve thee but poorly. Thou hast not only given us every green herb, and the fruits of the trees to be to us for meat, but every moving thing that liveth even as the green herb. *Deuteronomy 30:20. Genesis 48:15. 1 Timothy 6:17. Genesis 1:29. Genesis 9:3.*

And blessed be God that now under the gospel we are taught to call nothing common or unclean, and that it is not that which goes into the man that defiles the man, but that every creature of God is good, and nothing to be refused; for God hath created it to be received with thanksgiving of them which believe and know the truth. *Acts 10:14, 15. Matthew 15:11. 1 Timothy 4:4, 3.*

We acknowledge we are not worthy of the least crumb that falls from the table of thy providence: Thou mightest justly take away from us the stay of bread, and the stay of water, and make us to eat our bread by weight, and to drink our water by measure, and with astonishment; because when we have been fed to the full, we have forgotten God our Maker. But let our sins be pardoned, we pray thee, that our table may not become a snare before us, nor that be made a trap, which should have been for our welfare. *Matthew 15:27. Isaiah 3:1. Ezekiel 4:16. Deuteronomy 32:15. Hosea 8:14. Psalm 69:22.*

We know that every thing is sanctified by the word of God and prayer; and that man lives not by bread alone, but by every word that proceedeth out of the mouth of God; and therefore, according to our Master's example, we look up to heaven, and pray for a blessing upon our food, Abundantly bless our provision. *1 Timothy 4:5. Matthew 4:4. Matthew 14:19. Psalm 132:15.*

Lord, grant that we may not feed ourselves without fear, that we may not make a god of our belly, that our hearts may never be overcharged with surfeiting or drunkenness, but that whether we eat or drink, or whatever we do, we may do all to the glory of God. *Jude 12. Philippians 3:19. Luke 21:34. 1 Corinthians 10:31.*

IN RETURNING THANKS AFTER OUR MEAT

OW we have eaten and are full, we bless thee for the good land thou hast given us. Thou preparest a table for us in the presence of our enemies, thou anointest our head, and our cup runs over. *Deuteronomy 8:10. Psalm 23:5.*

Thou, Lord, art the portion of our inheritance and of our cup, thou maintainest our lot, so that we have reason to say, The lines are fallen to us in pleasant places, and we have a goodly heritage. *Psalm 16:5, 6.*

Especially we bless thee for the bread of life, which came down from heaven, which was given for the life of the world, Lord, evermore give us that bread; and wisdom to labour less for the meat which perisheth, and more for that which endures to everlasting life. *John 6:33, 34, 27.*

The Lord give food to the hungry, and send portions to them for whom nothing is prepared. *Psalm 146:7.*

Let us be of those blessed ones that shall eat bread in the kingdom of God, that shall eat of the hidden manna. *Luke 14:15. Revelation 2:17.*

WHEN WE ARE GOING A JOURNEY

ORD, keep us in the way that we go, and let no evil thing befall us: Let us have a prosperous journey by the will of God, and with thy favour let us be compassed where-ever we go as with a shield. *Genesis 28:20. Psalm 91:10. Romans 1:10. Psalm 5:12.*

Let us walk in our way safely, and let not our foot stumble, or dash against a stone. *Proverbs 3:23. Psalm 91:12.*

Direct our way in every thing, and enable us to order all our affairs with discretion, and the Lord send us good speed, and shew kindness to us. *1 Thessalonians 3:11. Psalm 112:5. Genesis 24:12.*

And the Lord watch between us when we are absent the one from the other. *Genesis 31:49.*

WHEN WE RETURN FROM A JOURNEY

BLESSED be the Lord God of Abraham, who hath not left us destitute of his mercy and his truth. *Genesis 24:27.*

All our bones shall say, Lord, who is like unto thee, for thou keepest all our bones. *Psalm 35:10. Psalm 34:20.*

It is God that girdeth us with strength, and maketh our way perfect. *Psalm 18:32.*

ON THE EVENING BEFORE THE LORD'S-DAY

OW give us to remember that to morrow is the sabbath of the Lord, and that it is a high day, holy of the Lord and honourable, and give us grace so to sanctify ourselves, that to morrow the Lord may do wonders among us; and to mind the work of our preparation now the sabbath draws on. *Exodus 16:23. John 19:31. Isaiah 58:13. Joshua 3:5. Luke 23:54.*

When thou sawest every thing that thou hadst made in six days, behold all was very good, but in many things we have all offended. O that by repentance and faith in Christ's blood we may wash not our feet only, but also our hands and our head, and our heart, and so may compass thine altar, O Lord. *Genesis 1:31. James 3:2. John 13:9. Psalm 26:6.*

Now give us to rest from all our own works, and to leave all our worldly cares at the bottom of the hill, while we go up into the mount to worship God, and return again to them. *Hebrews 4:10. Genesis 22:5.*

ON THE MORNING OF THE LORD'S DAY

E bless thee, Lord, who hath shewed us light, and that the light we see is the Lord's; that we see one more of the days of the Son of man; a day to be spent in thy courts, which is better than a thousand elsewhere. *Psalm 118:27. Luke 17:22. Psalm 84:10.*

We thank thee, Father, Lord of heaven and earth, that the things which were hid from the wise and prudent, are revealed unto us babes, even so, Father, because it seemed good in thine eyes: That our eyes see, and our ears hear that which many prophets and kings desired to see, desired to hear, and might not; That life and immortality are brought to light by the gospel. *Luke 10:21, 23, 24. 2 Timothy 1:10.*

And now, O that we may be in the Spirit on the Lord's day! that we may call the sabbath a delight, and may honour the Son of man, who is Lord also of the sabbath day, not doing our own ways, or finding our own pleasure, or speaking our own words. *Revelation 1:10. Isaiah 58:13. Mark 2:28. Isaiah 58:13.*

AT THE ENTRANCE UPON THE PUBLICK WORSHIP
ON THE LORD'S DAY BY THE MASTERS OF THE
ASSEMBLIES

HOU (O God) art greatly to be feared in the assembly of the saints, and to be had in reverence of all them that are about thee. O give us grace to worship thee with reverence and godly fear, because thou our God art a consuming fire. *Psalm 89:7. Hebrews 12:28, 29.*

This is that which thou hast said, that thou wilt be sanctified in them which come nigh unto thee, and before all the people thou wilt be glorified. Thou art the Lord that sanctifiest us, sanctify us by thy truth, that we may sanctify thee in our hearts, and make thee our fear and our dread. *Leviticus 10:3. Ezekiel 20:12. John 17:17. Isaiah 8:13.*

We come together to give glory to the great JEHOVAH, who in six days made heaven and earth, the sea and all that in them is, and rested the seventh day, and therefore blessed a sabbath day, and hallowed it. And our help stands in the name of the Lord, who made heaven and earth. *Exodus 20:11. Psalm 124 (v. 8).*

O let us be new creatures, thy workmanship created in Christ Jesus unto good works; And let that God who on the first day of the world commanded the light to shine out of darkness, on this first day of the week shine into our hearts, to give us the light of the knowledge of the glory of God in the face of Jesus Christ. *2 Corinthians 5:17. Ephesians 2:10. 2 Corinthians 4:6.*

We come together to give glory to the Lord Jesus Christ, and to sanctify this sabbath to his honour, who was the stone that the builders refused, but is now become the head stone of the corner. This is the Lord's doing, and it is marvellous in our eyes: This is the day which the Lord has made, we will rejoice and be glad in it: He is the first and the last, who was dead and is alive. *Psalm 118:22, 23, 24. Revelation 2:8.*

O that we may this day experience the power of Christ's resurrection, and may be planted together in the likeness of it, that as Christ was raised up from the dead by the glory of the Father; so we also may walk in newness of life, and may sit with him in heavenly places; and by seeking the things that are above, may make it to appear that we are risen with him. *Philippians 3:10. Romans 6:5, 4. Ephesians 2:6. Colossians 3:1.*

We come together to give glory to the blessed Spirit of grace, and to celebrate the memorial of the giving of that promise of the Father, in whom the apostles received power on the first day of the week, as on that day Christ rose. *Acts 1:4, 8. Acts 2:1.*

O that we may this day be filled with the Holy Ghost, and that the fruit of the Spirit in us may be in all goodness, and righteousness, and truth. *Ephesians 5:18, 9.*

We come together to testify our communion with the universal church, that though we are many, yet we are one; that we worship one and the same God, the Father, of whom are all things, and we in him, in the name of one Lord Jesus Christ, by whom are all things, and we by him; under the conduct of the same Spirit, one and the self-same Spirit, who divideth to every man severally as he will, walking by the same rule, looking for the same blessed hope, and the glorious appearing of the great God and our Saviour. *1 Corinthians 10:17. 1 Corinthians 8:6. 1 Corinthians 12:4, 11. Galatians 6:16. Titus 2:13.*

IN OUR PREPARATION FOR THE LORD'S SUPPER

OW we are invited to come eat of wisdom's bread, and drink of the wine that she has mingled, give us to hunger and thirst after righteousness; And being called to the marriage supper of the Lamb, give us the wedding garment. *Proverbs 9:5. Matthew 5:6. Revelation 19:9. Matthew 22:11.*

Awake, O north wind, and come thou south, and blow upon our garden, that the spices thereof may flow forth; and then let our beloved come into his garden, and eat his pleasant fruits. *Canticle (Song of Solomon) 4:16.*

Draw us, and we will run after thee; bring us into the chambers, that there we may be glad and rejoice in thee, and may remember thy love more than wine. And when the king sits at his table, let our spikenard send forth the smell thereof. *Canticle (Song of Solomon) 1:4, 12.*

And the good Lord pardon every one that prepareth his heart to seek God, the Lord God of his fathers, though he be not cleansed according to the purification of the sanctuary: Hear our prayers, and heal the people. *2 Chronicles 30:18, 19, 20.*

In the celebrating of the Lord's supper

Let this cup of blessing, which we bless, be the communion of the blood of Christ; let this bread which we break be the communion of the body of Christ, and enable us herein to shew the Lord's death, till he come. *1 Corinthians 10:16. 1 Corinthians 11:26.*

Now let us be joined to the Lord in an everlasting covenant; so joined to the Lord, as to become one spirit with him. Now let us be made partakers of Christ by holding fast the beginning of our confidence stedfast to the end. *Jeremiah 50:5. 1 Corinthians 6:17. Hebrews 3:14.*

Let Christ's flesh be meat indeed to us, and his blood drink indeed; and give us so by faith to eat his flesh, and drink his blood, that he may dwell in us, and we in him, and we may live by him. *John 6:55, 56, 57.*

Let the cross of Christ, which is to the Jews a stumbling block, and to the Greeks foolishness, be to us the wisdom of God and the power of God. *1 Corinthians 1:23, 24.*

Seal to us the remission of sins, the gift of the Holy Ghost, and the promise of eternal life, and enable us to take this cup of salvation, and to call on the name of the Lord. *Acts 2:38. 1 John 2:25. Psalm 116:13.*

After the celebrating of the Lord's supper

ND now, Lord, give us to hold fast that which we have received, that no man take our crown: And keep it always in the imagination of the thought of our heart, and prepare our hearts unto thee. *Revelation 3:11. 1 Chronicles 29:18.*

Give us grace, as we have received Christ Jesus the Lord, so to walk in him, that our conversation may be in every thing as becomes his gospel. *Colossians 2:6. Philippians 1:27.*

O that we may now bear about with us continually the dying of the Lord Jesus, so as that the life also of Jesus may be manifested in our mortal body, that to us to live may be Christ. *2 Corinthians 4:10. Philippians 1:21.*

Thy vows are upon us, O God: O that we may be daily performing our vows. *Psalm 56:12. Psalm 61:8.*

UPON OCCASION OF THE BAPTISM OF A CHILD

O thee, O God, whose all souls are, the souls of the parents and the souls of the children, we present this child a living sacrifice, which we desire may be holy and acceptable, and that it may be given up and dedicated to the Father, Son, and Holy Ghost. *Ezekiel 18:4. Romans 12:1. Matthew 28:19.*

It is conceived in sin, but there is a fountain opened: O wash the soul of this child in that fountain, now it is by thine appointment washed with pure water. *Psalm 51:5. Zechariah 13:1. Hebrews 10:22.*

It is one of the children of the covenant, one of the children that is borne unto thee, it is thy servant born in thy house: O make good thy ancient covenant, that thou wilt be a God to believers and to their seed; for this blessing of Abraham comes upon the Gentiles, and the promise is still to us and to our children. *Acts 3:25. Ezekiel 16:20. Psalm 116:16. Genesis 17:7. Galatians 3:14. Acts 2:39.*

Thou hast encouraged us to bring little children to thee; for thou hast said, that of such is the kingdom of God: Blessed Jesus, take up this child in the arms of thy power and grace, put thy hands upon it, and bless it; let it be a vessel of honour, sanctified, and meet for the master's use, and owned as one of thine in that day when thou makest up thy jewels. *Mark 10:14, 16. 2 Timothy 2:21. Malachi 3:17.*

O pour thy spirit upon our seed, thy blessing upon our offspring, that they may spring up as willows by the water-courses, and may come to subscribe with their own hands unto the Lord, and to surname themselves by the name of Israel. *Isaiah 44:3, 4, 5.*

Upon occasion of a funeral

LORD, give us to find it good for us to go to the house of mourning, that we may be minded thereby of the end of all men, and may lay it to our heart, and may be so wise as to consider our latter end; for we also must be gathered to our people, as our neighbours and brethren are gathered: And though whither those that are dead in Christ are gone we cannot follow them now, yet grant that we may follow them afterwards, every one in his own order. *Ecclesiastes 7:2. Deuteronomy 32:29. Numbers 27:13. John 13:36. 1 Corinthians 15:23.*

We know that thou wilt bring us to death, and to the house appointed for all living; but let us not see death, till by faith we have seen the Lord Christ, and then let us depart in peace according to thy word; And when the earthly house of this tabernacle shall be dissolved, let us have a building of God, a house not made with hands, eternal in the heavens. *Job 30:23. Luke 2:26, 29. 2 Corinthians 5:1.*

And give us to know that our redeemer liveth, and that though after our skins, worms destroy these bodies, yet in our flesh we shall see God; whom we shall see for ourselves, and our eyes shall behold, and not another. *Job 19:25, 26, 27.*

Upon occasion of a marriage

IVE to those that marry to marry in the Lord; and let the Lord Jesus by his grace come to the marriage, and turn the water into wine. *1 Corinthians 7:39. John 2:1, 2, 9.*

Make them helps meet for each other, and instrumental to promote one another's salvation, and give them to live in holy love, that they may dwell in God, and God in them. *Genesis 2:18. 1 Corinthians 7:16. 1 John 4:16.*

Let the wife be as a fruitful vine by the side of the house, and the husband dwell with the wife as a man of knowledge; and let them dwell together as joint heirs of the grace of life, that their prayers be not hindered. And make us all meet for that world where they neither marry, nor are given in marriage. *Psalm 128:3. 1 Peter 3:7. Luke 20:35.*

Upon Occasion of the Ordaining of Ministers

ET the things of God be committed to faithful men, who may be able also to teach others, and make them such burning and shining lights, as that it may appear it was Christ Jesus who put them into the ministry; and let not hands be suddenly laid on any. *2 Timothy 2:2. John 5:35. 1 Timothy 1:12. 1 Timothy 5:22.*

Give to those who are ordained to take heed to the ministry which they have received of the Lord, that they fulfil it, and to make full proof of it by watching in all things. *Colossians 4:17. 2 Timothy 4:5.*

Let those who in Christ's name are to preach repentance and remission of sins, be endued with power from on high, give them another spirit, and make them good ministers of Jesus Christ, nourished up in the words of faith and good doctrine. *Luke 24:47, 49. 1 Samuel 10:9. 1 Timothy 4:6.*

Upon occasion of the want of rain

THOU hast with-holden the rain from us, and caused it to rain upon one city, and not upon another, yet have we not returned unto thee. *Amos 4:7, 8.*

But thou hast said when heaven is shut up that there is no rain, because we have sinned against thee, if we confess thy name, and turn from our sins, thou wilt hear from heaven, and forgive our sin, and give rain upon our land. *1 Kings 8:35, 36.*

We ask of thee the former and later rain, and depend upon thee for it; for there are not any of the vanities of the heathen that can give rain, nor can the heavens give showers; but we wait on thee, for thou hast made all these things. *Zechariah 10:1. Jeremiah 14:22.*

Upon Occasion of Excessive Rain

ET the rain thou sendest be in mercy to our land, and not for correction; not a sweeping rain, which leaveth no food. *Job 37:13. Proverbs 28:3.*

Thou hast sworn that the waters of Noah shall no more return to cover the earth; Let fair weather therefore come out of the north, for with thee is terrible majesty. *Isaiah 54:9. Job 37:22.*

Upon Occasion of Infectious Diseases

AKE sickness away from the midst of us, and deliver us from the noisome pestilence. *Exodus 23:25. Psalm 91:3.*

Appoint the destroying angel to put up his sword into the sheath, and to stay his hand. *2 Samuel 24:16.*

UPON OCCASION OF FIRE

THOU callest to contend by fire, we bewail the burning which the Lord hath kindled: O Lord God, cease, we beseech thee, and let the fire be quenched, as that kindled in Israel was at the prayer of Moses. *Amos 7:4. Leviticus 10:6. Amos 7:5. Numbers 11:2.*

UPON OCCASION OF GREAT STORMS

LORD, thou hast the winds in thy hands, and bringest them out of thy treasures, even stormy winds fulfil thy word: O preserve us and our habitations, that we be not buried in the ruins of them, as Job's children were. *Proverbs 30:4. Psalm 135:7. Psalm 148:8. Job 1:19.*

Upon Occasion of the Cares, and Burdens, and Afflictions of Particular Persons: As,

1. *When we pray with or for those that are troubled in mind, and melancholy, and under doubts and fears about their spiritual state.*

LORD, enable those that fear thee, and obey the voice of thy servant, but walk in darkness, and have no light, to trust in the name of the Lord, and to stay themselves upon their God; And at evening time let it be light. *Isaiah 50:10. Zechariah 14:7.*

O strengthen the weak hands, confirm the feeble knees, say to them that are of a fearful heart, Be strong, fear not: Answer them with good words and comfortable words; saying unto them, Be of good cheer, your sins are forgiven you; Be of good cheer, it is I, be not afraid, I am your salvation; And make them to hear this voice of joy and gladness, that broken bones may rejoice. *Isaiah 35:3, 4. Zechariah 1:13. Matthew 9:2. Mark 6:50. Psalm 35:3. Psalm 51:8.*

Let those who now remember God and are troubled, whose spirits are overwhelmed, and whose souls refuse to be comforted, be enabled to trust in thy mercy, so that at length they may rejoice in thy salvation; though thou slay them yet to trust in thee. *Psalm 77:3, 2. Psalm 13:5. Job 13:15.*

Though deep calls unto deep, and all thy waves and thy billows go over them; yet do thou command thy loving-kindness for them in the daytime, and in the night let thy song be with them, and their prayer to the God of their life; Though their souls are cast down, and disquieted within them, give them to hope in God, that they shall yet praise him, and let them find him the health of their countenance and their God. *Psalm 42:7, 8, 11.*

O renew a right spirit within them, cast them not away from thy presence, and take not thy holy spirit from them, but restore unto them the joy of thy salvation, and uphold them with thy free spirit, that their tongues may sing aloud of thy righteousness, and shew forth thy salvation. *Psalm 51:10, 11, 12, 14. Psalm 71:15.*

O bring them up out of this horrible pit, and this miry clay, and set their feet upon a rock, establishing their goings, and put a new song into their mouth, even praises to our God: O comfort them again now after the time that thou hast afflicted them. *Psalm 40:2, 3. Psalm 90:15.*

Though for a small moment thou hast forsaken them, and hid thy face from them, yet gather them, and have mercy on them with everlasting kindness. *Isaiah 54:7, 8.*

O let thy Spirit witness with their spirits, that they are the children of God; and by the blood of Christ let them be purged from an evil conscience. *Romans 8:16. Hebrews 10:22.*

Lord, rebuke the tempter, even the accuser of the brethren, the Lord that hath chosen Jerusalem rebuke him, and let poor tempted troubled souls be as brands plucked out of the burning. *Revelation 12:10. Zechariah 3:2.*

2. *Those that are under convictions of sin, and begin to be concerned about their souls, and their salvation, and to enquire after Christ.*

Those that are asking the way to Zion with their faces thitherward, that are lamenting after the Lord, and are pricked to the heart for sin, O shew them the good and the right way, and lead them in it. *Jeremiah 50:5. 1 Samuel 7:2. Acts 2:37. 1 Samuel 12:23.*

To those who are asking what they shall do to inherit eternal life, discover Christ as the way, the truth and the life, the only true and living way. *Matthew 19:16. John 14:6.*

O do not quench the smoking flax, nor break the bruised reed, but bring forth judgment unto victory. Let the great shepherd of the sheep gather the lambs in his arms, and carry them in his bosom, and gently lead them, and help them against their unbelief. *Matthew 12:20. Isaiah 40:11. Mark 9:24.*

Let not the red dragon devour the man child as soon as it is born, but let it be caught up to God and to his throne. *Revelation 12:4, 5.*

3. *When we pray with or for those that are sick and weak, and distempered in body; that those who are sick and in sin may be convinced, those who are sick and in Christ comforted.*

Lord, thou hast appointed those that are sick to be prayed for, and prayed with, and hast promised that the prayer of faith shall save the sick; Lord, help us to pray in faith for the sick, and as being ourselves also in the body. *James 5:14, 15. Hebrews 13:3.*

When our Lord Jesus was here upon earth, we find that they brought to him all sick people that were taken with divers diseases and torments, and he healed all manner of sickness and all manner of disease among the people: And he hath still the same power over bodily diseases that ever he had; he saith to them, Go, and they go; Come, and they come; Do this, and they do it; and can speak the word, and they shall be healed. And he is still touched with the feeling of our infirmities; In the belief of this, we do by prayer bring our friends that are sick, and lay them before him. *Matthew 4:24, 23. Matthew 8:9, 8. Hebrews 4:15. Luke 5:18.*

Lord, grant that those who are sick may neither despise the chastening of the Lord, nor faint when they are rebuked of him; but that they may both hear the rod, and him that has appointed it, and may kiss the rod, and accept of the punishment of their iniquity. *Hebrews 12:5. Micah 6:9. Leviticus 26:41.*

Give them to see that affliction cometh not forth out of the dust, nor springs out of the ground, that they may therefore seek unto God, to the Lord more than to the physicians, because unto God the Lord belong the issues of life and death. *Job 5:6, 8. 2 Chronicles 16:12. Psalm 68:20.*

Lord, shew them wherefore thou contendest with them, and give them in their affliction to humble themselves greatly before the God of their fathers, and to repent and turn from every evil way, and make their ways and their doings good, that being judged and chastened of the Lord, they may not be condemned with the world. By the sickness of the body, and the sadness of the countenance let the heart be made better. *Job 10:2. 2 Chronicles 33:12. Jeremiah 18:11. 1 Corinthians 11:32. Ecclesiastes 7:3.*

O Lord, rebuke them not in thine anger, neither chasten them in thy hot displeasure: Have mercy upon them, O Lord, for they are weak: Lord heal them, for their bones are vexed, their souls also are sore vexed: Return, O Lord, and deliver their souls, save them for thy mercy's sake; and lay no more upon them than thou wilt enable them to bear, and enable them to bear what thou dost lay upon them. *Psalm 6:1-4. 1 Corinthians 10:13.*

When thou with rebukes dost chasten man for sin, thou makest his beauty to consume away like a moth; surely every man is vanity. But remove thy stroke, we pray thee, from those that are even consumed by the blow of thine hand: O spare a little, that they may recover strength before they go hence and be no more. *Psalm 39:11, 10, 13.*

Those that are chastened with pain upon their bed, and the multitude of their bones with strong pain, so that their life abhorreth bread, and their soul dainty meat, shew them thine uprightness, be gracious to them. Deliver them from going down to the pit, for thou hast found a ransom. *Job 33:19, 20, 23, 24.*

Let the eternal God be their refuge, and underneath them be the everlasting arms; Consider their frame, remember that they are but dust. *Deuteronomy 33:27. Psalm 103:14.*

O deliver those that are thine in the time of trouble, preserve them and keep them alive: O strengthen them upon their bed of languishing, and make all their bed in their sickness: Be merciful to them, and heal their souls, for they have sinned. *Psalm 41:1-4.*

O turn to them and have mercy upon them, bring them out of their distresses; look upon their affliction and their pain, but especially forgive all their sin. *Psalm 25:16, 17, 18.*

Make thy face to shine upon them, save them for thy mercy's sake: The God that comforteth them that are cast down, comfort them; and let the soul dwell at ease in thee, when the body lies in pain. *Psalm 31:16. 2 Corinthians 7:6. Psalm 25:13.*

————

(If it be the beginning of a distemper)

Lord, set bounds to this sickness, and say, Hitherto it shall come, and no further: Let it not prevail to extremity, but in measure when it shooteth forth do thou debate, and stay thy rough wind in the day of thine east wind; and by this let iniquity be purged, and let this be all the fruit, even the taking away of sin. *Job 38:11. Isaiah 27:8, 9.*

————

(If it have continued long)

Lord, let patience have its perfect work, even unto long-suffering, that those who have been long in the furnace may continue hoping and quietly waiting for the salvation of the Lord: Let tribulation work patience, and patience experience, and experience a hope that maketh not ashamed; and enable them to call even this affliction light and but for a moment, seeing it to work for them a far more exceeding and eternal weight of glory. *James 1:4. Lamentations 3:26. Romans 5:3, 4, 5. 2 Corinthians 4:17.*

————

(If there be hopes of recovery)

Lord, when thou hast tried them let them come forth like gold; Let their souls live, and they shall praise thee, let thy judgments help them: O deal bountifully with them that they may live, and keep thy word. In love to their souls deliver them from the pit of corruption, and cast all their sins behind thy back. Recover them, and make them to live. Speak the word, and they shall be healed; say unto them, Live, yea, say unto them, Live, and the time shall be a time of love. Father, if it be possible, let the cup pass away; however not as we will, but as thou wilt: The will of the Lord be done. Perfect that which concerns them; thy mercy, O Lord, endures for ever, forsake not the work of thine own hands; but whether they live or die, let them be the Lord's. *Job 23:10. Psalm 119:175, 17. Isaiah 38:17, 16. Matthew 8:8. Ezekiel 16:6, 8. Matthew 26:39. Acts 21:14. Psalm 138:8. Romans 14:8.*

———

(If they be in appearance at the point of death)

Now the flesh and the heart are failing, Lord, be thou the strength of the heart, and an everlasting portion: In the valley of the shadow of death, Lord, be thou present, as the good shepherd with a guiding rod, and a supporting staff. O do not fail them nor forsake them now. Be a very present help: Into thy hands we commit the departing spirit, as into the hands of a faithful Creator, by the hands of him who has redeemed it. Let it be carried by the angels into Abraham's bosom. Let it be presented to thee without spot, or wrinkle, or any such thing. Lord Jesus, receive this precious soul, let it come to the spirits of just men made perfect; when it is absent from the body, let it be present with the Lord! This day let it be with thee in paradise. Now let it be for ever comforted, and perfectly freed from sin; and prepare us to draw after, as there are innumerable before, that we may be together for ever with the Lord, there where there shall be no more death, and where all tears shall be wiped away. *Psalm 73:26. Psalm 23:4. Hebrews 13:5. Psalm 46:1. Psalm 31:5. 1 Peter 4 (v. 19). Luke 16:22. Ephesians 5:27. Acts 7:59. Hebrews 12:23. 2 Corinthians 5:8. Luke 23:43. Luke 16:25. Romans 6:7. Job 21:33. 1 Thessalonians 4 (v. 17). Revelation 21:4.*

4.   *When we pray with or for those that are deprived of the use of their reason.*

O look with pity upon those that are put out of the possession of their own souls, whose judgment is taken away, so that their soul chooseth strangling and death rather than life: O restore them to themselves and their right mind. Deliver them from doing themselves any harm: And whatever afflictions thou layest upon any of us in this world, preserve to us the use of our reason, and the peace of our consciences. *Luke 21:19. Job 27:2. Job 7:15. Luke 15:17. Mark 5:15. Acts 16:28.*

5.   *When we pray with or for sick children.*

Lord, we see death reigning even over them that have not sinned after the similitude of Adam's transgression; but Jesus Christ hath abolished death, and admitted even little children into the kingdom of God. O let sick children be pitied by thee, as they are by their earthly parents. They are come forth like flowers, O let them not be cut down again: Turn from them, that they may rest till they shall have accomplished as a hireling their day. Be gracious to us, and let the children live. However, Father, thy will be done. O let their spirits be saved in the day of the Lord Jesus. *Romans 5:14. 2 Timothy 1:10. Matthew 18:3. Psalm 103:13. Job 14:2, 6. 2 Samuel 12:22. Acts 21:14. 1 Corinthians 5:5.*

6.   *When we pray with or for families where death is, especially such as have lost their head.*

Visit the houses of mourning, as our Saviour did, and comfort them, by assuring them that Christ is the resurrection and the life, that their relations which are removed from them, are not dead, but sleep; and that they shall rise again, that they may not sorrow as those that have no hope: And enable them to trust in the living God, the rock of ages, and enjoy the fountain of living waters, when creatures prove broken reeds and broken cisterns. *John 11:25, 23. Matthew 9:24. 1 Thessalonians 4:13. 1 Timothy 6:17. Psalm 146:4, 5. Isaiah 26:4. Jeremiah 2:13.*

Be a Father to the fatherless, and a husband to the widows, O God, in thy holy habitation. With thee let the fatherless find mercy, keep them alive, and let the widows trust in thee, that they may be widows indeed, who being desolate, trust in God, and continue instant in prayer night and day. And where father and mother have forsaken, let the Lord take up the children, and not leave them orphans, but come to them. *Psalm 68:5. Hosea 14:3. Jeremiah 49:11. 1 Timothy 5:5. Psalm 27:10. John 14:18.*

7. *When we pray with or for those women that are near the time of travail, or in travail.*

Lord, thou hast past this sentence upon the woman that was first in the transgression, that in sorrow she shall bring forth children. But let this handmaid of thine be saved in childbearing, and continue in faith, and charity, and holiness, with sobriety. Enable her to cast her burden upon the Lord, and let the Lord sustain her; and what time she is afraid, grant that she may trust in thee, and may encourage herself in the Lord her God. O let not the root be dried up from beneath, nor let the branch be withered or cut off; but let both live before thee. Be thou her strong habitation, her rock, and her fortress, give commandment to save her. And when travail comes upon her, which she cannot escape; be pleased, O Lord, to deliver her: O Lord make haste to help her: Be thou thyself her help and deliverer, make no tarrying, O our God: Let her be safely delivered, and remember the anguish no more, for joy that a child is born into the world, is born unto thee. *1 Timothy 2:14. Genesis 3:16. 1 Timothy 2 (v. 15). Psalm 55:22. Psalm 56:3. 1 Samuel 30:6. Job 18:16. Psalm 71:3. 1 Thessalonians 5:3. Psalm 40:13, 17. John 16:21.*

8. *When we pray with or for those that are recovered from sickness, or are delivered in child-bearing, and desire to return thanks unto God for His mercy.*

We will extol thee, O Lord, upon the account of those whom thou hast lifted up, whose souls thou hast brought up from the grave, and kept them alive, that they should not go down to the pit. Those that were brought low thou hast helped, hast delivered their souls from death, their eyes from tears, and their feet from falling. Now give them grace to walk before thee in the land of the living, to offer to thee the sacrifice of thanksgiving, to call upon thy name, and to pay their vows unto the Lord. *Psalm 30:1, 2, 3. Psalm 116:6, 8, 9, 17, 18.*

The grave cannot thus praise thee, death cannot celebrate thee, they that go down to the pit cannot hope for thy truth; but the living, the living they shall praise thee, as we do this day. Lord, grant that those who are delivered from death may not be as the nine lepers, who did not return to give thanks, or as Hezekiah, who rendered not again according to the benefit done unto him, but that they may so offer praise, as to glorify thee, and so order their conversation, as to see the salvation of God. *Isaiah 38:18, 19. Luke 17:18. 2 Chronicles 32:25. Psalm 50:23.*

Those whom the Lord hath chastened sore, yet he has not delivered over unto death: O that they may therefore praise him, who is become their salvation. *Psalm 118:18, 21.*

9.   *When we pray with or for those parents, whose children are a grief to them, or such as they are in fear about.*

Lord, give to parents the desire of their souls concerning their children, which is to see them walking in the truth, form Christ in their souls. O give them betimes to know the God of their fathers, and to serve him with a perfect heart and a willing mind. Let children of the youth, that are as arrows in the hand, be directed aright, that those parents may have reason to think themselves happy, that have their quiver full of them, and they may never be arrows in the heart. *2 John 4. Galatians 4:19. 1 Chronicles 28:9. Psalm 127:4, 5.*

Let those foolish children, that are the grief of the father, and the heaviness of her that bare them, that mock at their parents, and despise to obey them, be brought to repentance; and let those that have been unprofitable now at length be made profitable. O turn the hearts of the children to the fathers, even the disobedient to the wisdom of the just, that they may be made ready a people prepared for the Lord. O shew them their work, and their transgression, that they have exceeded, and open their ear to discipline. *Proverbs 17:25. Proverbs 30:17. Philemon 11. Malachi 4:6. Luke 1:17. Job 36:9, 10. Isaiah 29:23, 24.*

10.   *When we pray with or for those that are in prison.*

Those that sit in darkness and in the shadow of death, being bound in affliction and iron, because they rebelled against the words of God, and contemned the counsel of the most High, give them grace to cry unto thee in their trouble, and in a day of adversity to consider. *Psalm 107:10, 11, 13. Ecclesiastes 7:14.*

In their captivity give them to bethink themselves, to humble themselves, and pray, and seek thy face, to repent, saying, We have sinned, and have done perversely, and to return unto thee with all their heart, and with all their soul; and thus bring their souls out of prison, that they may praise thy name: Bring them into the glorious liberty of the children of God, out of the bondage of corruption. Let the Son make them free, and then they shall be free indeed. *1 Kings 8:47, 48. Psalm 142:7. Romans 8:21. John 8:36.*

Those that are wrongfully imprisoned be thou with them, as thou wast with Joseph in the prison, and shew them mercy. Hear the poor, and despise not thy prisoners, but let their sorrowful sighing come before thee, and according to the greatness of thy power preserve those that are unjustly appointed to die. *Genesis 39:21. Psalm 69:33. Psalm 79:11.*

11.   *When we pray with or for condemned malefactors, that have but a little while to live.*

O look with pity upon those, the number of whose months is to be cut off in the midst for their sin: O give them repentance unto salvation, as thou didst to the thief upon the cross, that they may own the justice of God in all that is brought upon them, that he has done right, but they have done wickedly. O turn them, and they shall be turned, that being instructed they may smite upon the thigh, and may be ashamed, yea even confounded, because they do bear the reproach of their own iniquity. O pluck them as brands out of the fire; let them be delivered from the wrath to come. *Job 21:21. 2 Corinthians 7:10. Nehemiah 9:33. Jeremiah 31:18, 19. Jude 23. 1 Thessalonians 1:10.*

Enable them to give glory to God by making confession, that they may find mercy, and that others may hear and fear, and do no more presumptuously. *Joshua 7:19. Proverbs 28:13. Deuteronomy 17:13.*

Lord Jesus, remember them now thou art in thy kingdom: O let them not be hurt of the second death: Deliver them from going down to that pit! Though the flesh be destroyed, O let the spirit be saved in the day of the Lord Jesus. The God of infinite mercy be merciful to these sinners, these sinners against their own souls. *Luke 23:42. Revelation 2:11. Job 33:24. 1 Corinthians 5:5. Luke 18:13. Numbers 16:38.*

12.   *When we pray with or for those that are at sea.*

Let those that go down to the sea in ships, that do business in great waters, observe the works of the Lord there, and his wonders in the deep; And acknowledge what a great God he is whom the winds and the seas obey; who hath placed the sand for the bound of the sea, by a perpetual decree, that it cannot pass it; and though the waves thereof toss themselves, yet can they not prevail; though they roar, yet can they not pass over. *Psalm 107:23, 24. Matthew 8:27. Jeremiah 5:22.*

O preserve them through the paths of the seas, and in perils by waters, and perils by robbers. If the stormy wind be raised, which lifteth up the waves, so that they are at their wits end, deliver them out of their distresses, make the storm a calm, and bring them to their desired haven: And O that those who are delivered may praise the Lord for his goodness, and for his wonderful works to the children of men. *Psalm 8:8. 2 Corinthians 11:26. Psalm 107:25, 27-31.*

7

Conclusion of our Prayers

Conclusion of our Prayers

Of the conclusion of our prayers

We are commanded to pray always, to pray without ceasing, to continue in prayer, because we must always have in us a disposition to this duty, must be constant to it, and never grow weary of it, or throw it up; and yet we cannot be always praying, we must come down from this mount; nor may we be over-long, so as to make the duty a task or a toil to ourselves, or those that join with us. We have other work that calls for our attendance. Jacob wrestles with the angel; but he must go, for the day breaks: We must therefore think of concluding. The prayers of David the son of Jesse must be ended. But how shall we conclude, so as to have the impressions of the duty kept always in the imagination of the thought of our heart.

We may then sum up our requests in some comprehensive petitions, as the conclusion of the whole matter.

OW the God of peace, that brought again from the dead our Lord Jesus, that great shepherd of the sheep, through the blood of the everlasting covenant, make us perfect in every good work to do his will, working in us that which is well-pleasing in his sight through Christ Jesus. *Hebrews 13:20, 21.*

Now the Lord direct our hearts into the love of God, and into a patient waiting for Christ. *2 Thessalonians 3:5.*

And the God of all grace, who hath called us to his eternal glory by Christ Jesus, after that we have suffered a while, make us perfect, stablish, strengthen, settle us. *1 Peter 5:10.*

And now, Lord, what wait we for? Truly our hope is even in thee, and on thee do we depend to be to us a God all-sufficient. *Psalm 39:7. Genesis 17:1.*

Do for us exceeding abundantly above what we are able to ask or think, according to the power that worketh in us: And supply all our needs according to thy riches in glory by Christ Jesus. *Ephesians 3:20. Philippians 4:19.*

WE MAY THEN BEG FOR THE AUDIENCE AND ACCEPTANCE OF OUR POOR WEAK PRAYERS, FOR CHRIST'S SAKE

OW the God of Israel grant us the things we have requested of him. *1 Samuel 1:17.*

Let the words of our mouths and the meditations of our hearts be acceptable in thy sight, O Lord, our strength and our redeemer. *Psalm 19:14.*

Let thine eyes be open unto the supplication of thy servants, and unto the supplication of thy people Israel, to hearken unto them in all that they call unto thee for; for they be thy people and thine inheritance. *1 Kings 8:52, 51.*

O our God, let thine ears be attent unto the prayers that we have made: O turn not away the face of thine anointed; remember the mercies of David thy servant; even Jesus, who is at thy right hand making intercession for us. *2 Chronicles 6:40, 42. Romans 8:34.*

Lord, thou hast assured us that whatever we ask the Father in Christ's name, he will give it us: We ask all these things in that name, that powerful name which is above every name, that precious name which is as ointment poured forth. O make thy face to shine upon us for the Lord's sake, who is the Son of thy love, and whom thou hearest always: Good Lord, give to us to hear him, and be well pleased with us in him. *John 16:23. Philippians 2:9. Canticle (Song of Solomon) 1:3. Daniel 9:17. Colossians 1:13. John 11:42. Matthew 17:5.*

WE MAY THEN BEG FOR THE FORGIVENESS OF WHAT HAS BEEN AMISS IN OUR PRAYERS

ORD, we have not prayed as we ought; who is there that doth good, and sins not? Even when we would do good evil is present with us; and if to will be present, yet how to perform that which is good we know not, for the good that we would we do not; so that thou mightest justly refuse to hear even when we make many prayers. But we have a great high priest, who bears the iniquity of the holy things, which the children of Israel hallow in all their holy gifts; for his sake take away all that iniquity from us, even all the iniquity of our holy things, and receive us graciously, and love us freely; And deal not with us after our folly. *Romans 8:26. Ecclesiastes 7:20. Romans 7:21, 18, 19. Isaiah 1:15. Exodus 28:38. Hosea 14:2, 4. Job 42:8.*

WE MAY THEN RECOMMEND OURSELVES TO THE CONDUCT, PROTECTION AND GOVERNMENT OF THE DIVINE GRACE, IN THE FURTHER SERVICES THAT LIE BEFORE US, AND IN THE WHOLE COURSE OF OUR CONVERSATION

ND now let us be enabled to go from strength to strength, until we appear before God in Zion, and while we pass through this valley of Baca, let it be made a well, and let the rain of the divine grace and blessing fill the pools. *Psalm 84:7, 6.*

Now, speak, Lord, for thy servants hear. What saith our Lord unto his servants? Grant that we may not turn away our ear from hearing the law; for then our prayers will be an abomination; but may hearken unto God, that he may hearken unto us. *1 Samuel 3:9. Joshua 5:14. Proverbs 28:9. Judges 9:7.*

And now the Lord our God be with us, as he was with our fathers; let him not leave us nor forsake us; That he may incline our hearts unto him, to walk in all his ways, and to keep his commandments, and his statutes, and his judgments; And let our hearts be perfect with the Lord our God all our days, and continue so till the end be, that then we may rest, and may stand in our lot, and let it be a blessed lot in the end of the days. *1 Kings 8:57, 58, 61. Daniel 12:13.*

WE MAY CONCLUDE ALL WITH DOXOLOGIES, OR SOLEMN PRAISES OF GOD, ASCRIBING HONOUR AND GLORY TO THE FATHER, THE SON, AND THE HOLY GHOST, AND SEALING UP ALL OUR PRAISES AND PRAYERS WITH AN AFFECTIONATE AMEN

OW blessed be the Lord God of Israel, from everlasting to everlasting, Amen and Amen. *Psalm 41:13.*

For ever blessed be the Lord God, the God of Israel, who only doth wondrous things, and blessed be his glorious name for ever, and let the whole earth be filled with his glory, Amen and Amen. Yea, let all the people say, Amen, Hallelujah. *Psalm 72:18, 19. Psalm 106:48.*

To God only wise be glory through Jesus Christ for ever, Amen. *Romans 16:27.*

Now to God the Father, and our Lord Jesus Christ, who gave himself for our sins, that he might deliver us from this present evil world, according to the will of God and our Father, be glory for ever and ever, Amen. *Galatians 1:3, 4, 5.*

To God be glory in the church by Christ Jesus, throughout all ages, world without end, Amen. *Ephesians 3:21.*

Now to the King eternal, immortal, invisible, the only wise God, be honour and glory for ever and ever, Amen: To him be honour and power everlasting, to him be glory and dominion, Amen. *1 Timothy 1:17. 1 Timothy 6:16. 1 Peter 5:11.*

Now unto him that is able to keep us from falling, and to present us faultless before the presence of his glory with exceeding joy, to the only wise God our Saviour, be glory and majesty, dominion and power, now and ever, Amen. *Jude 24, 25.*

Hallelujah, salvation and glory, and honour, and power unto the Lord our God, Amen, Hallelujah. *Revelation 19:1, 4.*

And now, we prostrate our souls before the throne, and worship God, saying, Amen, blessing, and glory, and wisdom, and thanksgiving, and honour, and power, and might, be unto our God for ever and ever, Amen. *Revelation 7:11, 12.*

Blessing, and honour, and glory, and power, be unto him that sitteth upon the throne, and unto the Lamb for ever and ever; And let the whole creation say, Amen, amen. *Revelation 5:13. Psalm 150:6.*

IT IS VERY PROPER TO SUM UP OUR PRAYERS IN THAT
FORM OF PRAYER WHICH CHRIST TAUGHT HIS
DISCIPLES

Our Father which art in heaven;
Hallowed be thy name;
Thy kingdom come;
Thy will be done on earth as it is in heaven;
Give us this day our daily bread;
And forgive us our trespasses
as we forgive them that trespass against us;
And lead us not into temptation,
but deliver us from evil;

For thine is the kingdom, the power, and the glory, for ever and
ever, Amen. *Matthew 6:9-13.*

8

A Paraphrase on the Lord's Prayer

A Paraphrase on the Lord's Prayer

A PARAPHRASE ON THE LORD'S PRAYER, IN SCRIPTURE EXPRESSIONS

*T*HE *Lord's prayer being intended not only for a form of prayer itself, but a rule of direction, a plan or model in little, by which we may frame our prayers; and the expressions being remarkably concise, and yet vastly comprehensive, it will be of good use sometimes to lay it before us, and observing the method and order of it, to dilate upon the several passages and petitions of it, that when we use it only as a form, we may use it the more intelligently; of which we shall only here give a specimen in the assistance we may have from some other scriptures.*

Our Father Which Art In Heaven

O Lord our God, doubtless thou art our Father, though Abraham be ignorant of us, and Israel acknowledge us not; thou, O Lord, art our Father, our redeemer, thy name is from everlasting; And we will from this time cry unto thee, Our Father, thou art the guide of our youth. *Isaiah 63:16. Jeremiah 3:4.*

Have we not all one Father, has not one God created us? Thou art the Father of our spirits, to whom we ought to be in subjection and live. *Malachi 2:10. Hebrews 12:9.*

Thou art the Father of lights, and the Father of mercies, and the God of all consolation: The eternal Father, of whom, and through whom, and to whom are all things. *James 1:17. 2 Corinthians 1:3. Isaiah 9:6. Romans 11:36.*

Thou art the Father of our Lord Jesus Christ, whose glory was that of the only begotten of the Father, who is in his bosom, by him as one brought up with him, daily his delight, and rejoicing always before him. *Ephesians 1:3. John 1:14, 18. Proverbs 8:30.*

Thou art in Christ our Father, and the Father of all believers, whom thou hast predestinated to the adoption of children, and into whose hearts thou hast sent the Spirit of the Son, teaching them to cry, Abba, Father. Behold what manner of love the Father hath bestowed upon us, that we should be called the children of God; That the Lord God Almighty should be to us a Father, and we should be to him for sons and daughters; And that as many as receive Christ, to them thou shouldest give power to become the sons of God, even to them that believe on his name; which are born not of the will of man, but of God, and his grace. *Ephesians 1:5. Galatians 4:6. 1 John 3:1. 2 Corinthians 6 (v. 18). John 1:12, 13.*

O that we may receive the adoption of sons, and that as obedient and genuine children we may fashion ourselves according to the example of him who hath called us, who is holy; and may be followers of God as dear children, and conformed to the image of his Son, who is the first born among many brethren. *Galatians 4:5. 1 Peter 1:14, 15. Ephesians 5:1. Romans 8:29.*

Enable us to come to thee with humble boldness and confidence, as to a Father, a tender Father, who spares us as a man spares his son that serves him; and as having an advocate with the Father, who yet has told us, that the Father himself loves us. *Ephesians 3:12. Malachi 3:17. 1 John 2:1. John 16:27.*

Thou art a Father, but where is thine honour? Lord, give us grace to serve thee as becomes children, with reverence and godly fear. *Malachi 1:6. Hebrews 12:28.*

Thou art a Father, and if earthly parents, being evil, yet know how to give good gifts unto their children, how much more shall our heavenly Father give the Holy Spirit to them that ask him. Lord, give us the spirit of grace and supplication. *Luke 11:13. Zechariah 12:10.*

We come to thee as prodigal children that have gone from our Father's house into the far country; but we will arise and go to our Father, for in his house there is bread enough and to spare, and if we continue at a distance from him, we perish with hunger. Father, we have sinned against heaven and before thee, and are no more worthy to be called thy children, make us even as thy hired servants. *Luke 15:13, 17, 18, 19.*

Thou art our Father in heaven, and therefore unto thee, O Lord, do we lift up our souls. Unto thee lift we up our eyes, O thou that dwellest in the heavens: As the eyes of a servant are to the hand of his master, and the eyes of a maiden to the hand of her mistress, so do our eyes wait upon thee, O Lord our God; a God whom the heaven of heavens cannot contain, and yet whom we may have access to, having a high-priest that is passed into the heavens, as our forerunner. *Psalm 86:4. Psalm 123:1, 2. 1 Kings 8:27. Ephesians 3:12. Hebrews 4:14. Hebrews 6:20.*

Thou, O God, dwellest in the high and holy place, and holy and reverend is thy name. God is in heaven, and we are upon earth, therefore should we choose out words to reason with him; and yet through a mediator we have boldness to enter into the Holiest. *Isaiah 57:15. Psalm 111:9. Ecclesiastes 5:2. Job 9:14. Hebrews 10:19.*

Look down (we pray thee) from heaven, and behold from the habitation of thy holiness and of thy glory, and have compassion upon us and help us. *Isaiah 63:15. Mark 9:22.*

Heaven is the firmament of thy power: O hear us from thy holy heaven with the saving strength of thy right hand; send us help from the sanctuary, and strengthen us out of Sion. *Psalm 150:1. Psalm 20:6, 2.*

And O that since heaven is our Father's house; we may have our conversation there, and may seek the things that are above. *John 14:2. Philippians 3:20. Colossians 3:1.*

HALLOWED BE THY NAME

AND now what is our petition, and what is our request? What would we that thou shouldest do for us? This is our hearts desire and prayer in the first place, Father in heaven, let thy name be sanctified. We pray that thou mayest be glorified as a Holy God. *Esther 5:6. Matthew 20:32. Romans 10:1. Leviticus 10:3.*

We desire to exalt the Lord our God, to worship at his footstool, at his holy hill, and to praise his great and terrible name, for it is holy, for the Lord our God is holy. Thou art holy, O thou that inhabitest the praises of Israel. *Psalm 99:5, 3, 9. Psalm 22:3.*

We glory in thy holy name, and therefore shall our hearts rejoice, because we have trusted in that holy name of thine, to which we will always give thanks, and triumph in thy praise. *Psalm 105:3. Psalm 33:21. Psalm 106:47.*

Lord, enable us to glorify thy holy name for evermore, by praising thee with all our hearts, and by bringing forth much fruit, for herein is our heavenly Father glorified. O that we may be to our God for a name, and for a praise, and for a glory, that being called out of darkness, into his marvellous light, to be to him a peculiar people, we may shew forth the praises of him that hath called us. *Psalm 86:12. John 15:8. Jeremiah 13:11. 1 Peter 2:9.*

O that we may be thy children, the work of thy hands, that we may sanctify thy name, and sanctify the Holy One of Jacob, and fear the God of Israel, and may be to the praise of his glory. *Isaiah 29:23. Ephesians 1:12.*

Enable us, as we have received the gift, so to minister the same as good stewards of the manifold grace of God, that God in all things may be glorified through Jesus Christ: And if we suffer, enable us to suffer as Christians, and to glorify God therein; for this is our earnest expectation and hope, that always Jesus Christ may be magnified in our bodies in life and death. *1 Peter 4:10, 11, 16. Philippians 1:20.*

Lord, enable others to glorify thee, let even the strong people glorify thee, and the city of the terrible nations fear thee; but especially let the Lord be magnified from the border of Israel. Let them glorify the Lord in the fires, even the Lord God of Israel in the isles of the sea. O let all nations whom thou hast made come and worship before thee, O Lord, and glorify thy name; for thou art great, and dost wondrous things, thou art God alone. *Isaiah 25:3. Malachi 1:5. Isaiah 24:15. Psalm 86:9, 10.*

O let the Gentiles glorify God for his mercy, let his name be known and confessed among the Gentiles, and let them rejoice with his people. O let thy name be great among the Gentiles, and let all the ends of the world remember and turn to the Lord, and all the kindreds of the nations worship before thee; and let them declare thy righteousness to a people that shall be born. *Romans 15:9, 10. Malachi 1:11. Psalm 22:27, 31.*

Lord, do thou thyself dispose of all things to thy own glory, both as King of nations, and as King of saints: Do all according to the counsel of thy own will, that thou mayest magnify thyself, and sanctify thyself, and mayest be known in the eyes of many nations, that thou art the Lord. O sanctify thy great name, which has been profaned among the heathen, and let them know that thou art the Lord, when thou shalt be sanctified in them. *Jeremiah 10:7. Revelation 15:3. Ephesians 1:11. Ezekiel 38:23. Ezekiel 36:23.*

Father, glorify thine own name: Thou hast glorified it, glorify it yet again: Father, glorify thy Son, that thy Son also may glorify thee. O give him a name above every name, and in all places, in all things let him have the pre-eminence. *John 12:28. John 17:1. Philippians 2:9. Colossians 1:18.*

Lord, what wilt thou do for thy great name? Do this for thy great name; Pour out of thy spirit upon all flesh; and let the word of Christ dwell richly in the hearts of all. Be thou exalted, O Lord, among the heathen, be thou exalted in the earth; Be thou exalted, O God, above the heavens, let thy glory be above all the earth; Be thou exalted, O Lord, in thine own strength, so will we sing and praise thy power. Do great things with thy glorious and everlasting arm, to make unto thyself a glorious and an everlasting name. *Joshua 7:9. Joel 2:28. Colossians 3:16. Psalm 46:10. Psalm 57:11. Psalm 21:13. Isaiah 63:5, 12, 14.*

O let thy name be magnified for ever, saying, The Lord of hosts is the God of Israel, even a God to Israel. *1 Chronicles 17:24.*

THY KINGDOM COME

IN order to the sanctifying and glorifying of thy Holy name, Father in heaven, let thy kingdom come, for thine is the kingdom, O Lord, and thou art exalted as head above all: Both riches and honour come of thee; thou reignest over all, and in thine hand is power and might, in thine hand it is to make great, and to give strength unto all. And we desire to speak of the glorious majesty of thy kingdom, for it is an everlasting kingdom, and thy dominion endures throughout all generations. Thou rulest by thy power for ever, thine eyes behold the nations. O let not the rebellious exalt themselves, but through the greatness of thy power let thine enemies submit themselves unto thee. *1 Chronicles 29:11, 12. Psalm 145:11, 13. Psalm 66:7, 3.*

O make it to appear that the kingdom is thine, and that thou art the governor among the nations, so evident, that they may say among the heathen, The Lord reigneth; that all men may fear, and may declare the work of God, and may say, Verily he is a God that judgeth in the earth. Make all the kings of the earth to know that the heavens do rule, even that the most High ruleth in the kingdom of men, and giveth it to whomsoever he will, and to praise and extol and honour the King of heaven, all whose works are truth, and his ways judgment, and those that walk in pride he is able to abase. *Psalm 22:28. Psalm 96:10. Psalm 64:9. Psalm 58:11. Daniel 4:25, 26, 37.*

O let the kingdom of thy grace come more and more in the world, that kingdom of God which cometh not with observation, that kingdom of God which is within men. Let it be like leaven in the world, diffusing its relish till the whole be leavened, and like a grain of mustard-seed, which though it be the least of all seeds, yet when it is grown, is the greatest among herbs. *Luke 17:20, 21. Matthew 13:33, 31, 32.*

Let the kingdoms of the world become the kingdoms of the Lord and of his Christ: Take unto thyself thy great power, and reign, though the nations be angry. Set up thy throne there where Satan's seat is; let every thought be brought into obedience to thee, and let the law of thy kingdom be magnified and made honourable. *Revelation 11:15, 17, 18. Revelation 2:13. 2 Corinthians 10:5. Isaiah 42:21.*

Let that kingdom of God, which is not in word, but in power, be set up in all the churches of Christ. Send forth the rod of thy strength out of Zion, and rule by the beauty of holiness. *1 Corinthians 4:20. Psalm 110:2, 3.*

Where the strong man armed hath long kept his palace, and his goods are in peace, let Christ, who is stronger than he come upon him, and overcome him, and take from him all his armour wherein he trusted, and divide the spoil. *Luke 11:21, 22.*

O give to the Son of man dominion and glory, and a kingdom, that all people, nations, and languages may serve him, and the judgment may be given to the saints of the most High. *Daniel 7:14, 22.*

Let the kingdom of thy grace come more and more in our land, and the places where we live. There let the word of the Lord have free course and be glorified, and let not the kingdom of God be taken from us, as we have deserved it should, and given to a nation bringing forth the fruits thereof. *2 Thessalonians 3:1. Matthew 21:43.*

Let the kingdom of thy grace come into our hearts, that they may be the temples of the Holy Ghost. Let no iniquity have dominion over us: Overturn, overturn, overturn the power of corruption there, and let him come whose right our hearts are, and give them him; make us willing, more and more willing in the day of thy power. Rule in us by the power of truth, that being of the truth, we may always hear Christ's voice; and may not only call him Lord, Lord, but do the things that he saith. And let the love of Christ command us, and constrain us, and his fear be before our eyes, that we sin not. *1 Corinthians 3:16. Psalm 119:133. Ezekiel 21:27. Psalm 110:3. John 18:37. Luke 6:46. 2 Corinthians 5:14. Exodus 20:20.*

O let the kingdom of thy glory be hastened; we believe it will come, we look for the Saviour, the Lord Jesus, to come in the clouds of heaven with power and great glory; we hope that he shall appear to our joy; we love his appearing; we are looking for, and hasting to the coming of the day of God: Make us ready for it, that we may then lift up our heads with joy, knowing that our redemption draws nigh. And O that we may have such first fruits of the Spirit, as that we ourselves may groan within ourselves, waiting for the adoption, even the redemption of our body; and may have a desire to depart, and to be with Christ, which is best of all. *Philippians 3:20. Matthew 24:30. Isaiah 66:5. 2 Timothy 4:8. 2 Peter 3:12. Matthew 24:44. Luke 21:28. Romans 8:23. Philippians 1:23.*

Blessed Jesus, be with thy ministers and people (as thou hast said) always even unto the end of the world: And then (as thou hast said) surely I come quickly, even so, come, Lord Jesus, come quickly: When the mystery of God shall be finished, make haste, our beloved, and be thou like to a roe, or to a young hart upon the mountains of spices. *Matthew 28:20. Revelation 22:20. Revelation 10:7. Canticle (Song of Solomon) 8:14.*

THY WILL BE DONE ON EARTH
AS IT IS IN HEAVEN

AND as an evidence that thy kingdom comes, and in order to the sanctifying of thy name, Father in heaven, let thy holy will be done. We know, O Lord, that whatsoever thou pleasest, that thou dost in heaven, and in earth, in the seas, and in all deep places; Thy counsel shall stand, and thou wilt do all thy pleasure: Even so be it, Holy Father, not our will, but thine be done. As thou hast thought, so let it come to pass, and as thou hast purposed, let it stand. Do all according to the counsel of thine own will. Make even those to serve thy purposes, that have not known thee, and that mean not so, neither doth their heart think so. *Psalm 135:6. Isaiah 46:10. Luke 22:42. Isaiah 14:24. Ephesians 1:11. Isaiah 45:4. Isaiah 10:7.*

Father, let thy will be done concerning us and ours: Behold, here we are; It is the Lord, let him do to us as seemeth good unto him: The will of the Lord be done. O give us to submit to thy will in conformity to the example of the Lord Jesus, who said, Not as I will, but as thou wilt, and to say, The Lord gave, and the Lord hath taken away, blessed be the name of the Lord. Shall we receive good at the hand of the Lord, and shall we not receive evil also? *1 Samuel 3:12. 1 Samuel 3:18. 2 Samuel 15:26. Acts 21:14. Matthew 26:39. Job 1:21. Job 2:10.*

Father, let the scriptures be fulfilled; the scriptures of the prophets, which cannot be broken. Though heaven and earth pass away, let not one iota or tittle of thy word pass away. Do what is written in the scriptures of truth; and let it appear that for ever, O Lord, thy word is settled in heaven. *Matthew 26:56. John 10:35. Matthew 24:35. Matthew 5:18. Daniel 10:21. Psalm 119:89.*

Lord, give grace to each of us to know, and do the will of our Father which is in heaven. This is the will of God, even our sanctification. Now the God of peace sanctify us wholly. O let us be filled with the knowledge of thy will, in all wisdom and spiritual understanding, and make us perfect in every good work to do thy will. O let the time past of our life suffice us to have wrought the will of the flesh, and to have walked according to the course of this world; And from henceforth grant that it may always be our meat and drink to do the will of our Father, and to finish his work; not to do our own will, but his that sent us, that we may be of those that shall enter into the kingdom of heaven, and not those that shall be beaten with many stripes. *Matthew 12:50. 1 Thessalonians 4:3. 1 Thessalonians 5:23. Colossians 1:9. Hebrews 13:21. 1 Peter 4:3. Ephesians 2:2. John 4:34. John 6:38. Matthew 7:21. Luke 12:47.*

Lord, give grace to others also to know and do thy will; to prove what is the good and acceptable, and perfect will of God; not to be unwise, but understanding what the will of the Lord is; and then give them to stand perfect and complete in all the will of God: And let us all serve our generations according to that will. *Romans 12:2. Ephesians 5:17. Colossians 4:12. Acts 13:36.*

And when we have done the will of God, let us inherit the promises: And let that part of the will of God be done; Lord, let the word which thou hast spoken concerning thy servants be established for ever, and do as thou hast said. *Hebrews 10:36. 1 Chronicles 17:23.*

We rejoice that thy will is done in heaven, that the holy angels do thy commandments, and always hearken to the voice of thy word; that they always behold the face of our Father. And we lament it that thy will is so little done on earth, so many of the children of men being led captive by Satan at his will. O that this earth may be made more like to heaven! and saints more like to the holy angels! And that we who hope to be shortly as the angels of God in heaven, may now like them, not rest from praising him; may now like them, resist and withstand Satan, may be as a flame of fire, and fly swiftly, and may go straight forward whithersoever the spirit goes; may minister for the good of others, and thus may come into communion with the innumerable company of angels. *Psalm 103:20. Matthew 18:10. 2 Timothy 2:26. Matthew 22:30. Revelation 4:8. Daniel 10:13. Psalm 104:4. Daniel 9:21. Ezekiel 1:9, 12. Hebrews 1:14. Hebrews 12:22.*

Give Us This Day Our Daily Bread

THOU, O God, who hast appointed us to seek first the kingdom of God and the righteousness thereof, hast promised that if we do so, other things shall be added unto us: And therefore having prayed for the sanctifying of thy name, the coming of thy kingdom, and the doing of thy will, we next pray, Father in heaven, Give us this day, give us day by day our daily bread. *Matthew 6:33. Luke 11:3.*

Remove far from us vanity and lies; give us neither poverty nor riches, feed us with food convenient for us, lest we be full, and deny thee, and say, Who is the Lord? or lest we be poor and steal, and take the name of our God in vain. *Proverbs 30:8, 9.*

Lord, we ask not for dainties; for they are deceitful meat; nor do we pray that we may fare sumptuously every day, for we would not in our life-time receive our good things; but we pray for that bread which is necessary to strengthen man's heart. We desire not to eat the bread of deceit, nor to drink any stolen waters, nor would we eat the bread of idleness, but that if it be thy will we may eat the labour of our hands, that with quietness we may work, and eat our own bread; And having food and raiment, give us to be therewith content, and to say, We have all and abound. *Proverbs 23:3. Luke 16:19, 25. Psalm 104:15. Proverbs 20:17. Proverbs 9:17. Proverbs 31:27. Psalm 128:2. 2 Thessalonians 3:12. 1 Timothy 6:8. Philippians 4:18.*

Bless, Lord, our substance, and accept the work of our hands; and give us wherewithal to provide for our own, even for those of our own house; and to leave an inheritance, as far as is just, to our childrens children. Let the beauty of the Lord our God be upon us; prosper thou the work of our hands upon us, yea the work of our hands establish thou it. Bless, Lord, our land with the precious things of the earth, and the fulness thereof; but above all let us have the good-will of him that dwelt in the bush, even the blessing that was upon the head of Joseph, and upon the crown of the head of him that was separated from his brethren. *Deuteronomy 33:11. 1 Timothy 5:8. Proverbs 13:22. Psalm 90:17. Deuteronomy 33:13-16.*

But if the fig-tree should not blossom, and there should be no fruit in the vine, if the labour of the olive should fail, and the field should yield no meat, if the flock should be cut off from the fold, and there should be no herd in the stall, yet let us have grace to rejoice in the Lord, and to joy in the God of our salvation. *Habakkuk 3:17, 18.*

Father, we ask not for bread for a great while to come, but that we may have this day our daily bread; for we would learn, and the Lord teach us not to take thought for the morrow, what we shall eat, or what we shall drink, or wherewithal we shall be clothed; but we cast the care upon thee, our heavenly Father, who knowest that we have need of all these things; who feedest the fowls of the air, though they sow not, neither do they reap, and wilt much more feed us, who are of more value than many sparrows. *Matthew 6:31, 32, 26. Matthew 10:31.*

Nor do we pray for daily bread for ourselves only, but for others also. O satisfy thy poor with bread: Let all that walk righteously and speak uprightly, dwell on high: Let the place of their defence be the munitions of rocks, let bread be given to them, and let their waters be sure. *Psalm 132:15. Isaiah 33:15, 16.*

AND FORGIVE US OUR DEBTS AS WE FORGIVE OUR DEBTORS

AND, Lord, as duly as we pray every day for our daily bread, we pray for the forgiveness of our sins: For we are all guilty before God, have all sinned, and have come short of the glory of God: In many things we all offend every day; who can tell how oft he offends? If thou shouldest mark iniquities, O Lord, who shall stand? But there is forgiveness with thee that thou mayest be feared. God be merciful to us sinners! *Romans 3:19, 23. James 3:2. Psalm 19:12. Psalm 130:3, 4. Luke 18:13.*

We have wasted our Lord's goods, we have buried the talents we were intrusted with, nor have we rendered again according to the benefit done unto us, and thus we come to be in debt. The scripture has concluded us all under sin: We have done such things as are worthy of death, things for which the wrath of God comes upon the children of disobedience. Our debt is more than ten thousand talents, it is a great debt; and we have nothing to pay, so far are we from being able to say, Have patience with us, and we will pay thee all. Justly therefore might our adversary deliver us to the judge, and the judge to the officer, to be cast into prison, the prison of hell, till we should pay the last farthing. *Luke 16:1. Matthew 25:18. 2 Chronicles 32:25. Galatians 3:22. Romans 1:32. Ephesians 5:6. Matthew 18:24, 32, 25, 26. Matthew 5:25, 26.*

But blessed be God there is a way found out of agreeing with our adversary; for if any man sin, we have an advocate with the Father, even JESUS CHRIST THE RIGHTEOUS, and he is the propitiation for our sins. For his sake we pray thee blot out all our transgressions, and enter not into judgment with us. He is our surety, who restored that which he took not away, that blessed day's-man which hath laid his hand upon us both; through him let us be reconciled unto God, and let the hand-writing which was against us, which was contrary to us, be blotted out, and taken out of the way, being nailed to the cross of Christ, that we may be quickened together with Christ, having all our trespasses forgiven us. Be thou merciful to our unrighteousnesses, and our sins and our iniquities do thou remember no more. *1 John 2:1, 2. Psalm 51:1. Psalm*

143:2. *Hebrews 7:22. Psalm 69:4. Job 9:33. 2 Corinthians 5:20. Colossians 2:14, 13. Hebrews 8:12.*

And give us, we pray thee, to receive the atonement, to know that our sins are forgiven us; speak peace to us, and make us to hear joy and gladness. Let the blood of Christ thy Son cleanse us from all sin, and purge our consciences from dead works to serve the living God. *Romans 5:11. 1 John 2:12. Psalm 85:8. Psalm 51:8. 1 John 1:7. Hebrews 9:14.*

And as an evidence that thou hast forgiven our sins, we pray thee give us grace to forgive our enemies, to love them that hate us, and bless them that curse us; for we acknowledge that if we forgive not men their trespasses, neither will our Father forgive our trespasses: And therefore we forgive, Lord, we desire heartily to forgive, if we have a quarrel against any, even as Christ forgave us. Far be it from us to say that we will recompense evil, or that we should avenge ourselves. But we pray that all bitterness, and wrath, and anger, and clamour, and evil-speaking may be put away from us, with all malice; and that we may be kind one to another, and tender-hearted, forgiving one another, even as God for Christ's sake we hope hath forgiven us. O make us merciful as our Father which is in heaven is merciful, who hath promised that with the merciful he will shew himself merciful. *Matthew 5:44. Matthew 6:15. Mark 11:25. Colossians 3:13. Proverbs 20:22. Romans 12:19. Ephesians 4:31, 32. Luke 6:36. Psalm 18:25.*

AND LEAD US NOT INTO TEMPTATION, BUT DELIVER US FROM EVIL

AND, Lord, forasmuch as there is in us a bent to backslide from thee, so that when our sins are forgiven, we are ready to return again to folly, we pray that thou wilt not only forgive us our debts, but take care of us, that we may not offend any more: Lord, lead us not into any temptation. We know that no man can say when he is tempted, that he is tempted of God, for God tempteth not any man: But we know that God is able to make all grace abound towards us, and to keep us from falling, and present us faultless. We therefore pray that thou wilt never give us up to our own hearts lust, to walk in our own counsels, but restrain Satan, that roaring lion that goes about seeking whom he may devour: and grant that we may not be ignorant of his devices. O let not Satan have us to sift us as wheat, or however let not our faith fail. Let not the messengers of Satan be permitted to buffet us; but if they be, let thy grace be sufficient for us, that where we are weak there we may be strong, and may be more than conquerors through him that loved us. And the God of peace tread Satan under our feet, and do it shortly. And since we wrestle not against flesh and blood, but against principalities and powers, and the rulers of the darkness of this world, let us be strong in the Lord, and in the power of his might. *Hosea 11:7. Psalm 85:8. Job 34:32. James 1:13. 2 Corinthians 9:8. Jude 24. Psalm 81:12. 1 Peter 5:8. 2 Corinthians 2:11. Luke 22:31, 32. 2 Corinthians 12:7, 9, 10. Romans 8:37. Romans 16:20. Ephesians 6:12, 10.*

Lord, grant that we may never enter into temptation, but having prayed, may set a watch, and let thy wise and good providence so order all our affairs, and all events that are concerning us, that no temptation may take us, but such as is common to men, and that we may never be tempted above what we are able, to discern, resist, and overcome through the grace of God. Lord, do not lay any stumbling blocks before us, that we should fall upon them and perish. Let nothing be an occasion of falling to us, but give us that great peace which they have that love thy law, whom nothing shall offend. *Matthew 26:41. Nehemiah 4:9. 1 Corinthians 10:13. Jeremiah 6:21. Romans 14:13. Psalm 119:165.*

And lead us, we pray thee, into all truth; lead us in thy truth, and teach us, for thou art the God of our salvation. Shew us thy ways, O God, and teach us thy paths; the paths of righteousness; O lead us in those paths for thy name's sake, that so we may be led beside the still waters. *John 16:13. Psalm 25:5, 4. Psalm 23:3, 2.*

And deliver us, we pray thee, from the evil one; keep us that the wicked one touch us not, that he sow not his tares in the field of our hearts, that we be not ensnared by his wiles, or wounded by his fiery darts, let the word of God abide in us, that we may be strong, and may overcome the wicked one. *1 John 5:18. Matthew 13:25. Ephesians 6:11, 16. 1 John 2:14.*

Deliver us from every evil thing, we pray, that we may do no evil: O deliver us from every evil work, save us from our sins, redeem us from all iniquity, especially the sin that doth most easily beset us; Hide pride from us; Remove from us the way of lying; Let us not eat of sinners dainties; Incline our hearts to thy testimonies, and not to covetousness; And keep us that we never speak unadvisedly with our lips; but especially keep back thy servants from presumptuous sins, let not them have dominion over us. *2 Corinthians 13:7. 2 Timothy 4:18. Matthew 1:21. Titus 2:14. Hebrews 12:1. Job 33:17. Psalm 119:29. Psalm 141:4. Psalm 119:36. Psalm 106:33. Psalm 19:13.*

Preserve us, we pray thee, that no evil thing may befall us; let thy hand be with us, and keep us from evil, that it may not hurt us. O thou that savest by thy right hand them which put their trust in thee, from those that rise up against them, shew us thy marvellous loving-kindness, and keep us as the apple of thine eye, hide us under the shadow of thy wings. Keep that which we commit unto thee. Thou that hast delivered dost deliver, and we trust and pray that thou wilt yet deliver, wilt deliver us from all our fears. O make us to dwell safely, and grant that we may be quiet from the fear of evil. And bring us safe at last to that holy mountain, where there is no pricking brier, or grieving thorn; nothing to hurt or destroy. *Psalm 91:10. 1 Chronicles 4:10. Psalm 17:7, 8. 2 Timothy 1:12. 2 Corinthians 1:10. Psalm 34:4. Proverbs 1:33. Ezekiel 28:24. Isaiah 11:9.*

FOR THINE IS THE KINGDOM, THE POWER, AND THE GLORY FOR EVER, AMEN

ATHER in heaven, let thy kingdom come; for thine is the kingdom, thou art God in heaven, and rulest over all the kingdoms of the heathen: Let thy will be done, for thine is the power, and there is nothing too hard for thee: Let thy name be sanctified, for thine is the glory, and thou hast set thy glory above the heavens. *2 Chronicles 20:6. Jeremiah 32:17. Psalm 8:1.*

Father in heaven, supply our wants, pardon our sins, and preserve us from evil, for thine is the kingdom, the power, and the glory, and thou art Lord over all, who art rich to all that call upon thee; None can forgive sins but thou only; Let thy power be great in pardoning our sins; And since it is the glory of God to pardon sin, and to help the helpless, Help us, O God of our salvation, for the glory of thy name deliver us, and purge away our sins, for thy names sake. *Romans 10:12. Mark 2:7. Numbers 14:17. Proverbs 25:2. Psalm 79:9.*

We desire in all our prayers to praise thee, for thou art great, and greatly to be praised. We praise thy kingdom, for it is an everlasting kingdom, and endures throughout all generations, and the sceptre of thy kingdom is a right sceptre, thou lovest righteousness, and hatest wickedness, to thee belongeth mercy, and thou renderest to every man according to his work. We praise thy power, for thou hast a mighty arm, strong is thy hand, and high is thy right hand, and yet judgment and justice are the habitation of thy throne, mercy and truth shall go before thy face. We praise thy glory, for the glory of the Lord shall endure for ever. Glory be to the Father, to the Son, and to the Holy Ghost; as it was in the beginning, is now, and ever shall be. O let God be praised in his sanctuary, and praised in the firmament of his power, let him be praised for his mighty acts, and praised according to his excellent greatness: Let every thing that hath breath praise the Lord; Hallelujah. *Psalm 145:3, 13. Psalm 45:6, 7. Psalm 62:12. Psalm 89:13, 14. Psalm 104:31. Psalm 150:1, 2, 6.*

And forasmuch as we know that he heareth us, and whatsoever we ask, according to his will, in faith, we have the petitions that we desired of him, we will triumph in his praise. Now know we that the Lord heareth his anointed, and for his sake will hear us from his holy heaven with the saving strength of his right hand: And therefore in token, not only of our desire, but of our assurance to be heard in Christ's name, we say, Amen, amen. *1 John 5:15. Psalm 106:47. Psalm 20:6.*

Our Father which art in heaven, hallowed be thy name, &c.

9

Some forms of Prayer

Some forms of Prayer

SOME SHORT FORMS OF PRAYER FOR THE USE OF THOSE WHO MAY NOT BE ABLE TO COLLECT FOR THEMSELVES OUT OF THE FOREGOING MATERIALS

A PRAYER TO BE USED BY CHILDREN

God, thou art my God, early will I seek thee. Thou art my God and I will praise thee, my father's God and I will exalt thee.

Who is a God like unto thee, glorious in holiness, fearful in praises, doing wonders?

Whom have I in heaven but thee? and there is none upon earth that I desire besides thee. When my flesh and my heart fail, thou art the strength of my heart, and my portion for ever.

Thou madest me for thyself to shew forth thy praise.

But I am a sinner; I was shapen in iniquity, and in sin did my mother conceive me.

God be merciful to me a sinner.

O deliver me from the wrath to come, through Christ Jesus who died for me, and rose again.

Lord, give me a new nature. Let Jesus Christ be formed in my soul, that to me to live may be Christ, and to die may be gain.

Lord, I was in my baptism given up to thee; receive me graciously, and love me freely.

Lord Jesus, thou hast encouraged little children to come to thee, and hast said, that of such is the kingdom of God; I come to thee; O make me a faithful subject of thy kingdom, take me up in thy arms, put thy hands upon me, and bless me.

O give me grace to redeem me from all iniquity, and particularly from the vanity which childhood and youth is subject to.

Lord, give me a wise and an understanding heart, that I may know and do thy will in every thing, and may in nothing sin against thee.

Lord, grant that from my childhood I may know the Holy Scriptures, and may continue in the good things which I have learned.

Remove from me the way of lying, and grant me thy law graciously.

Lord, be thou a Father to me; teach me, and guide me; provide for me, and protect me; and bless me, even me, O my Father.

Bless all my relations [father, mother, brothers, sisters] and give me grace to do my duty to them in every thing.

Lord, prepare me for death, and give me wisely to consider my latter end.

O Lord, I thank thee for all thy mercies to me; for life and health, food and raiment, and for my education; for my creation, preservation, and all the blessings of this life; but above all for thine inestimable love in the redemption of the world by our Lord Jesus Christ, for the means of grace, and the hopes of glory.

Thanks be to God for his unspeakable gift; Blessed be God for JESUS CHRIST. None but Christ, none but Christ for me.

Now to God the Father, the Son, and the Holy Ghost, that great name into which I was baptized, be honour and glory, dominion and praise, for ever and ever, Amen.

Our Father which art in heaven, &c.

Another paraphrase on the Lord's prayer, in the words of the assemblies shorter Catechism

UR Father in heaven, we come to thee as children to a Father able and ready to help us.

We beseech thee, Let thy name be sanctified; enable us and others to glorify thee in all that whereby thou hast made thyself known, and dispose of all things to thine own glory.

Let thy kingdom come; Let Satan's kingdom be destroyed, and let the kingdom of thy grace be advanced; let us and others be brought into it, and kept in it, and let the kingdom of thy glory be hastened.

Let thy will be done on earth as it is done in heaven; make us by thy grace able and willing to know, obey, and submit to thy will in all things, as the angels do in heaven.

Give us this day our daily bread; of thy free gift let us receive a competent portion of the good things of this life, and let us enjoy thy blessing with them.

And forgive us our trespasses as we forgive them that trespass against us. We pray that for Christ's sake thou wouldest freely pardon all our sins, and that by thy grace thou wouldest enable us from the heart to forgive others.

And lead us not into temptation, but deliver us from evil: Either keep us (O Lord) from being tempted to sin, or support and deliver us when we are tempted.

For thine is the kingdom, the power, and the glory for ever. Lord, we take our encouragement in prayer from thyself only, and desire in our prayers to praise thee, ascribing kingdom, power, and glory to thee: And in testimony of our desires and assurance to be heard through Jesus Christ, we say Amen.

Our Father which art in heaven, &c.

ANOTHER PRAYER DRAWN OUT OF MY PLAIN CATECHISM FOR CHILDREN (WHICH WAS FIRST PUBLISHED IN THE YEAR 1703) WHICH WILL BE EASY TO THOSE CHILDREN WHO HAVE LEARNED THAT CATECHISM

Lord, thou art an infinite and eternal spirit, most wise and powerful, holy, just, and good.

Thou art the great God that madest the world, and art my Creator; and thou that madest me doest preserve and maintain me, and in thee I live and move and have my being. O that I may remember thee as my Creator in the days of my youth, and never forget thee.

Lord, give me grace to serve and honour thee, to worship and obey thee, and in all my ways to trust in thee and to please thee.

Lord, I thank thee for thy holy word, which thou hast given me to be the rule of my faith and obedience, and which is able to make me wise unto salvation.

I confess, O Lord, that the condition I was born in is sinful and miserable. I am naturally prone to that which is evil, and backward to that which is good, and foolishness is bound up in my heart; and I am by nature a child of wrath, so that if thou hadst not raised up a Saviour for me, I had been certainly lost and undone for ever. I have been disobedient to the command of God, and have eaten forbidden fruit.

But blessed and for ever blessed be God for the Saviour Jesus Christ, the eternal Son of God, and the only mediator between God and man, who took our nature upon him, and became man, that he might redeem and save us.

Lord, I bless thee for his Holy life, give me to follow his steps; I bless thee for the true and excellent doctrine which he preached, give me to mix faith with it; I bless thee for the miracles which he wrought to confirm his doctrine: And especially that he died the cursed death of the cross to satisfy for sin, and to reconcile us to God; and that he rose again from the dead on the third day, and ascended up into heaven, where he ever lives making intercession for us, and hath all power both in heaven and in earth; and that we are assured he will come again in glory to judge the world at the last day.

Lord, I thank thee that I am one of his disciples; for I am a baptized Christian; and I give glory to Father, Son, and Holy Ghost, in whose name I was baptized.

Lord, be thou in Christ to me a God, and make me one of thy people.

Be thou my chief good and highest end; let Jesus Christ be my Prince and Saviour; and let the Holy Ghost be my sanctifier, teacher, guide and comforter.

Lord, enable me to deny all ungodliness, and worldly fleshly lusts, and to live soberly, righteously, and godly in this present world, always looking for the blessed hope.

Work in me repentance towards God, and faith towards our Lord Jesus Christ; and give me to live a life of faith and repentance.

Lord, make me truly sorry that I have offended thee in what I have thought, and spoken, and done amiss, and give me grace to sin no more.

And enable me to receive Jesus Christ, and to rely upon him as my prophet, priest, and king, and to give up myself to be ruled, and taught, and saved by him.

Lord, grant unto me the pardon of my sins, the gift of the Holy Ghost, and eternal life.

And give me grace to manifest the sincerity of my faith and repentance by a diligent and conscientious obedience to all thy commandments.

Enable me to love thee with all my heart, and to love my neighbour as myself.

Give me grace always to make mention of thy name with reverence and seriousness, to read and hear thy word with diligence and attention, to meditate upon it, to believe it, and to frame my life according to it.

Lord, grant that I may receive all thy mercies with thankfulness, and bear all afflictions with patience and submission to thy holy will.

Lord, grant that my heart may never be lifted up with pride, disturbed with anger, or any sinful passion; and that my body may never be defiled with intemperance, uncleanness, or any fleshly lusts; and keep me from ever speaking any sinful words.

Lord, give me grace to reverence and obey my parents and governors; I thank thee for their instructions and reproofs: I pray thee bless them to me, and make me in every thing a comfort to them.

Lord, pity, help, and succour the poor, and those in affliction and distress.

Lord, bless my friends, forgive my enemies, and enable me to do my duty to all men.

Wherein I have in any thing offended thee, I humbly pray for pardon in the blood of Christ, and grace to do my duty better for the time to come, and so to live in the fear of God, as that I may be happy in this world, and that to come.

Lord, prepare me to die, and leave this world; O save me from that state of everlasting misery and torment, which will certainly be the portion of all the wicked and ungodly, and bring me safe to the world of everlasting rest and joy with thee and Jesus Christ.

And give me wisdom and grace to live a holy godly life, and to make it my great care and business to serve thee, and to save my own soul.

All this I humbly beg in the name and for the sake of Jesus Christ, my blessed Saviour and Redeemer, to whom with thee, O Father, and the eternal Spirit, be honour, glory, and praise henceforth, and for evermore. Amen.

Our Father which art in heaven, &c.

A MORNING PRAYER FOR A FAMILY

Lord our God, we desire with all humility and reverence to adore thee as a Being infinitely bright, and blessed, and glorious, that hast all perfection in thyself, and art the fountain of all being, power, life, motion, and perfection.

Thou art good to all, and thy tender mercies are over all thy works; and thou art continually doing us good, though we are evil and unthankful.

We reckon it an unspeakable privilege, that we have liberty of access to thee through Jesus Christ, and leave to call thee our Father in him. O look upon us now, and be merciful to us, as thou usest to do unto those that love thy name.

O give us all to account our daily worship of thee in our family the most needful part of our daily business, and the most pleasant of our daily comforts.

Thou art the God of all the families of Israel, be thou the God of our family, and grant that whatever others do, we and ours may always serve the Lord; that thou mayest cause the blessing to rest on our house from the beginning of the year to the end of it. Lord, bless us, and we are blessed indeed.

We humbly thank thee for all the mercies of this night past, and this morning, that we have laid us down and slept, and waked again, because thou hast sustained us; That no plague has come nigh our dwelling; but that we are brought in safety to the light and comforts of another day.

It is of thy mercies, O Lord, that we are not consumed, even because thy compassions fail not, they are new every morning; great is thy faithfulness.

We have rested and are refreshed, when many have been full of tossings to and fro till the dawning of the day: We have a safe and quiet habitation, when many are forced to wander and lie exposed.

We own thy goodness to us, and ourselves we acknowledge less than the least of all the mercy, and of all the truth thou hast shewed unto us.

We confess we have sinned against thee, we are guilty before thee, we have sinned and have come short of the glory of God: We have corrupt and sinful natures, and are bent to backslide from thee; backward to good and prone to evil continually.

Vain thoughts come into us, and lodge within us, lying down and rising up, and they defile or disquiet our minds, and keep out good thoughts. We are too apt to burden ourselves with that care which thou hast encouraged us to cast upon thee.

We are very much wanting in the duties of our particular relations, and provoke one another more to folly and passion than to love and to good works. We are very cold and defective in our love to God, weak in our desires towards him, and unsteady and uneven in our walking with him; and are at this time much out of frame for his service.

We pray thee forgive all our sins for Christ's sake, and be at peace with us in him who died to make peace, and ever lives making intercession.

There be many that say, Who will shew us any good? but, Lord, let not us be put off with the good of this world for a portion: for this is our heart's desire and prayer, Lord, lift up the light of thy countenance upon us, and that shall put gladness into our hearts more than they have whose corn and wine and oil increaseth.

Lord, let thy peace rule in our hearts, and give law to us, and let thy peace keep our hearts and minds, and give comfort to us; and let the consolations of God, which are neither few nor small, be our strength and our song in the house of our pilgrimage.

Lord, we commit ourselves to thy care and keeping this day: Watch over us for good; compass us about with thy favour as with a shield; preserve us from all evil, yea, the Lord preserve and keep our souls; preserve our going out and coming in.

Our bodies and all our worldly affairs we commit to the conduct of thy wise and gracious providence, and submit to its disposals. Let no hurt or harm happen to us; keep us in health and safety; bless our employments, prosper us in all our lawful undertakings, and give us comfort and success in them. Let us eat the labour of our hands, and let it be well with us.

Our precious souls and all their concerns we commit to the government of thy Spirit and grace. O let thy grace be mighty in us, and sufficient for us, and let it work in us both to will and to do that which is good, of thine own good pleasure.

O give us grace to do the work of this day in its day, according as the duty of the day requires, and to do even common actions after a godly sort; acknowledging thee in all our ways, and having our eye ever up to thee, and be thou pleased to direct our steps.

Lord, keep us from sin; give us rule over our own spirits, and grant that we may not this day break out into passion upon any provocation, or speak unadvisedly with our lips: Give us grace to live together in peace and holy love, that the Lord may command the blessing upon us, even life for evermore.

Make us conscientious in all our dealings, and always watchful against sin, as becomes those who see thine eye ever upon us: Arm us against every temptation, uphold us in our integrity, keep us in the way of our duty; and grant that we may be in thy fear every day, and all the day long.

In every doubtful case let our way be made plain before us; and give us that wisdom of the prudent, which is at all times profitable to direct; and let integrity and uprightness preserve us, for we wait on thee.

Sanctify to us all our losses, crosses, afflictions and disappointments, and give us grace to submit to thy holy will in them, and let us find it good for us to be afflicted, that we may be partakers of thy holiness.

Prepare us for all the events of this day, for we know not what a day may bring forth: Give us to stand complete in thy whole will; to deny ourselves, to take up our cross daily, and to follow Jesus Christ.

Lord, fit us for death, and judgment, and eternity, and give us grace to live every day as those that do not know but it may be our last day.

Lord, plead thy cause in the world; build up thy church into perfect beauty; set up the throne of the exalted Redeemer in all places upon the ruins of the Devil's kingdom. Let the reformed churches be more and more reformed, and let every thing that is amiss be amended; and let those that suffer for righteousness sake be supported and delivered.

Do us good in these nations; bless the queen and all in authority; guide publick counsels and affairs; over-rule all to thine own glory; let peace and truth be in our days, and be preserved to those that shall come after us.

Be gracious to all our relations, friends, neighbours, and acquaintance, and do them good according as their necessities are.

Supply the wants of all thy people. Dwell in the families that fear thee, and call upon thy name. Forgive our enemies, and those that hate us; give us a right and charitable frame of spirit towards all men, and all that is theirs.

Visit those that are in affliction, and comfort them, and be unto them a very present help. Recover the sick, ease the pained, succour the tempted, relieve the oppressed, and give joy to those that mourn in Zion.

Deal with us and our family according to the tenor of the everlasting covenant, which is well ordered in all things and sure, and which is all our salvation and all our desire; however it pleaseth God to deal with us and with our house.

Now blessed be God for all his gifts both of nature and grace, for those that concern this life, and that to come; especially for Jesus Christ the fountain and foundation of all; Thanks be to God for his unspeakable gift.

We humbly beseech thee for Christ Jesus sake to pardon our sins, accept our services, and grant an answer of peace to our prayers, even for his sake who died for us and rose again, who hath taught us to pray:

Our Father which art in heaven, &c.

An Evening Prayer for a Family

OST holy and blessed and glorious Lord God, whose we are, and whom we are bound to serve; for because thou madest us, and not we ourselves, therefore we are not our own but thine, and unto thee, O Lord, do we lift up our souls: Thy face, Lord, do we seek; whither shall we go for a happiness but to thee from whom we derive our being?

Thou art the great benefactor of the whole creation: Thou givest to all life and breath, and all things: Thou art our benefactor; the God that hast fed us, and kept us all our life long unto this day. Having obtained help of God, we continue hitherto, monuments of sparing mercy, and witnesses for thee that thou art gracious, that thou art God and not man; for therefore it is that we are not cut off.

One day tells another, and one night certifies to another, that thou art good and dost good, and never failest those that seek thee and trust in thee. Thou makest the outgoings of the morning and of the evening to praise thee.

It is through the good hand of our God upon us, that we are brought in safety to the close of another day, and that after the various employments of the day, we come together at night to mention the loving kindness of the Lord, and the praises of our God, who is good, and whose mercy endureth for ever.

Blessed be the Lord, who daily loads us with his benefits, even the God of our salvation; for he that is our God is the God of salvation. We have from thee the mercies of the day in its day, according as the necessity of the day requires, though we come far short of doing the work of the day in its day, according as the duty of the day requires.

We bless thee for the ministration of the good angels about us, the serviceableness of the inferior creatures to us, for our bodily health and ease, comfort in our relations, and a comfortable place of abode, and that thou hast not made the wilderness our habitation, and the barren land our dwelling; and especially that thou continuest to us the use of our reason, and the quiet and peace of our consciences.

We bless thee for our share in the publick tranquillity, that thou hast given us a good land, in which we dwell safely under our own vines and fig-trees.

Above all we bless thee for Jesus Christ, and his mediation between God and man, for the covenant of grace made with us in him, and all the exceeding great and precious promises and privileges of that covenant, for the throne of grace erected for us, to which we may in his name come with humble boldness, and for the hope of eternal life through him.

We confess we have sinned against thee; this day we have sinned and done foolishly: O God, thou knowest our foolishness, and our sins are not hid from thee: we misspend our time, we neglect our duty, we follow after lying vanities, and forsake our own mercies. We offend with our tongues: Are we not carnal and walk as men, below Christians? Who can understand his errors? Cleanse us from our secret faults.

We pray thee give us repentance for our sins of daily infirmity, and make us duly sensible of the evil of them, and of our danger by them, and let the blood of Christ thy Son, which cleanseth from all sin, cleanse us from them, that we may lie down to night at peace with God, and our souls may comfortably return to him, and repose in him as our rest.

And give us grace so to repent every day for the sins of every day, as that when we come to die we may have the sins but of one day to repent of, and so we may be continually easy.

Do us good by all the providences we are under, merciful or afflictive; give us grace to accommodate ourselves to them, and by all bring us nearer to thee, and make us fitter for thee.

We commit ourselves to thee this night, and desire to dwell in the secret place of the most High, and to abide under the shadow of the Almighty. Let the Lord be our habitation, and let our souls be at home in him.

Make a hedge of protection (we pray thee) about us, and about our house, and about all that we have round about, that no evil may befall us, nor any plague come nigh our dwelling. The Lord be our keeper, who neither slumbers nor sleeps; Lord, be thou a sun and a shield to us.

Refresh our bodies (we pray thee) with quiet and comfortable rest, not to be disturbed with any distrustful disquieting cares or fears; but especially let our souls be refreshed with thy love and the light of thy countenance, and thy benignity, which is better than life.

When we awake, grant that we may be still with thee, and may remember thee upon our beds, and meditate upon thee in the night-watches, and may improve the silence and solitude of our retirements for communing with God and our own hearts; that when we are alone we may not be alone, but God may be with us, and we with him.

Restore us to another day in safety, and prepare us for the duties and events of it; and by all the supports and comforts of this life, let our bodies be fitted to serve our souls in thy service, and enable us to glorify thee with both, remembering that we are not our own, we are bought with a price.

And forasmuch as we are now brought one day nearer our end, Lord, enable us so to number our days, as that we may apply our hearts unto wisdom: Let us be minded by our putting off our clothes, and going to sleep in our beds, of putting off the body, sleeping the sleep of death, and of making our bed in the darkness shortly, that we may be dying daily in expectation of and preparation for our change, that when we come to die indeed, it may be no surprise or terror to us, but we may with comfort put off the body, and resign the spirit, knowing whom we have trusted.

Lord, let our family be blessed in him, in whom all the families of the earth are blessed, blessed with all spiritual blessings in heavenly things by Christ Jesus, and with temporal blessings as far as thou seest good for us: Give us health and prosperity, but especially let our souls prosper and be in health, and let all that belong to us belong to Christ, that we who live in a house together on earth, may be together for ever with the Lord.

Look with pity upon a lost world, we beseech thee, and set up Christ's throne there where Satan's seat is; send the gospel where it is not, make it successful where it is; let it be mighty through God to the pulling down of the strong holds of sin.

Let the church of Christ greatly flourish in all places; and make it to appear that it is built upon a rock, and that the gates of hell cannot prevail against it; and suffer not the rod of the wicked any where to rest upon the lot of the righteous.

Let the land of our nativity be still the particular care of thy good providence, that in the peace thereof we may have peace. Let glory dwell in our land, and upon all the glory let there be a defence.

Rule in the hearts of our rulers: We pray thee continue the queen's life and government long a publick blessing; make all that are in places of publick trust faithful to the publick interest; and all that bear the sword a terror to evil doers, and a protection and praise to them that do well. Own thy ministers in their work, and give them skill and will to help souls to heaven.

Be gracious to all that are dear to us: Let the rising generation be such as thou wilt own, and do thee more and better service in their day than this has done.

Comfort and relieve all that are in sorrow and affliction, lay no more upon them than thou wilt enable them to bear, and enable them to bear what thou dost lay upon them.

Do for us, we pray thee, abundantly above what we are able to ask or think, for the sake of our blessed Saviour Jesus Christ, who is THE LORD OUR RIGHTEOUSNESS. To him with the Father and the eternal Spirit be glory and praise now and for ever. Amen.

Our Father which art in heaven, &c.

A FAMILY PRAYER FOR THE LORD'S DAY MORNING

OST gracious God, and our Father in our Lord Jesus Christ: It is good for us to draw near to thee; the nearer the better, and it will be best of all when we come to be nearest of all in the kingdom of glory.

Thou hast thy Being of thyself, and thy happiness in thyself; we therefore adore thee as the great JEHOVAH: We have our being from thee, and our happiness in thee, and therefore it is both our duty and our interest to seek to thee, to implore thy favour, and to give unto thee the glory due to thy name.

We bless thee for the return of the morning light, and that thou causest the day-spring to know its place and time. O let the day-spring from on high visit our dark souls, and the Sun of righteousness arise with healing under his wings.

We bless thee that the light we see is the Lord's: That this is the day which the Lord hath made, hath made for man, hath made for himself, we will rejoice and be glad in it. That thou hast revealed unto us thy holy sabbaths, and that we were betimes taught to put a difference between this day and other days, and that we live in a land, in all parts of which God is publickly and solemnly worshipped on this day.

We bless thee that sabbath liberties and opportunities are continued to us; and that we are not wishing in vain for these days of the Son of man; that our candlestick is not removed out of its place, as justly it might have been, because we have left our first love.

Now we bid this sabbath welcome: Hosanna to the Son of David, blessed is he that cometh in the name of the Lord, Hosanna in the highest. O that we may be in the Spirit on this Lord's day; That this may be the sabbath of the Lord in our dwelling; in our hearts, a sabbath of rest from sin, and a sabbath of rest in God. Enable us, we pray thee, so to sanctify this sabbath, as that it may be sanctified to us, and be a means of our sanctification: That by resting to day from our worldly employments, our hearts may be more and more taken off from present things, and prepared to leave them; and that by employing our time to day in the worship of God, we may be led into a more experimental acquaintance with the work of heaven, and be made more meet for that blessed world.

We confess we are utterly unworthy of the honour, and unable for the work of communion with thee; but we come to thee in the name of our Lord Jesus Christ, who is worthy, and depend upon the assistances of thy blessed Spirit to work all our works in us, and so to ordain peace for us.

We keep this day holy to the honour of God the Father Almighty, the Maker of heaven and earth, in remembrance of the work of creation, that work of wonder, in which thou madest all things out of nothing, by the word of thy power, and all very good; and they continue to this day according to thine ordinance, for all are thy servants. Thou art worthy to receive blessing and honour and glory and power, for thou hast created all things, and for thy pleasure they are and were created. O thou who at first didst command the light to shine out of darkness, who saidst on the first day of the first week, Let there be light, and there was light; we pray thee shine this day into our hearts, and give us more and more of the light of the knowledge of the glory of God in the face of Jesus Christ; and let us be thy workmanship created in Christ Jesus unto good works; a kind of first fruits of thy creatures.

We likewise sanctify this day to the honour of our Lord Jesus Christ, the eternal Son of God, and our exalted Redeemer, in remembrance of his resurrection from the dead on the first day of the week, by which he was declared to be the Son of God with power. We bless thee that having laid down his life to make atonement for sin, he rose again for our justification, that he might bring in an everlasting righteousness. That the stone which the builders refused, the same is become the head-stone of the corner; this is the Lord's doing, and it is marvellous in our eyes. We bless thee that he is risen from the dead as the first fruits of them that slept, that he might be the resurrection and the life to us. Now we pray that while we are celebrating the memorial of his resurrection with joy and triumph, we may experience in our souls the power and virtue of his resurrection, that we may rise with him, may rise from the death of sin, to the life of righteousness, from the dust of this world to a holy, heavenly, spiritual and divine life. O that we may be planted together in the likeness of Christ's resurrection, that as Christ was raised from the dead by the glory of the Father, so we also may walk in newness of life.

We sanctify this day also to the honour of the eternal Spirit, that blessed Spirit of grace the Comforter, rejoicing at the remembrance of the descent of the Spirit upon the apostles on the day of Pentecost, the first day of the week likewise. We bless thee that when Jesus was glorified, the Holy Ghost was given to make up the want of his bodily presence, to carry on his undertaking, and to ripen things for his second coming; and that we have a promise that he shall abide with us for ever. And now we pray that the Spirit of him that raised up Jesus from the dead, may dwell and rule in every one of us, to make us partakers of a new and divine nature. Come, O blessed Spirit of grace, and breathe upon these dry bones, these dead hearts of ours, that they may live, and be in us a spirit of faith and love and holiness, a spirit of power and of a sound mind.

O Lord, we bless thee for thy holy word, which is a light to our feet, and a lamp to our paths, and which was written for our learning, that we through patience and comfort of the scriptures might have hope: That the scriptures are preserved pure and entire to us, and that we have them in a language that we understand. We beg that we may not receive the grace of God herein in vain. We bless thee that our eyes see the joyful light, and our ears hear the joyful sound of a Redeemer and a Saviour, and of redemption and salvation by him; that life and immortality are brought to light by the gospel. Glory be to God in the highest, for in and through Jesus Christ there is on earth peace, and good-will towards men.

We bless thee for the great gospel record, That God hath given to us eternal life, and this life is in his Son. Lord, we receive it as a faithful saying, and well worthy of all acceptation; we will venture our immortal souls upon it; and we are encouraged by it to come to thee, to beg for an interest in the mediation of thy Son. O let him be made of God to us wisdom, righteousness, sanctification and redemption; let us be effectually called into fellowship with him, and by faith be united to him, so that Christ may live in us, and we may grow up into him in all things who is the head; that we may bring forth fruit in him, and whatever we do in word or deed, we may do all in his name. O let us have the Spirit of Christ, that thereby it may appear we are his. And through him we pray that we may have eternal life, that we may none of us come short of it, but may all of us have the first fruits and earnests of it abiding in us.

We bless thee for the new covenant made with us in Jesus Christ; that when the covenant of innocency was irreparably broken, so that it was become impossible for us to get to heaven by that covenant, thou wast then pleased to deal with us upon new terms, that we are under grace and not under the law; that this covenant is established upon better promises in the hand of a mediator. Lord, we fly for refuge to it, we take hold of it as the hope set before us. O receive us graciously into the bond of this covenant, and make us accepted in the beloved, according to the tenor of the covenant. Thou hast declared concerning the Lord Jesus, that he is thy beloved Son in whom thou art well pleased, and we humbly profess that he is our beloved Saviour, in whom we are well pleased: Lord, be well pleased with us in him.

O that our hearts may be filled this day with pleasing thoughts of Christ, and his love to us, that great love wherewith he loved us. O the admirable dimensions of that love, the height, and depth, and length, and breadth of the love of Christ, which passeth knowledge: Let this love constrain us to love him and live to him, who died for us and rose again. O that it may be a pleasure and mighty satisfaction to us to think, that while we are here praying at the footstool of the throne of grace, our blessed Saviour is sitting at the right hand of the throne of glory interceding for us: We earnestly beg that through him we may find favour with thee our God, and may be taken into covenant and communion with thee.

We humbly pray thee for his sake forgive all our sins, known and unknown, in thought, word, and deed: Through him let us be acquitted from guilt, and accepted as righteous in thy sight: Let us not come into condemnation, as we have deserved; let our iniquity be taken away, and our sin covered; and let us be clothed with the spotless robe of Christ's righteousness, that the shame of our nakedness may not appear. O let there be no cloud of guilt to interpose between us and our God this day, and to intercept our comfortable communion with him. And let our lusts be mortified and subdued, that our own corruptions may not be as a clog to us, to hinder the ascent of our souls heaven-wards.

We pray thee assist us in all the religious services of this thine own holy day: Go along with us to the solemn assembly; for if thy presence go not up with us, wherefore should we go up? Give us to draw nigh to thee with a true heart, with a free heart, with a fixed heart, and in full assurance of faith. Meet us with a blessing: Grace thine own ordinances with thy presence, that special presence of thine which thou hast promised there where two or three are gathered together in thy name. Help us against our manifold infirmities, and the sins that do most easily beset us in our attendance upon thee: Let thy word come with life and power to our souls, and be as good seed sown in good soil, taking root, and bringing forth fruit to thy praise: And let our prayers and praises be spiritual sacrifices, acceptable in thy sight through Christ Jesus, and let those that tarry at home divide the spoil.

Let thy presence be in all the assemblies of good Christians this day: Grace be with all them that love the Lord Jesus Christ in sincerity; let great grace be upon them all. In the chariot of the everlasting gospel let the great REDEEMER ride forth triumphantly, conquering and to conquer, and let every thought be brought into obedience to him: Let many be brought to believe the report of the gospel, and to many let the arm of the Lord be revealed: Let sinners be converted unto thee, and thy saints edified and built up in faith, holiness and comfort, unto salvation: Complete the number of thine elect, and hasten thy kingdom.

Now the Lord of peace himself give us peace always by all means. The God of hope fill us with joy and peace in believing, for Christ Jesus sake our blessed Saviour and Redeemer, who hath taught us to pray,

Our Father which art in heaven, &c.

A FAMILY PRAYER FOR THE LORD'S DAY EVENING

Eternal and for ever blessed and glorious Lord God: Thou art God over all, and rich in mercy to all that call upon thee, Most wise and powerful, holy, just, and good; the King of kings and Lord of lords; our Lord and our God.

Thou art happy without us, and hast no need of our services, neither can our goodness extend unto thee; but we are miserable without thee, we have need of thy favours, and are undone, for ever undone, if thy goodness extend not unto us; and therefore, Lord, we intreat thy favour with our whole hearts; O let thy favour be towards us in Jesus Christ, for our happiness is bound up in it, and it is to us better than life. We confess we have forfeited thy favour, we have rendered ourselves utterly unworthy of it; yet we are humbly bold to pray for it in the name of Jesus Christ, who loved us, and gave himself for us.

We bewail it before thee, that by the corruption of our natures, we are become odious to thine holiness, and utterly unfit to inherit the kingdom of God; and that by our many actual transgressions we are become obnoxious to thy justice, and liable to thy wrath and curse. Being by nature children of disobedience, we are children of wrath, and have reason both to blush and tremble in all our approaches to the holy and righteous God. Even the iniquity of our holy things would be our ruin, if God should deal with us according to the desert of them.

But with thee, O God, there is mercy and plenteous redemption: Thou hast graciously provided for all those that repent and believe the gospel, that the guilt of their sin shall be removed through the merit of Christ's death, and the power of their sins broken by his Spirit and grace; and he is both ways able to save to the uttermost all those that come unto God by him, seeing he ever lives making intercession for us.

Lord, we come to thee as a Father by Jesus Christ the mediator, and earnestly desire by repentance and faith to turn from the world and the flesh to God in Jesus Christ, as our ruler and portion. We are sorry that we have offended thee, we are ashamed to think of our treacherous and ungrateful carriage towards thee. We desire that we may have no more to do with sin, and pray as earnestly that the power of sin may be broken in us, as that the guilt of sin may be removed from us: and we rely only upon the righteousness of Jesus Christ, and upon the merit of his death, for the procuring of thy favour. O look upon us in him, and for his sake receive us graciously, heal our backslidings, and love us freely; and let not our iniquity be our ruin.

We beg, that being justified by faith, we may have peace with God through our Lord Jesus Christ, whom God hath set forth to be a propitiation for sin, that he may be just, and the justifier of them which believe in Jesus. Through him who was made sin for us, though he knew no sin, let us who know no righteousness of our own, be accepted as righteous.

And the God of peace sanctify us wholly; begin and carry on that good work in our souls; renew us in the spirit of our minds, and make us in every thing such as thou wouldest have us to be. Set up thy throne in our hearts, write thy law there, plant thy fear there, and fill us with all the graces of thy Spirit, that we may be fruitful in the fruits of righteousness, to the glory and praise of God.

Mortify our pride, and clothe us with humility; mortify our passion, and put upon us the ornament of a meek and quiet spirit, which is in the sight of God of great price. Save us from the power of a vain mind, and let thy grace be mighty in us to make us serious and sober-minded. Let the flesh be crucified in us with all its affections and lusts, and give us grace to keep under our body, and to bring it into subjection to the laws of religion and right reason, and always to possess our vessel in sanctification and honour.

Let the love of the world be rooted out of us, and that covetousness which is idolatry; and let the love of God in Christ be rooted in us. Shed abroad that love in our hearts by the Holy Ghost, and give us to love thee the Lord our God with all our heart, and soul, and mind, and might; and to do all we do in religion from a principle of love to thee.

Mortify in us all envy, hatred, malice, and uncharitableness; pluck up these roots of bitterness out of our minds, and give us grace to love one another with a pure heart fervently, as becomes the followers of the Lord Jesus, who has given us this as his new commandment. O that brotherly love may continue among us, love without dissimulation.

We pray thee rectify all our mistakes; if in any thing we be in an error discover it to us, and let the Spirit of truth lead us into all truth, the truth as it is in Jesus, the truth which is according to godliness; and give us that good understanding which they have that do thy commandments; and let our love and all good affections abound in us yet more and more, in knowledge and in all judgment.

Convince us, we pray thee, of the vanity of this world, and its utter insufficiency to make us happy, that we may never set our hearts upon it, nor raise our expectations from it; and convince us of the vileness of sin, and its certain tendency to make us miserable, that we may hate it and dread it, and every thing that looks like it, or leads to it.

Convince us, we pray thee, of the worth of our own souls, and the weight of eternity, and the awfulness of that everlasting state which we are standing upon the brink of, and make us diligent and serious in our preparation for it, labouring less for the meat that perisheth, and more for that which endures to eternal life; as those who have set their affections on things above, and not on things that are on the earth, which are trifling and transitory.

O that time and the things of time may be as nothing to us in comparison with eternity, and the things of eternity; that eternity may be much upon our heart, and ever in our eye; that we may be governed by that faith which is the substance of things hoped for, and the evidence of things not seen; looking continually at the things that are not seen that are eternal.

Give us grace, we pray thee, to look up to the other world with such a holy concern, as that we may look down upon this world with a holy contempt and indifferency, as those that must be here but a very little while, and must be somewhere for ever; that we may rejoice as though we rejoiced not, and weep as though we wept not, and buy as though we possessed not, and may use this world as not abusing it, because the fashion of this world passeth away, and we are passing away with it.

O let thy grace be mighty in us, and sufficient for us to prepare us for that great change which will come certainly and shortly, and may come very suddenly, which will remove us from a world of sense to a world of spirits; from our state of trial and probation to that of recompence and retribution; and to make us meet for the inheritance of the saints in light, that when we fail we may be received into everlasting habitations.

Prepare us, we beseech thee, for whatever we may meet with betwixt and the grave: We know not what is before us, and therefore know not what particular provision to make, but thou dost; and therefore we beg of thee to fit us by thy grace for all the services and all the sufferings which thou shalt at any time call us out to; and arm us against every temptation which we may at any time be assaulted with, that we may at all times and in all conditions glorify God, keep a good conscience, and be found in the way of our duty, and may keep up our hope and joy in Christ, and a believing prospect of eternal life, and then welcome the holy will of God.

Give us grace, we pray thee, to live a life of communion with thee both in ordinances and providences, to set thee always before us, and to have our eyes ever up unto thee; and to live a life of dependance upon thee, upon thy power, providence, and promise, trusting in thee at all times, and pouring out our hearts before thee; and to live a life of devotedness to thee, and to thine honour and glory, as our highest end: And that we may make our religion not only our business, but our pleasure, we beseech thee enable us to live a life of complacency in thee, to rejoice in thee always; that making God our heart's delight, so we may have our heart's desire; and this is our heart's desire, to know, and love, and live to God, to please him, and to be pleased in him.

We beseech thee, preserve us in our integrity to our dying day, and grant that we may never forsake thee, or turn from following after thee, but that with purpose of heart we may cleave unto the Lord; and may not count life itself dear to us, so we may but finish our course with joy and true honour.

Let thy good providence order all the circumstances of our dying, so as may best befriend our comfortable removal to a better world; and let thy grace be sufficient for us then to enable us to finish well; and let us then have an abundant entrance ministered to us into the everlasting kingdom of our Lord and Saviour Jesus Christ.

And while we are here, make us wiser and better every day than other; more weaned from the world, and more willing to leave it; more holy, heavenly, and spiritual; that the longer we live in this world, the fitter we may be for another world, and our last days may be our best days, our last works our best works, and our last comforts our sweetest comforts.

We humbly pray thee accomplish all that which thou hast promised concerning thy church in the later days: Let the earth be filled with thy glory. Let the fulness of the Gentiles be brought in, and let all Israel be saved. Let the mountain of the Lord's house be established upon the top of the mountains, and exalted above the hills, and let all nations flow unto it.

Propagate the gospel in the plantations, and let the enlargement of trade and commerce contribute to the enlargement of thy church. Let the kingdom of Christ be set up in all places upon the ruins of the Devil's kingdom.

Hasten the downfall of the man of sin, and let primitive Christianity, even pure religion and undefiled before God and the Father, be revived, and be made to flourish in all places; and let the power of godliness prevail and get ground among all that have the form of it.

Let the wars of the nations end in the peace of the church, the shakings of the nations in the establishment of the church, and the convulsions and revolutions of states and kingdoms in the settlement and advancement of the kingdom of God among men, that kingdom which cannot be moved.

Let Great Britain and Ireland flourish in all their publick interests: Let thine everlasting gospel be always the glory in the midst of us, and let thy providence be a wall of fire round about us: Destroy us not, but let a blessing be among us, even a meat offering and a drink offering to the Lord our God.

Be very gracious to our sovereign lady the queen, protect her person, preserve her health, prolong her days, guide her counsels, let her reign be prosperous, and crown all her undertakings for the publick good.

Bless the privy counsellors, the nobility, the judges, and magistrates in our several counties and corporations; and make them all in their places faithful and serviceable to the interests of the nation, and every way publick blessings.

Bless all the ministers of thy holy word and sacraments; make them burning and shining lights, and faithful to Christ, and to the souls of men. Unite all thy ministers and people together in the truth, and in true love one to another; pour out a healing spirit upon them, a spirit of love and charity, mutual forbearance and condescension, that with one shoulder and with one consent all may study to promote the common interests of our great Master, and the common salvation of precious souls.

We pray thee prosper the trade of the nation, guard our coasts, disappoint the devices of our enemies against us, preserve the publick peace, and keep all the people of these lands in quietness among themselves, and due subjection to the authority God hath set over us; and let the Lord delight to dwell among us, and to do us good.

Bless the fruits of the earth, continue our plenty, abundantly bless our provision, and satisfy even our poor with bread.

We bless thee for all the mercies of this thine own holy day; we have reason to say that a day in thy courts is better than a thousand. How amiable are thy tabernacles, O Lord of hosts! Bless the word we have heard this day to us, and to all that heard it: Hear our prayers, accept our praises, and forgive what thy pure eye hath seen amiss in us and our performances.

Take us under thy protection this night, and enable us to close the day with thee, that we may lie down, and our sleep may be sweet. Be with us the week following in all our ways; forgive us that we brought so much of the week with us into the sabbath, and enable us to bring a great deal of the sabbath with us into the week, that we may be the fitter for the next sabbath, if we shall live to it.

Make us meet for the everlasting Sabbath, which we hope to keep within the vail, when time and days shall be no more: And let this day bring us a sabbath day's journey nearer heaven, and make us a sabbath day's work fitter for it.

As we began this Lord's day with the joyful memorials of Christ's resurrection, so we desire to conclude it with the joyful expectations of Christ's second coming, and of our own resurrection then to a blessed immortality; triumphing in hope of the glory of God.

Bless the Lord, love the Lord, O our souls, and let all that is within us love and bless his holy name; for he is good, for his mercy endures for ever. In praising God we desire to spend as much as may be of our time, that we may begin our heaven now; for in this good work we hope to be spending a happy eternity.

Now unto the King eternal, immortal, invisible, the only wise God, and our God in three persons, Father, Son, and Holy Ghost, be honour and glory, dominion and praise henceforth and for ever. Amen.

Our Father which art in heaven, &c.

A PRAYER PROPER TO BE PUT UP BY PARENTS FOR THEIR CHILDREN

 Lord our God, the God of the spirits of all flesh; all souls are thine, the souls of the parents and the souls of the children are thine, and thou hast grace sufficient for both.

Thou wast our father's God, and as such we will exalt thee; thou art our childrens God, and that also we will plead with thee; for the promise is to us and our children; and thou art a God in covenant with believers, and their seed.

Lord, it is thy good providence that hath built us up into a family: We thank thee for the children thou hast graciously given thy servants; the Lord that hath blessed us with them make them blessings indeed to us, that we may never be tempted to wish we had been written childless.

We lament the iniquity which our children are conceived and born in; and that corrupt nature which they derive through our loins.

But we bless thee that there is a fountain opened for their cleansing from that original pollution, and that they were betimes by baptism dedicated to thee, and admitted into the bonds and under the blessings of thy covenant; that they are born in thy house, and taken in as members of thy family upon earth.

It is a comfort to us to think that they are baptized, and we desire humbly to plead it with thee. They are thine, save them; enable them as they become capable to make it their own act and deed, to join themselves unto the Lord, that they may be owned as thine in that day when thou makest up thy jewels.

Give them a good capacity of mind, and a good disposition, make them towardly and tractable, and willing to receive instruction; incline them betimes to religion and virtue: Lord, give them wisdom and understanding, and drive out the foolishness that is bound up in their hearts.

Save them from the vanity which childhood and youth is subject to, and fit them every way to live comfortably and usefully in this world. We ask not for great things in the world for them:

Give them, if it please thee, a strong and healthful constitution of body, preserve them from all ill accidents, and feed them with food convenient for them, according to their rank.

But the chief thing we ask of God for them is, that thou wilt pour thy spirit upon our seed, even thy blessing, that blessing, that blessing of blessings upon our off-spring, that they may be a seed to serve thee, which shall be accounted unto the Lord for a generation: Give them that good part, which shall never be taken away from them.

Give us wisdom and grace to bring them up in thy fear, in the nurture and admonition of the Lord, with meekness and tenderness, and having them in subjection with all gravity. Teach us how to teach them the things of God as they are able to bear them, and how to reprove and admonish, and when there is need to correct them in a right manner; and how to set them good examples of every thing that is virtuous and praise-worthy, that we may recommend religion to them, and so train them up in the way wherein they should go, that if they live to be old, they may not depart from it.

Keep them from the snare of evil company, and all the temptations to which they are exposed, and make them betimes sensible how much it is their interest as well as their duty to be religious: And, Lord, grant that none that come of us may come short of eternal life, or be found on the left hand of Christ in the great day.

We earnestly pray that Christ may be formed in their souls betimes, and that the seeds of grace may be sown in their hearts while they are young; and we may have the satisfaction of seeing them walking in the truth, and setting their faces heaven-wards. Give them now to hear counsel and receive instruction, that they may be wise in their latter end: and if they be wise, our hearts shall rejoice, even ours.

Prosper the means of their education; let our children be taught of the Lord, that great may be their peace; and give them so to know thee the only true God, and Jesus Christ whom thou hast sent, as may be life eternal to them.

O that they may betimes get wisdom, and get understanding, and never forget it: As far as they are taught the Truth as it is in Jesus, give them to continue in the things which they have learned.

It is our heart's desire and prayer that our children may be praising God on earth when we are gone to praise him in heaven, and that we and they may be together for ever serving him day and night in his temple.

If it should please God to remove any of them from us while they are young, let us have grace submissively to resign them to thee, and let us have hope in their death.

If thou remove us from them while they are young, be thou thyself a Father to them, to teach them and provide for them, for with thee the fatherless findeth mercy.

Thou knowest our care concerning them; we cast it upon thee; ourselves and ours we commit to thee. Let not the light of our family religion be put out with us, nor that treasure be buried in our graves, but let those that shall come after us do thee more and better service in their day than we have done in ours, and be unto thee for a name and a praise.

In these prayers we aim at thy glory: Father, let thy name be sanctified in our family, there let thy kingdom come, and let thy will be done by us and ours as it is done by the angels in heaven; for Christ Jesus sake our blessed Saviour and Redeemer, whose seed shall endure for ever, and his throne as the days of heaven. Now to the Father, Son, and Holy Ghost, that great and sacred name into which we and our children were baptized, be honour and glory, dominion and praise henceforth and for ever. Amen.

Our Father which art in heaven, &c.

A PRAYER FOR THE USE OF A PARTICULAR PERSON, BEFORE THE RECEIVING OF THE SACRAMENT OF THE LORD'S SUPPER

OST holy, and blessed, and gracious Lord God, with all humility and reverence I here present myself before thee, to seek thy face, and intreat thy favour, and as an evidence of thy good will towards me, to beg that I may experience thy good work in me.

I acknowledge myself unworthy, utterly unworthy, of the honour; unfit, utterly unfit for the service to which I am now called. It is an inestimable privilege that I am admitted so often to hear from thee in thy word, and to speak to thee in prayer, and yet as if this had been a small matter, I am now invited into communion with thee at thy holy table, there to celebrate the memorial of my Saviour's death, and to partake by faith of the precious benefits which flow from it. I who deserve not the crumbs, am called to eat of the childrens bread.

O Lord, I thank thee for the institution of this blessed ordinance, this precious legacy and token of love, which the Lord Jesus left to his church, that it is preserved to this age; that it is administered in this land, that I am admitted to it, and have now before me an opportunity to partake of it; Lord grant that I may not receive thy grace herein in vain.

O thou who hast called me to the marriage-supper of the Lamb, give me the wedding-garment; work in me a disposition of soul, and all those pious and devout affections which are suited to the solemnities of this ordinance, and requisite to qualify me for an acceptable and advantageous participation of it. Behold the fire and the wood, all things are now ready; but where is the lamb for the burnt-offering? Lord provide thyself a Lamb, by working in me all that which thou requirest of me upon this occasion. The preparation of the heart, and the answer of the tongue are both from thee; Lord, prepare my unprepared heart for communion with thee.

Lord, I confess I have sinned against thee, I have done foolishly, very foolishly, for foolishness is bound up in my heart; I have sinned and have come short of the glory of God; I have come short of glorifying thee, and deserve to come short of being glorified with thee. The imagination of my heart is evil continually, and the bias of my corrupt nature is very strong towards the world and the flesh, and the gratifications of sense, but towards God and Christ and heaven I move slowly, and with a great many stops and pauses. Nay, there is in my carnal mind, a wretched aversion to divine and spiritual things. I have mis-spent my time, trifled away my opportunities, have followed after lying vanities, and forsaken my own mercies. God be merciful to me a sinner! for how little have I done since I came into the world of the great work that I was sent into the world about.

Thou hast taken me into covenant with thee, for I am a baptized Christian, set apart for thee, and sealed to be thine; thou hast laid me, and I also have laid myself under all possible obligations to love thee, and serve thee, and live to thee. But I have started aside from thee like a deceitful bow, I have not made good my covenant with thee, nor hath the temper of my mind, and the tenor of my conversation been agreeable to that holy religion which I make profession of, to my expectations from thee, and engagements to thee. I am bent to backslide from the living God; and if I were under the law I were undone; but I am under grace, a covenant of grace which leaves room for repentance, and promiseth pardon upon repentance, which invites even backsliding children to return, and promiseth that their backslidings shall be healed. Lord, I take hold of this covenant, seal it to me at thy table. There let me find my heart truly humbled for sin, and sorrowing for it after a godly sort: O that I may there look on him whom I have pierced and mourn, and be in bitterness for him; that there I may sow in tears, and receive a broken Christ into a broken heart: And there let the blood of Christ, which speaks better things than that of Abel, be sprinkled upon my conscience, to purify and pacify that: there let me be assured that thou art reconciled to me, that mine iniquities are pardoned, and that I shall not come into condemnation. There say unto me, Be of good cheer, thy sins are forgiven thee.

And that I may not come unworthily to this blessed ordinance, I beseech thee lead me into a more intimate and experimental acquaintance with Jesus Christ, and him crucified; with Jesus Christ and him glorified; that knowing him, and the power of his resurrection, and the fellowship of his sufferings, and being by his grace planted in the likeness of both, I may both discern the Lord's body, and shew forth the Lord's death.

Lord, I desire by a true and lively faith to close with Jesus Christ, and consent to him as my Lord, and my God; I here give up myself to him as my prophet, priest and king, to be ruled and taught and saved by him; this is my beloved, and this is my friend. None but Christ, none but Christ. Lord increase this faith in me, perfect what is lacking in it; and enable me in receiving the bread and wine at thy table by a lively faith to receive Christ Jesus the Lord. O let the great gospel doctrine of Christ's dying to save sinners, which is represented in that ordinance, be meat and drink to my soul, meat indeed and drink indeed. Let it be both nourishing and refreshing to me, let it be both my strength and my song, and be the spring both of my holiness and of my comfort. And let such deep impressions be made upon my soul, by the actual commemoration of it, as may abide always upon me, and have a powerful influence upon me in my whole conversation, that the life I now live in the flesh I may live by the faith of the Son of God, who loved me, and gave himself for me.

Lord, I beseech thee fix my thoughts; let my heart be engaged to approach unto thee, that I may attend upon thee without distraction. Draw out my desires towards thee; give me to hunger and thirst after righteousness that I may be filled; and to draw near to thee with a true heart, and in full assurance of faith; and since I am not straitened in thee, O let me not be straitened in my own bosom.

Draw me, Lord, and I will run after thee. O send out thy light and thy truth, let them lead and guide me; pour thy spirit upon me, put thy Spirit within me, to work in me both to will and to do that which is good; and leave me not to myself. Awake O north wind, and come thou south, and blow upon my garden, come O blessed Spirit of grace, and enlighten my mind with the knowledge of Christ, bow my will to the will of Christ, fill my heart with the love of Christ, and confirm my resolutions to live and die with him.

Work in me (I pray thee) a principle of holy love and charity towards all men, that I may forgive my enemies, (which by thy grace I heartily do) and may keep up a spiritual communion in faith, hope and holy love, with all that in every place call on the name of Jesus Christ our Lord. Lord bless them all, and particularly that congregation with which I am to join in this solemn ordinance. Good Lord, pardon every one that engageth his heart to seek God, the Lord God of his fathers, though not cleansed according to the purification of the sanctuary. Hear my prayers, and heal the people.

Lord, meet me with a blessing, a Father's blessing at thy table; grace thine own institutions with thy presence; and fulfil in me all the good pleasure of thy goodness, and the work of faith with power, for the sake of Jesus Christ my blessed Saviour and Redeemer, to him with the Father, and the eternal Spirit, be everlasting praises. Amen.

Our Father which art in heaven, &c.

ANOTHER AFTER THE RECEIVING OF THE LORD'S SUPPER

Lord, my God and my Father in Jesus Christ, I can never sufficiently admire the condescension of thy grace to me; what is man that thou dost thus magnify him, and the son of man that thou visitest him! Who am I? and what is my house that thou hast brought me hitherto; hast brought me into thy banqueting house, and thy banner over me hath been love? I have reason to say, That a day in thy courts, an hour at thy table, is better, far better, than a thousand days, than ten thousand hours elsewhere; it is good for me to draw near to God. Blessed be God for the privileges of his house; and those comforts with which he makes his people joyful in his house of prayer.

But I have reason to blush and be ashamed of myself, that I have not been more affected with the great things which have been set before me, and offered to me at the Lord's table. O what a vain foolish trifling heart have I! when I would do good, even then evil is present with me; good Lord be merciful to me, and pardon the iniquity of my holy things, and let not my manifold defects in my attendance upon thee be laid to my charge, or hinder my profiting by the ordinance.

I have now been commemorating the death of Christ, Lord grant that by the power of that, sin may be crucified in me, the world crucified to me, and I to the world; and enable me so to bear about with me continually the dying of the Lord Jesus, as that the life also of Jesus may be manifested in my mortal body.

I have now been receiving the precious benefits which flow from Christ's death, Lord grant that I may never lose, may never forfeit those benefits, but as I have received Christ Jesus the Lord, give me grace so to walk in him, and to live as one that am not my own, but am bought with a price, glorifying God with my body and spirit which are his.

I have now been renewing my covenant with thee, and engaging myself a-fresh to thee to be thine, now Lord give me grace to perform my vow. Keep it always in the imagination of the thought of my heart, and establish my way before thee; Lord preserve me by thy grace that I may never return again to folly; after God hath spoken peace, may never by my loose and careless walking undo what I have been doing to day: But having my heart enlarged with the consolations of God, give me to run the way of thy commandments with cheerfulness and constancy, and still to hold fast my integrity.

This precious soul of mine, which is the work of thine own hands, and the purchase of thy Son's blood, I commit into thy hands, to be sanctified by thy Spirit and grace, and wrought up into a conformity to thy holy will in every thing: Lord set up thy throne in my heart, write thy law there, shed abroad thy love there, and bring every thought within me into obedience to thee, to the commanding power of thy law, and the constraining power of thy love; Keep through thine own name that which I commit unto thee, keep it against that day when it shall be called for; let me be preserved blameless to the coming of thy glory, that I may then be presented faultless with exceeding joy.

All my outward affairs I submit to the disposal of thy wise and gracious providence; Lord save my soul, and then as to other things do what thou pleasest with me; only make all providences to work together for my spiritual and eternal advantage. Let all things be pure to me, and give me to taste covenant-love in common mercies; and by thy grace let me be taught both how to want and how to abound, how to enjoy prosperity, and how to bear adversity as becomes a Christian; and at all times let thy grace be sufficient for me, and mighty in me, to work in me both to will and to do that which is good of thine own good pleasure.

And that in every thing I may do my duty, and stand complete in it, let my heart be enlarged in love to Jesus Christ, and affected with the height and depth, the length and breadth of that love of his to me, which passeth all conception and expression.

And as an evidence of that love let my mouth be filled with his praises; Worthy is the Lamb that was slain, to receive blessing and honour, and glory and power; for he was slain, and hath redeemed a chosen remnant unto God by his blood, and made them to him kings and priests. Bless the Lord, O my soul, and let all that is within me bless his holy name, who forgiveth all mine iniquities, and healeth all my diseases; who redeemeth my life from destruction, and crowneth me with loving kindness and tender mercy; who having begun a good work, will perform it unto the day of Christ. As long as I live I will bless the Lord, I will praise my God while I have any being; and when I have no being on earth, I hope to have a being in heaven to be doing it better. O let me be borne up in everlasting arms, and carried from strength to strength, till I appear before God in Zion; for Jesus sake, who died for me, and rose again, in whom I desire to be found living and dying. Now to God the Father, Son, and Spirit, be ascribed kingdom, power and glory, henceforth and for ever. Amen.

Our Father which art in heaven, &c.

AN ADDRESS TO GOD BEFORE MEAT

O Lord our God, in thee we live and move and have our being, and from thee we receive all the supports and comforts of our being: Thou spreadest our table and fillest our cup, and comfortest us with the gifts of thy bounty from day to day. We own our dependance upon thee, and our obligations to thee: Pardon our sins, we pray thee; sanctify thy good creatures to our use, and give us grace to receive them soberly and thankfully, and to eat and drink not to ourselves, but to thy glory, through Jesus Christ our blessed Lord and Saviour. Amen.

Our Father which art in heaven, &c.

ANOTHER

RACIOUS God, Thou art the protector and preserver of the whole creation, thou hast fed us all our life long unto this day with food convenient for us, though we are evil and unthankful. We pray thee forgive all our sins by which we have forfeited all thy mercies, and let us see our forfeited right restored in Christ Jesus: Give us to taste covenant-love in common mercies, and to use these and all our creature-comforts to the glory of our great benefactor, through the grace of our great REDEEMER. Amen.

Our Father which art in heaven, &c.

AN ADDRESS TO GOD AFTER MEAT

BLESSED be the Lord, who daily loads us with his benefits, and gives us all things richly to enjoy, though we serve him but poorly: O Lord, we thank thee for present refreshments in the use of thy good creatures, and for thy love to our souls in Jesus Christ, which sweetens all: We pray thee pardon our sins, go on to do us good, provide for the poor that are destitute of daily food, fit us for thy whole will, and be our God and guide, and portion for ever, through Jesus Christ our Lord and Saviour. Amen.

Our Father which art in heaven, &c.

ANOTHER

WE thank thee, Father, Lord of heaven and earth, for all the gifts both
of thy providence and of thy grace, for those
blessings which relate to the life that now is, and that
to come; for the use of thy good creatures at this
time: Perfect, O God, that which concerns us,
nourish our souls with the bread of life to
life eternal; and let us be of those that
shall eat bread in the kingdom of
our Father, for Christ Jesus
sake our Lord and
Saviour.
AMEN.

———

FINIS

PSALM 119

ALEPH.

BLESSED are the undefiled in the way,
who walk in the law of the LORD.
² Blessed are they that keep his testimonies,
and that seek him with the whole heart.
³ They also do no iniquity:
they walk in his ways.
⁴ Thou hast commanded us to keep thy precepts diligently.
⁵ O that my ways were directed to keep thy statutes!
⁶ Then shall I not be ashamed,
when I have respect unto all thy commandments.
⁷ I will praise thee with uprightness of heart,
when I shall have learned thy righteous judgments.
⁸ I will keep thy statutes:
O forsake me not utterly.

BETH.

WHEREWITHAL shall a young man cleanse his way?
by taking heed thereto according to thy word.
¹⁰ With my whole heart have I sought thee:
O let me not wander from thy commandments.
¹¹ Thy word have I hid in mine heart,
that I might not sin against thee.
¹² Blessed art thou, O LORD:
teach me thy statutes.
¹³ With my lips have I declared all the judgments of thy mouth.
¹⁴ I have rejoiced in the way of thy testimonies,
as much as in all riches.
¹⁵ I will meditate in thy precepts,
and have respect unto thy ways.
¹⁶ I will delight myself in thy statutes:
I will not forget thy word.

GIMEL.

DEAL bountifully with thy servant,
that I may live, and keep thy word.
¹⁸ Open thou mine eyes,
that I may behold wondrous things out of thy law.
¹⁹ I am a stranger in the earth:
hide not thy commandments from me.
²⁰ My soul breaketh for the longing
that it hath unto thy judgments at all times.
²¹ Thou hast rebuked the proud that are cursed,
which do err from thy commandments.
²² Remove from me reproach and contempt;
for I have kept thy testimonies.
²³ Princes also did sit and speak against me:
but thy servant did meditate in thy statutes.
²⁴ Thy testimonies also are my delight
and my counsellers.

DALETH.

MY soul cleaveth unto the dust:
quicken thou me according to thy word.
²⁶ I have declared my ways, and thou heardest me:
teach me thy statutes.
²⁷ Make me to understand the way of thy precepts:
so shall I talk of thy wondrous works.
²⁸ My soul melteth for heaviness:
strengthen thou me according unto thy word.
²⁹ Remove from me the way of lying:
and grant me thy law graciously.
³⁰ I have chosen the way of truth:
thy judgments have I laid before me.
³¹ I have stuck unto thy testimonies:
O LORD, put me not to shame.
³² I will run the way of thy commandments,
when thou shalt enlarge my heart.

HE.

T EACH me, O LORD, the way of thy statutes;
and I shall keep it unto the end.
34 Give me understanding, and I shall keep thy law;
yea, I shall observe it with my whole heart.
35 Make me to go in the path of thy commandments;
for therein do I delight.
36 Incline my heart unto thy testimonies,
and not to covetousness.
37 Turn away mine eyes from beholding vanity;
and quicken thou me in thy way.
38 Stablish thy word unto thy servant,
who is devoted to thy fear.
39 Turn away my reproach which I fear:
for thy judgments are good.
40 Behold, I have longed after thy precepts:
quicken me in thy righteousness.

VAU.

L ET thy mercies come also unto me, O LORD,
even thy salvation, according to thy word.
42 So shall I have wherewith to answer him that reproacheth me:
for I trust in thy word.
43 And take not the word of truth utterly out of my mouth;
for I have hoped in thy judgments.
44 So shall I keep thy law continually
for ever and ever.
45 And I will walk at liberty:
for I seek thy precepts.
46 I will speak of thy testimonies also before kings, and will not be
ashamed.
47 And I will delight myself in thy commandments, which I have
loved.
48 My hands also will I lift up unto thy commandments, which I
have loved;
and I will meditate in thy statutes.

ZAIN.

R EMEMBER the word unto thy servant,
upon which thou hast caused me to hope.
⁵⁰ This is my comfort in my affliction:
for thy word hath quickened me.
⁵¹ The proud have had me greatly in derision:
yet have I not declined from thy law.
⁵² I remembered thy judgments of old, O LORD;
and have comforted myself.
⁵³ Horror hath taken hold upon me because of the wicked that
forsake thy law.
⁵⁴ Thy statutes have been my songs in the house of my pilgrimage.
⁵⁵ I have remembered thy name, O LORD, in the night, and have kept
thy law.
⁵⁶ This I had,
because I kept thy precepts.

CHETH.

T HOU art my portion, O LORD:
I have said that I would keep thy words.
⁵⁸ I intreated thy favour with my whole heart:
be merciful unto me according to thy word.
⁵⁹ I thought on my ways,
and turned my feet unto thy testimonies.
⁶⁰ I made haste, and delayed not to keep thy commandments.
⁶¹ The bands of the wicked have robbed me:
but I have not forgotten thy law.
⁶² At midnight I will rise to give thanks unto thee
because of thy righteous judgments.
⁶³ I am a companion of all them that fear thee,
and of them that keep thy precepts.
⁶⁴ The earth, O LORD, is full of thy mercy:
teach me thy statutes.

TETH.

T HOU hast dealt well with thy servant, O LORD,
according unto thy word.
⁶⁶ Teach me good judgment and knowledge:
for I have believed thy commandments.
⁶⁷ Before I was afflicted I went astray:
but now have I kept thy word.
⁶⁸ Thou art good, and doest good;
teach me thy statutes.
⁶⁹ The proud have forged a lie against me:
but I will keep thy precepts with my whole heart.
⁷⁰ Their heart is as fat as grease;
but I delight in thy law.
⁷¹ It is good for me that I have been afflicted;
that I might learn thy statutes.
⁷² The law of thy mouth is better unto me
than thousands of gold and silver.

JOD.

T HY hands have made me and fashioned me:
give me understanding, that I may learn thy commandments.
⁷⁴ They that fear thee will be glad when they see me;
because I have hoped in thy word.
⁷⁵ I know, O LORD, that thy judgments are right,
and that thou in faithfulness hast afflicted me.
⁷⁶ Let, I pray thee, thy merciful kindness be for my comfort,
according to thy word unto thy servant.
⁷⁷ Let thy tender mercies come unto me, that I may live:
for thy law is my delight.
⁷⁸ Let the proud be ashamed; for they dealt perversely with me
without a cause:
but I will meditate in thy precepts.
⁷⁹ Let those that fear thee turn unto me,
and those that have known thy testimonies.
⁸⁰ Let my heart be sound in thy statutes;
that I be not ashamed.

CAPH.

M Y soul fainteth for thy salvation:
but I hope in thy word.
⁸² Mine eyes fail for thy word,
saying, When wilt thou comfort me?
⁸³ For I am become like a bottle in the smoke;
yet do I not forget thy statutes.
⁸⁴ How many are the days of thy servant?
when wilt thou execute judgment on them that persecute me?
⁸⁵ The proud have digged pits for me,
which are not after thy law.
⁸⁶ All thy commandments are faithful:
they persecute me wrongfully; help thou me.
⁸⁷ They had almost consumed me upon earth;
but I forsook not thy precepts.
⁸⁸ Quicken me after thy lovingkindness;
so shall I keep the testimony of thy mouth.

LAMED.

F OR ever, O LORD, thy word is settled in heaven.
⁹⁰ Thy faithfulness is unto all generations:
thou hast established the earth, and it abideth.
⁹¹ They continue this day according to thine ordinances:
for all are thy servants.
⁹² Unless thy law had been my delights,
I should then have perished in mine affliction.
⁹³ I will never forget thy precepts:
for with them thou hast quickened me.
⁹⁴ I am thine, save me;
for I have sought thy precepts.
⁹⁵ The wicked have waited for me to destroy me:
but I will consider thy testimonies.
⁹⁶ I have seen an end of all perfection:
but thy commandment is exceeding broad.

MEM.

O How love I thy law!
it is my meditation all the day.
98 Thou through thy commandments hast made me wiser than mine enemies:
for they are ever with me.
99 I have more understanding than all my teachers:
for thy testimonies are my meditation.
100 I understand more than the ancients,
because I keep thy precepts.
101 I have refrained my feet from every evil way,
that I might keep thy word.
102 I have not departed from thy judgments:
for thou hast taught me.
103 How sweet are thy words unto my taste!
yea, sweeter than honey to my mouth!
104 Through thy precepts I get understanding:
therefore I hate every false way.

NUN.

T HY word is a lamp unto my feet,
and a light unto my path.
106 I have sworn, and I will perform it,
that I will keep thy righteous judgments.
107 I am afflicted very much:
quicken me, O LORD, according unto thy word.
108 Accept, I beseech thee, the freewill offerings of my mouth, O LORD,
and teach me thy judgments.
109 My soul is continually in my hand:
yet do I not forget thy law.
110 The wicked have laid a snare for me:
yet I erred not from thy precepts.
111 Thy testimonies have I taken as an heritage for ever:
for they are the rejoicing of my heart.
112 I have inclined mine heart to perform thy statutes alway, even unto the end.

SAMECH.

I Hate vain thoughts:
but thy law do I love.
114 Thou art my hiding place and my shield:
I hope in thy word.
115 Depart from me, ye evildoers:
for I will keep the commandments of my God.
116 Uphold me according unto thy word, that I may live:
and let me not be ashamed of my hope.
117 Hold thou me up, and I shall be safe:
and I will have respect unto thy statutes continually.
118 Thou hast trodden down all them that err from thy statutes:
for their deceit is falsehood.
119 Thou puttest away all the wicked of the earth like dross:
therefore I love thy testimonies.
120 My flesh trembleth for fear of thee;
and I am afraid of thy judgments.

AIN.

I Have done judgment and justice:
leave me not to mine oppressors.
122 Be surety for thy servant for good:
let not the proud oppress me.
123 Mine eyes fail for thy salvation,
and for the word of thy righteousness.
124 Deal with thy servant according unto thy mercy,
and teach me thy statutes.
125 I am thy servant; give me understanding,
that I may know thy testimonies.
126 It is time for thee, LORD, to work:
for they have made void thy law.
127 Therefore I love thy commandments
above gold; yea, above fine gold.
128 Therefore I esteem all thy precepts concerning all things to be
    right;
and I hate every false way.

PE.

T HY testimonies are wonderful:
therefore doth my soul keep them.
130 The entrance of thy words giveth light;
it giveth understanding unto the simple.
131 I opened my mouth, and panted:
for I longed for thy commandments.
132 Look thou upon me, and be merciful unto me,
as thou usest to do unto those that love thy name.
133 Order my steps in thy word:
and let not any iniquity have dominion over me.
134 Deliver me from the oppression of man:
so will I keep thy precepts.
135 Make thy face to shine upon thy servant;
and teach me thy statutes.
136 Rivers of waters run down mine eyes,
because they keep not thy law.

TZADDI.

R IGHTEOUS art thou, O LORD,
and upright are thy judgments.
138 Thy testimonies that thou hast commanded are righteous
and very faithful.
139 My zeal hath consumed me,
because mine enemies have forgotten thy words.
140 Thy word is very pure:
therefore thy servant loveth it.
141 I am small and despised:
yet do not I forget thy precepts.
142 Thy righteousness is an everlasting righteousness,
and thy law is the truth.
143 Trouble and anguish have taken hold on me:
yet thy commandments are my delights.
144 The righteousness of thy testimonies is everlasting:
give me understanding, and I shall live.

KOPH.

I Cried with my whole heart;
hear me, O LORD: I will keep thy statutes.
146 I cried unto thee; save me,
and I shall keep thy testimonies.
147 I prevented the dawning of the morning, and cried:
I hoped in thy word.
148 Mine eyes prevent the night watches,
that I might meditate in thy word.
149 Hear my voice according unto thy lovingkindness:
O LORD, quicken me according to thy judgment.
150 They draw nigh that follow after mischief:
they are far from thy law.
151 Thou art near, O LORD;
and all thy commandments are truth.
152 Concerning thy testimonies, I have known of old
that thou hast founded them for ever.

RESH.

C ONSIDER mine affliction, and deliver me:
for I do not forget thy law.
154 Plead my cause, and deliver me:
quicken me according to thy word.
155 Salvation is far from the wicked:
for they seek not thy statutes.
156 Great are thy tender mercies, O LORD:
quicken me according to thy judgments.
157 Many are my persecutors and mine enemies;
yet do I not decline from thy testimonies.
158 I beheld the transgressors, and was grieved;
because they kept not thy word.
159 Consider how I love thy precepts:
quicken me, O LORD, according to thy lovingkindness.
160 Thy word is true from the beginning:
and every one of thy righteous judgments endureth for ever.

SCHIN.

P RINCES have persecuted me without a cause:
but my heart standeth in awe of thy word.
162 I rejoice at thy word,
as one that findeth great spoil.
163 I hate and abhor lying:
but thy law do I love.
164 Seven times a day do I praise thee
because of thy righteous judgments.
165 Great peace have they which love thy law:
and nothing shall offend them.
166 LORD, I have hoped for thy salvation,
and done thy commandments.
167 My soul hath kept thy testimonies;
and I love them exceedingly.
168 I have kept thy precepts and thy testimonies:
for all my ways are before thee.

TAU.

L ET my cry come near before thee, O LORD:
give me understanding according to thy word.
170 Let my supplication come before thee:
deliver me according to thy word.
171 My lips shall utter praise,
when thou hast taught me thy statutes.
172 My tongue shall speak of thy word:
for all thy commandments are righteousness.
173 Let thine hand help me;
for I have chosen thy precepts.
174 I have longed for thy salvation, O LORD;
and thy law is my delight.
175 Let my soul live, and it shall praise thee;
and let thy judgments help me.
176 I have gone astray like a lost sheep; seek thy servant;
for I do not forget thy commandments.

My
AFFECTION

TO

THE FULNESS OF THE GODHEAD

IN

JESUS CHRIST
FULL OF GRACE
Colossians 2:9

A sceptre of righteousness, is the sceptre of your kingdom.
Hebrews 1:8; Psalm 45:6 & 72:1–4, 11-14 & 9:7; Jeremiah 33:15.

Abraham rejoiced to see your day.
John 8:56; Genesis 22:18; Galatians 3:8.

All things are given into your hand, and put under your feet.
Philippians 2:9-11; Ephesians 1:10, 19-22; Matthew 11:27 & 28:18; John 3:35 & 13:3 & 17:2; Romans 14:9; 1 Corinthians 15:27; Hebrews 2:8; 1 Peter 3:22; Daniel 7:13, 14; Revelation 17:14.

Before the beginning of your ways, you are wisdom brought forth.
Proverbs 8:12, 22 & 3:19; Luke 2:52; 1 Corinthians 1:24, 30; Ephesians 1:8; Colossians 2:3.

Before the mountains were settled, before the hills, you are brought forth to be forsaken by God.
Proverbs 8:25; Luke 22:44; Psalm 22:1 & 71:11.

Before you appointed the foundations of the earth, you are my Saviour who came forth to be condemned.
Hebrews 1:10; Mark 14:64; Proverbs 8:29; Luke 24:20.

Before you had formed the earth and the world, you are my Saviour to be spit upon and mocked.
Psalm 90:2 & 69:7; Matthew 27:29; Jeremiah 20:7; Mark 14:65 & 15:19.

Before you made a decree for the rain, and a way for the lightning of the thunder, you are brought forth to be wounded for my transgressions.
Isaiah 53:5; Job 28:26; Romans 4:25; 1 Corinthians 15:3; 1 Peter 2:24.

Before you prepared the heavens, you are sent of your Father to be scourged for me.
Proverbs 8:27; John 19:1; Matthew 20:19; Mark 10:34 & 15:15.

Before your works of old, you are brought forth to be crucified for me.
Matthew 27:35; Proverbs 8:22; Luke 24:20; 1 Peter 4:1.

Behold, you are alive for evermore, Amen.
Revelation 1:18 & 4:9 & 5:14; Hebrews 7:16.

By you, all things consist.
Colossians 1:17; Hebrews 1:3.

By you and for you, the worlds are made.
Colossians 1:16, 17; John 1:3, 10; Hebrews 1:2; Ephesians 3:9.

By your faith, I have peace with God.
Galatians 2:16, 20 & 3:22; Romans 3:21-24 & 5:1; Revelation 2:13 & 14:12; 1 Timothy 1:14; 1 Corinthians 6:11; 2 Corinthians 5:19-21; Philippians 3:9; 1 Peter 3:18.

Draw me, and I will run after you.
Song of Solomon 1:4; Jeremiah 31:3; Hosea 11:4; Psalm 119:32.

For of you, and through you, and to you, are all things.
Romans 11:36; 1 Chronicles 29:12; Psalm 33:6; Proverbs 16:4; Daniel 2:20-23 & 4:3 & 4:34; Acts 17:25, 26, 28; 1 Corinthians 8:6; Ephesians 4:6-10; Colossians 1:15-17; Revelation 21:6.

From everlasting to everlasting, you are God.
Psalm 90:2, 4 & 106:48; Hebrews 13:8; Revelation 1:17.

Gird your sword upon your thigh, O most mighty, with your glory and your majesty.
Psalm 45:3; Isaiah 9:6; 2 Peter 1:16; Jude 25.

Great and marvellous are your works, Lord God almighty.
Revelation 15:3 & 16:7.

He who has you, has life.
1 John 5:12; Galatians 2:20; John 1:4; Psalm 27:1.

I am complete in you.
Colossians 2:10 & 3:11; John 1:16; Hebrews 7:25.

In you are hid all the treasures of wisdom and knowledge.
Colossians 2:3; 1 Corinthians 1:24; Ephesians 3:9.

In you dwells all the fulness of the Godhead bodily.
Colossians 2:9 & 1:19; John 10:30, 38 & 17:21; 1 Timothy 3:16.

In you, I live and move, and have my being.
Acts 17:28, 25; 1 Samuel 25:29; Job 12:10 & 27:3 & 34:14, 15; Psalm 36:9 & 66:8, 9 & 104:29; Numbers 16:22; Genesis 2:7 & 6:17.

In your name, I am forgiven.
Luke 24:46, 47; Acts 10:43 & 22:16; 1 John 2:12.

In your name, I have life.
John 20:31 & 5:24 & 10:10; Luke 24:47; Acts 10:43.

It is written of you: As the living Father has sent me, and I live by the Father; so he who eats of me, even he shall live by me.
John 6:57, 63.

It is written of you: In the beginning was the Word.
John 1:1, 2; Genesis 1:1; 1 John 1:1.

It is written of you: The Word was God.
John 1:1 & 10:30–33 & 20:28; Isaiah 9:6 & 40:9–11; Matthew 1:23; Philippians 2:6; 1 Timothy 3:16; Titus 2:13; Hebrews 1:8–13; 1 John 5:7, 20.

It is written of you: The Word was with God.
John 1:1 & 1:18 & 16:28 & 17:5; Proverbs 8:30.

I will be still, and know; you are God.
(Psalm 46:10; 1 Kings 19:12); Psalm 4:4 & 27:14 & 62:5 & 130:5; Hosea 12:6; Habakkuk 2:20; Isaiah 40:31; Zechariah 2:13; 1 Thessalonians 1:10; Mark 4:39.

Let all the angels of God worship you.
Hebrews 1:6; Luke 2:13, 14; 1 Peter 3:22; Revelation 5:11, 12.

Let every thing that has breath, praise you Lord; saying, Holy, holy, holy, is the Lord of host, the whole earth is full of his glory.
Psalm 150:6; Isaiah 6:3 with John 12:41; Revelation 4:8.

Moses wrote of you.
John 5:46 & 1:45; Numbers 21:8 & 24:17; Deuteronomy 18:18.

Purge me with hyssop, and I shall be clean.
Psalm 51:7; 1 John 1:7; Revelation 1:5; John 15:3.

Take me up in your arms, and speak your peace unto me.
Mark 10:16 & 4:39; Isaiah 40:11; John 14:27 & 20:19; Psalm 85:8.

The government is upon your shoulder.
Isaiah 9:6, 7 & 22:21; Jeremiah 23:5; Psalm 22:28.

The Lord has declared the decree: You are my Son, this day have I begotten you.
Psalm 2:7; Acts 13:33; Hebrews 1:5.

The people say, you are one of the prophets.
Matthew 16:14; John 9:17; Luke 9:18, 19; Mark 6:15.

There is no unrighteousness in you.
John 7:18; 1 John 3:3.

The scriptures testify of you.
John 5:39, 46 & 1:45; Luke 24:27, 44.

The title of your accusation is written above you; Jesus of Nazareth the King of the Jews.
John 19:19; Matthew 27:37; Mark 15:26; Luke 23:38.

The words of your mouth are a sharp sword.
Isaiah 49:2 & 11:4; Hosea 6:5; Revelation 19:15, 21; Hebrews 4:12.

Through you Lord Jesus, I have peace with God.
Romans 5:1; Colossians 1:20; Ephesians 2:13, 14; Isaiah 53:5; Ezekiel 34:25.

Unto you, I lift up mine eyes, unto you who dwells in the heavens.
Psalm 123:1 & 25:15 & 121:1 & 141:8 & 11:4 & 113:5 & 115:3; Luke 18:13; Isaiah 57:15 & 66:1; Matthew 6:9.

Unto you, O Lord, do I lift up my soul.
Psalm 25:1 & 86:4 & 143:8; 1 Samuel 1:15; Lamentations 3:41.

Upon you, the angels of God are ascending and descending.
John 1:51; Matthew 25:31; 2 Thessalonians 1:7; Genesis 28:12.

When there was no depths, or fountains abounding with water, you came forth to be betrayed for me.
Proverbs 8:24; Matthew 27:3 & 17:22; Luke 22:4.

While as yet you had not made the earth, or the fields, or the highest part of the dust of the world, you are brought forth being the lamb who is sacrificed for me.
1 Corinthians 5:7; Proverbs 8:26; Revelation 13:8.

You abide for ever.
John 8:35; Psalm 61:6, 7 & 9:7 & 29:10; 1 Timothy 1:17; Hebrews 7:17.

You alone are holy.
Revelation 15:4 & 3:7 & 6:10; 1 Samuel 2:2; Psalm 22:3 & 99:5.

You alone are worthy.
Revelation 5:9, 12 & 4:11; Psalm 18:3; Hebrews 3:3.

You are above all, and through all, and in us all.
*Ephesians 4:6 & 1:21; Genesis 14:19; 1 Chronicles 29:11, 12; Psalm 95:3;
Romans 11:36; Revelation 4:8–11; John 14:23; 2 Corinthians 6:16; 1 John
4:12–15.*

You are a buckler to all them that trust in you.
2 Samuel 22:31; Psalm 18:2, 30 & 91:4.

You are a buckler to them that walk uprightly.
Proverbs 2:7 & 30:5; Psalm 84:11.

You are a bundle of myrrh.
Song of Solomon 1:13; Psalm 45:8.

You are a consuming fire.
*Hebrews 12:29 & 10:27; Exodus 24:17; Numbers 11:1 & 16:35;
Deuteronomy 4:24 & 9:3; Psalm 50:3 & 97:3; Isaiah 66:15; Daniel 7:9; 2
Thessalonians 1:8.*

You are a glorious throne to your Father's house.
Isaiah 22:23 & 60:13; Luke 22:29; Revelation 3:21; Exodus 15:6.

You are a Nazarene.
Mark 14:67 & 16:6.

You are a polished shaft.
Isaiah 49:2 & 50:4 & 11:3; Psalm 45:5.

You are a precious stone.
1 Peter 2:4, 6; Proverbs 17:8.

You are a priest for ever.
Hebrews 5:6 & 6:20 & 7:3, 17, 21, 24.

You are a royal diadem.
Isaiah 62:3; Zechariah 9:16; 1 Peter 2:4.

You are a Son over your own house.
Hebrews 3:6; Psalm 2:6; Ephesians 1:22 & 5:23; Colossians 1:18.

You are a stone of stumbling, and a rock of offence.
1 Peter 2:8; Romans 9:33; Isaiah 8:14.

You are a tried stone.
Isaiah 28:16; Hebrews 2:10 & 4:15 & 5:8.

You are a well of living water.
Song of Solomon 4:15; Psalm 36:8, 9; John 4:14; Isaiah 12:3.

You are a witness to the people.
Isaiah 55:4; John 18:37; 1 Timothy 6:13; Revelation 1:5 & 3:14.

You are all, and in all.
Colossians 3:11; 2 John 9; John 15:5 & 6:57 & 14:23.

You are Alpha and Omega, the beginning and the ending.
Revelation 1:8, 11 & 21:6 & 22:13; Isaiah 46:9, 10; John 1:1; Colossians 1:18; Hebrews 1:10; Romans 10:4.

You are Alpha and Omega, the first and the last.
Revelation 1:11, 8, 17; Isaiah 44:6 & 41:4.

You are altogether lovely.
Song of Solomon 5:16; Psalm 45:2; John 12:3.

You are an offering and a sacrifice to God for me.
Ephesians 5:2; John 15:13; Galatians 1:4 & 2:20; 1 Peter 2:21.

You are at the right hand of God exalted.
Act 2:33 & 5:31; Philippians 2:9; Hebrews 1:3.

You are before all things.
Colossians 1:17; John 8:57 & 17:5; (Isaiah 44:6 with Revelation 1:8, 17).

You are begotten of God.
1 John 5:1 & 3:9 & 4:7 & 5:18.

You are blessed for ever.
2 Corinthians 11:31; Romans 1:25 & 9:5; John 12:13; Luke 13:35; Psalm 118:26.

You are born, king of the Jews.
Matthew 2:2; John 18:37; Isaiah 9:6; Luke 2:11.

You are both Lord and Christ.
Acts 2:36 & 4:26; Revelation 11:15.

You are carried up into heaven.
Luke 24:51; Mark 16:19; Acts 1:9; Ephesians 4:10; Hebrews 4:14.

You are chosen out of the people.
Psalm 89:19; 1 Kings 11:34.

You are Christ Jesus my Lord.
Romans 8:39; 1 Corinthians 15:31; Ephesians 3:11; 1 Timothy 1:12; 2 Timothy 1:2; 2 Corinthians 4:5; Colossians 2:6.

You are Christ Jesus.
Acts 19:4; Romans 3:24 & 8:1; 1 Corinthians 1:2, 30; Hebrews 3:1; 1 Peter 5:10, 14; 1 Timothy 1:15.

You are Christ my king.
Luke 23:2; Mark 14:61, 62 & 15:32.

You are Christ my Passover.
1 Corinthians 5:7; John 1:29, 36 & 19:14; Acts 8:32, 33; Revelation 5:12.

You are Christ the Lord.
Luke 2:11; Philippians 2:11; Colossians 2:6.

You are consecrated for evermore.
Hebrews 7:28 & 2:10 & 5:9; Luke 13:32; John 19:30.

You are crowned with a crown of pure gold.
Psalm 21:3; 2 Samuel 12:30; Exodus 39:30.

You are crowned with glory and honour.
Hebrews 2:9; Psalm 8:5; 1 Timothy 1:17; 2 Peter 1:17.

You are crowned with many crowns.
Revelation 19:12 & 6:2; Psalm 8:5 & 132:18; Isaiah 62:3.

You are crucified, king of the Jews.
John 19:14, 19 & 18:39; Matthew 27:29; Mark 15:12.

You are David my king.
Jeremiah 30:9; Ezekiel 37:24, 25; Hosea 3:5.

You are fairer than the children of men.
Psalm 45:2; Zechariah 9:17; Matthew 17:2; Hebrews 1:3; Revelation 1:13-18.

You are faithful and just.
1 John 1:9; Hebrews 10:23; Deuteronomy 7:9; Romans 3:26; Revelation 15:3.

You are faithful.
1 Thessalonians 5:24; 2 Timothy 2:13; 2 Thessalonians 3:3; 1 Corinthians 10:13; Lamentations 3:22, 23.

You are from above, but I am of the earth; you must increase, but I must decrease.
*John 3:13, 30, 31 & 8:23; 1 Corinthians 6:19, 20 & 15:47; Isaiah 9:7;
Matthew 13:31–33; Daniel 2:35; Acts 13:36; 2 Timothy 1:8; Philippians
3:7-10; Colossians 3:1-5; 2 Corinthians 12:7-10.*

Your goings forth have been from of old, from everlasting.
*Micah 5:2; Psalm 102:25 & 90:2; Colossians 1:17; Hebrews 13:8 & 1:2, 10
& 11:3; Proverbs 8:22, 25; John 1:1-3.*

You are full of grace and truth.
John 1:14 & 14:6; Luke 2:40; Acts 15:11; Romans 15:8; Malachi 2:6.

You are glorified.
Act 3:13; John 12:16 & 13:31 & 17:1-5.

You are glorious.
Isaiah 4:2 & 49:5; Exodus 15:6; Psalm 76:4; Philippians 3:21.

You are God blessed for ever.
Romans 9:5; Psalm 21:6 & 45:2.

You are God manifest in the flesh.
1 Timothy 3:16; 1 Corinthians 15:47; Philippians 2:6; John 1:14.

You are God with us.
Matthew 1:23; John 1:14; 2 Corinthians 5:19.

You are God.
*Isaiah 40:3; Matthew 1:23; John 1:1 & 5:18; Hebrews 1:8; Romans 9:5; 1
Timothy 3:16; 1 John 5:20; Jude 25; Philippians 2:6.*

You are God's own Son.
Romans 8:32 & 5:10; 1 John 4:10.

You are goodness.
Psalm 27:13 & 31:19 & 33:5 & 52:1& 144:2.

You are gracious.
1 Peter 2:3; Psalm 9:10; Exodus 22:27; Luke 4:22; Jonah 4:2.

You are greater than Jonah.
Matthew 12:41.

You are greater than Solomon.
Matthew 12:42.

You are greater than the temple.
Matthew 12:6.

You are harmless.
Hebrews 7:26; Luke 23:22, 41.

You are higher than the heavens.
Hebrews 7:26 & 1:3; Ephesians 4:10.

You are higher than the kings of the earth.
Psalm 89:27 & 72:11; Revelation 19:16 & 21:24.

You are holy.
Hebrews 7:26; Revelation 3:7 & 15:4; Luke 4:34.

You are holy, harmless, undefiled, separate from sinners, and made higher than the heavens.
Hebrews 7:26.

You are immortal.
1 Timothy 1:17; Psalm 90:2.

You are in heaven.
Matthew 26:64; Acts 2:33 & 7:55; Romans 8:34; Ephesians 1:20; Colossians 3:1; Hebrews 1:13 & 8:1 & 10:12 & 12:2; 1 Peter 3:22; Psalm 110:1; Mark 16:19; Daniel 7:13; Matthew 24:30; John 14:2, 3; 1 Timothy 6:14-16; 1 Thessalonians 4:16, 17 & 1:10; 2 Thessalonians 1:10; Revelation 1:7 & 19:11-14; Job 19:25.

You are in your glory, the glory that you had with your Father before the world was.
Luke 24:26; John 17:5, 24.

You are Israel.
Isaiah 49:3 & 44:23.

You are the Lord God of hosts.
Hosea 12:5; Psalm 80:19 & 89:8.

You are the Lord my God.
Zechariah 14:5; Matthew 16:27.

You are the Lord of hosts.
Isaiah 6:3; John 12:41.

You are the Lord, mighty in battle.
Psalm 24:8; Revelation 6:2; Colossians 2:15.

You are the Lord, strong and mighty.
Psalm 24:8 & 45:3; Luke 11:21, 22.

You are Jehovah.
(Exodus 3:14 & 6:3 with John 8:58; Hebrews 13:8; Revelation 1:8); Isaiah 12:2 & 26:4 & 40:3; John 17:5, 24.

You are Jesus Christ my Saviour.
Titus 3:6 & 1:4; Luke 2:11; John 4:42; 2 Peter 1:11.

You are Jesus Christ of Nazareth.
Acts 4:10 & 22:8; Mark 10:47; Luke 24:19.

You are Jesus Christ our Lord.
Romans 1:3 & 5:21 & 6:11, 23 & 7:25.

You are Jesus Christ the righteous.
1 John 2:1; Revelation 16:5; Hebrews 7:2.

You are Jesus Christ.
Hebrews 13:8; Matthew 1:1; John 1:17 & 17:3 and others.

You are Jesus of Galilee.
Matthew 26:69 & 21:11.

You are Jesus of Nazareth.
John 1:45 & 18:5, 7 & 19:19; Acts 22:8.

You are Jesus, the Son of God.
Hebrews 4:14; Mark 1:1; 1 Corinthians 1:9; Matthew 8:29; 1 John 5:5, 20; John 20:31.

You are Jesus, the Christ.
Matthew 16:20; 1 John 2:22; John 6:69.

You are Jesus, the son of Joseph.
John 6:42 & 1:45; Luke 4:22.

You are Joshua.
Hebrews 4:8.

You are just.
1 Peter 3:18; Zechariah 9:9; Matthew 27:19, 24; 1 John 1:9; Acts 7:52.

You are justified in the Spirit.
1 Timothy 3:16; Isaiah 50:5–7; Matthew 3:16, 17.

You are King, over all the earth.
Zechariah 14:9; Psalm 2:6–8 & 47:2–9; Daniel 7:27; Revelation 11:15.

You are light.
John 12:35, 46 & 1:5-9; 1 John 1:5; Isaiah 2:5; Ephesians 5:14; Psalm 27:1.

You are like a cluster of camphire.
Song of Solomon 1:14.

You are like a hen that gathers her young under her wings.
Matthew 23:37; Psalm 17:8 & 91:4 & 57:1.

You are like a tender plant.
Isaiah 53:2; Zechariah 6:12.

You are like a wall of fire.
Zechariah 2:5 & 9:8; Isaiah 4:5.

You are like an apple tree, among the trees of the wilderness.
Song of Solomon 2:3; Mark 8:24; 1 Chronicles 16:33; Psalm 96:12; Isaiah 7:2.

You are like fullers' soap.
Malachi 3:2; Isaiah 1:18 & 4:4; Revelation 1:5.

You are like the refiner's fire.
Malachi 3:2; Zechariah 13:9; Matthew 3:10–12; 1 Corinthians 3:13–15; Revelation 3:18.

You are Lord, both of the dead and living.
Romans 14:9; John 5:28, 29; Acts 10:42; 2 Timothy 4:1; 1 Peter 4:5.

You are Lord of all.
Acts 10:36; Romans 10:11–13; Philippians 2:9-11.

You are Lord of the Sabbath.
Mark 2:28; Matthew 12:8; Luke 6:5; John 9:14.

You are Lord over all things.
Romans 10:12 & 14:9; Revelation 17:14.

You are Lord.
John 13:13; 1 Corinthians 12:3; Philippians 2:11; Acts 2:36.

You are lowly in heart.
Matthew 11:29; Zechariah 9:9; Philippians 2:7, 8.

You are made unto me wisdom, and righteousness, and sanctification, and redemption.
1 Corinthians 1:30; Romans 4:25; 2 Corinthians 5:21; Colossians 2:3.

You are meek.
Matthew 11:29 & 21:5; 2 Corinthians 10:1.

You are mighty to save.
Isaiah 63:1; Hebrews 7:25; John 10:28-30.

You are The Lord Jesus Christ; who is, and who was, and who is to come.
Revelation 1:4, 8.

You are most blessed for ever.
Psalm 21:6 & 72:17; Romans 9:5; Luke 19:38.

You are my advocate with the Father.
1 John 2:1; Hebrews 7:25.

You are my all, and in all.
Colossians 3:11 & 2:10; Ephesians 1:23.

You are my beloved, and you are my friend.
Song of Solomon 5:16; John 15:14, 15.

You are my beloved.
*Song of Solomon 2:3, 10 & 4:16 & 5:1, 4 & 6:3 & 7:10, 11 & 8:13, 14;
Psalm 127:2; Ephesians 1:6.*

You are my blessed and only potentate.
1 Timothy 6:15; Revelation 19:16.

You are my blessed hope.
Titus 2:13 & 3:7; Colossians 1:5; Hebrews 6:18, 19.

You are my bridegroom.
John 3:29; Matthew 9:15 & 25:6; Revelation 21:9.

You are my brother.
Mark 3:35; Hebrews 2:11, 12.

You are my Christ crucified.
1 Corinthians 1:23 & 2:2; Matthew 28:5; Luke 24:20.

You are my consolation and comfort.
Luke 2:25; 1 Corinthians 2:3-5; Psalm 119:76; Isaiah 61:2.

You are my covert from the tempest.
Isaiah 32:2 & 4:6 & 25:4.

You are my diadem of beauty.
Isaiah 28:5.

You are my eternal life.
*1 John 1:2 & 2:25 & 5:11-13, 20; John 10:28 & 17:2, 3; Romans 5:21 & 6:23;
Jude 21; Psalm 27:1.*

You are my example, to do as you have done.
John 13:15; Philippians 2:5; 1 Peter 2:21; 1 John 2:6.

You are my exceeding great reward.
Genesis 15:1; Proverbs 11:18; Revelation 22:12.

You are my faithful creator.
1 Peter 4:19; Psalm 138:8 & 146:6; Isaiah 40:28.

You are my faithful high priest.
Hebrews 2:17 & 3:2 & 4:15 & 5:2; Isaiah 11:5.

You are my forerunner.
Hebrews 6:20 & 2:10; John 14:2, 3; Matthew 26:32.

You are my fortress.
Psalm 31:3 & 71:3 & 91:2.

You are my fountain of living waters.
Jeremiah 2:13 & 17:13; John 4:10 & 7:37.

You are my friend, who loves at all times.
Proverbs 17:17; Matthew 28:20; John 14:21.

You are my friend, who sticks closer than a brother.
Proverbs 18:24; Hebrews 13:5.

You are my friend.
Song of Solomon 5:16; John 15:15; Exodus 33:11; Proverbs 18:24 & 22:11;
(Isaiah 41:8; 2 Chronicles 20:7 with Galatians 3:28, 29).

You are my God and Saviour.
2 Peter 1:1; Luke 1:47; Titus 2:13; 2 Samuel 22:3; Isaiah 12:2; 1 Timothy
1:1 & 2:3; Jude 25; Titus 1:3 & 2:10 & 3:4.

You are my great high priest, who is passed into the heavens.
Hebrews 4:14 & 9:24; Romans 8:34; Acts 1:11; Mark 16:19.

You are my guide.
Psalm 48:14 & 25:9 & 31:3 & 32:8; Luke 1:79; John 16:13.

You are my healer.
Matthew 8:5-7; Jeremiah 3:22 & 30:17; Psalm 41:4; Hosea 14:4; Luke 4:18.

You are my help and my deliverer.
Psalm 70:5 & 40:17 & 144:2; 2 Samuel 22:2.

In you Jesus, is my help.
*Hosea 13:9; Psalm 10:14 & 22:19 & 28:7 & 30:10 & 33:20 & 35:2 & 38:22
& 46:1 & 63:7 & 94:17 & 119:173 & 121:1, 2 & 124:8; Isaiah 41:10, 13 &
49:8 & 50:9; Acts 26:22; Romans 8:26; Hebrews 4:16 & 13:6.*

You are my hidden manna.
Revelation 2:17.

You are my hiding place from the wind.
Isaiah 32:2.

You are my high tower.
Psalm 18:2 & 144:2.

You are my hope of glory.
Colossians 1:27; 2 Corinthians 2:14.

You are my hope, O Lord God.
*1 Timothy 1:1; Colossians 1:27; Psalm 16:9 & 22:9 & 31:24 & 33:18, 22 &
38:15 & 39:7 & 71:5, 14 & 119:43, 49, 81, 114, 166 & 147:11; Romans 15:4,
13; Hebrews 6:18; 1 Peter 1:21.*

You are my intercessor.
Hebrews 7:25 & 9:24; Romans 8:34.

You are my interpreter.
Job 33:23; Luke 24:27, 32, 45; Genesis 40:8.

**You are my King, who is without father, without mother, without
descent; having neither beginning of days nor end of life.**
Hebrews 7:2, 3.

You are my life, and I am hid with you in God.
Colossians 3:3, 4; John 14:6; Psalm 27:1.

You are my Lord and master.
John 13:13 & 11:28; Philippians 2:11.

You are my Lord and my God.
John 20:28; 1 Timothy 3:16; Isaiah 9:6; Psalm 45:6.

You are my Lord and Saviour Jesus Christ.
2 Peter 1:11 & 3:18.

You are my Lord Jesus Christ.
Galatians 1:3; James 2:1; Acts 16:31; Romans 5:1.

You are my maker.
Isaiah 54:5; Job 36:3; Psalm 95:6; Hebrews 11:10.

You are my master.
Matthew 23:8, 10; Ephesians 6:9.

You are my mediator.
1 Timothy 2:5; Hebrews 8:6 & 9:15 & 12:24.

You are my merciful and faithful high priest.
Hebrews 2:17 & 3:2 & 4:15 & 5:2; Psalm 41:4; Luke 18:13.

You are the only foundation.
1 Corinthians 3:11; Isaiah 28:16.

You are my Passover lamb, who is sacrificed for me.
Exodus 12:21; 1 Corinthians 5:7; Isaiah 53:7; Revelation 5:6, 12 & 13:8.

You are my peace.
Ephesians 2:14; Colossians 1:20; Acts 10:36; Ezekiel 34:25.

You are my peaceable habitation.
Isaiah 32:18 & 60:18; Hebrews 4:9; Jeremiah 33:16.

You are my physician.
Jeremiah 8:22; 2 Chronicles 16:12; Matthew 9:12; Mark 5:25-28.

You are the portion of my inheritance.
Psalm 16:5 & 73:26 & 119:57 & 142:5; Lamentations 3:24; Jeremiah 10:16.

You are my purifier.
Malachi 3:3; Psalm 51:7; Daniel 12:10; Ephesians 5:26; Titus 2:14; John 15:2.

You are my quiet resting place.
Isaiah 32:18; Hebrews 4:9; Matthew 11:29; Psalm 23:2.

You are my redemption.
1 Corinthians 1:30; Ephesians 1:7; Hebrews 9:12.

You are my refiner.
Malachi 3:3; Hebrews 12:6, 11; Proverbs 3:12; Isaiah 48:10; Zechariah 13:9; John 15:2.

You are my refuge and strength, a very present help in trouble.
Psalm 46:1; Deuteronomy 4:7.

You are my refuge from the avenger.
Joshua 20:3; Hebrews 6:18.

You are my refuge from the storm.
Isaiah 25:4 & 4:6 & 32:2.

You are my restingplace.
Jeremiah 50:6 & 6:16; Psalm 94:13 & 116:7; Song of Solomon 1:7; Matthew 11:28, 29; Hebrews 4:3, 9, 10; Revelation 14:13.

You are my righteousness.
1 Corinthians 1:30; 2 Corinthians 5:21; Romans 10:4; Jeremiah 51:10.

You are my rock and my fortress.
Psalm 18:2 & 31:3 & 71:3 & 144:2.

You are my salvation in the time of trouble.
Isaiah 33:2; Psalm 37:39 & 46:1 & 50:15 & 60:11; Jeremiah 14:8; 2 Corinthians 1:3, 4.

You are my salvation.
Luke 2:30; Isaiah 49:6 & 52:10; Genesis 49:18; Acts 4:12.

You are my Saviour before the world was.
John 1:2 & 17:5, 24; Matthew 25:34; 1 Peter 1:20; Revelation 13:8; Proverbs 8:22–31.

You are my Saviour who lives, and was dead; and, behold, you are alive for evermore, Amen.
Revelation 1:18 & 4:9; Romans 6:9.

You are my Saviour, and I will look to no other.
Matthew 11:2-6; Acts 4:12; John 3:36 & 14:6; 1 Corinthians 3:11; 1 Timothy 2:5; Hebrews 12:25; 1 John 5:11, 12; Revelation 20:15.

You are my Saviour.
2 Samuel 22:3; Isaiah 60:16 & 43:3; Luke 1:47; Acts 4:12.

You are my shadow from the heat.
Isaiah 25:4 & 4:6 & 32:2.

You are my shepherd.
Psalm 23:1 & 80:1; John 10:14; Isaiah 40:11; Jeremiah 23:3, 4; Ezekiel 34:11, 12, 23.

You are my shield.
Genesis 15:1; Psalm 3:3 & 5:12 & 18:35 & 84:9.

You are my spiritual drink.
1 Corinthians 10:4; John 6:56, 57, 63.

You are my spiritual meat.
1 Corinthians 10:3; John 6:57, 58, 63.

You are my strength and my redeemer.
Psalm 19:14 & 18:1, 2 & 28:7, 8 & 118:14; Philippians 4:13.

You are my strong habitation.
Psalm 71:3 & 26:8 & 31:2 & 27:5; Isaiah 33:16.

You are my strong rock.
Psalm 31:2 & 94:22 & 95:1; Matthew 16:18.

You are my strong tower.
Psalm 61:3; Proverbs 18:10; Micah 4:8; Judges 9:51.

You are my sure dwelling place.
Isaiah 32:18 & 4:5; 1 John 4:16; John 14:2, 3.

You are my sure foundation.
Isaiah 28:16; 1 Corinthians 3:11; Ephesians 2:20; 2 Timothy 2:19.

You are my wedding garment.
Matthew 22:12; Revelation 7:14 & 19:7, 8 & 21:9-11; Luke 15:22; Isaiah 61:10.

You are my wellbeloved.
Song of Solomon 1:13; Isaiah 5:1; Mark 12:6.

You are not of this world.
John 8:23 & 17:14 & 18:36.

You are ointment poured forth.
Song of Solomon 1:3; John 19:34; Romans 5:5; Titus 3:6.

You are one Lord.
Ephesians 4:5; 1 Corinthians 8:6; Deuteronomy 6:4; Zechariah 14:9.

You are our Lord Jesus Christ himself.
2 Thessalonians 2:16; Romans 1:7; 1 Thessalonians 3:11; Luke 24:15.

You are over all things.
Romans 9:5 & 10:12; Psalm 103:19; Philippians 2:10, 11; 1 Peter 3:22; Ephesians 1:20-23; Colossians 1:18.

You are made perfect.
Hebrews 5:9 & 2:10; Luke 13:32.

You are most precious.
Revelation 21:11; 1 Peter 2:6, 7.

You are pure.
1 John 3:3; Hebrews 7:26; John 7:18.

You come down like rain upon the mown grass.
Psalm 72:6; Deuteronomy 32:2; Proverbs 19:12; Hosea 6:3 & 14:5.

You are rivers of water, in a dry place.
Isaiah 32:2 & 35:6, 7 & 41:18 & 43:20.

You are sent of the Father.
John 10:36 & 5:36, 37 & 8:42.

You are separate from sinners.
Hebrews 7:26; 1 Peter 1:19 & 2:22.

You are set up from everlasting, to die for me.
1 John 3:16; Titus 2:14; 1 Thessalonians 5:10; Ephesians 5:2; 1 Corinthians 5:7.

You are Shiloh.
Genesis 49:10; 1 Samuel 3:21; Ezekiel 21:27.

You are strength to the children of God.
Joel 3:16; 1 Samuel 15:29; Psalm 29:11.

You are strength to the needy in distress.
Isaiah 25:4; Psalm 12:5 & 35:10 & 72:4, 13.

You are strength to the poor.
Isaiah 25:4 & 26:4 & 41:17; Job 5:15, 16; Psalm 35:10 & 107:41.

You are that Christ, the Son of the living God; this I believe, and I am sure.
John 6:69 & 11:27; Matthew 16:16; Mark 8:29; Luke 9:20.

You are the altar, where you offer yourself.
Revelation 8:3 & 11:1; Hebrews 7:27 & 13:10; John 10:17, 18 & 15:13; Galatians 1:4 & 2:20; Titus 2:14; Ephesians 5:2; 1 Peter 2:21.

You are the angel of the Lord.
Genesis 16:7-11 & 21:17 & 22:15 & 31:11 & 48:16; Exodus 14:19, 20.

You are the angel of the Lord's presence, who saves me.
Isaiah 63:9; Exodus 14:19.

You are the angel, who redeems me from all evil.
Genesis 48:16; Exodus 23:20-23.

You are the anointed of God.
Psalm 2:2 & 45:7; Acts 4:27; Isaiah 61:1.

You are the apostle, and high priest of my profession.
Hebrews 3:1 & 6:20; John 20:21; Romans 15:8.

You are the arm of the Lord.
Isaiah 51:9 & 53:1; Psalm 45:3; 1 Corinthians 1:24; Romans 1:4.

You are the author and finisher of my faith.
Hebrews 12:2 & 10:14; Mark 9:24; Luke 17:5; Psalm 138:8; 1 Corinthians 1:8; Philippians 1:6.

You are the author of my eternal salvation.
Hebrews 5:9 & 2:3 & 9:12; Isaiah 45:22 & 49:6; 2 Timothy 2:10.

You are the babe, lying in a manger.
Luke 2:16; 2 Corinthians 8:9.

You are the balm of Gilead.
Jeremiah 8:22 & 46:11 & 51:8; Luke 5:31, 32.

You are the beginning and the ending.
Revelation 1:8 & 21:6 & 22:13.

You are the beginning of the creation of God.
Revelation 3:14; Colossians 1:15; John 1:1-3.

You are the beginning.
Colossians 1:18; John 1:1; 1 John 1:1; Revelation 1:8 & 3:14 & 21:6 & 22:13.

You are the beloved Son of God, in whom his soul is well pleased.
Matthew 3:17 & 12:18 & 17:5; 2 Peter 1:17.

You are the branch of the Lord.
Isaiah 4:2 & 60:21; Jeremiah 23:5; Zechariah 6:12.

You are the branch, that grows out of the roots.
Isaiah 11:1; Zechariah 6:12; Jeremiah 33:15.

You are the branch that you make strong for yourself.
Psalm 80:15 & 89:21; Isaiah 49:5.

You are the bread of God.
John 6:33, 38, 58.

You are the bread of life.
John 6:35, 48–58.

You are the bread that came down from heaven.
John 6:41, 33, 51, 58.

You are the bread that comes down from heaven, that I may eat of, and not die.
John 6:50, 58 & 8:51 & 11:25, 26; Romans 8:10.

You are the bright and morning star.
Revelation 22:16 & 2:28; Numbers 24:17; 2 Peter 1:19.

You are the brightness of God's glory.
Hebrews 1:3; John 1:14 & 14:9, 10; 2 Corinthians 4:6; Matthew 17:2.

You are the captain of my salvation.
Hebrews 2:10; Isaiah 55:4; Micah 2:13.

You are the captain of the host of the Lord.
Joshua 5:13, 14; Exodus 23:20–22; Revelation 19:11–14.

You are the carpenter.
Mark 6:3; Matthew 13:55.

You are the chief corner stone.
1 Peter 2:6; Ephesians 2:20.

You are the chief shepherd.
1 Peter 5:4 & 2:25; John 10:11; Hebrews 13:20.

You are the chiefest among ten thousand.
Song of Solomon 5:10; Philippians 2:9–11; Colossians 1:18.

You are the child Jesus.
Luke 2:27, 43; Acts 4:30.

You are the child who is born.
Isaiah 9:6; Luke 1:35 & 2:11.

You are the child who knows to refuse the evil, and choose the good.
Isaiah 7:16; Luke 2:43, 46, 48, 49, 52.

You are the chosen of God.
1 Peter 2:4; Luke 23:35.

You are the Christ.
Matthew 1:16 & 2:4 & 16:16 & 23:8; 1 John 5:1.

You are the city of refuge.
Numbers 35:25; Joshua 21:13; Hebrews 6:18; Psalm 91:2.

You are the corn of wheat, that falls into the ground and dies.
John 12:24; 1 Corinthians 15:36.

You are the covenant of your people.
*Isaiah 42:6 & 49:8; Luke 1:69–72; Romans 15:8; Galatians 3:17; Hebrews
8:6 & 12:24 & 13:20.*

You are the creator of all things.
Colossians 1:16, 17; John 1:3, 10; 1 Corinthians 8:6; Hebrews 1:2, 10 &
11:3; Ephesians 3:9; Revelation 3:14.

You are the crown of glory.
Isaiah 28:5 & 45:25 & 62:3; Zechariah 6:13.

You are the day star of my heart.
2 Peter 1:19; 2 Corinthians 4:6; 1 John 5:10; Revelation 2:28 & 22:16.

You are the daysman between God and men, laying your hand
upon us both.
Job 9:33; 1 Samuel 2:25; 1 John 2:1.

You are the dayspring from on high.
Luke 1:78; Malachi 4:2; Revelation 22:16; Numbers 24:17; Psalm 85:11; 2
Peter 1:19.

You are the dear Son of the Father.
Colossians 1:13; Isaiah 42:1; Matthew 3:17 & 17:5; John 3:35 & 17:24;
Ephesians 1:6.

You are the desire of the nations.
Haggai 2:7; Genesis 3:15 & 22:18 & 49:10; Zechariah 9:10; Luke 2:10;
Romans 15:9–15; Galatians 3:8.

You are the dew and the small rain, upon the tender herb.
Hosea 14:5; Deuteronomy 32:2; Job 29:19; Psalm 72:6; Proverbs 19:12;
Isaiah 18:4 & 55:10, 11; Hebrews 6:7.

You are the door of the sheep.
John 10:7, 9; Ephesians 2:18; Hebrews 10:19–21; John 14:6; Romans 5:1.

You are the elect of God, in whom his soul delights.
Isaiah 42:1; Psalm 18:19 & 22:8; Proverbs 8:30.

You are the elect stone.
1 Peter 2:6; Psalm 89:19; Isaiah 42:1.

You are the end of the law for righteousness to me.
Romans 10:4 & 3:25–31 & 8:3; Isaiah 53:11; Matthew 5:17; Acts 13:39;
Hebrews 10:14.

You are the ensign for your people.
Isaiah 11:10, 12 & 59:19; Genesis 49:10; John 3:14 & 12:32.

You are the everlasting God.
Isaiah 40:28 & 57:15; Genesis 21:33; Deuteronomy 33:27; Jeremiah 10:10;
Romans 16:26.

You are the everlasting light.
Isaiah 60:19, 20; Revelation 21:23; Psalm 27:1.

You are the express image of God's person.
Hebrews 1:3; 2 Corinthians 4:4; Colossians 1:15; John 14:9.

You are the faithful and true witness.
Revelation 1:5 & 3:14 & 3:7 & 19:11; Jeremiah 42:5; Psalm 89:37; John 18:37; 1 Timothy 6:13; 1 John 5:7–10.

You are the first and the last.
Revelation 1:11, 17 & 2:8 & 22:13.

You are the first begotten of the dead.
Revelation 1:5, 18; Colossians 1:18; Acts 26:23; 1 Corinthians 15:20–23.

You are the firstbegotten.
Hebrews 1:5, 6; Revelation 1:5; Proverbs 8:24, 25; John 1:14.

You are the firstborn among many brethren.
Romans 8:29; Psalm 89:27; Matthew 12:50 & 25:40; John 20:17; Hebrews 2:11–15.

You are the firstborn of every creature.
Colossians 1:15; Revelation 3:14.

You are the firstborn.
Psalm 89:27 & 2:7; Colossians 1:18; Romans 8:29; Hebrews 12:23.

You are the firstborn son of the virgin Mary.
Luke 2:7; Isaiah 7:14; Matthew 1:25.

You are the firstfruits, of them that sleep.
1 Corinthians 15:20, 23; Acts 26:23; Romans 8:11; 1 Peter 1:3.

You are the fountain opened.
Zechariah 13:1; Psalm 51:2, 7; Isaiah 1:16–18; Ezekiel 36:25; John 1:29 & 19:34; 1 Corinthians 6:11; Ephesians 5:25–27; Titus 3:5; 1 John 1:7; Revelation 1:5 & 7:14.

You are the friend of publicans and sinners.
Luke 7:34, 37-39 & 15:2 & 19:7; Matthew 9:11.

You are the gift of God.
John 4:10 & 3:16; Isaiah 9:6 & 42:6 & 49:6; Romans 8:32; 2 Corinthians 9:15; 1 Corinthians 1:30; Acts 8:20.

You are the glory in the midst of us.
Zechariah 2:5; Luke 2:46; Matthew 18:20; John 20:26; Revelation 7:17.

You are the glory of the Lord.
Isaiah 40:5 & 6:3 & 35:2 & 60:1; Psalm 72:19 & 102:16; Habakkuk 2:14;
John 1:14 & 12:41; 2 Corinthians 4:6; Hebrews 1:3.

You are the glory of your people.
Luke 2:32; Psalm 85:9; Isaiah 4:2 & 45:25; Zechariah 2:5.

You are the God of Abraham, the God of Isaac, and the God of Jacob.
Exodus 3:6; Jeremiah 31:33; Matthew 22:32; Acts 7:31, 32.

You are the God of the whole earth.
Isaiah 54:5; Zechariah 14:9; Romans 3:29; Revelation 11:15; Psalm 47:7.

You are the golden altar, that is before the throne.
Revelation 8:3 & 9:13; Exodus 40:26.

You are the good master.
Matthew 19:16; Mark 10:17; John 13:13, 14.

You are the good shepherd, who calls me by name and leads me.
John 10:11, 14 & 16:13; Psalm 31:3 & 25:5 & 43:3 & 139:24 & 143:10;
Nehemiah 9:12; Isaiah 49:10; Luke 1:79; 1 Peter 5:4; Revelation 7:17.

You are the governor, who rules God's people.
Matthew 2:6; Isaiah 9:6, 7; Colossians 1:18; Revelation 2:27 & 11:15.

You are the great God and my Saviour.
Titus 2:13 & 3:4; 1 Timothy 1:1 & 2:3 & 4:10.

You are the great high priest.
Hebrews 4:14 & 8:1 & 9:11.

You are the great King.
Matthew 5:35; Psalm 48:2 & 47:7, 8; Malachi 1:14.

You are the great light.
Isaiah 9:2 & 60:1–3, 19; Micah 7:8; Matthew 4:16; Ephesians 5:14; 1 Peter 2:9; John 8:12.

You are the great prophet.
Deuteronomy 18:18; Luke 7:16; John 6:14.

You are the great shepherd of the sheep.
Hebrews 13:20; Ezekiel 34:23 & 37:24; John 10:11, 14; 1 Peter 5:4.

You are the head of all principality and power.
Colossians 2:10 & 1:16–18; Ephesians 1:20–23 & 4:15; Philippians 2:9–11;
1 Peter 3:22; Revelation 5:9–13.

You are the head of every man.
1 Corinthians 11:3; Ephesians 1:22 & 4:15; Philippians 2:10, 11; Colossians 2:10, 18, 19.

You are the head of the body, the church.
Colossians 1:18; Ephesians 1:22 & 4:15, 16 & 3:21; Acts 20:28.

You are the head of the corner.
Matthew 21:42; Psalm 118:22; Mark 12:10; Acts 4:11; Ephesians 2:20; 1 Peter 2:4–8.

You are the head, in and over all things.
Ephesians 1:22 & 4:15; Hebrews 2:7; Colossians 1:18; Numbers 1:50; 1 Chronicles 26:26; Psalm 8:6; Daniel 11:43.

You are the head stone of the corner.
Psalm 118:22; Acts 4:11; Matthew 21:42; 1 Peter 2:7.

You are the heir of all things.
Hebrews 1:2; Matthew 21:38; John 3:35 & 13:3 & 16:15; Romans 8:17; Philippians 2:9–11.

You are the heir of the world.
Romans 4:13; Genesis 12:3 & 17:4, 5, 16 & 22:17, 18 & 28:14; Psalm 2:8 & 72:11.

You are the heritage of your people.
Isaiah 58:14; Psalm 105:9–11 & 135:12 & 136:21 & 16:5, 6; Colossians 1:12; 1 Peter 1:4; Ephesians 1:10, 11.

You are the high priest, after the order of Melchisedec.
Hebrews 2:17 & 3:1 & 4:14, 15 & 5:5, 10 & 6:20 & 7:26 & 8:1 & 9:11 & 10:21.

You are the high priest who offers himself.
Hebrews 2:17 & 3:1 & 4:14, 15 & 5:6, 10 & 7:17, 20, 21, 24, 26 & 8:1 & 9:11 & 10:21.

You are the Highest.
Luke 1:76, 35 & 6:35 & 19:38; Psalm 87:5 & 18:13; Acts 16:17; Matthew 21:9.

You are the holy child, who is anointed.
Acts 4:27, 30; Luke 1:35; Isaiah 61:1.

You are the holy thing who is born.
Luke 1:31, 32, 35; Isaiah 9:6.

You are the hope of your people.
Joel 3:16; Isaiah 4:6 & 25:4; Acts 28:20; 1 Timothy 1:1; Romans 15:13; Colossians 1:27; 2 Thessalonians 2:16; 1 Peter 1:3, 21.

You are the horn of my salvation.
Psalm 18:2 & 132:17; Luke 1:69; Ezekiel 29:21.

You are the image of God.
2 Corinthians 4:4, 6; Hebrews 1:3; John 14:9 & 15:24.

You are the image of the invisible God.
Colossians 1:15; Hebrews 11:27; 1 Timothy 1:17 & 6:16.

You are the judge of all the earth.
Genesis 18:25; John 5:22, 23; 2 Corinthians 5:10; Psalm 58:11 & 94:2 & 98:9.

You are the judge of Israel.
Micah 5:1; 1 Samuel 8:5, 6; Isaiah 33:22.

You are the judge of the quick and the dead.
Acts 10:42; 2 Timothy 4:1; Romans 14:9; 1 Peter 4:5; Revelation 20:11–15.

You are the king and only wise God.
1 Timothy 1:17; Jude 25; Romans 16:27; Ephesians 3:10; Colossians 2:3.

You are the king eternal, immortal, invisible, the only wise God, be honour and glory for ever and ever, Amen.
1 Timothy 1:17 & 6:15, 16; Psalm 10:16 & 47:6–8 & 145:13; Hebrews 1:8–13; Revelation 19:16; Matthew 6:13.

You are the king in his beauty.
Isaiah 33:17; 2 Chronicles 32:23; Psalm 45:2 & 27:4 & 90:17; Song of Solomon 5:10; Zechariah 9:17; Matthew 17:2; John 17:24; 2 Samuel 14:25; Hosea 14:6.

You are the king of glory.
Psalm 24:7-10 & 97:6 & 145:11; Luke 19:38; 1 Timothy 1:17.

You are the King of kings.
1 Timothy 6:15; Revelation 17:14 & 19:16.

You are the king of the daughters of Sion.
John 12:15; Isaiah 62:11; Micah 4:8; Zechariah 2:9–11.

You are the king of Israel.
John 1:49 & 12:13-15; Zephaniah 3:15; Matthew 27:42; Isaiah 44:6.

You are the king, the Lord of hosts.
Isaiah 6:5 & 44:6; Psalm 24:10 & 84:3; Jeremiah 46:18 & 48:15 & 51:57; Zechariah 14:16; Malachi 1:14.

You are the king, who comes in the name of the Lord.
Luke 19:38 & 13:35; Psalm 72:17–19 & 118:26; Matthew 21:9.

You are the lamb in the midst of the throne.
Revelation 7:17 & 5:6; Numbers 16:44-48; Psalm 46:5 & 47:8; John 19:18.

You are the lamb of God, who takes away the sin of the world.
*John 1:29, 36; Genesis 22:7, 8; Isaiah 53:7, 11; Acts 8:32; 1 Peter 1:19;
Revelation 1:5 & 5:12; 1 Corinthians 15:3; 2 Corinthians 5:21; Galatians
3:13; 1 John 2:2 & 3:5; Leviticus 16:21, 22.*

You are the lamb who is slain, from the foundation of the world.
Revelation 5:6, 12 & 13:8 & 17:8; Ephesians 1:4; Titus 1:2; 1 Peter 1:19, 20.

You are the lamb, who overcomes all things.
*Revelation 17:14; John 16:33 & 12:31; Psalm 68:18; Romans 8:37;
Galatians 1:4.*

You are the lamb without blemish, and without spot.
*1 Peter 1:19; Exodus 12:5; 1 Peter 2:22, 23; Song of Solomon 4:7; Hebrews
9:14.*

**You are the lamb, foreordained before the foundation of the
world.**
*1 Peter 1:20; Psalm 132:17; Acts 10:42 & 17:31; 1 Corinthians 2:7; John
17:24.*

You are the lamb, who is the light of the city.
*Revelation 21:23; Isaiah 60:1–3, 19, 20; Ezekiel 43:2 with Revelation 18:1;
Luke 17:24; 2 Thessalonians 2:8.*

You are the lamb, who is the temple of the city.
Revelation 21:22; John 2:19-21 & 4:23.

You are the last Adam, made a quickening spirit.
*1 Corinthians 15:45; Romans 5:12–19; 1 John 5:11; John 1:4 & 4:10, 14 &
5:21, 25, 26 & 6:33, 39, 40, 54, 57, 63 & 10:10, 28 & 11:25, 26 & 17:2;
Philippians 3:21; Revelation 21:6.*

You are the lawgiver.
*Isaiah 33:22; James 4:12; 2 Corinthians 5:10; Genesis 49:10; Numbers
21:18; Psalm 60:7.*

You are the leader and commander to your people.
*Isaiah 55:4 & 49:8–10; Micah 5:2–4; Matthew 2:6 & 28:20; John 10:3, 27 &
15:10-12, 17; 2 Thessalonians 1:8; Hebrews 5:9.*

You are the life.
John 14:6, 19 & 1:4 & 6:33, 51, 57 & 8:51 & 11:25 & 17:2; 1 John 1:2;
Colossians 3:4; 1 John 5:11.

You are the light of men.
John 1:4 & 8:12 & 12:35; Isaiah 42:6; Luke 1:79; Ephesians 5:14.

You are the light of the morning, when the sun rises, a morning without clouds.
2 Samuel 23:4; Psalm 89:36; Isaiah 60:1 & 18–20; Malachi 4:2; Hosea 6:3.

You are the light of the world.
John 8:12 & 12:46 & 1:4–9 & 3:19 & 9:5; Acts 26:23.

You are the light to lighten the Gentiles.
Luke 2:32; Isaiah 9:2 & 42:6 & 60:1-3.

You are the lily of the valleys.
Song of Solomon 2:1 & 6:3; Psalm 85:11.

You are the lion of the tribe of Judah.
Revelation 5:5; Genesis 49:9, 10; Hebrews 7:14.

You are the living bread.
John 6:51-57 & 3:13; Exodus 16:4.

You are the living stone.
1 Peter 2:4; John 5:26 & 6:57 & 11:25 & 14:19; Romans 5:10.

You are the Lord Christ, whom I serve.
Colossians 3:24; Romans 14:18; 1 Corinthians 7:22; Galatians 1:10;
Ephesians 6:6.

You are the Lord from heaven.
1 Corinthians 15:47; John 3:12, 13, 31 & 6:33; Ephesians 4:10.

You are the Lord God omnipotent.
Revelation 19:6 & 11:15–18; Psalm 47:2, 7 & 97:1; Matthew 6:13.

You are the Lord Jehovah.
Isaiah 12:2 & 26:4; Psalm 83:18; John 8:58.

You are the Lord Jesus Christ my Saviour.
Titus 1:4 & Luke 2:11; John 4:42; 2 Peter 1:11 & 2:20 & 3:18.

You are the Lord Jesus.
Romans 10:9; Acts 7:59; Colossians 3:17.

You are the Lord, my holy one.
Isaiah 43:3, 15 & 41:14 & 45:11; Habakkuk 1:12.

You are the Lord my redeemer.
Isaiah 43:14 & 44:6 & 54:5; Psalm 19:14; Revelation 5:9.

You are the Lord of glory.
1 Corinthians 2:8; Psalm 24:7–10; Acts 7:2; James 2:1.

You are the Lord of hosts.
Isaiah 44:6 & 54:5; Jeremiah 50:34.

You are the Lord of lords.
1 Timothy 6:15; Revelation 17:14 & 19:16.

You are the Lord of peace, who gives me peace.
2 Thessalonians 3:16; Psalm 72:7; Isaiah 9:6, 7; John 14:27; Romans 15:33;
Numbers 6:26.

You are the Lord of the harvest.
Matthew 9:38 & 10:1; Acts 13:2; 2 Thessalonians 3:1; John 20:21.

You are the Lord's Christ.
Luke 2:26; John 20:31; Acts 2:36; Psalm 2:2.

You are the Lord's Son.
Psalm 2:7; Matthew 3:17; Acts 8:37.

You are the man approved of God.
Acts 2:22; Matthew 11:2–6; John 3:2 & 5:36 & 6:14, 27 & 7:31 & 12:17 &
14:11; Hebrews 2:4.

You are the man of God's right hand.
Psalm 80:15, 17 & 89:21 & 110:1; John 5:21–23.

You are the man, who is the Lord's fellow.
Zechariah 13:7; Matthew 11:27; John 5:17 & 10:30, 38 & 14:1 & 16:15;
Philippians 2:6.

You are the man whom God ordains.
Acts 17:31; 1 Corinthians 2:7; Matthew 28:18.

You are the mediator of a new and better covenant.
Hebrews 8:6-13 & 12:24; Jeremiah 31:31-33.

You are the mediator of the new and better testament.
Hebrews 9:15 & 7:22; 2 Corinthians 3:6; Matthew 26:28.

You are the mercy seat for my sins.
Romans 3:25; 1 John 2:2 & 4:10; Numbers 7:89.

You are the messenger of God.
Isaiah 42:19; Job 33:23; Malachi 2:7.

You are the messenger of the covenant.
Malachi 3:1; John 13:20 & 20:21.

You are the messiah.
Daniel 9:25, 26; John 1:41 & 4:25.

You are the minister of the circumcision.
Romans 15:8; Matthew 15:24 & 20:28; Acts 3:25, 26 & 13:46; Galatians 4:4, 5.

You are the minister of the sanctuary, and of the true tabernacle.
Hebrews 8:2 & 9:8–12, 23, 24 & 10:21.

You are the morning star.
Revelation 2:28 & 22:16; 2 Peter 1:19.

You are the nail fastened in a sure place.
Ezra 9:8; Isaiah 22:23; Zechariah 10:4; Ecclesiastes 12:11.

You are my one husband, whom I am espoused to.
2 Corinthians 11:2; Isaiah 54:5; Hosea 2:19, 20.

You are the one mediator between God and men.
1 Timothy 2:5; Job 9:33; John 14:16; 1 Samuel 2:25; Hebrews 7:25 & 8:6 & 9:15 & 12:24; 1 Corinthians 8:6.

You are the one shepherd, of the one fold.
John 10:2, 11, 16, 27 & 6:37; Ezekiel 37:22 & 34:23; Ephesians 2:14; Ecclesiastes 12:11; Hebrews 13:20.

You are the one shepherd, who leads me beside the still waters, and feeds me all my life long.
Ezekiel 34:23; Psalm 23:2 & 46:4; Revelation 21:6 & 7:17; Isaiah 49:9, 10; Genesis 48:15; Psalm 37:3; Ecclesiastes 2:24.

You are the one Son wellbeloved of God.
Mark 12:6 & 1:11; Matthew 17:5; John 3:35.

You are the only begotten of the Father.
John 1:14, 18; 1 John 4:9; Hebrews 1:5.

You are the only begotten Son, who is in the bosom of the Father.
John 1:18 & 3:16; Proverbs 8:30.

You are the only wise God our Saviour.
Jude 25; Psalm 104:24 & 147:5; Romans 11:33 & 16:27; Ephesians 3:10; 1 Timothy 1:17 & 2:3; Isaiah 45:21; Titus 1:3 & 2:10, 13 & 3:4; 2 Peter 1:1.

You are the path of righteousness.
Psalm 23:3 & 5:8 & 143:8–10; Proverbs 8:20; Isaiah 42:16; John 10:2-4.

You are the pearl of great price.
Matthew 13:46; Proverbs 2:4; Isaiah 33:6; Ephesians 3:8; Colossians 2:3; 1 John 5:11, 12; Revelation 21:21.

You are the plant of renown.
Ezekiel 34:29; Isaiah 4:2 & 11:1 & 53:2; Jeremiah 23:5 & 33:15; Zechariah 3:8 & 6:12; Psalm 72:17.

You are the precious corner stone.
Isaiah 28:5, 16; 1 Corinthians 3:11; Ephesians 2:20; 1 Peter 2:6, 7.

You are the preserver of men.
Job 7:20; Nehemiah 9:6; Psalm 36:6; Philippians 4:7; 2 Thessalonians 3:3; Jude 24; John 10:29.

You are the prince among us.
Ezekiel 34:24; Isaiah 9:6; Micah 5:2; Acts 3:15 & 5:31.

You are the prince and Saviour, whom God exalts with his right hand, to give repentance and forgiveness of sins.
Acts 5:31; Psalm 89:19, 24; Ephesians 1:20–23; Philippians 2:9–11; 1 Peter 3:22; Acts 11:18; Ezekiel 36:25–37; Luke 24:47; Romans 11:27; Acts 3:19 & 13:38; Mark 2:10; Ephesians 1:7; Colossians 1:14.

You are the prophet mighty in deed and word.
Luke 24:19 & 7:16; John 3:2 & 6:14 & 7:40; Acts 2:22 & 10:38 & 7:22.

You are the prophet of Nazareth of Galilee.
Matthew 21:11 & 2:23; Deuteronomy 18:15–19; Luke 7:16; John 7:40 & 1:45 & 6:14; Acts 3:22, 23.

You are the resurrection and the life.
John 11:25 & 5:21, 26 & 6:39, 40, 44 & 1:4 & 14:6, 19; Romans 5:17–19 & 8:2; 1 Corinthians 15:20–26, 45-47; 2 Corinthians 4:14; Psalm 36:9; Isaiah 38:16; Colossians 3:3, 4; 1 John 1:1; Revelation 22:1, 17.

You are the righteous branch.
Jeremiah 23:5; Psalm 80:15; Isaiah 4:2; Ezekiel 17:2–10, 22-24.

You are the righteous judge.
2 Timothy 4:8; Genesis 18:25; Romans 2:5; 2 Thessalonians 1:5, 6; Revelation 19:11.

You are the righteous man.
Luke 23:41, 47; Matthew 27:4, 19, 24; 1 Peter 1:19.

You are the righteous servant of the Lord.
Isaiah 53:11 & 42:1 & 49:3; 1 John 2:1; (see, you are without sin).

You are the rock of ages.
Isaiah 26:4 & 17:10; Deuteronomy 32:4, 15; 1 Samuel 2:2; Psalm 18:2 & 135:13.

You are the rock of my refuge.
Psalm 94:22 & 62:2 & 18:2; Isaiah 33:16.

You are the rock of my salvation.
2 Samuel 22:47; Psalm 89:26 & 18:46 & 62:2, 6, 7 & 95:1; Isaiah 50:7–9.

You are the rock of my strength.
Psalm 62:7 & 18:2 & 94:22 & 95:1; Philippians 4:13; Isaiah 26:4 & 17:10.

You are the rock, that is higher than I.
Psalm 61:2 & 18:46 & 27:5 & 40:2 & 62:2; Isaiah 32:2.

You are the rock, that your church is built upon.
Matthew 16:18; Isaiah 28:16; 1 Corinthians 3:10, 11; Ephesians 2:19–22; Revelation 21:14; Zechariah 6:12, 13; Hebrews 3:3, 4.

You are the rod out of the stem of Jesse.
Isaiah 11:1; Psalm 110:2.

You are the root of Jesse.
Isaiah 11:10; Romans 15:12; Revelation 22:16.

You are the root out of the dry ground.
Isaiah 53:2; Luke 9:58; Philippians 2:7; Ezekiel 17:22–24.

You are the rose of Sharon.
Song of Solomon 2:1; Isaiah 35:1, 2 & 4:2; Hosea 14:6.

You are the ruler of your people.
Micah 5:2; Genesis 49:10; 1 Chronicles 5:2; Isaiah 9:6, 7; Ezekiel 37:22–25.

You are the sacrifice to God, for a sweetsmelling savour.
Ephesians 5:2; Romans 8:3; 1 Corinthians 5:7; Hebrews 10:12; Genesis 8:21; Leviticus 1:9, 13, 17 & 3:16; 2 Corinthians 2:15.

You are the salvation of God, for all to see.
Luke 3:6 & 2:10, 30-32; Psalm 98:2, 3; Isaiah 40:5 & 49:6 & 52:10; Mark 16:15; Romans 10:12, 18.

You are the salvation of the daughters of Zion.
Isaiah 62:11 & 40:9; Zechariah 9:9; Matthew 21:5; John 12:15.

You are the same yesterday, and to day, and for ever.
Hebrews 13:8 & 1:12; Psalm 90:2 & 102:27 & 103:17; Isaiah 41:4 & 44:6; Malachi 3:6; John 8:56–58; James 1:17; Revelation 1:4, 8, 11, 17, 18.

You are the same, and your years shall not fail.
Hebrews 1:12 & 7:24; Psalm 102:27 & 90:4 & 110:4; James 1:17; Job 36:26; Romans 6:9.

You are the sanctuary.
Isaiah 8:14 & 26:20; Psalm 46:1, 2; Proverbs 18:10; Ezekiel 11:16.

You are the Saviour of all men.
1 Timothy 4:10 & 2:4, 6; Psalm 36:6 & 107:2, 6; Isaiah 45:21, 22; John 1:29 & 3:15–17 & 5:24; 1 John 2:2 & 4:14.

You are the Saviour of the body.
Ephesians 5:23; Acts 20:28; 1 Thessalonians 1:10; Revelation 5:9; Colossians 2:19.

You are the Saviour, who is Christ the Lord.
Luke 2:11; Philippians 2:11 & 3:8; Colossians 2:6; John 6:69 & 7:25, 26 & 20:31.

You are the sceptre rising out of Israel.
Numbers 24:17; Genesis 49:10; Psalm 45:6 & 110:2; Isaiah 9:7; Luke 1:32, 33; Hebrews 1:8.

You are the second man, the Lord from heaven.
1 Corinthians 15:45, 47; John 3:13, 31 & 6:33; Matthew 1:23; Acts 10:36; Ephesians 4:9, 10; 1 Timothy 3:16.

You are the seed of Abraham.
Galatians 3:16, 19, 27-29; Genesis 12:7 & 22:17 & 13:15 & 17:7.

You are the seed of David.
Romans 1:3; Matthew 1:1 & 9:27 & 12:23 & 15:22; John 7:42; Acts 2:30 & 13:22, 23; 2 Timothy 2:8.

You are the servant of Israel.
Isaiah 49:3 & 42:1 & 52:13 & 53:11.

You are the servant of rulers.
Isaiah 49:7; Matthew 20:28; Luke 22:27; Philippians 2:4, 5; Hebrews 5:8.

You are the servant of the Lord.
Isaiah 42:1 & 43:10 & 52:13; Philippians 2:7; Matthew 12:18–20.

You are the shade upon my right hand.
Psalm 121:5 & 109:31 & 16:8; Isaiah 4:6 & 25:4 & 32:2.

You are the shadow of a great rock, in a weary land.
Isaiah 32:2; Psalm 31:2 & 63:1.

You are the shepherd and bishop of my soul.
1 Peter 2:25 & 5:4; Psalm 23:1–3 & 80:1; Song of Solomon 1:7, 8; Ezekiel 34:11–16; John 10:11–16; Hebrews 13:20.

You are the shepherd of the Lord.
Zechariah 13:7; Jeremiah 31:10; Hebrews 13:20.

You are the showers that water the earth.
Psalm 72:6; Deuteronomy 32:2; Proverbs 16:15 & 19:12; Ezekiel 34:25, 26; Hosea 6:3 & 14:5.

You are the Son from heaven.
1 Thessalonians 1:10; Acts 1:11; 1 Corinthians 1:7; Philippians 3:20; 2 Thessalonians 1:7; Revelation 1:7.

You are the son of a carpenter.
Matthew 13:55; Isaiah 53:2; Mark 6:3; 1 Peter 2:4.

You are the son of Abraham.
Matthew 1:1.

You are the son of David.
Matthew 1:1 & 12:23 & 9:27; Luke 1:32; Revelation 22:16.

You are the Son of God most high.
Luke 8:28.

You are the Son of God, who walks in the midst of the fire with us.
Daniel 3:25; Isaiah 43:2; Matthew 28:20; Zechariah 13:9; Malachi 3:2, 3; Luke 21:12–18; 1 Corinthians 3:13–15; Hebrews 11:33–38; 1 Peter 4:12, 13.

You are the son of Mary.
Mark 6:3; Matthew 1:16 & 13:55; Acts 1:14.

You are the Son of the blessed.
Mark 14:61; John 5:18–25; 1 Timothy 6:15; Matthew 26:63.

You are the Son of the Father.
2 John 3; 1 John 1:3 & 2:23, 24 & 4:10; Matthew 11:27; John 3:35 & 5:23.

You are the Son of the King.
Psalm 72:1; 1 Kings 1:47 & 2:1–4; Jeremiah 23:5.

You are the Son of the living God.
Matthew 16:16; John 6:69.

You are the Son of the most high God.
Mark 5:6, 7.

You are the Son who is given.
Isaiah 9:6; John 1:14 & 3:16, 17; Romans 8:32; 1 John 4:10–14.

You are the Son.
Matthew 11:27 & 28:19; Colossians 1:13; 1 John 4:14; Luke 1:32; John 3:36.

You are the spiritual rock, that follows your people in the wilderness.
1 Corinthians 10:4; Exodus 17:6; Numbers 20:11; Psalm 78:15, 20 & 105:41.

You are the stone cut out of the mountain, without hands.
Daniel 2:34, 45; Psalm 118:22; Isaiah 28:16; Acts 4:11; Zechariah 4:6; John 1:13; 2 Corinthians 5:1; Hebrews 9:24.

You are the stone laid of God.
Isaiah 28:16; Genesis 49:24; Matthew 21:42; 1 Corinthians 3:11.

You are the stone that the builders reject.
Matthew 21:42; Psalm 118:22; Acts 4:11; 1 Peter 2:7.

You are the strength of my heart.
Psalm 73:26 & 18:2 & 27:14 & 138:3; Isaiah 40:29–31; 2 Corinthians 12:9, 10.

You are the sure mercies of David.
Isaiah 54:8 & 55:3; Acts 13:34; Psalm 89:28, 35-37; Matthew 9:27 & 15:22 & 20:31.

You are the surety of a better testament.
Hebrews 7:22 & 8:6–12 & 9:15–23 & 12:24.

You are the teacher who has come from God.
John 3:2 & 8:42 & 13:3; Matthew 22:16.

You are the temple.
Revelation 21:22; John 2:19–21 & 10:30; Colossians 1:19 & 2:9; Hebrews 9:1–12; Psalm 29:9.

You are the tender grass, springing out of the earth, by the clear shining after rain.
2 Samuel 23:4; Deuteronomy 32:2; Psalm 72:6; Isaiah 4:2; Micah 5:7.

You are the testator for your people.
Hebrews 9:16, 17; Genesis 48:21; John 14:27.

You are the tower of my salvation.
2 Samuel 22:51; Psalm 3:3 & 21:1 & 48:3 & 89:26 & 91:2.

You are the tree of life, in the midst of the paradise of God.
Genesis 2:9 & 3:22; Revelation 2:7 & 22:2, 14; Proverbs 3:18; Ezekiel 47:12; John 6:48.

You are the true bread from heaven.
John 6:32, 33, 35, 41, 50, 58.

You are the true God.
1 John 5:20; Isaiah 9:6 & 44:6 & 45:14, 15, 21–25 & 54:5; Jeremiah 10:10 & 23:6; John 1:1–3 & 14:9 & 20:28; Acts 20:28; Romans 9:5; 1 Timothy 3:16; Titus 2:13; Hebrews 1:8.

You are the true light.
John 1:9, 4, 7 & 12:46; 1 John 2:8; Psalm 36:9 & 18:28; Isaiah 49:6 & 42:16; Matthew 6:23 & 4:16; 1 Peter 2:9.

You are the true vine.
John 15:1; Genesis 49:10, 11; Psalm 80:8; Isaiah 4:2 & 5:1.

You are the true witness.
Revelation 3:14 & 1:5 & 19:11 & 22:6; John 18:37; Isaiah 55:4; Jeremiah 42:5.

You are the truth.
John 14:6 & 1:14, 17 & 18:37; Psalm 31:5; Romans 15:8; 1 John 5:20; Revelation 3:7 & 19:11.

You are the unspeakable gift of God.
2 Corinthians 9:15; James 1:17; Romans 5:18 & 6:23; Hebrews 5:1 & 6:4 & 8:3; Ephesians 4:7.

You are the veil into the most holy place.
Hebrews 10:20 & 9:12; Leviticus 16:2, 15; Matthew 27:51; 1 Peter 3:18.

You are the vine.
John 15:5; Romans 12:5 & 6:22 & 7:4; 1 Corinthians 12:12; Hosea 14:8; Philippians 1:11.

You are the way, the truth, and the life; no man comes unto the Father, but by you.
John 14:6 & 10:7, 9; Acts 4:12; Romans 15:16; 1 Peter 2:4 & 3:18; 1 John 2:23; 2 John 9; Revelation 5:9 & 20:15.

You are the way.
John 14:6 & 10:9; Isaiah 35:8; Hebrews 10:19, 20 & 7:25 & 9:8 & 10:19–22; Matthew 11:27; Acts 4:12; Romans 5:1, 2; Ephesians 2:16-18; 1 Peter 1:21.

You are the wisdom of God.
1 Corinthians 1:24, 30; Colossians 2:3; Revelation 5:12; Proverbs 8:1, 22-30; Matthew 10:26.

You are the Word made flesh.
John 1:14; Isaiah 7:14; Romans 1:3 & 9:5; 1 Corinthians 15:47; Galatians 4:4; Philippians 2:6–8; 1 Timothy 3:16; Hebrews 2:11, 14-17 & 10:5; 1 John 4:2; 2 John 7.

You are the young child, whom wise men worship.
Matthew 2:11 & 14:33; Psalm 2:12 & 95:6; John 5:22, 23.

You are undefiled.
Hebrews 7:26; John 14:30; 1 Peter 2:22; (see, you are without sin).

You are upholding all things, by the word of your power.
Hebrews 1:3 & 11:3; Psalm 33:6 & 119:25, 28 & 147:15-18 & 148:8; Isaiah 40:26; Ecclesiastes 8:4; Matthew 8:8; 2 Peter 3:5.

You are very Christ.
Acts 9:22 & 17:3 & 18:5, 28; Luke 24:44; Galatians 3:1.

You are without sin.
John 8:46; 1 John 3:5; 2 Corinthians 5:21; 1 Peter 2:21, 22 & 1:19; Hebrews 9:13, 14 & 7:26 & 4:15.

You alone are worthy to receive power, and riches, and wisdom, and strength, and honour, and glory, and blessing.
Revelation 5:12, 9 & 4:11 & 7:12 & 19:1; Matthew 28:18; John 3:35 & 17:2; 1 Timothy 1:17.

You are: I AM THAT I AM.
Exodus 3:14.

You are: I AM.
(Exodus 3:14 with John 8:24, 28, 58); Matthew 14:27 & Mark 6:50 & 14:62; John 4:26 & 6:20 & 6:35 & 6:48, 51 & 8:12 & 8:18 & 8:58 & 10:7, 9 & 10:11, 14 & 11:25 & 13:19 & 14:6 & 15:1, 5 & 18:4–5, 6, 8.

You are: Messiah the Prince.
Daniel 9:25; Acts 5:31.

You are: The Almighty.
Revelation 1:8 & 4:8 & 11:17; Psalm 91:1; Isaiah 9:6.

You are: The Amen.
Revelation 3:14; Isaiah 65:16; 2 Corinthians 1:20.

You are: The Ancient of days.
Daniel 7:9; Psalm 90:2 & 93:2; Habakkuk 1:12; Hebrews 13:8; Revelation 1:8.

You are: The Branch of righteousness.
Jeremiah 33:15; Psalm 80:15; Isaiah 11:1–5; Ezekiel 34:29; Zechariah 6:12, 13.

You are: The Christ of God.
Luke 9:20; John 20:31; Matthew 16:16.

You are: The Deliverer.
Romans 11:26; 1 Samuel 17:37; Job 33:24; Galatians 1:4; 2 Peter 2:9; 1 Thessalonians 1:10.

You are: The Door.
John 10:9 & 14:6; Ephesians 2:18.

You are: The Head.
Colossians 2:19; Ephesians 4:15.

You are: The Holy One and the Just.
Acts 3:14; Revelation 3:71; 1 Peter 3:18.

You are: The Holy One of God.
Mark 1:24; Acts 2:27.

You are: The Holy One of Israel.
Psalm 89:18; Isaiah 41:14 & 49:7 & 54:5.

You are: The Holy One.
Psalm 16:10; Acts 2:27 & 3:14; Luke 4:34.

You are: The Judge.
Acts 10:42 & 17:31; John 5:22; Revelation 19:11.

You are: The King of nations.
Jeremiah 10:7; Revelation 15:4 & 11:15; Psalm 22:28 & 72:11 & 86:9; Isaiah 2:4; Zechariah 2:11.

You are: The King of peace.
Hebrews 7:2; Romans 5:1; Micah 5:5; 1 Kings 4:24; 1 Chronicles 22:9; Mark 4:39; John 14:27.

You are: The King of righteousness.
Hebrews 7:2; Psalm 72:1-3 & 45:4–7; Isaiah 32:1 & 45:22–25; Jeremiah 23:5, 6; Romans 3:26 & 5:18.

You are: The King of saints.
Revelation 15:3; Isaiah 33:22; Zechariah 9:9; John 19:14, 15; Matthew 25:34.

You are: The King of Salem.
Hebrews 7:2; Genesis 14:28.

You are: The King.
Zechariah 9:9 & 14:16; Psalm 2:6; Matthew 21:5; Luke 19:38.

You are: The Lord's servant, the Branch.
Zechariah 3:8; Isaiah 52:13 & 42:1 & 4:2.

You are: The Man Christ Jesus.
1 Timothy 2:5; Hebrews 2:6, 7.

You are: The mighty One of Jacob.
Isaiah 49:26 & 60:16.

You are: The mighty One.
Isaiah 60:16 & 1:24 & 30:29 & 49:26.

You are: The Offspring of David.
Revelation 22:16; Matthew 22:42; Romans 1:3.

You are: The Power of God.
1 Corinthians 1:24; Romans 1:4; Revelation 5:12, 13.

You are: The Prince of life.
Acts 3:15; John 5:26 & 17:2.

You are: The Prince of princes.
Daniel 8:25; Revelation 19:16.

You are: The Prince of the kings of the earth.
Revelation 1:5; Psalm 72:11 & 89:27; Proverbs 8:15, 16; Ephesians 1:20–22; 1 Timothy 6:15.

You are: The Prophet.
John 7:40 & 6:14; Acts 3:22, 23; Deuteronomy 18:15–18; Luke 7:16.

You are: The Redeemer.
Isaiah 59:20 & 54:5; Job 19:25; Jeremiah 50:34; Psalm 19:14; Ephesians 1:7.

You are: The Root of David.
Revelation 5:5 & 22:16.

You are: The Saviour of the world.
John 4:42 & 3:16, 17; 1 John 4:14; Isaiah 45:22 & 52:10.

You are: The Shepherd of Israel.
Psalm 80:1; Ezekiel 34:23.

You are: The Son of God.
Matthew 2:15 & 14:33 & 27:43; John 1:34, 49; Hebrews 4:14; Luke 1:35; Daniel 3:25; Mark 1:1; Acts 9:20; Romans 1:4; 1 John 4:15.

You are: The Son of man.
John 1:51 & 5:27 & 13:31; Daniel 7:13; Luke 22:69; Mark 10:33; Acts 7:56; Revelation 1:13 & 14:14.

You are: The Star out of Jacob.
Numbers 24:17; Matthew 2:2; Revelation 22:16.

You are: The Sun of righteousness.
Malachi 4:2; Isaiah 9:2; Luke 1:78.

You are: The Word of life.
1 John 1:1; John 5:26; Revelation 19:13.

You are: The Word with God.
John 1:1, 18 & 16:28 & 17:5; Proverbs 8:22–30; 1 John 1:2.

You are: The Word.
John 1:1 & 14; Genesis 1:1; 1 John 1:1 & 5:7; Revelation 19:13.

You blot out the handwriting of ordinances, that is against me.
Colossians 2:14; Numbers 5:23; Psalm 51:1, 9; Isaiah 43:25 & 44:22; Acts 3:19; Ephesians 2:14–16; Hebrews 10:9.

You build the house of God.
Hebrews 3:3; Matthew 16:18; Zechariah 3:8.

You come in the glory of your Father.
Matthew 16:27; Mark 8:38; Luke 9:26.

You come unto your own, and your own despise and reject you.
Isaiah 53:3; John 1:11; Matthew 21:42; Mark 8:31.

You command the winds and the waves, and they obey you.
Mark 4:37-41; Psalm 33:7-9 & 89:9 & 104:1-14; Jeremiah 5:22; Nahum 1:4; Proverbs 8:29 & 30:4; Genesis 1:9, 10; Matthew 8:26, 27; Luke 4:36 & 8:23-25; Job 38:8-11.

You deliver me from wrath.
1 Thessalonians 1:10 & 5:9; John 3:36; Matthew 1:21 & 3:7; Romans 5:9; Galatians 3:13; Hebrews 10:27.

You did no sin, neither was guile found in your mouth.
1 Peter 2:22; Isaiah 53:9; (see, you are without sin).

You dwell among us.
John 1:14 & 20:19; Matthew 18:20.

You expound the scriptures.
Luke 24:27, 45; 1 John 5:20.

You fill all in all.
Ephesians 1:23 & 4:10; 1 Corinthians 12:6.

You gather the wind in your fists.
Proverbs 30:4; Psalm 104:2; Isaiah 40:12; Mark 4:39.

You dwell in the high and holy place.
Isaiah 57:15; Psalm 11:4 & 68:4, 5 & 113:4–6 & 115:3 & 123:1; Zechariah 2:13; Matthew 6:9; 1 Timothy 6:16; John 3:13.

You give grace unto the humble.
1 Peter 5:5; James 4:6; Proverbs 3:34; Isaiah 57:15.

You give grace.
John 1:17; Acts 15:11; Romans 1:4, 5 & 12:3 & 15:15; 1 Corinthians 1:4; 2 Corinthians 12:8, 9.

You give light.
Isaiah 9:2; Luke 1:79; John 1:4, 9 & 8:12; Psalm 27:1.

You give living water.
John 4:10; Jeremiah 2:13; Isaiah 44:3; Zechariah 14:8.

You give your life, a ransom for me.
Mark 10:45; Hosea 13:14; Isaiah 53:10–12; Job 33:24; 1 Timothy 2:6.

You give yourself for me, an offering and a sacrifice to God, for a sweetsmelling savour.
Ephesians 5:2; John 10:11, 15; Romans 8:3; 1 Corinthians 5:7; Hebrews 10:12; Genesis 8:21; Leviticus 1:9, 13, 17 & 3:16; 2 Corinthians 2:15.

You have a more excellent name.
Hebrews 1:4; Luke 2:11; John 13:13 & 14:13 & 20:28; Acts 2:36; Isaiah 45:23–25; Romans 14:11; 1 John 4:15; Philippians 2:9, 10.

You have come a light into the world.
John 12:46, 35, 36 & 3:19 & 1:4 & 8:12 & 9:5; Psalm 36:9; Matthew 4:16; Luke 1:79 & 2:32; Acts 26:18; 1 John 2:8; Isaiah 42:7; Ephesians 5:14.

You have come being humble and obedient unto death, even the death of the cross.
Philippians 2:8; Proverbs 15:33; Acts 8:33; Hebrews 5:5–8 & 12:2; Matthew 26:39, 42; John 4:34 & 15:10 & 10:18.

You have come to be a brother born for adversity.
Proverbs 17:17; Matthew 11:6.

You have come to be a man.
John 19:5; 1 Timothy 2:5; Galatians 4:4; Hebrews 2:14-17; Philippians 2:8.

You have come to be a worm, and no man.
Psalm 22:6 & 69:7–12; Job 25:6; Isaiah 41:14 & 53:3; Lamentations 3:30.

You have come to be accursed of God for me.
Deuteronomy 21:23; Galatians 3:13; 1 Peter 2:24; Psalm 69:9; 2 Corinthians 5:21.

You have come to be both a stranger and a foreigner.
Psalm 69:8 & 31:11; Matthew 8:20 & 10:36; John 1:10, 11 & 7:5; Job 19:13–19.

You have come to be bruised for my iniquities.
Isaiah 53:5, 10; Genesis 3:15; 1 Peter 2:24; Luke 22:44; Hebrews 5:7.

You have come to be despised in my place.
Isaiah 53:3 & 49:7 & 50:6; Zechariah 11:13; Matthew 26:67 & 27:9; Acts 3:13–15; Psalm 22:6–8 & 69:10–12, 19, 20; Micah 5:1; Luke 8:53 & 16:14; John 8:48.

You have come to be made of a woman.
Galatians 4:4; Hebrews 2:14; Genesis 3:15; Isaiah 7:14.

You have come to be obedient unto death.
Philippians 2:8; Hebrews 5:8; Matthew 26:39, 42; John 4:34 & 15:10 & 10:18.

You have come to be received up into your own glory.
1 Timothy 3:16; John 17:5 & 13:1 & 16:28; Mark 16:19; Luke 9:51 & 24:50, 51; Acts 1:10, 11; Hebrews 4:14; 1 Peter 3:22.

You have come to be reviled and mocked, in my place.
Mark 15:18-20 & 29-32 & 10:34; Jeremiah 20:7; 1 Peter 2:23; John 9:28 & 10:10 & 19:3 & 20:31; Matthew 26:49 & 27:29, 31, 39, 41-44; Luke 18:32 & 23:11, 36, 37.

You have come to be smitten, that I might have life.
Isaiah 53:4; Job 16:10; Psalm 102:4; 1 Peter 2:24; Matthew 26:37; John 19:7; Lamentations 1:12.

You have come to be stricken for me.
Isaiah 53:3, 4, 8 & 50:6 & 52:14; Matthew 26:37, 67; Luke 22:44, 63, 64; Job 30:10; Micah 5:1; John 18:22; Hebrews 12:2.

You have come to be tempted like as I am, yet without sin.
Hebrews 4:15 & 2:18; Luke 4:2-11 & 22:28; John 4:6 & 13:21 & 14:30 & 11:33-35.

You have come to be the king, crowned with a crown of thorns.
Matthew 27:29; Psalm 69:7, 19, 20; Hebrews 12:3; John 19:1-5; Mark 15:17.

You have come to be the man of sorrows.
Isaiah 53:3, 4, 10; Psalm 69:29; Matthew 26:38; Luke 19:41; John 11:35; Hebrews 5:7.

You have come to be the righteous servant.
Isaiah 53:11 & 42:1 & 49:3; Matthew 20:28; 1 John 2:1; Romans 3:22-24 & 5:18, 19.

You have come to be the seed of the woman.
Genesis 3:15; Matthew 1:23; Psalm 132:11; Galatians 3:16, 19 & 4:4; Hebrews 2:14, 16; Jeremiah 31:22; 2 Timothy 2:8.

You have come to be touched with the feeling of my infirmities, yet without sin.
Hebrews 4:15 & 2:18; Luke 4:2-11 & 22:28; John 4:6 & 13:21 & 14:30 & 11:33-35.

You have come to offer yourself.
Hebrews 7:27; John 10:17, 18; Galatians 1:4; Titus 2:14.

You have come with peace, and we have oppressed you.
Hebrews 7:2; John 14:27 & 20:21; Acts 10:36; Isaiah 53:7; Psalm 17:8, 9 & 42:9 & 119:121, 122.

You have obtained eternal redemption for me.
Hebrews 9:12 & 5:9; Daniel 9:24; 1 Thessalonians 1:10; Psalm 37:18; 2 Timothy 2:10.

You have power over all flesh.
John 5:21-29 & 17:2 & 3:35; Philippians 2:9, 10; Psalm 2:6-12 & 110:1; Daniel 7:14; Matthew 11:27 & 28:18; 1 Corinthians 15:25; Hebrews 1:2 & 2:8; 1 Peter 3:22.

You have risen from the dead, on the third day.
Matthew 16:21 & 28:7; Luke 24:46; 1 Corinthians 15:4, 20; Acts 17:3.

You have risen.
Luke 24:6, 34, 46; Acts 17:3; Matthew 28:6; Mark 16:6; Romans 8:34.

You have the keys of hell and of death.
Revelation 1:18 & 3:7; Psalm 68:20; Isaiah 22:22.

You have the preeminence in all things.
Colossians 1:18; Psalm 45:2–5 & 89:27; John 3:31; Isaiah 52:13; 1 Corinthians 15:25; Revelation 5:9–13 & 11:15.

You have the words of eternal life.
John 6:63, 68; Psalm 19:7–10; 1 Thessalonians 2:13; Hebrews 4:12; James 1:18, 21; 1 Peter 1:23.

You intreat the Father for me.
1 Samuel 2:25; John 14:16; 1 Timothy 2:5; Hebrews 7:25.

You keep me from falling.
Jude 24; Psalm 18:35 & 63:8 & 73:23 & 140:7; Song of Solomon 2:6.

You keep me in your Father's name.
John 17:12 & 6:37 & 10:28, 29; Hebrews 2:13.

You lead me, and guide me.
Isaiah 40:11; Psalm 5:8 & 23:2, 3 & 25:5 & 27:11 & 31:3 & 43:3 & 61:2 & 139:10 & 143:10; Proverbs 6:22 & 8:20; Isaiah 42:16 & 48:17 & 49:10 & 57:18; Mark 9:2; John 10:3; Romans 2:4; Hebrews 8:9; Revelation 7:17.

You make all things new.
Revelation 21:5; 2 Corinthians 5:17; Isaiah 42:9 & 43:19 & 65:16, 17; John 5:21, 24-29, 33, 51, 57; Psalm 40:3; Lamentations 3:22, 23.

You make me free.
John 8:36; Galatians 5:1; Romans 6:6, 7, 16-18 & 8:2; Matthew 17:25.

You make the worlds.
Hebrews 1:2; Proverbs 8:22–31; Isaiah 44:24 & 45:12, 18; John 1:3; 1 Corinthians 8:6; Ephesians 3:9; Colossians 1:16.

You open and no man shuts, and shuts and no man opens.
Revelation 3:7; Isaiah 22:22; Matthew 16:19; Job 12:14.

You open the scriptures unto me; give your child understanding.
Luke 24:32, 45; Proverbs 2:6; Job 32:8.

You overcome all things for me.
Revelation 17:14; Luke 11:21, 22; 1 John 4:4; 2 Samuel 22:40; Psalm 18:39, 47.& 44:5.

You overcome the world, and inherit all things.
John 16:33; Isaiah 65:9; Psalm 82:8.

You perfect for ever, them that are sanctified.
Hebrews 10:14 & 7:19, 25 & 2:11 & 13:12; Acts 20:32; Romans 15:16; 1 Corinthians 1:2; Ephesians 5:26; Jude 1.

You plead the Father for me.
Job 16:21; Psalm 119:154; Jeremiah 50:34; Lamentations 3:58; Micah 7:9.

You present me faultless before God.
Jude 24; 2 Corinthians 11:2; Ephesians 5:27; Colossians 1:22, 28; Hebrews 13:20, 21; Revelation 14:5.

You quicken whom you will.
John 5:21 & 11:25 & 17:2.

You ransom me from the power of the grave.
Hosea 13:14 & 6:2; Job 19:25–27 & 33:24; Psalm 30:3 & 49:15 & 71:20 & 86:13; Ezekiel 37:11–14.

You redeem me from death, and its plagues.
Hosea 13:14; Isaiah 26:19; 1 Corinthians 15:21, 22, 52-57; 2 Corinthians 5:4; Philippians 3:21.

You restore my soul.
Psalm 23:3 & 119:25, 37 & 19:7 & 51:10, 12 & 85:4–7; Job 33:30; Jeremiah 32:37–42; Micah 7:8, 9.

You save to the uttermost.
Hebrews 7:25; John 10:29; 2 Timothy 1:12; Jude 24.

You say; Peace be still, and there is a great calm.
Mark 4:37-41.

You sit King for ever.
Psalm 29:10 & 10:16 & 145:1; 1 Timothy 1:17.

You speak of heavenly things.
John 3:12 & 6:68.

Your countenance is as Lebanon, excellent as the cedars.
Song of Solomon 5:15.

Your countenance is as the sun shines in his strength.
Revelation 1:16; Malachi 4:2; Acts 26:13.

Your glorious high throne from the beginning, is the place of our sanctuary.
Jeremiah 17:12; Psalm 96:6.

Your house is filled with glory.
Haggai 2:7; 1 Kings 8:11; Ezekiel 10:4 & 44:4.

Your name is remembered in all generations, therefore shall your people praise you for ever and ever.
Psalm 45:17 & 72:17-19; Malachi 1:11.

Your name is secret.
Judges 13:18.

Your name is: Counsellor.
Isaiah 9:6.

Your name is: Eliakim.
Isaiah 22:20.

Your name is: Emmanuel.
Matthew 1:23.

Your name is: Faithful and True.
Revelation 19:11 & 3:14; Jeremiah 42:5.

Your name is: Immanuel.
Isaiah 7:14 & 8:8; Matthew 1:23.

Your name is: Jehovah.
Exodus 6:3; Psalm 83:18; Isaiah 26:4.

Your name is: Jesus.
Matthew 1:21; Luke 2:21.

Your name is: Our Lord Jesus Christ.
1 Corinthians 1:10 & 5:4; Acts 15:26; Romans 5:1; Galatians 6:14.

Your name is: Rabbi.
John 3:2.

Your name is: Rabboni.
John 20:16.

Your name is: Saviour, Jesus.
Acts 13:23.

Your name is: The everlasting Father.
Isaiah 9:6.

Your name is: The holy child Jesus.
Acts 4:30.

Your name is: The King of kings, and Lord of lords.
Revelation 19:16 & 17:14; 1 Timothy 6:15.

Your name is: The Lord Our Righteousness.
Jeremiah 23:6; Isaiah 45:24 & 54:17.

Your name is: The mighty God.
Isaiah 9:6.

Your name is: The Nazarene.
Matthew 2:23.

Your name is: The Prince of peace.
Isaiah 9:6.

Your name is: The Son of the Highest.
Luke 1:32; Mark 5:7.

Your name is: The Word of God.
Revelation 19:13.

Your name is: True.
Revelation 19:11 & 3:7.

Your name is: Wonderful.
Isaiah 9:6.

Your resurrection has begotten me again, unto a lively hope.
1 Peter 1:3; 1 Corinthians 1:18.

Your resurrection is with power.
Philippians 3:10; 2 Corinthians 13:4; John 10:18.

Your throne is established of old: you are from everlasting.
Psalm 93:2 & 90:2 & 145:13; (Psalm 45:6 with Hebrews 1:8-12); Proverbs 8:22, 23; Micah 5:2; Hebrews 13:8; Revelation 1:8.

Your throne, O God, is for ever and ever.
Hebrews 1:8; Psalm 45:6 & 89:29, 36; Luke 1:33.

Your truth makes me free.
John 8:31, 32; Romans 6:18, 22; Galatians 5:1.

Your words will never pass away.
Luke 21:33; Isaiah 40:8; 1 Peter 1:25; Psalm 119:89–91, 160.

Your yoke is easy, and your burden is light.
Matthew 11:30; Galatians 5:1; 1 John 5:3; Philippians 4:13.

You were made flesh, and dwelt among us.
John 1:14; 1 Timothy 3:16.

You wipe away all tears from my eyes.
Revelation 7:17 & 21:4; Isaiah 25:8 & 30:19 & 35:10 & 60:20 & 65:19.

There are also many other things which Jesus did, the which, if they should be written every one, I suppose that even the world itself could not contain the books that should be written. Amen.
John 21:25.

GLOSSARY

HOLY BIBLE

The entrance of thy words giveth light.
Psalm 119:130

Ab: Fifth month in the Hebrew calendar; our July-August.

Abaddon: Meaning, destruction; the angel of the bottomless pit.

Abase: To make or bring low; to humble.

Abate: To restrain; to lessen; to diminish: or, to become sensible; to ease.

Abba: Father; figuratively meaning a superior.

Abhor: To hate extremely, or with contempt; to loathe, detest or abominate; to despise or neglect; to cast off or reject.

Abib or Nisan: First month in the Hebrew calendar; our March-April.

Abide: To rest, or dwell; to tarry or stay for a short time: or, to continue permanently or in the same state: or, to be firm and immovable: or, to wait for; to be prepared for: or, to endure or sustain.

Abjects: Hypocritical mockers; outcasts; striking out with the tongue.

Ablution: The act of cleaning or washing something; purging by water.

Abode: A place of continuance; a dwelling place; a habitation; lodged; stayed.

Abolish: To disannul; to take away; the conclusion of something.

Abominable: That which is filthy; detestable.

Abomination: Strange gods; images; idols; extreme hatred; detestation; moral defilement, idols and idolatry, are called an abomination in Scripture.

Abound: Be plentiful; to have an abundance.

About: Engaged in; relating to; in respect of: or, around; on the outer area or surface of something.

Abraham's bosom: A figure of speech to refer to a place for the spirits of the righteous dead and their comforts.

Abroad: Wide spread; away from home; outside the area; circulated.

Abstain: To set aside; to keep yourself from something; to be sober in mind; to refuse.

Abstinence: To separate from something; to forbid or restrain yourself.

Abuse: To use something improperly or misuse gifts given; to insult and mock; being ill-treated by another; a shameful and cruel death of someone.

Acceptation: To accept and believe something with favor.

Accord, (one): Gather together as one; having all things in common.

Accord, (own): Doing and thinking on your own.

Accursed: Doomed to destruction and misery; separated from the faithful; detestable; having the stain of sin.

Accuser: The devil; a prosecutor.

Aceldama: Meaning, the field of blood.

Acquaint: To gain a personal or exacting knowledge of something/one.

Acquit: To hold not guilty to the debt load of sin.

Acre: A measure of an area, 4,840 square yards.

Adamant: A hard stone: or, a picture of something unshakable or unbreakable.

Adar: Twelfth month in the Hebrew calendar; our February-March.

Adder: A deadly serpent; a viper.

Addicted: To be attached to something in a freely and voluntarily way; willingly give up yourself, and be addicted to aiding others.

Adjure: To command; to charge with a promise.

Admiration: Amazement; to be in wonder.

Admire: To marvel at something/one.

Admonish: To correct; to caution: or, to teach.

Admonition: Learning; nurture; instruction; warning.

Ado: Weeping and wailing; making a noise with trouble.

Adoption: An act of God's grace by which he brings men into the number of his redeemed family, and makes them partaker's of all the blessings he has provided for them.

Adorn: To clothe; to array; to cover.

Adria: The Adriatic Sea.

Adultery: Sexual behavior of a person, being married or unmarried with a married person; two people having sexual union that is outside of God's decree of marriage.

Adventure: A possibility; a risk; to try by chance; a possible hazard; that of which one has no direction.

Adversary: An enemy; an individual turning against another.

Adversity: Suffering; in troubles, affliction, distress; a state of unhappiness.

Advertise: To tell, inform, counsel: or, to give caution; to take or give notice of something.

Advise: To think about; to consider well.

Advisement: Information; consideration; taking advice and counsel.

Advocate: One who pleads for another; one who defends, vindicates, or supports a cause, by argument.

Affect: An act of aspiring to do something and having an influence and effect on it.

Affinity: A marriage contract, involving faithfulness to the end: or, friendship; being outgoing.

Affording: Providing; furnishing.

Affrighted: Afraid; horrified; shocked.

Afoot: By foot; walking with your feet.

Afore: Before; away from and out in front of something.

Aforetime: In time past; beforehand; being prepared in advance.

Afresh: Again; anew.

After: Being mindful of something; in the direction and influence of something: or, to talk of a plan or goal toward something.

Afterward: In time following, something which is a process.

Afterwards: At a later time, some particular thing.

Against: In contrast to; opposite in place; in an opposite direction; toward, facing or in front of something: or, in resistance to something.

Agar: Hagar.

Agate: A beautifully veined semi-transparent precious stone; a variety of quartz.

Aggravate: To stir up for action; to magnify circumstances.

Agone: Time gone by; to be far in the past, and gone forever.

Agony: The condition of great resist and pressure of soul.

Aground: Being on the ground by going downwards or falling: or, like the bottom of a ship that rests on the ground.

Ague: A fever; an extreme burning, and having cold and hot sweats.

Ah: A sigh of sorrow.

Aha: A cry of possession, triumph, and contempt by someone's loss; or simple surprise.

Ail: Nervousness; having torture of heart and mind.

Alabaster box: A bottle or container to protect ointment.

Alamoth: A high-note in music played on a harp.

Alas: Howling; a cry of mourning, despair, or regret.

Albeit: Meaning, even though it be; although it be.

Algum (almug): Possibly a sandalwood tree or juniper.

Alien: A person of another nation or race.

All to: To do entirely; to do something totally.

Allege: Being evident; to proclaim as right.

Allegory: A figure of speech; a picture of another thing.

Alleluia: Praise the LORD! (The Greek form of Hallelujah).

Allied: To be securely bound or united; coupled.

Allow: To permit; to let; to grant a thing.

Allure: To entice and attract; to tempt and draw away from something.

Alms: Good works; alms deeds; a charitable donation, as an aid to the poor.

Almug, (algum): Possibly a sandalwood tree or juniper.

Aloof: To be afar off; willfully turning away from others.

Alpha: First; beginning; the first letter of the Greek alphabet.

Alway: All the time; all the way; the whole way; endlessly.

Always: At every time; on every occasion.

Amazed: To be terrified with trembling; afraid; fearful; to be very heavy in mind.

Amazement: A loss of wits or presence of mind by a dynamic event.

Ambassador: A spokesperson; one that is sent on the behalf of another.

Ambassage: One sent, who wishes conditions of peace and the coming together, to end a war.

Amber: Yellow in color.

Ambush: To hide, and lie in wait to shock the adversary, and to overtake them.

Amen: So let it be; faithful; truth; sure.

Amend: To repair; recover; having improvement, by removing the difficulty.

Amends: To mend; making things right by being satisfied with fairness; to be active in repairing.

Amerce: To punish by fine or charge, at the sympathy of the court.

Amethyst: A precious gem of purple or blue-violet.

Amiable: Something dear; being lovely in conduct; to be agreeable.

Amiss: Do things wrong; being in error.

Amongst: Moving around in the midst of things or individuals.

Anathema: Accursed by God; someone removed for destruction.

Ancient of days: The God of eternity.

Ancients: The elders.

Angels, (evil): The false, refused and condemned angels; in light, in ways, in truth and life.

Angels: Messengers of and for God; ministering spirits sent forth to minister for them who shall be heirs of salvation.

Angle, (cast): Stretching nets upon the waters.

Angle: A fishhook.

Anguish: To be in agony; to travail; pain of mind or body.

Anoint: To rub in and rub on oil, on the head or body, making something separate for a holy task or service.

Anon: Immediately; without delay; at once.

Answer: A reply to a charge or a question.

Antichrist: One contrary to, and a replacement of Christ.

Antiquity: The ancients; the people of ancient times: or, someone is old in years.

Anvil: A hard base of iron, to form and work metal.

Apace: Fast paced; moving quickly.

Apollyon: The destroyer; the angel of the bottomless pit.

Apostle: A messenger; one sent to carry out a service.

Apothecary: One who makes and sells spices and perfumes.

Apparel: Clothes that serve a particular service.

Apparently: Coming more into view; being plainer and clearer to see or understand.

Appeal: Approaching and asking for an answer from someone.

Appease: To pacify; to satisfy; to create peace.

Appertain: Something belonging to a subject or an issue.

Apple of the eye: Pupil of the eye; someone special.

Apprehend: To take hold of; to grasp: or, to get hold of something with the mind.

Apron: A garment worn on the front part of the body; a covering.

Apt: Being able; suitable; something that is fitting for an occasion.

Archangel: The most powerful angel; the highest class among others.

Archer: A person whose job it is to shoot bows.

Arcturus: A bright star.

Ariel: Two lion-like men of Moab: or, the top of the altar on which the priests burned sacrifices, as a lion devours its prey: or, another name for Jerusalem.

Aright: Moving smoothly or evenly in good order: or, a proper or correct path; going straight to the point.

Ark: A box or chest; a large floating boat or vessel.

Arm of the LORD: To make bare his holy arm, that is, to reveal Christ.

Armageddon: The city or hill of Megiddo.

Armholes: Armpits.

Array: Putting in order, people, or property: or, the action of putting on clothing; to dress.

Art: Are; the second person singular.

Artificer: A craftsman or creator, who makes things by talent or skillfulness.

Artillery: Weapons of battle; gear; equipment.

Ascend: Go away upward; to raise or climb to a higher end.

Ascribe: The act of adding words by writing, your own thoughts or something that is heard or seen.

Aside: Away from the main direction.

Asp: A small poisonous snake; a serpent.

Ass: Tall-eared, 4-footed beast, smaller than a horse that carries a load.

Assay: To attempt; to take on; to test or try someone with heartiness.

Assent: To be in agreement upon or with something, with all your heart.

Assure: Making something certain or secure.

Asswage: To settle down; to subside; restrain; to make a thing more agreeable.

Astonied: Inwardly puzzled and confused.

Astonished: Wonderment; being stunned toward a particular thing.

Astrologer: Looking to the stars for information, and not to Christ; an action forbidden by God.

Asunder: Apart; into parts or pieces; separately; in a divided state, one from another with might.

Athirst: Thirsty.

Atonement: An act of God, making someone at peace with himself: or, a cover that makes amends for an unjust action.

Attain: To gain; to achieve or accomplish by touch or reach; to come to or arrive at something by motion; brave action or efforts towards a place or object.

Attent: Being mindful and attentive, and reaching toward something/one.

Attire: Clothing set out or put on, in an orderly way.

Audience: An official hearing, with a crowd of people or to one person.

Augment: To amplify or enlarge; to make greater in size and power.

Augustus: A title of someone being royal.

Aul: A pointed device to create holes.

Austere: To be unforgiving; cruel; demanding.

Author: One who makes or develops things, or who starts things and owns them.

Authority: Having authorization, order, permission; having power derived from opinion, respect, or esteem; having influence of character; dominion over, lordship over; the right to charge others.

Avail: Gives or brings forth; the performance and skill of a person, to be of valuable service.

Avenge: Getting revenge, with intense punishment, on behalf of someone else.

Avenger of blood: Someone taking revenge because of a brutal act done to them.

Averse: Turning away from something, because of a lack of interest.

Avoid: To withdraw; to escape; the action of refusing and moving away from something.

Avouched: Declared or professed; to have cited someone as evidence, or an assurance for some cause or reason.

Aware: Refers to perceiving; to be watchful.

Away with: To take away; to bear with; to endure; to tolerate.

Awe: Fear mingled with reverence and wonder, a state of mind inspired by something terrible or sublime.

Axletree: The spindle of a wheel.

Baal: A lord or master; a Canaanite male idol god.

Baali: Meaning, my lord; a name of a prophet.

Baalim: Plural number for baal.

Baal-zebub: A Philistines deity; lord of flies, as in mud or manure.

Babbling: Making sounds, no one can understand; as a baby trying to utter words.

Babe: A child; a baby in the womb, or a baby one day to a few months old: or, "babes in Christ" are men of little spiritual growth, carnal as opposed to spiritual; is also used of a child as a minor or infant in the eye of the law.

Babylon: Babel; the Gate of God; the language of Babylon is mixed and confused. In the Assyrian tablets, it means, the city of the scattering of the tribes.

Babylonish garment: A mantle of deep colors.

Backbiting: Evil speaking; to slander someone and give sharp wounds to their reputation, when they are not looking.

Backslide: Having turned aside or fallen back from a union with Christ.

Bade: Called; invited; told; a strong request for a response or action: (past tense of bid).

Bag: A small pack or money purse.

Bakemeats: The workings of a baker.

Baken: Baked.

Balances: Scales; refers to both sides of a set of scales.

Balm: A medication; gum/rosin from a shrub.

Band: A small assembly of people or a group of cattle that are united together.

Banishment: To condemn and cast out as a fugitive.

Bank: The margin of a watercourse; the raised ground bordering a lake, river, or sea, or the forming of an edge; a mound, pile or ridge of earth raised above the surrounding plain, either as a defense or for other purposes.

Banner: Like a flag, attached to a pole and held up high and set in view for others to see, such as a military ensign or flag.

Banqueting: A drinking party; gluttony: or, a feast of food, wine, and amusement.

Baptize: To apply water to a saved person, showing the death and resurrection of Christ.

Bar: The son of; a parents son.

Barbarian: A non-Greek person; the talking and traditions are different from Greeks.

Barbarous people: Foreign and uncivilized in speaking.

Barked: Peeled; to strip off the bark of a tree.

Barley: A grain for the feeding of animals, and bread-corn for the food of the poor.

Barn: A storehouse, where things are gathered and safely kept.

Barren: Desolate; waste: or, unfruitful, in the land, in the womb, or in knowledge.

Base: Lowly; meek: or, a dishonorable and hateful person: or, something being established upon it, as a base or false foundation.

Bason: A hollow, round vessel, holding different fluids or water.

Bastard: Polluted; an unlawful child, born out of wedlock, not born in a home.

Bath: About 6 to 9.3 gallons.

Battered: Something broken down; something weakened by beating or wearing.

Battleaxe: A hammer; a heavy war club.

Battlement: A retaining fence; a low safety-wall built on top of a flat-roofed house.

Bay horse: Reddish-brown color.

Bay: The laurel tree.

Bdellium: A tree that makes gum, yellow to light red in color.

Beacon: A fire or an ensign made to be as a warning on the top of a hill.

Beam: A long piece of wood shaped to carry out a task.

Bear: The act of holding or carrying something.

Became him: Suited or fitting for him; was appropriate to him.

Beckon: To signal someone for consideration, by using a hand or head.

Bedstead: A metal or wooden framework for supporting a bed.

Beelzebub: Prince or ruler of the devils.

Beer: A place where a well is dug.

Beeves: Plural for beef; horned cattle made for plowing.

Befall: To happen to; to occur to; the action of intense falling, usually into some evil.

Before: In front of or first in position.

Beforetime: Formerly; of old time.

Begat: Brought forth; generated, (past tense of beget).

Beget: Bring forth, physical or spiritual birth.

Beggarly: Being poor and unable to function, from having weakness of the body or mind.

Begotten: Generated; brought forth.

Beguile: To be spoiled by deceiving; being led astray by crafty words or actions.

Behalf: A person on the side or next to someone, who takes the place of another, in their interest.

Behemoth: A huge, strong animal.

Behold: See, or look; to keep or continue a grasp on something important.

Behoove: To do something of necessity or of duty, or of convenience: or, to be proper or needful for something.

Bekah: A half-shekel, 0.22 ounces.

Bel: The name of the highest Babylonian deity.

Belial: Ungodly; evil; wicked; vain; children of the devil.

Belied: Talking falsely; knowingly causing deception by lying.

Bellow: Making a roaring noise like a bull or cow.

Bellows: The action of casting metal; a piece of equipment for making a blast of air, to make the flames hotter.

Belly: The place of one's affections of Christ.

Bemoan: A passionate objection over some loss, with moaning.

Benefactors: A person who is wealthy, having been given benefits from others.

Benevolence: Maintaining the happiness of another.

Bereave: The taking away of goods or a persons, with some kind of aggression: or, to express the loss of a friend.

Beryl: A precious stone, light blue/green in color.

Beseech: To call upon; pleading sincerely after someone.

Beset: Go around; to surround; to circle around someone: or, obstruct; to press on all sides, to confuse and entangle someone.

Besides: In addition to; over and above in number.

Besiege: Enclosed around; a very severe long-term attack against a city or an enemy.

Besom: The sweeper of destruction; an aggressive sweeping rain that leaves no food, but ruin.

Besought: Entreated; to have asked; called to someone, (past tense of beseech).

Bestead: Being hard pressed, distressed or perplexed; being forcibly set in place by another.

Bestir: To put someone into a quick or lively action.

Bestow: To gather together; to put or place things in storage; to collect together possessions: or, to offer or provide a blessing.

Bethink: Lay it to heart; to think about, with turnings of consideration.

Betimes: Early; or quickly; or seasonably; an important or urgent occasion.

Betray: To give someone over into the adversaries' hand.

Betrothed: Someone who is engaged to be married.

Betwixt: Between; being in an in-between space, between two things.

Bewail: To lament; in deep sadness.

Bewitched: To charm; to mislead with words; relating to witchcraft.

Bewray: To make clear, obvious, and evident.

Bid: To ask; to request; to invite: or, to command; to order or direct: or, to wish or pray: or, to proclaim; to make known by a public voice.

Bier: A carriage on which dead bodies are placed and brought to the grave; like an open coffin.

Billow: The swelling of waves; a mound of water.

Bind: Making secure by a band, cord or a bond.

Birthright: Having peculiar privileges and benefits, belonging to the first-born.

Bishop: An overseer, in the congregation.

Bishoprick: A protector of the faith; the office of overseeing.

Bit: A restraint put into the mouth of horses, to control them.

Blains: A swollen skin tumor; a boil breaking forth with blains.

Blaspheme: To curse, revile or speak reproachfully of God.

Blaze: To make known information or publish news throughout the country, like a spreading flame.

Bleating: The crying sound of sheep.

Blemish: Being not perfect; to injure or weaken anything that is well formed, or excellent: or, to reproach and disgrace that which would harm the character of a person.

Blessed: Happy; having Gods favor because of the blood of Jesus Christ.

Blossom: To flourish and prosper.

Blot: To be shamed with a blot, from a wicked man: or, a blot in reputation, a stain, a disgrace, a reproach: or, to blot out, to destroy, to consume: or, a blot of the world, prosperity from unrighteousness or ill gotten gains.

Boil: A tumor upon the flesh, together with soreness and swelling.

Boisterous: Mighty and powerful; loud and roaring.

Bolled: Blossomed; bolled in the seed/shell of a flower.

Bolster: A head-rest or cushion.

Bond: A responsibility of any kind: or, in a state of servitude or slavery, being a captive: or, the cause of union; the strength that unites.

Bondage: Oppression; under a burden or load; being afflicted to serve with rigor.

Bonnet: A turban or cap worn by a priest; a headdress worn by women.

Booth: A hut made of branches.

Booty: The collection of captives, livestock, or objects of worth, taken in war from the enemy.

Borne: Something carried or sent out; to support something.

Bosom: In a figurative sense, it means intimacy, tender care and watchfulness, or closest intimacy and most perfect knowledge, or "into their bosom" indicates the bosom as the seat of thought and reflection.

Bosses: A knob at the center of a shield, or any circular rounded projection: or, a round or knob like swelling on the body.

Botch: A boil; swelling of the skin.

Bottle: A potter's vessel that holds wine, water or tears.

Bottom, (in the): A low ground; a valley.

Boughs: Large branches on a tree.

Bound: To be connected by moral ties: or, confined or restrained: or, a limit; a landmark: or, to bind.

Bounty: The riches of good things.

Bowels: The innermost part of the affections.

Box: A vial; a box that holds precious ointment.

Box tree: A beautiful evergreen, growing in many parts of Europe and Asia, its hard wood is much prized by engravers; is supposed by some, to mean a species of cedar.

Bramble: A thorny bush.

Brandish: Waving a sword in an aggressive way.

Brasen: Brass.

Brawler: One who is likely and fit to brawl.

Bray a fool: To strike and bruise a fool.

Bray: To press; to grind something, as in a mortar: or, to moan; to wail; to make a foul sound.

Breach: A break or disunion in spirit; a gap; a violation; to harm something.

Breaches: Bays; harbors; creeks.

Breeches: Trousers; pants; clothing that covers.

Bribe: Something given in order to distort justice and blind the eyes of the wise.

Bridechamber: A bridal room or the nuptial apartment; possibly for the bridegroom only.

Bridle: A muzzle to rule and direct, used in the mouth of an animal.

Brier: Any wild thorny-type bush.

Brigandine: A coat of body armor; a coat of mail; a breastplate.

Brim: The upper edge of a vessel; the rim or lip of any vessel or other thing.

Brimstone: Sulfur and fire.

Brink: The exact border where the ground meets the water.

Broad: A certain measurement in the distance across something.

Broided: To adorn with braided hair interwoven with pearls, gold etc.

Broidered: Embroidery done with decorative needlework on clothing.

Brood: A group of young fowls.

Brook: A violent flow of water; a stream.

Brow: Ridge; the edge of a steep place; or the ridge over the eye.

Bruit: Information; a rumor; a description of something.

Brute: Being dull; unreasonable and thick headed.

Brutish: Stupid; having the understanding as an animal.

Buckler: A kind of shield or piece of defensive armor; often was four feet high and covered the whole body.

Buffet: To strike with a closed hand.

Bul: Eighth month in the Hebrew calendar; our October- November.

Bullock: A bull, steer, or ox.

Bulrush: A large bush growing in wet soil.

Bulwark: A shielding structure; that which secures against an enemy or any outside danger; a screen or shelter; a means of protection and safety.

Bunch: Things tied together; a collection.

Bunches of camels: Humps on a camel's back.

Burning: An inflaming illness; living flesh that burns, having a white bright spot on the skin.

Burnished: Metal brightly polished and made shiny.

Bushel: A container; anything that may hide or cover, so hindering light and usefulness; used to measure grain, about 2 gallons.

Busybody: One who meddles or gets involved in other people's business and concerns.

Butler: A servant in charge of wine; a cupbearer.

Butlership: The office of a cupbearer.

Buttocks: A person's bottom; the rear end.

By and by: To do at once; to be immediately done.

By: Against; next to someone.

Byway: Curved, winding, bending paths or side roads.

Byword: Words or expressions, showing something/one to be of no worth or substance.

Cab: About 1.36 to 2 quarts.

Cabin: An arched small room: or, a dungeon, like a prison.

Calamity: Having very serious damage done to something; a horrible tragedy.

Calamus: A reed or cane, for producing sacred oil or perfume.

Caldron: A pan; a kettle; a pot.

Calkers: One who mends the seams on a vessel.

Calve: The act of an animal giving birth to a calf.

Camphire: A plant of white or yellow blossoms, giving a sweet-smelling scent.

Candlestick: A lamp stand that holds a candle.

Canker: A slow dying of something; rotting; being consumed away slowly.

Cankerworm: A licking, hopping locust.

Captain: Chief or head; a prince or leader over others.

Carbuncle: A deep red gemstone; a precious stone, flashing in color.

Carcase: A slain or slaughtered body.

Careful: Full of cares; watchful; being troubled about many things: or, being careful with all care.

Careless: Free from concerns; falsely secure and being at peace.

Carnal: Fleshly; refers to the fallen human nature of the body.

Carpenter: A worker in wood, stone, iron, and copper.

Carriage: Carrying luggage or some load; or carrying people.

Case: An event that happens to an individual.

Casement: A lattice; a window made of window panes, placed in front of a window, and opens out, hinged on one side.

Cassia: A spice to make anointing oil.

Cast a mount: To build a fort or buckler against someone; a raised defense.

Cast about: To turn round; to turn back.

Cast angle: To fish with a pole or hook and line.

Cast in the teeth: To insult or scorn someone in their face.

Cast: Something worn-out; aged.

Cast: To throw, toss or to send: or, to sow seed; to scatter seed: or, to drive or push by violence: or, to shed or throw off: or, to throw away, as worthless: or, to dig, raise, or form: or, to cast down, to throw down, to deject or depress the mind: or, to form into a particular shape.

Castaway: Seen as unworthy by others; rejected of others.

Castle: A military fortress; a tower.

Castor: A god of Greek mythology, one of the twin sons of Jupiter, has supposed power to save men in danger at sea.

Caul: The fatty lobe attached above the liver: or, embroidered work; netting worn by a woman to set hair in.

Causeless: Without just grounds, reason or motive; as causeless hatred; causeless fear.

Causeway: A dry raised walkway, over wet or marshy ground: or, a raised way, an ascent by steps.

Celestial: In the heavens above; the idea of superior brilliance, delight, and purity.

Cellar: A room that supplies wine and oil.

Censer: An instrument used for burning incense.

Centurion: A commanding officer of a hundred men.

Certify: Making something set, established, or sure.

Chafed: To be upset or angry because of irritation.

Chaff: The refused part of winnowed corn; dried out grass or hay.

Chalcedony: A quartz-type of stone, milky or grayish in color.

Chalkstones: Pieces of chalk; limestone pieces.

Chamber: A small room for visitors, with a vaulted-ceiling.

Chambering: Sexual immorality with wantonness; lewdness and sin inside a bedroom.

Chamberlain: A steward and assistant over a stately bedchamber: or, any particular officer or attendant to the king.

Chamois: Like a wild goat, deer, or antelope.

Champaign: A flat dry land, usually with few trees; a level countryside.

Chancellor: One who has legal power; a governor for the king.

Changeable: Can be changed; having changes of dress, being a sign of wealth.

Channel: The bottom of the sea or river.

Chant: Singing of hymns or psalms.

Chapiter: The upper part of a column; the top of a pillar.

Chapmen: Merchantmen; buying and selling of goods.

Chapt: Cleft; opened; cracked.

Charge: To command: or, to give confidence to someone; to build up.

Chargeable: Burdensome; to be troublesome.

Charged: Burdened; to be weighed down.

Charger: A large dish; a platter.

Chariot: A vehicle for battle and other purposes.

Charity: The sacrificing love of Christ that a Christian has toward God; a Christ like disposition of heart that inclines one Christian to think favorably on another.

Charmed: Controlled or restrained by a charmer.

Charmer: A magician using tricks by the means of devils, to influence, control, and persuade people.

Chaste: Untouched; living an undefiled life as a virgin.

Chasten: To apply suffering, discipline or corrective punishment for the use of moral cleansing: or, to discipline; to educate; to instruct.

Chastise: A father punishing and shaping his child in love, to a preferred end.

Chatter: Making repeated sounds, like a bird.

Check: A charge; rebuke; to scold someone with reproach.

Chemarims: Idolatrous priests.

Chemosh: A deity worshipped by the Moabites and Ammonites.

Cherub, (s): A kind of heavenly being having wings, who is a servant to God.

Chesnut: Chestnut; or plane tree.

Chide: To contend with; to struggle and resist someone: or, to rebuke harshly, with scolding noises of irritation.

Chief: The first or most outstanding person of a group.

Chisleu: Ninth month in the Hebrew calendar; our November-December.

Chode: Complained, (past tense of chide).

Choler: Anger; hostility.

Christ: Anointed One; Jesus the Christ.

Christian: A person who belongs to Jesus Christ.

Chrysolite: A brilliant yellow precious stone.

Chrysoprasus: A stone of an apple green color.

Church: An assembly of people severing God.

Churl: A rude, deceitful person; a man of the lowest class of people.

Churlish: A mean; stubborn; ill-tempered person.

Churning: Turning; the work of churning milk, to create butter.

Cieled: To overlay something; to panel a wall; to cover a wall on the inside.

Circuit: To go around in a circle; a roundabout type of travel.

Circumcision of Christ, (the heart): Made without hands; cutting away of sin.

Circumcision: Cutting around or cutting off the foreskin.

Circumspect, (be): Pay attention to; give strict consideration.

Cistern: A pit; a well dug in the ground.

Clad: An outer wrap-around piece of clothing, similar to a cloke.

Clamour: An outcry; an objection with the crying of dissatisfaction.

Clave: To split; to break through; tear, (past tense of cleave).

Claw: The cloven hoof of an ox, sheep, or goat.

Cleanness of teeth: A famine from anything.

Cleave: To attach close to; adhere to; joining together: or, to cut open; to separate.

Cleft: Something split.

Clemency: Mercy; a state of being mild and compassionate.

Cliff: The steep face of a mountain.

Clift: An opening; a gap.

Clods: Two or more solid chunks of earth.

Cloke: Raiment; a loose-fitting robe, worn as an outer-piece of clothing, over other clothing.

Closet: A private, secret room where the bride prays.

Clouted: Patched.

Clouts: Parts of clothing used for patches; old rotten rags for mending.

Cloven: Separated; divided into two.

Cluster: A collected group of like things.

Coast: A county or an area of land: or, the border of a body of water; the shoreline: or, the border of the land.

Cock: A male native bird.

Cockatrice: A deadly viper; a serpent.

Cockle: A weed similar to wheat.

Coffer: A small box alongside the Ark of the Covenant.

Cogitations: Turning thoughts.

Collops: Lumps of fatty flesh.

Colour: Figuratively, a cover up for the actual reason or motive; a false appearance.

Comely: Beauty; becoming; appropriate.

Commend: To entrust; to give into the hand of another for secure keeping.

Commission: Giving orders to someone, and sending them away to fulfill it.

Commit: The trusting action of joining something together with another thing.

Commodious: Being suitable and useful.

Common: Being equally bound or owned, by two or more people: or, universal; belonging to all: or, something/one lower in rank or estimation: or, a picture of uncleanness.

Commonwealth: A common state of happiness and wealth, with a body of people.

Commotions: Civil uprisings, with strong emotional turnings.

Commune: Having views and feelings the same as others.

Communicate: To share or have things in common.

Communion: Friendship with God.

Companied: Accompany; being friendly in the company of others.

Compass, (fetch a): Go round about; encircle around something.

Compass: To border around something; make a circuit; surround.

Compel: To drive or urge someone with authority or things that are appealing; to constrain; to require; to demand, either by physical or moral force.

Complete: Having no need; to be overflowing; being full to the top; to stand perfect and whole, wanting nothing.

Composition: The act of putting together; forming a whole by placing together and uniting different things, parts, or ingredients.

Conceal: To cover by hanging something in front of the object hidden.

Conceit: An opinion; a conception, relating to vanity, as thoughts or plans.

Concision: A cutting off; a fake circumcision; a disfigurement.

Concluded: Shut together; to enclosed; included.

Concord: In harmony; companionship; communion; spiritual union.

Concourse: A gathering; a crowd of people assembled.

Concubine: A secondary or less important wife.

Concupiscence: Irregular lustful desires; strong carnal passions, especially of a sexual nature.

Condemn: A legal expression, someone is established as guilty; someone not honorable.

Condescend: Jesus stooped down, and with his finger wrote on the ground.

Conduit: A waterway or channel; a pipe.

Coney: Rabbit like, a hyrax; a rock badger that lives in stony places.

Confectionaries: Ointment or perfumers: or, cooks and bakers of sweet meats.

Confederacy: At peace with another, by making an agreement, a league, or union.

Confer: To have a discussion; to talk together. .

Conformable: To be fashioned or shaped in a like or similar disposition as someone else.

Confound: The action of mixing things together, so that the elements cannot be well known: or, to ruin or overthrow; to put or cast down: or, to throw the mind into disorder; to make ashamed, to perplex with terror, to terrify, to dismay, to astonish.

Confusion: A state of disorder and tumult, having shame and being confounded, overthrown, defeated, and ruined.

Congeal: Frozen or becoming solid as one.

Conquer: To subdue opposition or resistance of the will by moral force; to overcome by argument, persuasion or other influence.

Conscience: Internal or self-knowledge, to make judgments of right and wrong, by power or principle within us.

Consecrate: To regard as set apart; separated for holy purposes.

Consent: An agreement in feelings and opinions with others.

Consist: Standing together, being firm, and solid.

Consolation: The act or state of being greatly comforted.

Consort: To associate; to unite in company; to keep company.

Conspiracy: Plotting together for evil purposes.

Constantly: Standing firm; strong in mind.

Constrain: To compel someone to do something: or, drawing something tightly together.

Consult: Gathering together with others for making a decision and to take advice.

Consume: To devour; completely using up something.

Consummation: The end or conclusion of the present system of things.

Consumption: A wasting away; a disease causing decay and destruction of the body.

Contemn: To despise with mockery and scorn: or, to hold someone in contempt.

Contempt: The act of disgracing, scorning, or despising someone.

Contemptible: Disgraceful; worthy of nothing.

Contend: To be in distress, when interfering with others: or, struggling strongly with someone for control.

Content: To be satisfied so as to have no complaint.

Contentious: Loving to quarrel; being fond of strife and division.

Contrary: Being in opposition or striving against someone.

Contrite: A heart that is crushed and ground into powder: or, broken and bruised in spirit.

Controversy: A mental-emotional turning of one person against another, or against a group, causing contention and dispute.

Convenient: Being proper; appropriate; suitable.

Conversant: Being familiar with others; living or spending much time in a certain place with others.

Conversation: One's conduct; manner of life, behavior or lifestyle.

Convert: To change the heart and moral character; God alone turns the heart around, or changes man's character or nature.

Convey: To carry; to move, bear or transport.

Convicted: Proved or determined to be guilty, either by the verdict of a jury or by the decision of conscience.

Convince: To persuade or satisfy the mind by evidence; to subdue the mind of the opposition to truth: or, to convict; to prove guilty; to constrain a person to admit or acknowledge himself to be guilty.

Convocation: A calling together; an assembly of people.

Coping: The very top level of brickwork on a wall.

Copulation: The condition of being joined together in sexual union.

Cor: A measure of 53 to 55 gallons.

Coral: The red coral being esteemed the most precious; was used for ornamental purposes.

Corban: A gift or offering to God.

Coriander: A plant with small round white spicy seeds, the leaves and seeds are used for cooking and medicine.

Cormorant: A large sea raven.

Corn floor: The threshing floor for corn.

Corn: A general term for grain, mostly wheat.

Cornet: A wind instrument; horn; trumpet.

Corpse: A dead body being human or animal, killed or eaten with violence.

Corrupt: Being completely destroyed from its state of purity.

Cote: A livestock shed; a shed where a group of animals rest.

Couch: A bed; a place for rest or sleep.

Couched: To hide; to lie down in secret or in ambush.

Couching: To stoop under a burden; to bend the body or back in labor.

Couchingplace: A stable where animals lie down together.

Coulter: An iron blade, being part of a plough.

Countenance: A person's appearance; the face, showing the attitude or state of mind.

Countervail: To be made equal; to counterbalance; to compensate for something.

Coupling: That which connects together; uniting in couples; fastening or embracing.

Course, (by): In portion; in part; in turn.

Cousin: Kinsman, kinswoman.

Covenant: An agreement between two persons or parties; usually an agreement involving God.

Covert: A cover; a shelter: or, a carefully planned hiding place.

Covet: To long after; actively try to gain; related to lust and idolatry.

Cracknel: A small dry cake; a cracker.

Crafty: Being skillful in devising and executing underhanded, evil schemes.

Crag: The rough, broken projecting part of a rock.

Crane: Like a stork or heron.

Creature: A created thing.

Creditor: A person who is owed money to, by a borrower.

Crew: The past-tense action of the cry of a rooster.

Crib: A place where cattle are fattened.

Crimson: A deep red color.

Crisping pins: Small curling rods for the hair.

Crookbackt: Having a twisted back; a hunchback or humpback.

Crop: To pluck or break off.

Cruse: A small jar or cup for water or oil.

Crystal: It is a stone of the flint kind, the most refined kind of quartz.

Cubit: Of a man (ordinary cubit), Old Testament length from elbow to fingertip 17.5 inches: A royal cubit, ordinary cubit plus a hand- breadth 20.5 inches: New Testament length 18 inches.

Cuckow: A gull; any bird of the genus Cuculus known for its coo-cooing sounds.

Cud: A portion of newly eaten food, brought up from the first stomach of an animal, to be chewed on and digested.

Cumbered: To be distracted with cares, and unable to think clearly.

Cumbereth: To make useless; to make vain and waste, causing great trouble and distress.

Cumbrance: That which makes motion or action difficult and toilsome.

Cummin: A seed like fennel, bearing aromatic seeds; for medicine and cooking.

Cunning: Being learned; having the ability, knowledge, and wisdom to do things skillfully: or, being crafty in a deceitful way.

Cunningly: Artfully; craftily; being divisive with subtly; using well-planned stories.

Curdled: The past-tense action of turning milk into cheese.

Curious arts: Divination; witchcraft; magic; all are forbidden by God.

Curious: Being made with great care and diligence to fine detail and workmanship.

Current: Money that is in use, in a certain place and time.

Curse: God disapproving someone; invoking or calling down destruction on someone/thing.

Custom: A tax; tribute or toll, forced by the Romans.

Cut in sunder: To cut into pieces.

Cutting: An idolatrous practice; part of idol-worship.

Cypress: A cone-bearing evergreen tree.

Dagon: The main idol of the Philistines.

Dainty meats: A picture of the fruits of the wicked.

Dale: A low place between hills; a vale or valley.

Dam: A mother of birds or animals.

Damnation: Receiving damnation after being condemned from a judgment passed; the process or condition of being damned and receiving punishment.

Damned: Being condemned; being judged and condemned as guilty.

Damsel: A young girl of a marrying age; a servant.

Dandled: To be soothed; to be caressed; to fondle.

Darkness over the land: An eclipse, a token of God's anger.

Darling: Only one beloved; singular affection to someone.

Dart: An instrument of war; a light spear.

Dash: To strike violently, and break something in pieces.

Daub: To cover or plaster something.

Days journey: 1 day-24 miles or 42,000 paces or 127,000 feet.

Daysman: A judge; a moderator; bringing two together as a mediator.

Dayspring: The beginning of a new thing: or, the dawn of the morning; at daybreak.

Daystar: The appearance of Christ in the soul, imparting spiritual light and comfort.

Deacon: Servant or attendant; one who serves or waits on others.

Dearth: The cutting off of rain, causing a famine; making things limited, and costly.

Debase: To degrade, reduce or lower in quality, purity, or value; to pollute.

Debtor: Someone who owes something to another.

Deceit: Something that is deceptive or purposely misleading.

Deceive: Trapping someone by getting them to believe what is false.

Decision: The act of making a choice by cutting; to cut away and separate between two things.

Deck: To adorn; to array with clothing: or, to provide or furnish: or, to over spread with something; to cover something.

Declare: Taking something obscure, and making it very clear, plain, or obvious.

Decline: To leave the path of truth or justice, or the course given, and then to move away; to avoid or shun; to refuse; not to comply with something.

Decree: An official decision or declaration such as a law.

Decrees of God: His eternal, sovereign, unchangeable, holy, and wise purposes.

Deemed: Thought; believe; judged; supposed; has formed an opinion.

Deep: Being hidden or secret; being distant from understanding: or, to be still; sound; not easily broken or disturbed: or, to be unknown; unintelligible: or, something being thick, black, not to be entered by sight: or, meaning the grave or the abyss.

Defame: To slander; to speak evil of someone; getting a bad name by a false report.

Defer: To delay; to put off; to set aside.

Defied: Putting away your trust and hope in someone.

Defile: Angrily polluting something by smashing it, and grinding it to powder.

Defraud: Taking someone's goods, in a deceitful way.

Degenerate: Having fallen from a desirable state.

Degrees, (song of): A song of steps; journeying closer towards the temple in steps.

Delectable: An attractive and desirable idol-god, which is valued, and prized highly by its maker.

Delicacies: A handful of small, expensive, enchanting items.

Delicately: Doing something tenderly and in a fragile manner, with polite regard to propriety and the feelings of others: or, with elegance and luxury.

Delicates: Someone given over to a life of luxury, (kings, princes, and nobles).

Deliciously: Living in a manner to please the taste and gratify the mind.

Delusion: The act or fact of deceiving someone while pretending to be honest with them.

Demand: The action of urgent asking, with proper authority.

Den: A place where wild beasts or harmful creatures live: or, a cave to be inhabited for a time.

Denounce: To make known or announce publicly that someone is evil.

Deny: The action of refusing completely.

Deposed: The past-tense action of laying or putting someone down, (like a king down from his throne).

Deprived: The past-tense action of totally releasing or taking something/one from someone.

Deputed: A man having been separated and set aside for a special purpose.

Deputy: One set up over others; an officer in legal and financial affairs.

Deride: Putting someone down by scoffing and scorning at them.

Derision: To laugh at; to mock at the enemies' threats.

Describe: The action of writing down words: or, to divide; to mark out.

Descry: To spy out; discovering an enemies position by observing it and revealing it.

Desert: A wilderness, a place of utter abandonment and barrenness.

Deserts: Recompense or reward, for something earned.

Deserve: To be worthy of; to merit by an evil act, as to deserve blame or punishment.

Desired: What you wished for, coveted, requested, or entreated.

Desolate: Being utterly alone or forsaken.

Despair: The state of mind where there is no hope, and nothing to look forward to.

Despise: To have contempt and look down upon someone with scorn and think of them as worthless.

Despite: An act of malice or contempt; to trodden under foot, with violent hatred.

Destitute: Being abandoned, deserted, or put away from other people.

Destroy: The willful undoing of the building process, as in pulling down something/one.

Destroyer, (the): A destroying angel of God.

Destruction: Eternal death; to be murdered, slaughtered, and to have ruin eternally: or, the cause of destruction is a consuming plague or a destroyer.

Detain: Holding someone back from where they were intending to go.

Determine: To resolve; to conclude; to come to a decision: or, to fix on; to settle or to establish: or, to end or settle a point in the mind.

Detest: To utterly abhor; to hate extremely.

Device: That which is a carefully prepared plan and formed by design or invented; a scheme.

Devil, (hath a): To say that a person is crazy or insane.

Devil: The slanderer; the father of lies; the false accuser.

Devise: To invent; to arrange and set up; to form in the mind by new combinations of ideas, new applications of principles, or new arrangement of parts.

Devote: To take something for one's own use by vow; to set apart or dedicate by a solemn act; to consecrate.

Devotions: Two or more religious affections that have been devoted to Jesus.

Devour: Eating up eagerly like a beast, in a reckless greedy way.

Devout: Being devoted or given over, to divine worship and service of Jesus Christ.

Dew: Moisture that has condensed out of the sky; a symbol of blessing.

Diadem: A band or wreath bound across the forehead, worn as a sign of royalty or dignity.

Dial, (sun): For the measurement of time by the sun, shining down on a dial placed on the ground.

Diamond: A gem of crystallized carbon, the most valued, and brilliant of precious stones, remarkable for its hardness.

Die the death: Meaning, to surely die.

Diet: A daily allowance of food and water.

Dignities: Two or more people of noble standing or high position in life.

Dignity: The quality of being worthy, noble or excellent.

Diligence: To give constant effort to accomplish what is undertaken; to care; to heed.

Diligent: Giving strict and careful attention to do something right.

Diligently: Being done in a very careful and attentive manner.

Dim: Being dark or obscure; the eyes see things darkly and not clear, because of having dim, heavy eyes.

Diminish: To lessen; thoroughly making something smaller.

Dine: To furnish with the main meal.

Dirt: Something foul and worthless, such as mire or dung.

Disallowed: Disapproved; rejected; not granted, permitted or admitted.

Disannul: To condemn a vow; to turn back; to utterly reduce something into nothing, like putting it out of existence.

Discern: To wholly separate and distinguish between things or people.

Discharge: The action of unloading, (wagon, ship, or animal): or, to be relieved or delivered, of a duty or debt or a benefit, and possibly has been retained before.

Disciple: One who learns by careful consideration and study; a follower and learner of Christ.

Discomfited: To be scatter, defeated, confused: or, having been destroyed or ripped apart.

Discontent: Being uneasy and dissatisfied.

Discord: When people's hearts are turned from each other, in anger and disagreement, or misunderstanding.

Discover: To uncover or reveal something that has been earnestly covered up.

Discovered: Uncover; to come into view of something.

Discreet: Showing wise discernment in picking and choosing ones words and actions.

Discretion: The ability to make decisions of right and wrong.

Disdain: To look upon or consider someone to be unworthy of notice, care, regard, or esteem.

Disgrace: To bring to shame; to dishonor.

Disguise: To put on other raiment from one's normal clothes, so that no eye shall perceive or known.

Disinherit: Reversing the process of making someone an heir.

Dismayed: Having had one's ability to perform, broken down, or destroyed.

Disobedience: Not listening nor submitting to instructions.

Dispatch: The action of cutting loose and sending off.

Dispensation: God's affairs towards men: or, having stewardship and to distribute affairs; the operation or function of managing a person's affairs.

Disperse: To scatter all around in different directions; to scatter abroad.

Displease: To be vexed, irritated and provoked; it usually expresses less than anger; applied to God, it is the same as anger.

Disposing: The act of arranging, ruling, directing; to put something where it belongs.

Disposition: Administration; method; arrangement; by the ministry (disposition) of angels; the condition of things having been put where they belong.

Dispossess: To remove someone from their property, (take away their ownership).

Disputation: The act of disputing; to reason or oppose in disagreement to something.

Dispute: The action of pulling something into pieces and considering all the parts.

Disquiet: The act to destroy the calm of something; to make uneasy or restless; to disturb and irritate the body; to fret or vex the mind.

Dissemblers: Pretenders; hypocrites, hiding their true plans and character, causing separation.

Dissension: Thinking and feeling different in a very emotional way with others, causing disagreement in opinion, usually a disagreement which is violent, producing warm debates or angry words.

Dissimulation: The act of dissembling; concealing true thoughts and intentions by falsehood and hypocrisy.

Distaff: A rod to hold wool for hand spinning clothing.

Distil: The action of dripping away from; to drop; to fall in drops.

Divers: Differing, in a plural number; unequal; assorted: or, two or more persons that are different in character or quality from other people.

Diverse: Different; in a singular number.

Divination: The act of divining and foretelling future events by the means of devils; or discovering things secret or obscure, by other than human means.

Divine, (to): To use or practice divination and magic to interpret dreams and visions, by the means of devils.

Divine: Pertaining to the true God, as the divine nature; divine perfections.

Do to wit: To make known.

Doctor: A well-studied teacher who gives instruction in some area of knowledge.

Doctrine: A lesson or group of lessons that are taught.

Dog: A term of reproach and shame; an unclean animal; the character of a wicked person or fool; a whore of sodomy.

Doleful: Howling; shrieking; having grief and sorrow.

Dominion: Being over something/one; governing control over things.

Dote: To speak or act foolishly, out of weakness.

Doth: To do; to produce; to make.

Doting: To appear to be ill or sick with excessive fondness over something.

Doubletongued: Saying two things that are not agreeable with each other.

Doubt: The action of hesitation and wavering in opinion.

Dove's dung: Some sort of lentil or vegetable or parched pulse.

Dowry: The price paid for a wife, and in addition some wealth or service given.

Drag: A net-like device attached to ropes, to catch or collect fish.

Dragon: A large snake; sea serpent or whale: or, a jackal.

Drams: Gold or silver coins, a ⅛ part of an ounce or the amount of coins that can be held in one hand.

Draught: A catch of food or prey, from hunting or fishing: or, the latrine; the outhouse; a public toilet: or, a drain or sewer.

Drave: To send something with a reasonable, driving force.

Dread: Fearing greatly, with terror and awe.

Dregs: Sediment; any foreign matter from liquors that go to the bottom of a vessel, and is waste or worthless: or, a picture of God's fury.

Dress: Arranging and setting in order food or sacrifice.

Dromedary: A camel or horse.

Dropsy: A disease that causes massive build up of fluids within the body.

Dross: Waste formed and separated by melting metal; any worthless thing separated from the better part.

Drove: A large number of animals, driven as one large group.

Drowsiness: The condition of heavy sluggishness.

Drunkard: A person who normally or frequently is drunk.

Dryshod: Having dry shoes and feet.

Due: Things that are owed to other people.

Duke: A head of a family or tribe or country.

Dulcimer: Musical instrument made with strings over an open box, and played like a guitar.

Dull: Being slow in understanding, thinking, or teachings.

Dumb: Unable or unwilling to speak.

Dung: Used as fertilizer: or, to be cast out as dung is a figurative expression, meaning to be rejected as unprofitable and worthless.

Dungeon: Harsher than a prison; a deep cell or container.

Dunghill: A shameful or foul dwelling place; to sit on a dunghill is a sign of the deepest dejection.

Dureth: To endure; to last; going on in action.

Durst: The past action of dare; to take action in a presuming daring way; having the heart filled with courage and strength, to take on something.

Dwarf: A withered looking person or a person short in size.

Each: Individual.

Ear: The spike or head-part of a cereal plant, as wheat or barley: or, to work, till, or plow the ground.

Earing: The plowing of a field into long open rows.

Earnest: A down payment; a pledge or token given as the guarantee of the fulfillment of an agreement or promise.

Earring: A jewel worn in the ear.

Ease: Spiritual slothfulness and decay.

East: The rising of the sun, from the view of Israel.

Easter: A pagan goddess; a springtime celebration to a fertility goddess: or, remembering our Saviour's resurrection.

Ebenezer: Meaning, hitherto hath the LORD helped us.

Eden: Meaning, pleasure or delight.

Edify: To create; build up or establish, another's spiritual well-being.

Edst, (ending on words): The second person, the one spoken to.

Effect: The thing accomplished or produced by some cause.

Effectual: Producing a planned or proposed effect; having enough power or force to produce the effect.

Effeminate: A man acting like a woman; unmanly; causing confusion to children.

Elder: An older spiritual companion: or, someone older; greater in age.

Elect: Having been chosen or picked out of a group.

Elements: First principles or building blocks of this universe.

Elias: Elijah.

Eliseus: Elisha.

Eloquent: Speaking well, in a fluent, strong convincing way.

Elul: Sixth month in the Hebrew calendar; our August-September.

Embalm: The process of preserving a body by means of balm and spices.

Embolden: To have added courage and being bold.

Embrace: Taking one up in your arms: or, to receive; to admit; to find; to take; to accept: or, to seize eagerly; to lay hold on.

Embroider: A maker of sacred robes, with fancy stitching.

Emerald: A transparent precious gemstone, with deep green color.

Emerods: Tumors; hemorrhoids; a swollen blood vessel, causing pain.

Eminent: Famous; something/one that is raised up high.

Emmanuel: Meaning, God with us.

Emulation: Having jealousy in envying someone; an attempt to equal or excel others in that which is praise-worthy, without the desire of depressing others.

Encamp: For a defense around something: or, to set up a resting place when traveling.

Enchantment: Secret arts; tricks of deceit, by the means of devils.

Encourage: To add strength of heart to someone; a lifting up.

Endamage: To cause injury or damage to someone: or, to cause or suffer loss.

Endeavour: Putting yourself in action to accomplish something.

Endow: The act of providing a payment, (see dowry).

Endued: To give someone a quality or ability: or, having brought or lead something to someone.

Engines: Battering rams; machines; inventions that are skillfully made into weapons.

Engrafted: Imparting or implanting a word in union with someone and it becomes natural, being firmly establish.

Engrave: To use carving or digging, to write names or make pictures in wood or stone.

Enjoin: A charge to put something in action; to join two things together.

Enlargement: The product of making something more abundant or bigger: or, having freedom or relief.

Enmity: An enemy; the hostility or hatred of two parties.

Enquire: Looking into or asking a question about a topic.

Ensample: A sample that can be internalized through specific personal knowledge of the object looked at.

Ensign: A banner or sign, as a memorial borne by an officer at the head of a company, troop, or other band; any signal to a troop to assemble or to give a notice.

Ensue: To seek and follow after and overtake.

Enterprise: Purposes and plans; a work or project, in hand to finish.

Entertain: Public feasts; festivals: or, the act or thought of supporting, preserving or maintaining a thing.

Entice: One's passions are given life; to tempt; to incite; to urge or lead astray; to seduce; to persuade to sin, by promises or persuasions.

Entreat: To treat; to use: or, to make an earnest petition or request.

Entreaties: Pleadings; making humble requests.

Envious: Feeling or showing envy; feeling uneasiness at a view of the excellence, prosperity, or happiness of another.

Environ: To surround; to encompass around.

Envy: The act of looking against someone with hatred and ill will, because of greed or resentment.

Ephah: About 8 gallons.

Ephod: A high priest embroidered cape, worn over their other clothing.

Epistle: A letter written and sent by an apostle of Jesus Christ, in the first 95 years of the New Testament church.

Equity: Uprightness, righteousness, and fairness, in a moral or legal sense.

Ere: Before; or until.

Err: To stray or wander away, from uprightness and truth.

Errand: An oral message; a mandate or order; something to be told or done.

Error: A transgression of the law, by vain and foolish mistakes.

Esaias: Isaiah.

Eschew: To avoid; to shun; to turn aside from.

Especially: Something happening in a particular way; principally; chiefly; in an uncommon way or measure.

Espoused: To be asked and promised in marriage; a time of betrothal.

Espy: To see or view from a distance, and to examine and make secret observations.

Est, (ending on words): The second person, the one spoken to.

Estate: The position or station of something; how or where a thing lives.

Estates: The chief estates, meaning, great men: or, estate of the elders, meaning, holding office as elders.

Esteem: The act of putting a moral value on a thing.

Estimate: The act of setting a financial value on a thing.

Estranged: To be a stranger or outsider.

Eth, (ending on words): The third person, the one spoken about.

Ethanim: Seventh month in the Hebrew calendar; our September-October.

Eunuch: A castrated man trusted to work in the king's court.

Euroclydon: A furious, northeasterly wind.

Evangelist: A messenger of the gospel of Jesus Christ.

Eve: Meaning, "living".

Even: Evening: or, the word "even" is positioned in-between two words that have the same meaning, as a comparison.

Eveningtide: Evening time at the end of the day, when shadows lengthen, until after the sun sets and there is no more light.

Eventide: Evening time when the sun is just setting.

Evermore: Always; at all times; having no end of time.

Every several: Each one separately.

Every whit: The whole of something; all of a thing.

Evidently: Plainly; clearly.

Evil eye: Figuratively, the envious or covetous person.

Evil: The Devil; everything not agreeable to God.

Evilfavouredness: Having a blemish; ugliness; having a deformity.

Ewe: A female sheep.

Exact: Using force to get something out of a thing.

Exactor: An overseer; a tax collector.

Example: An outward sample, (see ensample).

Exchanger: A moneychanger or banker.

Exclude: To thrust out or eject.

Execration: A curse declared; the act of cursing.

Execute: To perform a work, duty, or judgment, and pursue it to the end.

Executioner: One who carries into effect a judgment of death.

Exempt: Being free or not liable to any service, charge, or burden.

Exercised: Made familiar with something by applying, training, and disciplining yourself; becoming skilled in God's precepts by use.

Exhortation: Giving encouragement; counsel.

Exile: Banishment; the state of being expelled from one's native country.

Exorcist: Casting out devils without Christ.

Expecting: Waiting.

Expedient: To quickly promote an object or plan that is suitable for a purpose.

Expel: To drive or force out from any enclosed place.

Experiment: Proving; a trial; an act or operation designed to discover some unknown truth.

Expire: To come to an end; to cease; to terminate; to close or conclude.

Exploit: Brave and strong achievements, done in an honorable way.

Expound: To set forth; to declare and open something.

Extinct: Being at an end; having ceased a family or race.

Extol: To lift up; to esteem; the highest praise to God.

Extortioner: A greedy, ravenous person; a stranger who takes from another by strife, greed, and oppression that which does not lawfully belong to him.

Extremity: The utmost point; the highest or furthest degree.

Eyesalve: Ointment for the eyes, as to open the eyes to see salvation.

Eyeservice: Doing good work or service, only while being watched.

Ezekias: Hezekiah.

Fable: Cunningly devised traditions and speculations; an idle story of fiction.

Fain: To be glad or pleased to do something under some kind of necessity: or, to desire earnestly; to long for; to fix the mind or desire on.

Fairs: Wares; something received or purchased, referring to exports.

Fallow ground: Figuratively, evil habits in the heart.

Fallow: Pale; pale yellow; yellowish red or brown: or, uncultivated; untilled land.

Familiar spirit: An evil spirit, used by sorcerers and necromancers; a devil in them or under the power of them.

Familiars: Intimate friends.

Famished: To have suffered hunger of any kind.

Fan: An agricultural tool; a winnowing shovel to divide the chaff from the wheat.

Fanners: Winnowers; people who are like a destroying wind, to scatter and separate their enemies out of their dwellings, as wheat and chaff are separated.

Fare: To be in any state or condition in life, good or bad.

Farthing: A small coin of little worth, about ¼ of $0.01.

Fast: Abstaining from something for a short time: or, being firm and immovable: or, firmly being close to something.

Fat: Dull; heavy; stupid; unable to teach: or, rich; fertile, as fat soil: or, abounding in spiritual grace and comfort: or, the best or richest part of a thing: or, vulgar; gross: or, rich; wealthy.

Fathom: About 6-7 feet, the utmost extent of both arms when stretched out.

Fatling: A young animal fattened for slaughter.

Fats: A large vessel, tub, or vat; a cistern used for various purposes.

Feeble minded: Weak minded; carried about with every wind of doctrine.

Feign: Deceitful; false: or, to devise in one's mind; imagine a false thing: or, to pretend; disguise a false thing.

Fell: To chop down.

Feller: One who cuts or knocks down trees; a tree surgeon.

Felloe: The outside rim of a wheel.

Fenced: Being protected; enclosed with a fence; guarded; fortified.

Fens: Marshes; swamps.

Fervent: Earnest; intense; excited in action, thoughts, or plans.

Fetched a compass: To travel around something in a circuit; wandered up and down; to go around about something.

Fetters: Bonds; chains; shackles; metal bands that confines or restrains someone from moving.

Fidelity: Faithfulness; careful and exact performance of duty, or performance of obligations.

File: A grindstone to sharpen metals or iron.

Fillet: Ornamental silver threads encircling the top of the pillars of the temple.

Filleted: Ornamented with silver threads.

Fillets: Curtain rods placed between the columns of the temple.

Finger's breadth: About ¾ inch.

Fining, finer: Clarifying; refining or purifying something, with fire to remove dross or with God's chastising love to remove the lust of the flesh, and the lust of the eyes, and the pride of life.

Firebrand: A torch; a piece of wood kindled or on fire; a picture of someone who causes contention and mischief.

Firkin: About 9 gallons.

Firmament: The heavens; the sky.

Firstling: First offspring; the first one born.

Fitch: A poor quality of wheat: or, an aromatic seeded plant; fennel.

Fitly: Suitably; properly; well placed; the appropriate time.

Flag: A type of marshy grass; reeds; weeds.

Flagon: A bottle; a vessel to carry liquid in.

Flakes: Folds of flesh, muscles, or scales.

Flank: The fleshy or muscular part of the side of an animal.

Flax: A plant of a single slender stalk, the height of 2 to 3 feet, it has blue flowers and very fibrous stalks; can be used to make linen.

Flay: To skin; to strip off the skin of an animal, as to flay an ox.

Fleece: The wool of sheep, whether shaved off or still attached to the skin.

Flesh: Human nature; carnality; a carnal state; the state of the unrenewed nature of man: or, being one flesh with another, denotes intimate relation: or, an arm of flesh, human strength or aid.

Fleshhook: A hook to draw flesh from a pot or caldron.

Flint: A well-known hard stone, a variety of quartz; for making knives; a picture of hardness.

Floats: A body or collection of timber; boards or planks fastened together and conveyed down a stream.

Flowers: Menstrual flow of blood.

Flux, (a bloody): An intestinal disease; dysentery; pain of the bowels.

Flux: The flow of blood.

Fodder: A mixture of various grains, hay, grass, straw, provender.

Fold: A flock of sheep, one fold and one shepherd: or, an enclosure for flocks to rest.

Folden: Interwoven; something bundled together.

Folk: Certain ones that are different from others; people or animals.

Foot breadth: The sole of a man's foot can measure.

Footman: A foot soldier.

Forasmuch: In consideration that; seeing that; since; because that.

Forbad: Past tense of forbid.

Forbare: Past tense of forbear.

Forbear: To cease; to let alone; to be silent.

Forbearance: Self-restraint.

Forbearing: Having patience; being slow to anger.

Forbore: Past tense of forbear.

Forborn: Ceased from action.

Ford: A place of dry ground in a river that can be walked on and crossed by foot.

Forecast: To scheme; to arrange; to plan before the execution of something.

Foreigner: A Gentile born in a different country other than Israel.

Forepart: The part most advanced, or first in time or in a place.

Forerunner: Someone going before or entering in something before others.

Foresaw: Saw before.

Foresee: To foreknow; to see or know before.

Foreship: The bow or front of a ship.

Forfeit: To be devoted to sacred uses, to be put into the treasury of the temple, and used in the service of it, and therefore never to be returned; something to which the right is lost.

Forge: To form or create, especially by concentrated effort: or, to devise and work plans within yourself.

Fornication: The lewdness of unmarried persons; sexual immorality: or, towards God, it means to forsake him, and turn to following after idols.

Forsaken: To leave in an abandoned condition.

Forsook: To have left in an abandoned condition.

Forswear: To swear falsely under an oath.

Forthwith: Immediately.

Fortify: To surround with a wall, against the enemy; to furnish with strength, or for the means of resisting force, violence or assault: or, to strengthen and fortify the mind against sudden calamity; to fortify an opinion or resolution.

Fortress: Any fortified place; a fort; a castle; a strong hold; a place of defense or security or safety.

Forum: A market place.

Forward, (to be): To wish; to desire; to purpose.

Founder: A person who creates idols by pouring metal or glass in a mould.

Fourscore: Eighty.

Foursquare: Squared; four cornered; the idea of perfect proportions.

Fowler: One who hunts and captures birds.

Fowls: Birds.

Fox: One who is cunning and destructive.

Frame(d): Construction; to manage and form something; fitted together; completed.

Frankincense: An ingredient for the perfume of the sanctuary, and for incense.

Frankly: Liberally; openly; freely; without reserve; without constraint.

Fray: To make afraid; to scare; to cast out; cause to tremble.

Fret: To be grieved; troubled; displeased: or, to gnaw away; to corrode way.

Frontier: At the extreme part of the land, upon the border of the country.

Frontlets: A headband or brow band, worn to keep in mind and in your sight, statutes, and precepts.

Froward: Perverse; deceitful; contrary; self willed.

Fuel: Every combustible matter.

Fuller: A launderer; a person who cleans clothing.

Furbish: To sharpen; to clean and polish metal.

Furlong: 1 mile or 200 paces or 600 feet.

Furniture: Equipment; a harness for horses.

Furrow: A groove in the earth made by a plough.

Gaddest: To have roamed about the land; to go away.

Gainsay: An opposing answer; to speak against; to contradict.

Gall: Anger; bitterness of mind: or, venom or the poison of snakes: or, of a person, the seat of life.

Gallant: Showing splendor; extravagant.

Gallery: A terrace; a projection; a ledge.

Galley: A low flat-built vessel, with one deck, and navigated with sails and oars; used in the Mediterranean.

Gallows: Trees used for the purpose of punishment, to kill someone by hanging.

Gape: To open wide the mouth.

Garlands: The victims of heathen sacrifices were adorned with this.

Garner: A barn; a storehouse; a grain store.

Garnish: To adorn: or, to set in order; to prepare something.

Garrison: A guard; a watchman or a patrol.

Gat: Got.

Gay: Brilliant in colors; splendid; fine; richly dressed.

Gazingstock: Something or someone stared at with contempt and wonder.

Gender: To breed; to beget; to father children: or, to produce; to encourage; to lead.

Genealogy: Pedigree; generation; an account or history of the descent of a person or family from an ancestor.

Generation of: A description of a certain kind of people.

Generation: History; family register.

Gentiles: The people of the world outside of Jesus Christ; the nations and the heathens.

Gerah: A Hebrew coin, $1/20$ of a shekel, $1/50$ ounce.

Ghost, (give up the): Died; expired one's life.

Ghost, Holy: One of three persons of the Godhead.

Ghost: Breath, life, spirit of man.

Giants: Known as men of violence; robbers; tyrants; monsters; Anakims or Emims, men of Ashtaroth and Edrei, Philistines.

Gier eagle: A species of vulture.

Gift: A thank-offering; to secure favor.

Gin: A noose; snare to catch animals; a net; a trap.

Gird: To fasten and secure clothing with a belt or band: or, to equip; to prepare.

Girdle: A band or belt; something drawn around the waist of a person.

Girt: Belted; wrapped.

Gittith: A stringed instrument; a harp.

Give place: Make room for; give way or yield to someone.

Glass: A mirror.

Glean: To gather; to collect what the reapers drop at harvest time.

Glede: Vulture; buzzard.

Glistering: Something sparking brilliantly.

Glutton: Riotous over eaters.

Gnash: To grind the teeth; showing rage or sorrow.

Go to: Come now! Advising; exhorting; stirring up and encouraging.

Goad: A sharp pointed pole to direct cattle; eight feet long, on one end was a sharp prickle for driving the oxen, and at the other end a small spade, or paddle of iron, for cleansing the plough from the clay.

Goblet: A bowl or large cup for drinking or mixing wine.

God speed: May God prosper you; I bid you or wish you good speed.

Goddess: A female heathen deity.

Godhead, (the): The essential being or nature of God.

Godliness: The whole of practical piety.

Godward: One's affection towards God.

Goeth about, going about: The action of attempting; trying.

Good, (proper): A persons goods.

Goodly trees: Probably the olive tree.

Goodly: Fine looking; a beautiful countenance.

Goodman: Husband; householder; master of the house.

Gopher wood: Perhaps wood of cypress; fir; or cedar.

Gore: To pierce with the point of an animal's horn.

Gorgeous: Strikingly beautiful or magnificent.

Gospel: God's news to the world; glad tidings of the word of God.

Gotten: Got; have obtained.

Gourd: A species of castor-oil plant, having very large broad leaves; when cut or injured it withers away quickly.

Governor: A prominent person; chief of the temple.

Grace: The free unmerited love and favor of God, the spring and source of all the benefits men receive from him; God showing kindness; favor; and mercy.

Graff, graffed: Graft; used to show union of two groups; to plant or introduce something foreign into that which is native, for the purpose of development.

Grant: To give; to bestow something on someone without reward, particularly in answer to prayer or request: or, to transfer the title of a thing to another, for a good or valuable consideration.

Graven, (graving): To cut or engrave to make images: or, to carve or cut letters or figures on stone to write a message.

Gravity: Seriousness; the consequence of behavior; dignity in matters of life.

Greaves: A section of defensive armor for the legs.

Grecians: Greek-speaking Jews.

Grieved: To be afflicted; to be suffering in a condition of sorrow.

Grievous: Something that is hard to bear; burdensome.

Grisled: Gray; grayish; sprinkled or mixed with gray; of a mixed white and black.

Gross: Fat; thick: or, horrible and dreadful.

Grove: A wooden image or a pillar set up among trees.

Grudge: To be discontented at another's enjoyments or advantages; to be envious.

Guile: Deceit; craftiness.

Guilty of: Worthy of.

Gutter: Where the outcasts live: or, a watercourse.

Ha, ha: The cry for speed to horses.

Habergeon: A coat of armor; a breastplate.

Haft: The handle of a dagger.

Hail: A greeting of joy and peace.

Hale: To draw; to drag with force.

Half-homer: About 5 ½ bushels.

Hallelujah: Praise the LORD!

Hallowed: Something that is holy; set apart from common.

Halt: Lame; crippled in the feet; to limp; to stop.

Handbreadth or palm: A measure of four fingers, about 3 inches.

Handmaid: A personal servant.

Handstave: Staffs or poles used as weapons.

Hap: To happen; to befall; to come by chance.

Haply: Perhaps; by chance; possibly it should happen.

Hard after: To cleave to; to stick firmly to something/one.

Hard by: Beside; being next to something.

Hard language: Rude taking; speaking words that are unpolished or not understandable.

Hard: Near; close.

Hardly: Doing something with difficulty.

Hare: A rodent of the genus Lepusan; with long ears, like a rabbit but slightly larger.

Harlot: A woman consecrated or devoted to prostitution for abominable worship.

Harness: Defensive armor that covers the body: or, to put necessary gear on horses.

Harnessed: To walk in an orderly manner.

Harrow: A sharp threshing instrument, for leveling and breaking up the lumpy soil, and to cover seed when sown; to break or tear with a harrow.

Hart: A male deer or hind.

Hast: Have.

Haste: To hurry; to urge on quickly.

Hath: Has.

Haughty: Proud; arrogant; a person who lifts up himself with pride.

Haunt: To inhabit; to visit or dwell frequently.

Haven: A harbor; a port; a bay; a safe station or shelter for ships.

Havock: Waste; devastation; wide and general destruction.

Headlong: Head first: or, acting rashly without consideration; or acting hurriedly without delay or relief.

Heady: Reckless; hasty; headstrong.

Hearken: Calling out, to come near and hear.

Hearth: A container made of brick or stone on which a fire is made to warm a room.

Heath: A species of juniper; a picture of parched places in the wilderness.

Heathen: Peoples; the nations; a pagan; a Gentile; one who worships idols, or is unaware of the true God.

Heave offering: Among the Jews, an offering consisting of the tenth of the tithes that the Levites received, or of the first of the dough, which was to be heaved or elevated.

Heaviness: Sadness; sorrow; dejection of mind; depression of spirits.

Hedge: A group of thorn-bushes or other shrubs or small trees; used to obstruct an adversary or surround a house for defense; to enclose for preventing escape.

Heed: To be careful to consider; to mind; to regard with care; to take notice of; to give care; attention.

Heifer: A young cow untrained to the yoke; symbolic for the beautiful woman of Samaria.

Heinous: Something that is hatefully, offensive or sinful; unashamed; odious; giving great offense, applied to deeds or character.

Heir: One who succeeds to the estate of a former owner; one who is entitled to possess: in Scripture, saints are called heirs of the promise, heirs of righteousness, and heirs of salvation.

Hell: The valley of Hinnom; the abode of unsaved souls.

Helm: The instrument by which a ship is steered.

Helve: The handle of an axe.

Hemlock: Gall; poison; venom; a bitter poisonous plant.

Hence: From this place; from this time; in the future; from this cause or reason; from this source or original.

Henceforth: From this time forth; from now on.

Henceforward: From this time forward; henceforth.

Herald: One who makes public proclamations to challenge a battle, to proclaim peace, and to bear messages from the commander of an army.

Herb: Any green plant; vegetables.

Hereafter: In time to come; in some future time.

Hereby: By this.

Herein: In this.

Hereof: Of this; from this.

Heresy: Self-willed, self-chosen doctrines not spoken from God.

Heretick: Heretic; one who chooses wrong beliefs, differing from Scripture; one who causes divisions and internal conflict.

Heretofore: Before; previously.

Hereunto: To here; to this.

Herewith: With this.

Heritage: Allotment; possession; in Scripture, the saints or people of God are called his heritage, as being claimed by him, and the objects of his special care.

Heron: A common large, unclean bird; with an angry character.

Hew: To shape by cutting or chopping.

Higgaion: A musical sign; a pause, interlude; a meditation.

Highminded: Puffed up with pride.

Hin: About 1 to 1.5 gallons.

Hind: A deer; the word speaks of gentleness.

Hinder: Latter; rear; something behind.

Hip and thigh: To be overpowered and utterly overthrow or defeated.

Hireling: A laborer employed on hire for a limited time.

Hiss: The same as wagging the head; to express contempt or to call.

Hither: To this place; here; to this point; to this argument or topic; to this end; nearest; towards the person speaking.

Hitherto: To this time; yet; in any time, or every time until now; in the time preceding the present; to this place; to a prescribed limit.

Ho: A call for attention.

Hoary: White colored; frosty white showing old age.

Hoised: To lift up; to rise up.

Hold to: Cleave to; cling to something.

Hold: A fortified place; a fort; a castle; often called a strong hold: or, to maintain, as an opinion; to proceed in a course; a grasp with the hand; an embrace with the arms: or, a prison; a place of confinement.

Holden: Held.

Hollow: The palm; a cup; containing an empty space natural or artificial, within a solid substance.

Holpen: Past tense of helped.

Holy of Holies: The innermost shrine of the sanctuary; behind the curtain; it contains the Ark of the Covenant, and it is where Christ sits.

Homage: Worship; devotion; honor.

Homer: About 90 to 100 gallons.

Honest: Being truthful and honorable; good.

Horn: A symbol of strength and power.

Hosanna: Save now; save I pray.

Hosen: Tunics; slacks; undergarments.

Hospitality: The act or practice of receiving and entertaining strangers or guests without reward, or with kind and generous charity.

Hough: To disable something by cutting a leg muscle.

Howbeit: Be it as it may; nevertheless; notwithstanding; yet; but; however.

Humility: Lowliness of mind; a deep sense of one's own unworthiness in the sight of God.

Hungerbitten: Famished.

Hungred: Having been hungry.

Husbandman: A farmer; one who tills the ground.

Husk: The skin of a grape.

Hymn: The singing of psalms, (psalm 113-118), for devotions.

Hypocrite: Masking yourself to be what you are not.

Hyssop: A bitter herb; a plant used in the Jewish observances; was used in sprinkling the unclean.

Idle: Unoccupied with business; inactive or trifling; vain; of no importance.

Idol: Anything on which we set our affections; that to which we indulge an excessive and sinful attachment.

Idolatry: Image-worship or divine honor paid to any created object.

Ignominy: Contempt; shame; dishonor.

Ignorance: Being absence or destitution of knowledge; not knowing.

Illuminate: God giving understanding by knowledge or grace.

Imagery: Idolatry; the worship of painted or carved images.

Immanuel: Meaning, God with us.

Immortality: Incorruptible; an imperishable state; never ceasing to live or exist.

Immutable: Unchangeable; unalterable; not capable of change.

Impart: To give, grant or communicate; to give the knowledge of something; to make known.

Impediment: That which hinders progress or motion; an obstruction; an obstacle.

Impenitent: Someone being without remorse; not repenting of sin; not contrite; of a hard heart.

Imperious: Marked by arrogant assurance; proud, behaving as if expecting to be obeyed.

Implacable: Unyielding; the condition of not being able to be pleased.

Implead: To bring a claim or plead against someone.

Importunity: A constant or pressing demand.

Impotent: A cripple being without strength, who never had walked.

Impoverish: To make poor; to reduce to poverty; to exhaust strength, richness or fruitfulness.

Impudent: Stubborn; hard-faced; shameless; lacking modesty.

Impute: To reckon or to assign; to set to the account of something/one.

In any wise: Surely; in any way, or by any means.

In no wise: By no means; assuredly not.

Inasmuch: To such an extent or degree; in like manner; for or since.

Incarnation: Whereby Christ took our human nature into union with his divine person, and became man.

Inclose: To surround; to shut in; to confine on all sides; to encompass.

Incontinency: Lack of self-control; uncontrolled passions or appetites.

Incontinent: Unbridled; uncontrollable; not restrained from glorifying yourself, and living deliciously.

Indignation: Anger or extreme anger, mingled with contempt, disgust, or abhorrence; holy displeasure at one's self for sin.

Indite: To control or dictate what is to be written.

Inditing: Referring to a person, overflowing; boiling over.

Industrious: Given to productive business; characterized by diligence.

Infamous: Hateful; terrible; offensive; held in abhorrence; branded with infamy by conviction of a crime.

Infamy: Extremely bad reputation; public reproach: or, strong condemnation as the result of a shameful, criminal, or outrageous act.

Infidel: Unbelieving; disbelieving the inspiration of the Scriptures or the divine institution of Christianity.

Infinite: Without limits; unbounded; boundless; that will have no end; God is infinite in his presence, being omnipresent, and his perfections are infinite.

Infirmity: As sickness or bodily disease: or, imperfections and weakness of the body: or, moral and spiritual weaknesses and defects.

Infolding: Rolling and folding within itself; involving; wrapping up itself.

Ingathering: Harvest time; the act or business of collecting and securing the fruits of the earth.

Iniquity: Crookedness, perverseness; evil regarded as that which is not straight, upright and moral; to distort, to bend, to make crooked, to pervert truth, even as the truth is in Jesus.

Inkhorn: Vessel or cup containing ink.

Inn: A guest-chamber for travelers.

Inordinate: Without restraint; immoderate.

Inquire: To make examination; to seek for particular information.

Inquisition: Inquiry; examination; a search or investigation.

Inscription: Something written or engraved to communicate knowledge, that would last a long time.

Insomuch: So that; to that degree.

Inspiration: The supernatural action of the Holy Spirit on the mind of the sacred writers whereby the Scriptures were not merely their own but the word of God. Scripture not merely contains but is the word of God. As the whole Godhead was joined to the whole manhood, and became the Incarnate Word, so the written word is at once perfectly divine and perfectly human; infallibly authoritative because it is the word of God, intelligible because in the language of men. If it were not human, we should not understand it; if it were not divine, it would not be an unerring guide.

Instant: Quick; making no delay; pressing; urgent; persistent; earnest.

Instantly: Immediately; without any intervening time; at the moment or with diligence and earnestness.

Insurrection: A rising against civil or political authority.

Intercession: Mediation; to communicate between parties that are different from each other, with a view to reconciliation.

Intermeddle: To take part in a matter; to meddle.

Interpret: To explain the meaning of words to a person who does not understand them; lay open what is concealed.

Intreat: To make an earnest petition or request; to offer a treaty; to discourse.

Iron: Different pointed weapons; figuratively, a yoke of iron denotes hard service; a rod of iron, a stern government; a pillar of iron, a strong support; a furnace of iron, severe labor; a bar of iron, strength; fetters of iron, affliction; giving silver instead of iron, prosperity.

Isle: A tract of land surrounded by water or a detached portion of land enclosed protectively in the ocean, in a lake or river.

Issue: To proceed, as having children; a discharge, a flux or running fluid; produce of the earth, or profits of land; a sending out; a passage out, an outlet.

Italian band: An army consisted of volunteers from Italy.

Jacinth: A precious stone; reddish-orange gemstone.

Jah: Shortened form of JEHOVAH.

Jangling: Foolish talking; empty talk; babbling.

Jasper: A precious stone; a quartz of various colors.

JEHOVAH: The Scripture name of the Supreme Being; I AM THAT I AM.

JEHOVAH-JIREH: The Lord will provide or The Lord will see; in the mount of the LORD it shall be seen.

JEHOVAH-NISSE: The Lord is my refuge or the LORD hath sworn that the LORD will have war with Amalek from generation to generation.

JEHOVAH-SHALOM: The Lord of peace or peace be unto thee; fear not thou shalt not die.

Jeopardy: Exposure to death, loss, or injury; hazard; danger; peril.

Jeremias: Jeremiah.

Jeremy: Jeremiah.

Jeshurun, Jesurun: A poetical name of affection, for the people of Israel.

Jesting: Joking; artfully turned discourses or words that are important, to deride or joke at; to make things light and trifling by making sport.

Jewry: Judea; Judaea.

Joined hard: To border; be lying near to something.

Joinings: Clamps; fittings.

Jonas: Jonah.

Jot: The smallest Hebrew letter; an iota; the smallest letter of the Greek alphabet, used metaphorically or proverbially for the smallest thing.

Jubile: The 50th Jubile, after seven weeks of years, when alienated lands returned to the original owners and Hebrew bondservants were freed.

Judge: A chief magistrate, with civil and military powers.

Jurisdiction: The power, right, or authority to interpret and apply the law.

Justification: A law term, the legal act of God; one is declared just in the presence of God, by Christ.

Justify: To pardon and clear form guilt; to absolve or acquit from guilt and merited punishment, and to accept as righteous on account of the merits of the Saviour; by the application of Christ's atonement to the offender.

Justle: To strike or push against; to clash.

Kerchief: A long headdress; an item of clothing or ornament applied to the head of the idolatrous women of Israel.

Kernel: The edible substance contained in the shell of a nut or grape husk.

Kettle: A vessel for cooking or sacrificial purposes.

Kid: A young goat; a kid of the goats.

Kin: Family.

Kindred: Tribe; family, by birth, marriage, or blood.

Kine: Cows; cattle.

Kinsfolk: Relations; kindred; persons of the same family.

Kinsman: A man of the same race or family; the nearest male blood relation alive.

Kinswoman: A female relation.

Kite: A keen-sighted bird of prey.

Knops: A knob, shaped like a flowering bud: or, part of the decoration of the golden candlestick.

Know: In Scripture, to have sexual intercourse with: or, to approve; to learn; to acknowledge with due respect; to choose; to favor or take an interest in; to commit; to have; to have full assurance of; to have satisfactory evidence of any thing, though short of certainty; to have clear and certain perception; not to be doubtful.

Lace: A thread or wire used as a fastener.

Lad: A male person of any age between early boyhood and maturity.

Lade: To burden; to load.

Laden: Loaded; burdened.

Lain: Laid.

Lame: Crippled or disabled in a limb, or otherwise injured to be unsound and impaired in strength.

Lament: To mourn; to grieve; to weep or wail; to express sorrow.

Lamentation: Expression of sorrow; cries of grief; the act of bewailing.

Lance: A small spear or a dart.

Lancet: A surgical instrument, sharp-pointed and two-edged.

Languish: Wither; to be made weak; to be or become dull; feeble or spiritless.

Lap up: The act of licking up water.

Lap, (shake the): To shake out, and emptied.

Lapwing: The lapwing bird has a crest, and resembled in size and color the hoopoe; it appears in the list of abominable birds.

Lasciviousness: Unbridled sensuality; excessive lust.

Latchet: A thong or strap of leather.

Latter: Last; coming or happening after something else.

Lattice: Lace-work before a window or balcony, to screen the view of the woman.

Laud: To applaud; to praise; commendation; extolling in words.

Laver: A basin for washing.

Lavish: To spare no expense for a desired end; to give with excess.

Lawyer: A person skilled in the Law of Moses.

Layeth at: Strike at.

League: A treaty or alliance; an agreement between two.

Leasing: Lying; falsehood; deceit.

Leathern: Something made of skin.

Leaven: Fermented dough; yeast; a picture of increase.

Ledge: A shelf; the word in the sense of side-projection in connection with the bases of Solomon's molten sea: or, short staves or bars of brass that stood upright in the temple.

Leeks: A plant related to the onion, and eaten as a vegetable; grass; herb; hay.

Lees: Sediment or dregs; the substance on the bottom of the wine glass, expressing ease and self-indulgence that is undisturbed.

Left hand: Denoting the north.

Lefthanded: One unable to use the right hand skillfully.

Legion: An indefinite large number; a Roman legion is 3,000 to 6,000 soldiers.

Leisure: Convenience of time; available time; time free from employment.

Lentiles: Red pottage made with small beans.

Leprosy: A foul, easy to catch disease, appearing in dry, white, thin, scurvy scabs, attended with violent itching.

Lest: That not; for fear that.

Let: To hinder; obstruct; prevent; to give rest.

Leviathan: Dragon; a piercing serpent; a river or sea monster.

Levy: Men drafted to do hard labor; the act of collecting men for military, or other public service, as by enlistment, enrollment, or other means.

Lewdness: Villainy; wickedness; lascivious; ignorant and unlearned persons.

Liberal: Bountiful; generous; ample; large; not selfish; enlarged; embracing other interests than one's own.

Libertine: One set at liberty, from being a slave.

Lien: Past tense of lie down; to recline.

Lieutenants: A local ruler.

Lign aloes: A tree whose soft resinous wood was burned as a perfume.

Ligure: A precious stone, possibly an orange zircon.

Liking: A good state of body; healthy appearance; plumpness.

Lineage: The line of paternal family descent.

Linger: To delay; to remain or wait long; to be slow; slumber.

Lintel: The upper doorpost.

Listeth: To choose; to will; listed.

Litter: A covered wagon; a cart carried by others with poles.

Lively: Living; as a lively youth.

Lo: Look; see; behold; observe; this word is used to excite particular attention in a hearer to some object of sight, or subject of discourse.

Loathe, lothe: To hate; to look on with hatred or abhorrence; to feel disgust or nausea.

Loathsome: Causing an extreme dislike for food: or, exciting extreme disgust, hatred, or abhorrence; being offensive, odious, and detestable.

Lock: A strand or cluster of hair.

Loft: The roof; the upper level in a house.

Lofty: Elevated in strength and height, as a lofty tower, a lofty mountain: or, The High and Lofty One, referring to God: or, someone elevated in condition or character; someone proud, haughty, having lofty looks.

Log: About 1 pint.

Loins: The lower back; the waist: or, the seat of strength and vigor.

Look to: Look upon.

Lop: To cut off.

Lot: A part, division, or portion, which falls to one by chance, that is, by divine determination: or, the smallest stone for casting lots: or, to allot; to assign; to distribute; to sort; to catalogue; to portion.

Lowing: Mooing; making cow noises.

Lowliness: Freedom from pride; having humility and humbleness of mind.

Lowring: To appear gloomy; overcast in describing weather.

Lucifer: A brilliant star, a title given to the king of Babylon.

Lucre, (filthy): Gain or advantage by corruption.

Lucre: Ill-gotten or unlawful gain or advantage.

Lukewarm: Neither cold nor hot.

Lunatick: A person having mental illness; supposed to be influenced by the position of the moon.

Lurk: To lie hid; to lie in wait for blood.

Lust: Sinful longings, strong desires of any kind.

Lusty: Stout; vigorous; robust; healthy; able of body.

Mad: Expressing passion or excitement in foolish plans or ways.

Made manifest: To be made visible; to make clear; to reveal.

Made whole: Healed.

Madness: A derangement proceeding either from weakness and misdirection of intellect or from ungovernable violence of passion.

Magic: The science or practice of stirring up devils, or to stir up the evil powers of nature to produce effects apparently supernatural.

Magician: One skilled in magic; one who practices the black arts, by the means of devils; an enchanter; a necromancer; a sorcerer or sorceress.

Magistrate: A judge or ruler; authority in the most general sense.

Magnifical: Magnificent; showing fame and glory exceedingly.

Maiden: A young unmarried woman or a virgin; a female servant.

Mail, (coat of): A coat of armor that protects the body, and is made of steel net-work.

Maimed: Crippled, or deprived of some body part.

Malefactor: One who commits a crime; one guilty of violating the law.

Malice: A disposition to injure others without cause, from mere personal gratification or from a spirit of revenge.

Malignity: Extreme enmity and hatred, or evil dispositions of heart towards another.

Mallows: Saltwort, an uneatable plant, found in waste and desolate wildernesses'.

Mammon: Earthly goods; property; riches; money personified.

Mandrake: Some beautiful fruit or flower with a sweet smell; this plant is said to excite love; provoke lust; and help conception.

Maneh: A portion by weight, about 2 to 3 pounds; of silver about $34, of gold $510.

Manger: A crib or feeding trough.

Manifest: To make openly known; to appear, to reveal.

Manifold more: Many times more.

Manifold: Of divers kinds; many in number; numerous; multiplied.

Manna: A small round thing, like the hoarfrost on the ground, and like coriander seed, of the color of bdellium, and in taste like wafers made with honey.

Manner: Kind; sort; or, custom; habit.

Mansions: Abiding or dwelling places.

Manslayer: One who was guilty of accidental murder, and was entitled to flee to a city of refuge.

Mantle: A loose garment to be worn over other clothing; a cover; that which conceals.

Mar: To mar, the means to destroy; to disfigure; to damage.

Maranatha: Meaning, our Lord comes, or is coming.

Marishes: Marshes; ponds; a miry place.

Marketplace: A public place in a city or town for buying and selling, and other activities.

Marriage: Marriage is honorable in all, and the bed undefiled; the marriage relation is used to represent the union between God and his people; in the New Testament, the same figure is used in representing the love of Christ to his saints; the church of the redeemed is the "Bride, the Lamb's wife."

Mart: A market; a coming together of people to buy and sell.

Martyr: A slain witness for Jesus Christ.

Marvel: To wonder, and causes a person to stand or gaze, or to pause.

Maschil: A song enforcing some lesson of wisdom or piety, with understanding.

Mason: A man whose occupation is to lay bricks and stones, or to construct the walls of buildings, chimneys and the like, which consist of bricks or stones.

Masteries, (strive for): To compete or contend; the act of mastering.

Mate: A companion; an associate; denotes an assistant.

Matrix: The womb.

Matter: Timber; forest; or fuel.

Mattock: A pickaxe; a hoe; shovel; a farming tool.

Maul: A war club or mallet.

Maw: Probably the stomach or liver of an animal.

Mazzaroth: The 12 lodgings or stopping places in which the sun repeatedly stays or appears to stay in the sky: or, the 12 constellations of the Zodiac.

Mean men: Common men; low in rank or birth: or, obscure and unknown men.

Mean: Obscure; unknown; insignificant.

Measure: The whole extent or dimensions of a thing, including length, breadth, and thickness; determined extent or length; the limit; extent of power or office; to allot or distribute by measure.

Meat: Food in general.

Meddle: To act in the concerns of others; to contend and distress with others.

Media: Plural for medium.

Mediator: One who communicate between two parties.

Meek: Gentle; tender; free from pride.

Meet: Agreeable; fitting; proper: or, being qualified.

Mend: To bring to a new condition.

Mensteolers: Kidnappers; taking men and selling them as slaves.

Menstruous: Something/one defiled and unclean by blood; filthy rags.

Merchant: A man who traffics or carries on trade with foreign countries.

Mercurius: A Roman god; being the god of eloquence.

Mercy seat: The lid of the Ark of the Covenant; where the blood of the yearly atonement was sprinkled by the high priest.

Mess: A portion of food; a gift; a dish of food.

Messenger: An angel; a carrier of news; a prophet of God; a herald or forerunner.

Messias: Messiah; the anointed One.

Mete: To measure; to deal out.

Meteyard: A measuring stick.

Midwife: The older female relatives and friends of the mother; attending mothers at childbirth.

Milch: An animal giving suck to her young; milking.

Mile: A Roman mile, 4,986 feet.

Millet: A grain used for breads and cereals.

Millstone: A stone used for grinding grain.

Mincing: Taking short quick steps; tripping.

Mingle: To mix things or people together, yet keeping the parts separate.

Minish: To make or become less, in a present state; (see diminish).

Minister: Servants; to attend and serve; to perform service in any office.

Ministration: Service; the act or process of serving or aiding.

Minstrel: Flute players employed as professional mourners at a funeral.

Mire: Mud; clay-like soil.

Mirror: Made of mixed metal, mostly copper, made with great skill, and shined to a bright luster.

Mirth: Gladness; rejoicing.

Miry: Muddy.

Miserable: A state of misery; poorness; to be pitied.

Mistress: A woman who governs; who rules her servants, slaves, or subjects.

Mite: A small Jewish coin; about ⅛ of $0.01.

Mitre: Turban; a headdress worn by the high priest.

Mixt: A subject inside another object, that is, intermixed, as a mixt of divers people.

Mock: To laugh at; to ridicule; to treat with scorn or contempt: or, to disappoint; to deceive.

Moist: Something fresh; a picture of preserving life.

Mole: The mole rat.

Mollify: To be softened; to make something tender.

Moloch: The name of the god of the Ammonites, to whom children are sacrificed by fire, being the fire god.

Molten: Past tense of melt; made by melting and casting in a mould; as a molten image.

Monster, (sea): A great dragon; all large and cruel creatures; or, a picture of the king of Egypt or the king of Tyre.

Morrow: The next day; tomorrow in the morning.

Mortar: A vessel of wood, metal or stone in the form of an inverted bell, in which substances are crushed or pounded with a pestle.

Morter: Cement like substance.

Mortify: To put to death; to take away; to destroy the life of.

Mote: A small dry speck of dust.

Motions: Impulses; internal action and moving of the heart.

Mount: A mound; a bank of earth.

Muffler: An ornament worn by women; a veil or scarf that covers the lower part of the face.

Munition: A fortress or stronghold.

Murrain: Pestilence; a cattle plague.

Muse: To meditate; to gaze on, and meditate and be in awe.

Musician, (chief): Choir leaders; were heads of schools of sacred inspired music; Asaph, Heman and Jeduthun.

Muster: To number; to inspect; or to assemble or gather troops.

Mutter: Murmur; obscure utterance; a voice used by the necromancers in uttering their falsehoods.

Myrrh: A fragrant resin from the Cistus or rock rose, a common Palestine shrub; used for holy anointing oil, embalming and perfume.

Naked: Being discovered or made manifest: or, exposed to shame and disgrace: or, destitute of worldly goods: or, guilty and exposed to divine wrath.

Napkin: A small cloth; a handkerchief.

Naught, naughty: Of no value; worthless; bad.

Naughtiness: Badness, wickedness.

Nave: A wheel hub.

Navel: The center of the lower part of the abdomen: or, a word used for the whole being.

Nay: No.

Nazarene: One separated and given up to God from the womb.

Necromancer: One who pretends to inquire of the dead, by the means of devils.

Neesings: Sneezings.

Neigh: To utter the voice of a horse, expressive of want or desire.

Nephew: A grandson.

Nether: Lower; the regions below.

Nethermost: Lowest; the lowest hell.

Nettle: Thorny shrub; a prickly weed.

Nibhaz: The barker; a deity of the Avites, in the figure of a dog, or a dog-headed man.

Nigh: In relation to time, meaning, soon; being nigh means being close: Near is usually used in relation to space, location, relationships, feelings, and states.

Nitre: A mineral; the carbonate of soda.

No little kindness: Exceptional or much kindness.

Nobleman: An officer of state in the service of Herod Antipas.

Noe: Noah.

Noised abroad: To be widely reported; before the public at large.

Noised: Testimony is spread by report; information going out to others by being much talked about.

Noisome: Foul; evil; hurtful; destructive.

North country: A general name for the countries that lay north of Palestine; the location of God's adversaries.

Northward: Toward the north; the image of jealousy was toward the north, that is, Babylon.

Nose jewels: A jewel that hung from the forehead upon a lace or ribbon between the eyes down upon the nose.

Not a whit: Not the least bit.

Notable: A great thing worthy of observation; known or apparent: or, notorious; terrible; prominent; sightly; as a notable horn.

Nought: Nothing.

Novice: A person newly planted in the Christian faith.

O: A call.

Oath: A solemn affirmation or declaration, made with an appeal to God for the truth of what is affirmed.

Obeisance: Homage or reverence to any one; bow down the head; a kiss.

Oblation: An offering; a sacrifice.

Obscure: Shrouded in or hidden by darkness.

Obstinate: Stubborn; hardened in heart and mind.

Occupy: To do business; to trade and traffic.

Occurrent: Occurrence; happening; taking place; no occurrent is no action of adversary or enemy.

Odious: Hateful; to stink; being disgusting.

Offend: To cause someone to stumble or sin.

Offscouring: Someone rejected by society; something that is scoured off; that which is vile or despised.

Oft: Often; frequently.

Oh: A sigh.

Omega: The last; the end of something; the last letter of the Greek alphabet.

Omer: About 6.5 pints.

Omnipotent: All-powerful; all mighty.

On this wise: In this manner.

Onycha: One of the ingredients of the sacred composition, which gave a sweet smell when burned.

Onyx: A veined and shelled quartz.

Open place: By the way side; a place where two ways or more met; by the roadside.

Oracle: A divine utterance delivered to man; the word of God; the Scriptures are called living oracles: or, the inner sanctuary, the Holy of Holies.

Oration: A speech; an elaborate discourse delivered in a formal and dignified manner.

Ordain: This word relates to a variety of ideas such as God's work and providence; the appointment to an office or a task; and the establishment of laws, principles, places, or observances.

Ordinance: A rule established by authority; ceremonial and religious regulation; a decree or a rule of action.

Or ever: Before.

Organ: A general term for all wind instruments.

Orion: A brilliant constellation dedicated to Nimrod or Merodach.

Ornament: Finely embroidered or decorated fabrics, various rings, bracelets, and chains.

Osee: Hosea.

Ospray: The sea eagle or fish hawk.

Ossifrage: The large bearded vulture known as the lammer-geier.

Ouches: Settings for gems; sockets; settings.

Ought: Should; to be held or bound in duty or moral obligation: or, to be necessary.

Outgoings: Limits or boundaries.

Outlandish: Of foreign origin; not native; having a foreign appearance.

Outmost: Farthest out.

Outwent: To go before in advance, (past tense of outgo).

Overcharged: To be weighed down; loaded; overburdened.

Overlay: To smother or suffocate by lying upon someone; to overlie.

Overlived: To outlive; out survived.

Overran: Outran.

Overrunning: Overflowing.

Paces: The space between the two feet in walking, about 2 ½ feet.

Pacify: To appease; to bring or restore to a state of peace or tranquility: or, to have quiet; calm.

Paddle: A small shovel or scraper.

Painful: Laborious; difficult.

Painfulness: To toil; to labor.

Palm: Of the hand-3.648 inches.

Palmerworm: A destructive locust that suddenly appears in large numbers, devouring herbage.

Palsy: To be paralyzed; the loss of sensation, or the power of motion or both, in any part of the body.

Pang: Pain and anguish; fearfulness; being bowed down; dismayed.

Pant: To long eagerly; to yearn.

Paper reed: The papyrus plant.

Paps: Bosoms; the nipple of the breast.

Parable: An utterance that involves a comparison; a riddle.

Paradise: The Garden of Eden, in which Adam and Eve were placed immediately after their creation.

Paramour: Forbidden male or female lovers; a concubine.

Parcel: A fragment; a portion of something.

Parched: Scorched; dried to extremity.

Parchment: Animal skins used to make scrolls for writing.

Pare: To trim off an outside or excess part of something; or irregular part.

Parlour: An upper room.

Partial: Showing favoritism and preference; having a liking for a person or thing.

Passage: A mountain pass; a river that can be crossed on foot.

Passion: Meaning, suffering; referring to the sufferings of our Lord.

Passover: An annual feast of the Israelites.

Pastor: One who feeds the flock; a shepherd.

Pate: Forehead; crown of the head.

Patriarch: The name given to the head of a family or tribe, in Old Testament times.

Patrimony: An inherited estate from one's father.

Pavement: A place paved with a mosaic of colored stones.

Pavilion: Tabernacle; a dwelling or enclosure, it probably denotes the canopy suspended over the judgment-seat of the king.

Peculiar: A special people, a possession or property of God.

Peeled: To make bald, bare, or smooth.

Peep: To chirp like a bird.

Pence: The plural of penny, when used of a sum of money or value.

Penny: Pennies mean the number of coins; pence the amount of pennies in value; the daily pay of a Roman soldier, about 17 cents, then later 15 cents.

Pentateuch: The first five books of the Old Testament.

Pentecost: In the Christian church, as the day on which the Spirit descended upon the apostles, fifty days after Passover.

Penury: Poverty; to be in need.

Peradventure: Perhaps; may it be possibly; by chance.

Perdition: Destruction; the utter loss of the soul or of final happiness in a future state; future misery or eternal death.

Perfect: Complete; spiritually full of age; being entire.

Peril: Being emotionally in the deep; an exposure of person or property to injury, loss, or destruction; danger; hazard.

Pernicious ways: Implies permanent harm done through evil doings, whose ways are sneaky, corrupting, and undermining.

Perpetual: Permanent; fixed; everlasting; endless.

Perplexed: Feeling desolate; troubled on every side.

Persecute: To pursue after in order to overtake someone.

Perseverance: Continuing in a state of persistence in anything undertaken.

Pestle: A club to pound things in a mortar.

Petition: A formal request or supplication.

Pharisee: A prominent sect of the Jews; and differing from the Sadducees, chiefly in its strict performance of religious ceremonies and practices, obedience to oral laws and traditions, and belief in an afterlife and the coming of a Messiah.

Phylacteries: Words of Scripture are rolled up and set in a small case, and tied around the wrist or elbow or the forehead.

Physician: Those who practiced heathen arts of magic, and rejects recognized methods of cure.

Pictures: Images carved in stone or wood.

Piece of money, (silver): A 4 day wage, $0.64.

Piety: Godliness; reverence of parents or friends, accompanied with affection and devotion to their honor and happiness.

Pilgrimage: The journey of human life.

Pillar: Monuments erected to celebrate events; monuments of idolatry: or, a foundation; a support; supporting the roof or other parts of a building.

Pilled: Peeled; to have stripped off skin or bark.

Pine away: To wear or fade away under any distress of anxiety of mind.

Pinnacle: Anything that runs out to a point.

Pipe: A name given to various kinds of wind instruments, as the pipe, flute, panpipes, etc.

Pit: Hell; the grave: or, a pool or waterhole; a cistern or well.

Pitch: A thick; dark; sticky substance; cement: or, setting up a tent; to arrange; to encamp.

Pitied, pitiful: Having compassion; to be full of pity.

Plague: A stroke of affliction, or disease sent as a divine chastisement: or, painful afflictions or diseases: or, severe calamity.

Plain: In a plain manner; without difficulty or vagueness: or, level or smooth ground; a low country.

Plaister: Plaster.

Plaiting: An elaborate gathering of the hair into a knot.

Plat: A plot of ground.

Platted: Braided; intertwined.

Platter: A dish.

Play: To fence in battle or game; to fight with swords.

Plea: To argue for or against a cause, as in a court of justice.

Pledge: Security given for future payment or conduct.

Pleiades: A cluster of stars.

Plough, (a): An instrument for plowing.

Plowshare: Cutting blades of a plough.

Plummet: A measuring line having a weight at the end.

Poetry: Defined as, the measured language of emotion.

Polled: To cut hair from the head.

Polls: Heads.

Pollux: A Greek mythological god, one of the twin sons of Jupiter, has supposed power to save men in danger at sea.

Pommel: Bowl or crown; anything round on the top of a column.

Pomp: A show of splendor and grandeur.

Ponder: To consider carefully; to meditate.

Pool: A pond, or reservoir, for holding water; an artificial cistern or tank.

Port: A door for the sheep pen.

Porter: A doorkeeper; gatekeeper.

Post: A runner; postman.

Potentate: One who possesses great power; a king; a ruler; a sovereign.

Potsherd: A piece of broken pottery.

Pottage: Any boiled dish or food; soup; stew.

Potters field: Called the field of blood; tradition places it in the valley of Hinnom.

Pound: New Testament currency, $20.00: Old Testament weight, 6.6 pounds.

Pourtray: A drawing or carving.

Praitorion: Judgment hall.

Prating: Speaking with ill-will words, in hearing and telling of news; babbling; chattering.

Precept: Any commandment or order intended as an authoritative rule of action.

Predestinated: To predetermine or foreordain; to appoint or ordain beforehand by an unchangeable purpose.

Preeminence: Superiority, especially in noble or excellent qualities; what is over and above.

Presbytery: An assembly of elders in a church.

Presently: Immediately.

Presidents: Governors; having management of the affairs of the kingdom.

Press: A crowd; a multitude of people crowded together: or, to constrain; to compel; to urge by authority or necessity: or, to urge or strain in motion; to urge forward with force.

Pressfat: A vessel collecting fats from oil or wine.

Presumptuous: Excess of confidence; willful; done with bold design, rash confidence or in violation of known duty.

Pretence: To profess something false rather than the real intention or purpose.

Prevent: Come before; going ahead; anticipate; to precede; to favor by anticipation or by hindering distress or evil.

Prey: Booty; spoil.

Prick: A goad; a rod with a sharp point for driving cattle.

Principal: Most important or considerable; first object to seek.

Principality: The highest powers; one invested with sovereignty.

Printed: Inscribed.

Prised: Priced; valued.

Privily: Secretly.

Privy: Secret or private chambers: or, taking part of something secretly: or, a males privates.

Procureth: To seek; to cause to draw near; to bring on.

Profane: Something common, unholy; to dishonor a thing.

Profound: To go deep into something; deep in skill or plan.

Progenitors: Ancestors; parents.

Prognosticator: Foretellers of the future, by the means of devils.

Prolong: To lengthen in time; to extend the duration of; to draw out in time by delay; to continue; to put off to a distant time.

Proper: Personal: or, one's own: or, handsome, beautiful.

Prophecy: A foretelling; prediction; a declaration of something to come. As God only knows future events with certainty, no being but God or some person informed by him can utter a real prophecy. The prophecies recorded in Scripture, when fulfilled, give most convincing evidence of the divine original of the Scriptures, as those who uttered the prophecies could not have foreknown the events predicted without supernatural instruction from the Lord Jesus Christ alone.

Prophesy: In Scripture, to preach; to instruct in religious doctrines; to interpret or explain Scripture or religious subjects; to exhort.

Propitiation: The wrath-ending sacrifice by which the Lord Jesus Christ secured his people's pardon.

Proselyte: A convert to Judaism.

Prospect: At the face of something; in front of.

Prove: To test; to try a thing.

Provender: Food or fodder for livestock or cattle.

Proverb: Dark sayings of the wise; a hidden mode of speaking, which conceals the sense under figurative expressions.

Provide: To consider beforehand; take thought for.

Providence: Forethought; God's preserving and governing all things.

Provocation: Rebelliousness; a hardened heart.

Prudent: A wise person, sensible in action and thought.

Psalm: A sacred song or hymn; a song composed on a divine subject and in praise of God; a melody.

Psaltery: A stringed musical instrument.

Publican: A tax collector.

Pulpit: A high object; a scaffolding or platform made of wood.

Pulse: Beans; vegetables or seed used for food.

Purchase: To obtain; to gain by seeking and pursuing.

Purge: To cleanse or purify by separating and carrying off whatever is impure.

Purloining: To carry something away for one's self; take by theft.

Purse: A bag or sack.

Pursue: To follow with hostility; to persecute; to continue.

Purtenance: Animal intestines; the inwards of an animal.

Put to: Apply to; to use.

Putrifying: Pertaining to gangrene; decaying.

Pygarg: A kind of goat or antelope.

Quarry: Area of land where stones were extracted for building various objects and buildings.

Quaternion: A company of four soldiers of an army.

Queen of heaven: The moon goddess, Ashtaroth or Astarte.

Quench: The word is used of fire or of thirst; to extinguish; to suppress; to cool.

Quick: Alive; a living person.

Quicken: Bring to life; God making the dead alive; raised up.

Quicksands: To be stuck and stranded upon the shores in quicksand.

Quit you like men: To show one's self like a man.

Quit: To be blameless or innocent; to be released from an oath or contract.

Quiver: A case or sheath for carrying arrows.

Rabbi: Master; teacher.

Rabboni: My master; my teacher.

Raca: Fool; senseless; vain; empty-headed.

Rahab: A poetical name of Egypt, meaning, fierceness, insolence, and pride, as a mythological monster.

Rahel: Rachel.

Rail: Reproaches; a scoff; an insult; to blaspheme.

Railer: An abusive person who scoffs and insults at others.

Raiment: Clothing; apparel; a covering.

Rampart: A low outer wall of earth, around a fort as a defense; a fortification.

Ranges: A cooking furnace for two or more pots: or, a series of mountains: or, ranks of soldiers in a line.

Ranging: Running to and fro; wandering; roving.

Rank: Fat and full grown; healthy; ripe: or, different kinds of people: or, to march in perfect order and in straight lines, none crossing the other's track.

Ransom: The price paid for obtaining the pardon of sins and the redemption of the sinner from punishment; to rescue; to deliver.

Rase: To demolish; to strip bare.

Ravening: Eagerness for plunder and tearing in pieces; to devour: or, food obtained by violence.

Ravin: To devour an animal like a wolf.

Ravish: To rape; to lie with; to humble.

Reap: To gather; to obtain or to receive as a reward or as the fruit of labor or of works, in a good or bad sense; as, to reap a benefit from actions made.

Rebuke: To reprimand; strongly warn; to restrain.

Receipt of custom: The tax office; the place of toll.

Recompence: That which is paid back, (noun).

Recompense: The action of paying back, (verb).

Reconciliation: A person brought into a state of favor with God, after natural estrangement or enmity.

Recorder: One who keeps rolls or records of events and history: or, who is invested with judicial powers.

Redeemed: Ransomed; delivered from bondage, penalty, and accountability: or, from the possession of another.

Redeemer: One charged with the duty of restoring the rights of another and avenging his wrongs.

Redemption: The forgiveness of sins.

Redound: Rebound; to surge up praise to God.

Reed: A water plant, used as a measuring device of six cubits or about 9 to 10 feet; a picture of weakness.

Refiner: The refiner's art was to the working of precious metals, in the separation of the dross from the pure metal.

Reform: To abandon that which is evil or corrupt, and return to a good state; to be amended or corrected.

Refrain: To hold back; to keep from behavior.

Refresh: To freshen up: (see afresh).

Refuge: That which shelters or protects from danger, distress, or calamity; a strong hold that protects by its strength, or a sanctuary that secures safety by its sacredness; any place inaccessible to an enemy.

Regeneration: The implanting of a new principle or disposition in the soul by God; the imparting of spiritual life to those who are by nature, dead in trespasses and sins.

Rehearse: To recite; to repeat the words of a passage or composition; to narrate or recount events or transactions.

Reign: Dominion; to possess or exercise sovereign power or authority; to rule.

Reins: The heart; innermost parts of the feelings and emotions and mind of man.

Remeth: The same as Ramoth, signifying high or lofty.

Remission: Forgiveness; to release.

Remit: To dismiss; to set free.

Remnant: Residue; that which is left after the separation, removal or destruction of a part.

Remphan: The star-god Saturn or Moloch.

Rend: To divide; to break or tear apart.

Renounce: To disown; to cast off or reject, as a connection or possession; to forsake.

Renown: A great name or a well-known person.

Rent: Divided; broke or tore apart.

Repent (God): To be grieved at the heart; to turn again.

Repent: To change one's mind; purpose; regret with sorrow of heart.

Replenish: To recover former fullness.

Reproach: To treat with scorn or contempt; the cause of disgrace and shame.

Reprobate: Being unapproved; to be rejected and unfit after testing; abandoned to sin.

Reproof: To reply with scolding; to rebuke.

Reprove: To convict of wrongdoings or to disprove of something or reject someone.

Repute: Reputation; good character.

Require: To demand; to ask, as of right and by authority; to ask as a favor; to request.

Requite: To return; to restore: or, repaying good or evil with reward or punishment.

Rereward: Towards the rear; the rearguard.

Respect: To look to or to look upon.

Respite: A temporary period of relief.

Rest: Jesus gives rest; rest from afflictions; quiet; repose; a state free from motion or disturbance; a state of reconciliation to God.

Resurrection: The state of a person who is raised from the dead.

Revelation: The supernatural communication of God's truth to the mind; to which is revealed.

Revellings: A feast resulting in noisy partying, with drinking and dancing.

Revenue: Income; increase.

Reverence: To regard with reverence; to regard with fear mingled with respect and affection.

Revile: To abuse; to attack with evil words.

Revolt: To renounce allegiance and subjection to one's prince or state; to reject the authority of a sovereign.

Ribband: A cord; twisted thread; a ribbon on clothing.

Rid: To free; to deliver; to clear away; to remove; to separate.

Riddance: Something that is devoured; or gathered away.

Riddle: Used as a test of wit; a mystifying, misleading, or puzzling question.

Rie: Rye; a grain like wheat.

Rifle, (to): To plunder; to spoil.

Rigour: The action or instance of strictness; harshness; or cruelty.

Ring: Rings were used as a signet; on the fingers, arms, wrists, and also the ears and the nose.

Ringstraked: Round steaks or stripes on something.

Riotous: Reckless; self-indulgent behavior.

Rising: Swelling; a tumor; a boil.

Rite: A prescribed form or manner governing the words or actions for a ceremony.

River of God: Meaning, that God's divine resources are inexhaustible.

Road, (made a): An army raiding the enemy's camp, they rushed in, or poured in and spread themselves.

Roe: A gazelle.

Roebuck: A species of antelope.

Roll: A scroll; the usual form of manuscript in biblical times.

Roller: A bandage; a long and broad bandage used in surgery.

Room: Space; a place at the table.

Rosh: Chief; the head of the nomadic tribe of Benjamin.

Round: On all sides; to go round about something.

Rouse: To put into action; to agitate someone for action.

Rover: A robber or a pirate.

Rubbish: Useless waste or rejected matter.

Ruby: A precious stone; a mineral of a carmine red color, sometimes verging to violet.

Rudder bands: Ancient ships had two great broad-bladed oars for rudders, they were tied up with these, when the rudders were not used.

Rude in speech: Untaught; ignorant; not skilled in speaking.

Rudiment: A first principle or element; that which is to be first learned.

Rue: A garden herb; used for medicinal and cooking purposes.

Ruinous: Laid waste; sudden violence or plague or ruin.

Rush: A reed growing in moist places.

Rye: A small grain grown in Egypt.

Sabaoth: Meaning, Lord of hosts or Lord God of hosts.

Sabbath day's journey: 6 miles or 1,000 paces or about 3,000 feet.

Sabbath: A rest; a refreshing; a break in any occupation or accomplishments.

Sackbut: A stringed musical instrument; like a harp.

Sackcloth: Clothing made of camel's hair, worn to show sorrow.

Sacrilege, (commit): The crime of violating or profaning sacred things; robbers of temples.

Sadducees: A religious sect; or school, among the Jews at the time of Christ.

Saints: Saved men and women of God.

Saith: Say; said.

Salutation: A greeting given in person, orally or in writing.

Salute: The act of expressing kind wishes or respect; a salutation; a greeting.

Salvation: The saving of a sinner from the righteous judgment of God.

Sanctification: God making a thing pure by separation.

Sanctify: To be sacred and set apart.

Sanctuary: The holy land; the temple; the tabernacle; the holy place, the place of the Ark of the Covenant.

Sapphire: A precious stone, apparently of a bright-blue color.

Sardine: A gem of a blood-red color; from Sardius.

Sardius: A precious red stone; carnelian.

Sardonyx: The sardonyx consists of a white opaque layer, superimposed upon a red transparent stratum of the true red sard.

Satan: Adversary; the father of lies.

Satiate: To satisfy; to be filled.

Satyr: He-goat.

Save: Except; besides.

Saviour: God alone who saves to the uttermost.

Savour: To like, to delight in, to favor: or, the cause or occasion of something: or, a smell; a taste: or, to think; to understand.

Savourest: To seek out and search, then to enjoy and appreciate thoroughly.

Scabbard: A case or covering for a sword.

Scall: A scaly skin eruption; a flare-up.

Scant measure: Hardly or scarcely sufficient in measure.

Scapegoat: The priest made atonement over the scapegoat, laying Israel's guilt upon it, and then sent it away; a picture of Jesus Christ.

Scarce: Being few in number and scattered; something rare or uncommon.

Scarlet: A bright red color, as a scarlet cloth or thread.

Sceptre: A staff held by a king as a sign of authority.

Schism: A formal division inside a religious group.

Schoolmaster: The law that brings us to Christ.

Scoff: Showing contempt by insulting words or actions; it combines bitterness with ridicule.

Scorn: Scorn is a crueler emotion than disdain or contempt; someone having an arrogant sense of self-esteem, and scorns others.

Scourge, (a): A whip made of small cords.

Scourge, (to): To whip; to lash a person.

Scrabble: To scratch or scrape, as with nails or hands.

Scrip: A bag or sack.

Scripture: The Bible consists of two great parts, called the Old and New Testaments, separated by an interval of nearly four hundred years. These Testaments are further divided into sixty-six books, thirty-nine in the Old Testament and twenty-seven in the New. These books are a library in themselves being written in every known form of old literature. Twenty-two of them are historical, five are poetical, eighteen are of prophecy, and twenty-one are epistles. They contain logical arguments, poetry, songs and hymns, history, biography, stories, parables, fables, eloquence, law, letters and philosophy. There are at least thirty-six different authors, who wrote in three continents, in many countries, in three languages, and from every possible human standpoint. Among these authors were kings, farmers, tentmakers, scientific men, lawyers, generals, fishermen, ministers and priests, a tax-collector, a doctor, some rich, some poor, some city bred, some country born -thus touching all the experiences of men extending over 1500 years.

Scroll: A roll of paper, for writing words.

Scurvy: An itchy, scaly disease of the scalp.

Sea of glass: A figurative expression; a calm, glass-like sea, in which is never a storm.

Sea, (molten): The great laver made by Solomon for the use of the priests in the temple.

Seared: Scorched; a heart unable to feel.

Seatward: Toward the mercy seat.

Sebat: Eleventh month in the Hebrew calendar; our January-February.

Sect: A group or division of people separated from others; a cluster.

Secure, securely: Free from being full of cares or anxiety.

Sedition: An uproar of violence; an insurrection; a rise in rebellion.

See to: Look upon.

Seed: Offspring; that from which anything springs; first principle; original; as the seeds of virtue or vice.

Seemly: An agreeably fashion; fitting, suitable.

Seer: Another word for prophet.

Seethe: To cook; to boil well.

Selah: A pause in the voices singing, while the instruments perform alone: or, silence or pause.

Selfsame: Being the one mentioned or the same one in question.

Selvedge: The end or edge; the end of a curtain.

Senate: The elders of Israel, who formed a larger part of the Sanhedrin.

Senators: A counselor; a judge or magistrate.

Sepulchre: A place of burial; a grave.

Seraphim: An order of celestial beings; plural of seraph, each of them having three pairs of wings.

Serjeants: A title of a particular office or function at the court of a monarch.

Servant: The subject of a king, as the servants of David; a person employed or used as an instrument in accomplishing God's purposes of mercy or wrath, as Nebuchadnezzar is called the servant of God; one who yields and serves from the heart to another, the saints are called servants of God, and the wicked are called the servants of sin.

Servile: Laborious; relating to servitude or forced labor.

Servitor: Attendant; as a servant.

Set forward: To oversee.

Set light by: To dishonor; treat with contempt or shame.

Set on: To attack.

Set to his seal: Affixed his seal; firmly believing and confirming what is said.

Settle: Ledge: or, a pedestal block; a base: or, to establish; a fixed establishment in the faith; a fixed determination.

Sevenfold: Multiplied by seven.

Sever: To separate and put in different places or orders: or, to make a separation or distinction; to distinguish.

Several house: A separate house; a separate place.

Severally: Separately; individually.

Severity: Harshness; sharpness of punishment.

Shalt: Shall.

Shambles: Meat market.

Shamefacedness: Modesty; a person humbled from sin.

Share: A sharp steel or iron wedge that cuts loose the top layer of soil; part of a plough.

Sheaf: Any bundle or collection; stalks of wheat, rye, grain, etc.

Sheath: A case or covering for a sword.

Sheepcote: Sheep pen.

Sheepfold: A place where sheep are collected or confined.

Shekel: -Weight; standard about 0.44 ounce. -of the sanctuary 0.5 ounce. -after the king's weight; the exact weight is unknown; if standard, the entire weight would be about 6 pounds.

Sheminith: A musical term, the lowest note sung by men's voices.

Shepham: A place on the eastern boundary of the Promised Land.

Sherd: A broken piece, part, or fragment.

Sheriffs: Someone who knows and executes the law.

Shew: Show.

Shewbread: Consecrated unleavened bread ritually placed by the Jewish priests on a table in the sanctuary.

Shibboleth: The word probably has the sense of a stream.

Shiggaion: A poem composed under strong mental emotion.

Shiloah, (the waters of): A soft flowing stream.

Shipping, (took): Got into the boats.

Shittah tree: The wood of the shittah, same as shittim, used to make the ark of the Hebrew tabernacle.

Shivers: Pieces; splinters.

Shock: A stack of sheaves.

Shod: Furnished or equipped with a shoe.

Shone: The radiance or brightness caused by emitted or reflected light.

Shorn: Having the hair or wool cut off; sheared.

Shoshannim eduth: Probable the name of the melody to which the psalm was to be sung.

Shoshannim: A musical direction, to the leader of the temple choir.

Shrines, (silver): A structure or place consecrated or devoted to Diana.

Shroud: To cover; to shelter from danger or annoyance.

Shun: To keep away from; take pains to avoid: or, to decline; to neglect.

Shut up: Kept under; closed up.

Shuttle: An instrument used by weavers.

Sickle: A pruning hook type of tool, used for cutting grain.

Siege: A military blockade of a city or fortified place to compel it to surrender.

Sieve: A strainer; a tool for separating flour from bran; or the fine substance from the coarse; that which retains the corn, and shakes out the chaff.

Sift: To separate and to part by a sieve, as the fine part of a substance from the coarse; God sifts a particular soul, to purify it from its lusts and corruptions.

Signet: A seal or stamp.

Silly: Weak in intellect; empty of ordinary strength of mind.

Silverlings: Silver coins; a thousand shekels.

Similitude: A likeness; an image; a representation or something similar.

Simple: Ignorant or innocent; weak in intellect; not wise and being silly.

Sin: Any voluntary transgression of the divine law, or violation of a divine command.

Sincere: Pure; unmixed; not feigned.

Sinew: That which unites a muscle to a bone.

Single: Clear; sound; healthy; uncorrupt.

Sith: Since.

Situate: To be place, with respect to any other object; as a town situate on a hill or on the sea shore.

Sivan: Third month in the Hebrew calendar; our May-June.

Sixscore: 120.

Skill, (can or could): To know how, to be skilled.

Slander: To speak against someone's nature or person.

Slave: A person who is entirely subject to the will of another; one who has no will of his own, but whose person and services are wholly under the control of another, (see servant, different from slave): or, a drudge; one who labors like a slave.

Sleight: Trickery; entrapment by deceit.

Slightly: In a small degree; feebly; superficially.

Slime: A sticky cement made for brick laying.

Slips: Stems or roots cut from a plant and used for grafting or planting.

Slothful: An inactive, sluggish, lazy slothful idle person.

Slow bellies: Idle gluttons.

Sluggard: A person always lazy; idle and inactive.

Sluices: A stream of water; an artificial channel for conducting water, controlled at the head by a gate.

Smart: To be sore distressed; to feel a strong pain of mind.

Smite: To strike; beat.

Smote off: To have taken off or away.

Snuffdishes: Used to catch the trimmed wick.

Snuffed: To snort; to inhale air with violence or with noise; as dogs and horses.

Snuffers: A device similar to a pair of scissors for cropping and holding the snuff of a candle.

Sobriety: Self-restraint; discretion; having prudence.

Sodden: Cooked; boiled.

Sodering: Soldering; to unite and make solid.

Sodoma: Sodom.

Sodomite: This word does not denote the inhabitants of Sodom; but those who practiced, as a religious rite, the abominable and unnatural vice, from which the inhabitants of Sodom and Gomorrah have derived their lasting infamy.

Sojourn: To dwell or live in a place as a temporary resident.

Solace: To delight in; to rejoice oneself in.

Solemnity: A rite or ceremony annually performed with religious reverence.

Solemnly: Religious seriousness and reverence.

Solitary: Living alone; not having company; being still and silent.

Sometime(s): Formerly; at one time; once.

Soothsayer: A foreteller of the future by the means of devils.

Soothsaying: Fortune-telling.

Sop: A morsel of food dipped in broth or liquid food, and intended to be eaten.

Sorcery: Relating to witchcraft, divination by the means of devils; belonging to the works of the flesh.

Sore: Doing things by difficulties; hardship; or exertion.

Sort: Manner, form of being or acting: or, class or order; as men of the wiser sort.

Sottish: Foolish; stupid; dull with drinking.

Sow: The female of the hog type or of swine.

Spake: Past tense of speak.

Span: A measure of length equal to about 9-11 inches.

Sped: Found or find.

Spikenard: The fragrant oil of an Indian plant.

Spindle: The pin used in spinning wheels for twisting the thread when sewing.

Spite: To be ill-willed or desire to hurt or offend.

Spittle: Spit; saliva.

Spoil: Booty; prey; things gathered from a defeated enemy.

Spoken for: Asked in marriage.

Sport: That which makes merry; to represent any kind of play or diversion; the cause of amusement by mockery.

Sprig: A small shoot or twig of a tree.

Spring: The dawn; the spring of the morning.

Spue: To vomit out.

St, (ending on words): The second person, the one spoken to.

Stablish: Establish; to make steadfast.

Stacte: A sweet aromatic gum, which is used to make the holy incense.

Stammer: To make involuntary stops and repetitions in speaking.

Stanched: Stopped; stood still.

Stand upon: Attack.

Standard: An ensign of war; a staff with a flag of colors: or, that which is established by sovereign power as a rule or measure by which others are to be adjusted.

Standard-bearer: One who carried the flag/banner in time of war.

Stargazers: Those who pretend to tell what will occur by looking upon the stars, by the means of devils.

Stately: Lofty; dignified; majestic.

Stature: Maturity and measure of life; the natural height of the human body.

Stature, (every): Meaning, every kind of person, young or old.

Staves: Rods; clubs: or, poles; staffs.

Stay: Something one relies upon and is a support; upholds something: or, to stop; hold back.

Stayed: Detained; held.

Stead, (in the): In the place of, or room of.

Stealth: A secret manner of acting; cunning or underhanded dealings.

Stedfast: Firm; fixed; steady.

Stern: The rear end of a boat.

Steward: Manager; a man employed in managing.

Stirs: Noises; tumults.

Stock: A wooden block or log.

Stoicks: A sect of atheists and philosophers.

Stomacher: A richly ornamented triangular piece of cloth, worn as a covering for the chest or stomach.

Stonesquarers: The inhabitants of Gebal, a place near Zidon, famous for artificers and architects, formed stones into squares.

Stoop: To yield; to be inferior.

Stout(ness): Hard(ness); bold(ness) and proud; strong.

Straightway: Immediately.

Strait: Narrow; a restricted and narrow path or road.

Straitened: Hindered; limited; restricted; distressed.

Straitly: Intimately; strictly; a position of difficulty or distress.

Straits, (in): Be in distress.

Strake sail: Lowered sail.

Strake: To make a line; a streak.

Strange: Something that is not of God, as a strange god; any thing or person that is foreign: or, to make yourself hard and disagreeable to someone.

Strawed: To scatter; to spread about, (past tense of to strew).

Stricken in age, (years): A person being aged.

Striker: One apt to inflict blows or hit others.

Striketh hands: Becoming a surety (a security) for another: or, the concluding of an agreement.

Stripling: A young man; a youth.

Strive: To make efforts; to use exertions; to endeavor with earnestness of the body or mind: or, to contend; to contest; to struggle in opposition to another; to be in contention or dispute.

Strong drink: Any intoxicating liquor; liquor made of honey and dates, of wheat and barley.

Strove: To make strong efforts toward any goal.

Strowed: To cast.

Subdue: To destroy the force of something; to overcome.

Suborned men: Men who are bribed and set up as false witnesses.

Suborned: Induced; bribed.

Subtil, subtilty: Crafty; deceitful; cunning: or, being insightful with good perception.

Suburbs: A building outside the walls of a city.

Subvert: To corrupt; to confound; to pervert the mind, and turn it from the truth.

Succour: To help; to aid.

Suffer: To allow; to permit; to endure; to support; to sustain: or, not to forbid or hinder.

Suffice: To be enough or sufficient.

Suit: A petition about a cause; a seeking for something by petition or application.

Sumptuously: Splendidly; extremely costly, rich, and luxurious.

Sunder: To break or cause something to break apart or in pieces.

Sundry: Various; many different; diverse.

Sup up: Gather up or together; to assemble.

Sup: To dine, to eat a meal; to drink.

Superfluity: Super abundance; overflowing.

Superfluous: Over and above; having more than enough.

Superscription: An inscription; a title; writing.

Superstition: The doing of things not required by God or abstaining from things not forbidden; having the fear of God towards created things, and not towards Jesus Christ alone.

Supplant: To remove or displace by deceiving or defrauding.

Supple: To clean by washing.

Suppliant: A worshipper, asking earnestly and submissively of God.

Supplication: A petition; an expression of need.

Suppose: A fact that may exist or be true.

Surety: The security or pledge for a person.

Surfeiting: Intoxication; overindulgence in food.

Surmisings: Suspicions; to think or conclude without certain or strong evidence.

Surname: An added name taken from someone's occupation or other circumstance.

Sustenance: That which supports life; food; victuals; provisions.

Swaddle: Clothes bound tight around the body.

Swaddling clothes: Clothes used for wrapping.

Swaddlingband: A long piece of clothing for swaddling an infant.

Swear: To utter or affirm with a solemn appeal to God for the truth of a declaration, as to swear an oath.

Swelling of Jordan: An earthly picture for the swelling of the heart.

Swellings: Being puffed-up; inflated attitudes; conceits.

Swine: Pig; regarded as the most unclean and the most abhorred of all animals: or, a picture of a person who is unclean before God, being unsaved.

Swoon: To pass out from weakness, physical or emotional.

Sworn: To make a solemn declaration or affirmation as true under an oath.

Synagogue: A gathering; an assembly for worship.

Syriack: The Syriac and the Chaldee language.

Tabering: To strike or beat, on a small drum or the tabret: or, upon the chest.

Tabernacle: A tent; a booth or dwelling.

Table: A writing tablet.

Tablets: Ornaments or jewelry worn on different parts of the body.

Tabret: A tambourine; a small drum.

Taches: Hooks; fasteners; clasps.

Tackling: Gear and rope used on ships.

Take up: To lift up and take to yourself; to obtain on credit.

Take: To trap; to catch.

Tale: A carefully counted number; a number of things; a list or series; a count or total.

Talebearer: A wounding whisperer, one who spreads hurtful stories or idle tales, with slandering gossip.

Talent: In the Old Testament, generally a disk of precious metal (gold, silver, etc.) weighing one talent: or, an Old Testament weight standard, 66 pounds: or, a New Testament currency, $1,200: or, a New Testament weight, 75 pounds.

Tales: A story or information given; idle tales.

Talitha cumi: A Syriac or Aramaic expression, meaning, little maid arise.

Tammuz: Forth month in the Hebrew calendar; our June-July.

Tanner: A trade to tan animal skins for clothing.

Tapestry: A kind of woven hangings of wool and silk, showing figures of men, animals, or landscapes.

Tares: Weeds found with grain; it bears the closest likeness to wheat until the ear appears, and only then, the difference is discovered.

Target: A small shield or buckler.

Tarry: To stay; to abide; to continue; to lodge.

Tartak: Prince of darkness; one of the gods of the Avite or Avite colonists of Samaria; being worshipped under the form of an ass.

Tartan: The title of the highest official next to the king; the commander-in-chief.

Tattler: One who tattles; an idle talker; one that tells tales.

Taunt: An object of scorn, disdain and disregard.

Tavern: A village or station; a public house for travelers and others.

Taxation: A required payment.

Taxing: A registration; a census.

Teats: Breasts.

Tebeth: Tenth month in the Hebrew calendar; our December-January.

Tedious: Being tiresome because of the length of time in some action, having slowness or dullness in the mind.

Teil tree: An oak tree.

Tell: To number; to count.

Temper: To mingle; to mix; to sprinkle; or to moisten.

Temperance: Self-control or moderation.

Temperate: To exercise power or self-control; moderate in the indulgence of the appetites and passions.

Tempest: A storm; whirlwind; hard winds.

Tempestuous: As tempestuous weather; blowing with violence; as a tempestuous wind.

Temporal: Relating to time, not to eternity; relating to earthly life.

Tempt: To try; to test; to prove; to put to trial for proof; to incite or solicit to an evil act; to entice to something wrong by presenting arguments that are plausible or convincing, or by the offer of some pleasure or apparent advantage as the attraction.

Temptation: The act of tempting; enticement to evil by arguments, by flattery, or by the offer of some real or apparent good.

Tempter: Satan is the great tempter of mankind; and by his promise of reward.

Tend: To be directed to any end or purpose; to aim at; to have or give a leaning to; to apply oneself to the care of something.

Tenon: Projections on a piece of wood, which fit into corresponding holes to make a joint.

Tenor: Stamp; the character of a subject; the general course or thought.

Tenth deal: About a gallon, equal to one-tenth of an ephah; a tenth to give out as a share or portion.

Teraphim: Idols for worship; images in human form.

Termed: A state of acceptance or understanding.

Terrestrial: Things of the earth.

Terrible: God is terrible by reason of his awful greatness, His infinite power, His perfect holiness.

Testament: A covenant; an agreement; a will.

Testator: One who has made a legally valid will before death.

Testimony: A witness; evidence; proof of some fact.

Tetrarch: A ruler over the fourth part of a country.

Th, (ending on words): The third person, the one spoken about.

Theatre: A place of amusement; a place where public plays, games, and battles were acted in honor of the goddess Diana.

Thee: You.

Thee-ward: Toward you.

Thence: There; that place.

Theophilus: The person to whom the evangelist Luke sent his gospel and the Acts of the Apostles; his name means, a lover of God.

Thereabout: About that.

Thereat: At that place.

Thereby: By that; by it; as a result of that.

Therefrom: From that.

Therein: In that.

Thereinto: Into that.

Thereof: Of that.

Thereon: On that.

Thereout: Out of that.

Thereto: To that.

Thereunto: Unto that.

Thereupon: Upon that.

Therewith: With it; with that.

Thicket: A thick or dense growth of trees or shrubs.

Thine: Your or yours.

Thistle: Thorns; a prickly plant.

Thither: To that place.

Thitherward: In that direction; towards a place.

Thong: A strap of leather, used for fastening anything.

Thou: You.

Thought, (no): The thoughts of this life; earthly thoughts.

Threescore: Sixty.

Threshing: The separation of grain or seeds from the husks and straw.

Thrice: Three times.

Throng: To crowd together; to press close together.

Thummim: A precious stones worn by the high priest upon his breastplate; meaning, lights and perfections.

Thy: Your.

Thyine wood: A sweet smelling wood.

Tidal: A man called, The King of nations.

Tidings: Giving or getting information, news, or notification, about something.

Till, Tillage: Cultivate; cultivation; preparing the land for seeding.

Tiller: Someone who tills or works the soil for farming: or, a box to keep money in.

Timbrel: A small drum or tambourine.

Tire: A turban; a head ornament: or, to put on a head ornament.

Tithe: The tenth part.

Tittle: A small stroke or mark on a Hebrew letter to denote accent: or, a picture of anything very small.

Toil: To labor; to work; to exert strength, with efforts of some continuance or duration.

Token: A sign; a symbol or visible representation of something.

Told out: Numbered; counted; tallied.

Toll: A tax paid for some liberty or privilege; a tribute.

Tombs: Made of solid rock, or were natural caves or made in gardens.

Tongues on the apostles: The reunion of the scattered nations; the gift of the Holy Spirit.

Tongues, (confusion of): At Babel, the cause of the early separation of mankind and their division into nations.

Topaz: It varies in color from a pale-green to a bottle green.

Torches: A hand lamp; a light usually carried in the hand; consists of some flammable substance at the top of a poll.

Tormentor: A torturer.

Tow: Coarse fibers of flax or hemp used for spinning.

Traffick: To pass goods from one person to another for an equivalent in goods or money; to barter; to buy and sell products.

Trance: A condition in which the mental powers are partly or wholly unresponsive to external impressions.

Transfigured: To change entirely the nature or appearance.

Transgression: Wrongdoing; a violation of a law.

Translate: To transfer; to take up to heaven; to carry or remove from one place to another.

Travail: To express extreme and painful sorrow; childbirth: or, the labor of one's daily work.

Traversing: Turning; interweaving; entangling.

Treacherous: Marked by unforeseen hazards; dangerous or deceptive.

Treason: A conspiracy; the betrayal of a trust or confidence.

Treatise: A brief narrative on a subject of interest.

Trespass: Wrong doings; any sin or violation of law, civil or moral.

Tribulation: A season of affliction, suffering, troubles, and distresses which proceed from persecution.

Tribute: A tax of 2 days' wages; a tax imposed by a king on his subjects.

Trimmest: Being diligent and industrious to make your way prosper.

Trodden: To trample; to walk over.

Trode: Trampled; stepped on.

Troublous: Full of trouble, disorder, and affliction.

Trough: A narrow open container, in which food or water for animals is put.

Trow: Think on; to suppose; to trust; think not.

Trump: Trumpet.

Tumultuous: Conduct full of uproar and disorder.

Turtle: A turtle dove.

Tutor: A private instructor; a guardian.

Twain: Two.

Twine: Two or more small threads twined together.

Twofold: Two of the same kind; two different things existing together; double; as twofold strength or desire.

Tyrus: City of Tyre.

Unawares, (at): Suddenly; unexpectedly; secretly; without previous preparation; without premeditated design.

Uncomely: Unsuitable; unpresentable; not in keeping with accepted standards of what is right or proper in polite society.

Unction: An anointing; divine or sanctifying grace; an allusion to the anointing oil under the law.

Undefiled: Being free from all guilt, disgrace, or shame.

Undergird: To form the basis or foundation of something; the strength of something.

Undergirding: Passing ropes under a ship to strengthen it.

Undersetter: Something used to prop; or as a support; like a pedestal to hold up things.

Undertake: To be a surety; to take upon or assume any business or province.

Unfeigned: Not counterfeit; not hypocritical; being real, sincere, true, and pure.

Ungirded: Loosed from something; to unbind; to unload.

Unicorn: A wild ox or bull.

Unlade: To discharge; to unload a burden.

Unperfect: Imperfect; unformed; unfolded.

Unruly: A person who does not like restraints; and no man can tame.

Unsatiable: Someone in a condition of not being satisfied.

Unseemly: Inappropriate; not becoming; indecent.

Unshod: Barefooted; not wearing shoes.

Untempered: Referring to mortar made with clay instead of slaked lime; houses made with untempered things can be broken down by a push or a heavy rainstorm.

Untimely: Happening before the natural time; premature.

Untoward: Perverse; unruly; unteachable persons.

Unwashed: Not cleansed by water for holy duties.

Upbraid: To scold; to reproach; reprimand.

Urim: A precious stone worn by the high priest upon his breastplate; meaning, lights and perfections.

Usurer: A person who lent money and took interest for it.

Usurp: To seize and take hold of; or take over.

Usury: Interest on money lent.

Usward: Towards us.

Utmost: Outermost part; the extreme; being at the furthest point or extremity; being in the greatest or highest degree; the most that can be; the greatest power, degree or effort.

Utter court: Outer court.

Utter gate: Outer gate.

Utter: Outer.

Utter: To speak; to pronounce; to express; as, to utter words.

Utterly: Completely; absolutely; entirely.

Uttermost: Outermost: or, in the most extensive degree; fully; extreme.

Vagabond: Wandering; one being in an everlasting unsettledness and fear; in a reprobate or rejected state.

Vail: A cloth that covers something.

Vain: Empty; foolish; useless.

Vainglory: Extreme self-pride and boastfulness; empty glory or pride.

Vale: A valley; a tract of low ground.

Valiant: Mighty men; possessing or displaying courage.

Valley of the shadow of death: In the midst of trouble; having depression.

Valour: Having courage or bravery.

Vanity: Falsehoods; what is fleeting; unsatisfying; and profitless.

Vapour: A substance in the gas like state; different from liquid or solid.

Variableness: Likely to change or vary; being changeable.

Variance: Contention; strife; the quality of being unlike or dissimilar.

Vaunt: To boast; lifting up oneself.

Vehemently: Violently; intensely; forcefully.

Veil: In relation to something being uncovered or revealed.

Vein: Lengthy and regularly shaped occurrence of ore in stone.

Venison: The flesh of a hunted game animal used as food; deer meat.

Venture: An undertaking that is risky or of uncertain outcome: or, at random; at chance, without seeing the end or mark.

Verily: Truly; surely; indeed; amen.

Verity: Truth; an offer that is a fact.

Vermilion: Mercuric sulfide used as a bright red pigment.

Vestments: Official garments; clothing; robes.

Vestry: A wardrobe; storeroom for robes.

Vesture: A garment the priest in the temple wore; a cloke; clothing.

Vex: To trouble; disturb; to agitate; cause to be perplexed or confounded: or, to crush or harm.

Vexation: Trouble; distress; affliction.

Vial: A shallow bowl or dish; vials of God's wrath in Scripture, are the execution of his wrath upon the wicked for their sins.

Victuals: Food; sustenance.

Vigilant: Watchful.

Vile: Wicked; filthy: or, lowly.

Vilest: Lowest; despised.

Villany: Emptiness; folly and wickedness.

Vine: A plant that produces grapes, in a great number of varieties; The expression "vine of Sodom" means "a vine whose juices and fruits were not fresh and healthy, but tainted by the corruption of which Sodom was the type" Figurative: Every man "under his vine and under his fig-tree" was a sign of national peace and prosperity. To plant vineyards and eat the fruit thereof implied long and settled habitation. To plant and not eat the fruit was a misfortune and might be a sign of God's displeasure. Not to plant vines might be a sign of deliberate avoidance of permanent habitation. A successful and prolonged vintage showed God's blessing, and a fruitful wife is compared to a vine; a failure of the vine was a sign of God's wrath; it might be a test of faith in Him. Joseph "is a fruitful bough,... his branches run over the wall". Israel is a vine brought out of Egypt; At a later period vine leaves or grape clusters figure prominently on Jewish coins or in architecture. Three of our Lord's parables are connected with vineyards, and He has made the vine ever sacred in Christian symbolism by His teaching regarding the true vine (Jn 15).

Vine-dresser: One who dresses, trims, prunes and cultivates vines.

Vine of Sodom: Meaning, the things coming from there; the wickedness of its inhabitants brought down upon it fire from heaven.

Vinegar: Could take away one's thirst; used as a picture of bitterness.

Vintage: The time of grape gathering.

Viol: A lyre; a stringed instrument; a kind of harp.

Violate: To break or disregard a law or promise.

Viper: Snake.

Virtue: Acting power and strength; something efficacious; that substance or quality that will produce effects on other bodies.

Virtuous: Characterized by or possessing virtue or moral excellence.

Visage: The appearance of a person; an expression; the look on the face; one's form.

Visitation: God viewing men's character and deeds and to give them their due lot or portion, whether of reward or of chastisement.

Vocation: A calling; an invitation; a summons.

Void: To vacate; to annul; to nullify; to render of no use or effect.

Volume: A roll or scroll; the Scriptures or sacred writings, bound in a single volume, is called the Bible.

Vow: A solemn promise; as the vows of unchangeable love and fidelity.

Vulture: A large bird of prey feeding mainly on dead bodies.

Wafers: Thin cakes; unleavened bread anointed with oil.

Wail: To lament with mournful sounds, because of grief or misery.

Wallow: To roll in; to tumble and roll in mud.

Want: Lack; be deficient or in need.

Wanton: Excessive; being rebellious, without restraint.

Wantonness: Extreme indulgence in sensual pleasures.

Ward, (being in): In prison; custody; under guard: or, on guard; on watch.

Ware: Aware: or, singular for wares.

Wares: Many products of riches and merchandise; art or craft, or farm produce.

Warp: The threads which are extended lengthwise in the loom, and crossed by the woof.

Wast: Were.

Watch: – first – 6.00pm to 9.00pm (not mentioned): second – 9.00pm to midnight: third – midnight to 3.00am: fourth – 3.00am to 6.00am: middle – 10.00pm to 2.00am: morning – 2.00am to 6.00am. (In pre-Roman times, the Jews had three watches of four hours).

Watchman: One who stands on the city walls or on the hilltops, to stand guard or keep watch.

Waterspouts: Waterfalls.

Wax: To grow; to become; to advance.

Wayfaring man: A traveler; a passer-by.

Waymark: A guidepost; a small stone pillar set on the roadside, with an indication of routes and distances.

Wayside: The outside limit of an object, area, or surface; the side or edge of a road.

Weaned: To detach from that which one is strongly attached to or devoted to.

Wedlock: The state of marriage; living in matrimony.

Wen: A running sore; a tumor.

Wench: A maidservant of a socially low class.

Wert: Were.

Whale: A picture of someone who has a wild, untamable nature: or, a sea monster.

What need: Why need.

Whelp: A baby animal.

When as: When.

Whence: From where.

Whereabout: About which.

Whereas: Although.

Whereby: By what.

Wherefore: Why? For what reason? For what cause?

Wherein: In which.

Whereinsoever: In whatever respect.

Whereinto: Into which.

Whereof: Of which.

Whereon: On which.

Whereto: To what; to which.

Whereunto: Unto what; unto which.

Whereupon: Upon what; upon which.

Wherewith: The things with which.

Wherewithal: How? By what means?

Whet: To sharpen; to rub for the purpose of sharpening, as an edged tool.

Whether is: Which of the two.

Which: Who.

Whiles: Describing when an action is taking place.

Whit, (every): Everything.

Whit, (not a): Not in anything.

Whit: A least bit; a point.

Whither: Where; in which place.

Whithersoever: Wherever.

Wholesome: Having soundness in body or mind, free from infirmity or disease.

Wholly: To the whole amount; to the full or entire extent.

Whore: To have unlawful sexual practices.

Whoremonger: A person who is joined with whores, who pays for goods or services.

Whorish: Being lewd, unchaste, addicted to forbidden sexual pleasures.

Wiles: The cunning devices, subtle, and methods of the devil.

Will: Wish; desire; to command; to direct.

Willows: Used in constructing booths at the feast of tabernacles; they spring up along watercourses.

Wilt: Will.

Wimples: A woman's garment; a hood or vail.

Winebibber: A drinker of wine; a drunkard.

Winefat, (vat): A collection trough beneath a winepress.

Winepress: A tub in which juice is taken from grapes by means of a plunger.

Wines on the lees: Wine fermented from its sediments.

Winked at: Overlooked, as took no notice of it.

Winnow: To throw up grain in the air so that the chaff may be separated from the wheat.

Wis: To think or imagine.

Wist: Knew; to have known; supposed.

Wit, (we do you to): We are letting you know.

Wit: To know; to become aware of: or, that is to say.

Witchcraft: Sorcery; enchantment; working craft by the means of devils.

Withal: At the same time; together with; also.

Wither: Where: or, to fade; to waste; to pine way.

Without: Outside.

Withs: Cords or ropes twisted.

Wits: Having sharp perception or judgment.

Wittingly: An action with knowledge: or, awareness of something.

Witty: Clever; skillful.

Wizard: Having magical influence or power, by the means of devils; it is forbidden by God.

Woe worth the day: Alas for the day.

Woe: An expression of grief or indignation.

Woeful: A condition of deep suffering from misfortune; affliction; or grief.

Wont: Accustomed; regularly; using or doing customarily.

Wood: The forest.

Woof: The yarn woven across the warp yarn in weaving.

Worldly: Fleshly; common; belonging to the world; as worldly actions; worldly ideas; the lust of the flesh, and the lust of the eyes, and the pride of life.

Wormwood: A bitter plant; a picture of bitterness.

Worship, (have): Have respect; have honor.

Worship: To adore; paying divine honors to; to reverence with supreme respect and veneration to God alone.

Worthy: Having worth, merit or value; being honorable or admirable.

Wot: To know; to be aware.

Would to God: Oh that!

Would: Will or desire to do.

Wrath: The just punishment of an offense or crime; his holy and just indignation against sin.

Wreathen: The twisting together of rope or chains.

Wrest: To wrench; to twist; to distort; to take truth and its natural meaning, and violently pervert it to vanity.

Wretched: Very miserable; sunk into deep affliction or distress: or, one that is hatefully, vile and contemptible.

Wring: Wrung; to force out; to squeeze out by twisting.

Wroth: To be provoked; to be angered.

Wrought: Worked; made.

Ye: You, (always plural in the bible).

Yea: Yes; certainly.

Yesternight: The last night.

Yield: To give place; to comply with; to permit or to grant permission: or, to produce crops, livestock, and fruits.

Yoke: A straight bar fastened to the necks of cattle, to keep them on a desired path; to couple; to join with another; to restrain; to confine.

Yokefellow: An associate or companion; being together in closeness.

Yonder: There; in that place.

You: (always plural in the bible).

Your: (always plural in the bible).

Youward: Toward or to you.

Zamzummims: A race of giants.

Zealous: Warmly engaged and a burning desire in the pursuit of an object.

Zif: Second month in the Hebrew calendar; our April-May.

Bible Reading Plan

By following this reading plan throughout the year, you will read the Old Testament through once and the New Testament twice.

January

1/1 _ Genesis 1-2 _ Psalms 1-2 _ Matthew 1-2
1/2 _ Genesis 3-4 _ Psalms 3-5 _ Matthew 3-4
1/3 _ Genesis 5-6 _ Psalms 6-8 _ Matthew 5
1/4 _ Genesis 7-8 _ Psalms 9-10 _ Matthew 6
1/5 _ Genesis 9-10 _ Psalms 11-13 _ Matthew 7
1/6 _ Genesis 11-12 _ Psalms 14-16 _ Matthew 8
1/7 _ Genesis 13-14 _ Psalms 17 _ Matthew 9
1/8 _ Genesis 15-16 _ Psalms 18 _ Matthew 10
1/9 _ Genesis 17-18 _ Psalms 19-21 _ Matthew 11
1/10 _ Genesis 19 _ Psalms 22 _ Matthew 12
1/11 _ Genesis 20-21 _ Psalms 23-25 _ Matthew 13
1/12 _ Genesis 22-23 _ Psalms 26-29 _ Matthew 14
1/13 _ Genesis 24 _ Psalms 30 _ Matthew 15
1/14 _ Genesis 25-26 _ Psalms 31 _ Matthew 16
1/15 _ Genesis 27 _ Psalms 32 _ Matthew 17
1/16 _ Genesis 28-29 _ Psalms 33 _ Matthew 18
1/17 _ Genesis 30 _ Psalms 34 _ Matthew 19
1/18 _ Genesis 31 _ Psalms 35 _ Matthew 20
1/19 _ Genesis 32-33 _ Psalms 36 _ Matthew 21
1/20 _ Genesis 34-35 _ Psalms 37 _ Matthew 22
1/21 _ Genesis 36 _ Psalms 38 _ Matthew 23
1/22 _ Genesis 37 _ Psalms 39-40 _ Matthew 24
1/23 _ Genesis 38 _ Psalms 41-43 _ Matthew 25
1/24 _ Genesis 39-40 _ Psalms 44 _ Matthew 26
1/25 _ Genesis 41 _ Psalms 45 _ Matthew 27
1/26 _ Genesis 42-43 _ Psalms 46-48 _ Matthew 28
1/27 _ Genesis 44-45 _ Psalms 49 _ Romans 1-2
1/28 _ Genesis 46-47 _ Psalms 50 _ Romans 3-4
1/29 _ Genesis 48-50 _ Psalms 51-52 _ Romans 5-6
1/30 _ Exodus 1-2 _ Psalms 53-55 _ Romans 7-8
1/31 _ Exodus 3-4 _ Psalms 56-57 _ Romans 9

February

2/1 _ Exodus 5-6 _ Psalms 58-59 _ Romans 10-11
2/2 _ Exodus 7-8 _ Psalms 60-61 _ Romans 12
2/3 _ Exodus 9 _ Psalms 62-63 _ Romans 13-14
2/4 _ Exodus 10 _ Psalms 64-65 _ Romans 15-16
2/5 _ Exodus 11-12 _ Psalms 66-67 _ Mark 1
2/6 _ Exodus 13-14 _ Psalms 68 _ Mark 2
2/7 _ Exodus 15 _ Psalms 69 _ Mark 3
2/8 _ Exodus 16 _ Psalms 70-71 _ Mark 4
2/9 _ Exodus 17-18 _ Psalms 72 _ Mark 5
2/10 _ Exodus 19-20 _ Psalms 73 _ Mark 6
2/11 _ Exodus 21 _ Psalms 74 _ Mark 7
2/12 _ Exodus 22 _ Psalms 75-76 _ Mark 8
2/13 _ Exodus 23 _ Psalms 77 _ Mark 9
2/14 _ Exodus 24-25 _ Psalms 78 _ Mark 10
2/15 _ Exodus 26 _ Psalms 79-80 _ Mark 11
2/16 _ Exodus 27 _ Psalms 81-82 _ Mark 12
2/17 _ Exodus 28 _ Psalms 83-84 _ Mark 13
2/18 _ Exodus 29 _ Psalms 85-86 _ Mark 14
2/19 _ Exodus 30 _ Psalms 87-88 _ Mark 15-16
2/20 _ Exodus 31-32 _ Psalms 89 _ 1 Corinthians 1-2
2/21 _ Exodus 33-34 _ Psalms 90-91 _ 1 Corinthians 3
2/22 _ Exodus 35 _ Psalms 92-93 _ 1 Corinthians 4-5
2/23 _ Exodus 36 _ Psalms 94-95 _ 1 Corinthians 6
2/24 _ Exodus 37 _ Psalms 96-99 _ 1 Corinthians 7
2/25 _ Exodus 38 _ Psalms 100-101 _ 1 Corinthians 8-9
2/26 _ Exodus 39-40 _ Psalms 102 _ 1 Corinthians 10
2/27 _ Leviticus 1-2 _ Psalms 103 _ 1 Corinthians 11
2/28 _ Leviticus 3-4 _ Psalms 104 _ 1 Corinthians 12-13

March

3/1 _ Leviticus 5-6 _ Psalms 105 _ 1 Corinthians 14
3/2 _ Leviticus 7 _ Psalms 106 _ 1 Corinthians 15
3/3 _ Leviticus 8 _ Psalms 107 _ 1 Corinthians 16
3/4 _ Leviticus 9-10 _ Psalms 108-109 _ 2 Corinthians 1-2
3/5 _ Leviticus 11 _ Psalms 110-112 _ 2 Corinthians 3-4
3/6 _ Leviticus 12-13 _ Psalms 113-114 _ 2 Corinthians 5-7
3/7 _ Leviticus 14 _ Psalms 115-116 _ 2 Corinthians 8-9
3/8 _ Leviticus 15 _ Psalms 117-118 _ 2 Corinthians 10-11
3/9 _ Leviticus 16 _ Psalms 119:1-40 _ 2 Corinthians 12-13

3/10 _ Leviticus 17-18 _ Psalms 119:41-80 _ Luke 1
3/11 _ Leviticus 19 _ Psalms 119:81-128 _ Luke 2
3/12 _ Leviticus 20 _ Psalms 119:129-176 _ Luke 3
3/13 _ Leviticus 21 _ Psalms 120-124 _ Luke 4
3/14 _ Leviticus 22 _ Psalms 125-127 _ Luke 5
3/15 _ Leviticus 23 _ Psalms 128-130 _ Luke 6
3/16 _ Leviticus 24 _ Psalms 131-134 _ Luke 7
3/17 _ Leviticus 25 _ Psalms 135-136 _ Luke 8
3/18 _ Leviticus 26 _ Psalms 137-139 _ Luke 9
3/19 _ Leviticus 27 _ Psalms 140-142 _ Luke 10
3/20 _ Numbers 1 _ Psalms 143-144 _ Luke 11
3/21 _ Numbers 2 _ Psalms 145-147 _ Luke 12
3/22 _ Numbers 3 _ Psalms 148-150 _ Luke 13-14
3/23 _ Numbers 4 _ Proverbs 1 _ Luke 15
3/24 _ Numbers 5 _ Proverbs 2 _ Luke 16
3/25 _ Numbers 6 _ Proverbs 3 _ Luke 17
3/26 _ Numbers 7 _ Proverbs 4 _ Luke 18
3/27 _ Numbers 8-9 _ Proverbs 5 _ Luke 19
3/28 _ Numbers 10 _ Proverbs 6 _ Luke 20
3/29 _ Numbers 11 _ Proverbs 7 _ Luke 21
3/30 _ Numbers 12-13 _ Proverbs 8-9 _ Luke 22
3/31 _ Numbers 14 _ Proverbs 10 _ Luke 23

April

4/1 _ Numbers 15 _ Proverbs 11 _ Luke 24
4/2 _ Numbers 16 _ Proverbs 12 _ Galatians 1-2
4/3 _ Numbers 17-18 _ Proverbs 13 _ Galatians 3-4
4/4 _ Numbers 19 _ Proverbs 14 _ Galatians 5-6
4/5 _ Numbers 20-21 _ Proverbs 15 _ Ephesians 1-2
4/6 _ Numbers 22-23 _ Proverbs 16 _ Ephesians 3-4
4/7 _ Numbers 24-25 _ Proverbs 17 _ Ephesians 5-6
4/8 _ Numbers 26 _ Proverbs 18 _ Philippians 1-2
4/9 _ Numbers 27 _ Proverbs 19 _ Philippians 3-4
4/10 _ Numbers 28 _ Proverbs 20 _ John 1
4/11 _ Numbers 29-30 _ Proverbs 21 _ John 2-3
4/12 _ Numbers 31 _ Proverbs 22 _ John 4
4/13 _ Numbers 32 _ Proverbs 23 _ John 5
4/14 _ Numbers 33 _ Proverbs 24 _ John 6
4/15 _ Numbers 34 _ Proverbs 25 _ John 7
4/16 _ Numbers 35 _ Proverbs 26 _ John 8
4/17 _ Numbers 36 _ Proverbs 27 _ John 9-10

4/18 _ Deuteronomy 1 _ Proverbs 28 _ John 11
4/19 _ Deuteronomy 2 _ Proverbs 29 _ John 12
4/20 _ Deuteronomy 3 _ Proverbs 30 _ John 13-14
4/21 _ Deuteronomy 4 _ Proverbs 31 _ John 15-16
4/22 _ Deuteronomy 5 _ Ecclesiastes 1 _ John 17-18
4/23 _ Deuteronomy 6-7 _ Ecclesiastes 2 _ John 19
4/24 _ Deuteronomy 8-9 _ Ecclesiastes 3 _ John 20-21
4/25 _ Deuteronomy 10-11 _ Ecclesiastes 4 _ Acts 1
4/26 _ Deuteronomy 12 _ Ecclesiastes 5 _ Acts 2
4/27 _ Deuteronomy 13-14 _ Ecclesiastes 6 _ Acts 3-4
4/28 _ Deuteronomy 15 _ Ecclesiastes 7 _ Acts 5-6
4/29 _ Deuteronomy 16 _ Ecclesiastes 8 _ Acts 7
4/30 _ Deuteronomy 17 _ Ecclesiastes 9 _ Acts 8

May

5/1 _ Deuteronomy 18 _ Ecclesiastes 10 _ Acts 9
5/2 _ Deuteronomy 19 _ Ecclesiastes 11 _ Acts 10
5/3 _ Deuteronomy 20 _ Ecclesiastes 12 _ Acts 11-12
5/4 _ Deuteronomy 21 _ Song of Solomon 1 _ Acts 13
5/5 _ Deuteronomy 22 _ Song of Solomon 2 _ Acts 14-15
5/6 _ Deuteronomy 23 _ Song of Solomon 3 _ Acts 16-17
5/7 _ Deuteronomy 24 _ Song of Solomon 4 _ Acts 18-19
5/8 _ Deuteronomy 25 _ Song of Solomon 5 _ Acts 20
5/9 _ Deuteronomy 26 _ Song of Solomon 6 _ Acts 21-22
5/10 _ Deuteronomy 27 _ Song of Solomon 7 _ Acts 23-24
5/11 _ Deuteronomy 28 _ Song of Solomon 8 _ Acts 25-26
5/12 _ Deuteronomy 29 _ Isaiah 1 _ Acts 27
5/13 _ Deuteronomy 30 _ Isaiah 2 _ Acts 28
5/14 _ Deuteronomy 31 _ Isaiah 3-4 _ Colossians 1
5/15 _ Deuteronomy 32 _ Isaiah 5 _ Colossians 2
5/16 _ Deuteronomy 33-34 _ Isaiah 6 _ Colossians 3-4
5/17 _ Joshua 1 _ Isaiah 7 _ 1 Thessalonians 1-2
5/18 _ Joshua 2 _ Isaiah 8 _ 1 Thessalonians 3-4
5/19 _ Joshua 3-4 _ Isaiah 9 _ 1 Thessalonians 5
5/20 _ Joshua 5-6 _ Isaiah 10 _ 2 Thessalonians 1-2
5/21 _ Joshua 7 _ Isaiah 11 _ 2 Thessalonians 3
5/22 _ Joshua 8 _ Isaiah 12 _ 1 Timothy 1-3
5/23 _ Joshua 9 _ Isaiah 13 _ 1 Timothy 4-5
5/24 _ Joshua 10 _ Isaiah 14 _ 1 Timothy 6
5/25 _ Joshua 11 _ Isaiah 15 _ 2 Timothy 1
5/26 _ Joshua 12 _ Isaiah 16 _ 2 Timothy 2

5/27 _ Joshua 13 _ Isaiah 17-18 _ 2 Timothy 3-4
5/28 _ Joshua 14 _ Isaiah 19 _ Titus 1-3
5/29 _ Joshua 15 _ Isaiah 20-21 _ Philemon 1
5/30 _ Joshua 16 _ Isaiah 22 _ Hebrews 1-2
5/31 _ Joshua 17 _ Isaiah 23 _ Hebrews 3-5

June

6/1 _ Joshua 18 _ Isaiah 24 _ Hebrews 6-7
6/2 _ Joshua 19 _ Isaiah 25 _ Hebrews 8-9
6/3 _ Joshua 20-21 _ Isaiah 26-27 _ Hebrews 10
6/4 _ Joshua 22 _ Isaiah 28 _ Hebrews 11
6/5 _ Joshua 23-24 _ Isaiah 29 _ Hebrews 12
6/6 _ Judges 1 _ Isaiah 30 _ Hebrews 13
6/7 _ Judges 2-3 _ Isaiah 31 _ James 1
6/8 _ Judges 4-5 _ Isaiah 32 _ James 2
6/9 _ Judges 6 _ Isaiah 33 _ James 3-4
6/10 _ Judges 7-8 _ Isaiah 34 _ James 5
6/11 _ Judges 9 _ Isaiah 35 _ 1 Peter 1
6/12 _ Judges 10-11 _ Isaiah 36 _ 1 Peter 2
6/13 _ Judges 12-13 _ Isaiah 37 _ 1 Peter 3-5
6/14 _ Judges 14-15 _ Isaiah 38 _ 2 Peter 1-2
6/15 _ Judges 16 _ Isaiah 39 _ 2 Peter 3
6/16 _ Judges 17-18 _ Isaiah 40 _ 1 John 1-2
6/17 _ Judges 19 _ Isaiah 41 _ 1 John 3-4
6/18 _ Judges 20 _ Isaiah 42 _ 1 John 5
6/19 _ Judges 21 _ Isaiah 43 _ 2 John- 3 John
6/20 _ Ruth 1-2 _ Isaiah 44 _ Jude 1
6/21 _ Ruth 3-4 _ Isaiah 45 _ Revelation 1-2
6/22 _ 1 Samuel 1 _ Isaiah 46-47 _ Revelation 3-4
6/23 _ 1 Samuel 2 _ Isaiah 48 _ Revelation 5-6
6/24 _ 1 Samuel 3 _ Isaiah 49 _ Revelation 7-9
6/25 _ 1 Samuel 4 _ Isaiah 50 _ Revelation 10-11
6/26 _ 1 Samuel 5-6 _ Isaiah 51 _ Revelation 12-13
6/27 _ 1 Samuel 7-8 _ Isaiah 52 _ Revelation 14
6/28 _ 1 Samuel 9 _ Isaiah 53 _ Revelation 15-16
6/29 _ 1 Samuel 10 _ Isaiah 54 _ Revelation 17-18
6/30 _ 1 Samuel 11-12 _ Isaiah 55 _ Revelation 19-20

July

7/1 _ 1 Samuel 13 _ Isaiah 56-57 _ Revelation 21-22
7/2 _ 1 Samuel 14 _ Isaiah 58 _ Matthew 1-2
7/3 _ 1 Samuel 15 _ Isaiah 59 _ Matthew 3-4
7/4 _ 1 Samuel 16 _ Isaiah 60 _ Matthew 5
7/5 _ 1 Samuel 17 _ Isaiah 61 _ Matthew 6
7/6 _ 1 Samuel 18 _ Isaiah 62 _ Matthew 7
7/7 _ 1 Samuel 19 _ Isaiah 63 _ Matthew 8
7/8 _ 1 Samuel 20 _ Isaiah 64 _ Matthew 9
7/9 _ 1 Samuel 21-22 _ Isaiah 65 _ Matthew 10
7/10 _ 1 Samuel 23 _ Isaiah 66 _ Matthew 11
7/11 _ 1 Samuel 24 _ Jeremiah 1 _ Matthew 12
7/12 _ 1 Samuel 25 _ Jeremiah 2 _ Matthew 13
7/13 _ 1 Samuel 26-27 _ Jeremiah 3 _ Matthew 14
7/14 _ 1 Samuel 28 _ Jeremiah 4 _ Matthew 15
7/15 _ 1 Samuel 29-30 _ Jeremiah 5 _ Matthew 16
7/16 _ 1 Samuel 31 _ Jeremiah 6 _ Matthew 17
7/17 _ 2 Samuel 1 _ Jeremiah 7 _ Matthew 18
7/18 _ 2 Samuel 2 _ Jeremiah 8 _ Matthew 19
7/19 _ 2 Samuel 3 _ Jeremiah 9 _ Matthew 20
7/20 _ 2 Samuel 4-5 _ Jeremiah 10 _ Matthew 21
7/21 _ 2 Samuel 6 _ Jeremiah 11 _ Matthew 22
7/22 _ 2 Samuel 7 _ Jeremiah 12 _ Matthew 23
7/23 _ 2 Samuel 8-9 _ Jeremiah 13 _ Matthew 24
7/24 _ 2 Samuel 10 _ Jeremiah 14 _ Matthew 25
7/25 _ 2 Samuel 11 _ Jeremiah 15 _ Matthew 26
7/26 _ 2 Samuel 12 _ Jeremiah 16 _ Matthew 27
7/27 _ 2 Samuel 13 _ Jeremiah 17 _ Matthew 28
7/28 _ 2 Samuel 14 _ Jeremiah 18 _ Romans 1-2
7/29 _ 2 Samuel 15 _ Jeremiah 19 _ Romans 3-4
7/30 _ 2 Samuel 16 _ Jeremiah 20 _ Romans 5-6
7/31 _ 2 Samuel 17 _ Jeremiah 21 _ Romans 7-8

August

8/1 _ 2 Samuel 18 _ Jeremiah 22 _ Romans 9
8/2 _ 2 Samuel 19 _ Jeremiah 23 _ Romans 10-11
8/3 _ 2 Samuel 20-21 _ Jeremiah 24 _ Romans 12
8/4 _ 2 Samuel 22 _ Jeremiah 25 _ Romans 13-14
8/5 _ 2 Samuel 23 _ Jeremiah 26 _ Romans 15-16

8/6 _ 2 Samuel 24 _ Jeremiah 27 _ Mark 1
8/7 _ 1 Kings 1 _ Jeremiah 28 _ Mark 2
8/8 _ 1 Kings 2 _ Jeremiah 29 _ Mark 3
8/9 _ 1 Kings 3 _ Jeremiah 30 _ Mark 4
8/10 _ 1 Kings 4-5 _ Jeremiah 31 _ Mark 5
8/11 _ 1 Kings 6 _ Jeremiah 32 _ Mark 6
8/12 _ 1 Kings 7 _ Jeremiah 33 _ Mark 7
8/13 _ 1 Kings 8 _ Jeremiah 34 _ Mark 8
8/14 _ 1 Kings 9 _ Jeremiah 35 _ Mark 9
8/15 _ 1 Kings 10 _ Jeremiah 36 _ Mark 10
8/16 _ 1 Kings 11 _ Jeremiah 37 _ Mark 11
8/17 _ 1 Kings 12 _ Jeremiah 38 _ Mark 12
8/18 _ 1 Kings 13 _ Jeremiah 39 _ Mark 13
8/19 _ 1 Kings 14 _ Jeremiah 40 _ Mark 14
8/20 _ 1 Kings 15 _ Jeremiah 41 _ Mark 15
8/21 _ 1 Kings 16 _ Jeremiah 42 _ Mark 16
8/22 _ 1 Kings 17 _ Jeremiah 43 _ 1 Corinthians 1-2
8/23 _ 1 Kings 18 _ Jeremiah 44 _ 1 Corinthians 3
8/24 _ 1 Kings 19 _ Jeremiah 45-46 _ 1 Corinthians 4-5
8/25 _ 1 Kings 20 _ Jeremiah 47 _ 1 Corinthians 6
8/26 _ 1 Kings 21 _ Jeremiah 48 _ 1 Corinthians 7
8/27 _ 1 Kings 22 _ Jeremiah 49 _ 1 Corinthians 8-9
8/28 _ 2 Kings 1-2 _ Jeremiah 50 _ 1 Corinthians 10
8/29 _ 2 Kings 3 _ Jeremiah 51 _ 1 Corinthians 11
8/30 _ 2 Kings 4 _ Jeremiah 52 _ 1 Corinthians 12-13
8/31 _ 2 Kings 5 _ Lamentations 1 _ 1 Corinthians 14

September

9/1 _ 2 Kings 6 _ Lamentations 2 _ 1 Corinthians 15
9/2 _ 2 Kings 7 _ Lamentations 3 _ 1 Corinthians 16
9/3 _ 2 Kings 8 _ Lamentations 4 _ 2 Corinthians 1-2
9/4 _ 2 Kings 9 _ Lamentations 5 _ 2 Corinthians 3-4
9/5 _ 2 Kings 10 _ Ezekiel 1 _ 2 Corinthians 5-7
9/6 _ 2 Kings 11-12 _ Ezekiel 2 _ 2 Corinthians 8-9
9/7 _ 2 Kings 13 _ Ezekiel 3 _ 2 Corinthians 10-11
9/8 _ 2 Kings 14 _ Ezekiel 4 _ 2 Corinthians 12-13
9/9 _ 2 Kings 15 _ Ezekiel 5 _ Luke 1
9/10 _ 2 Kings 16 _ Ezekiel 6 _ Luke 2
9/11 _ 2 Kings 17 _ Ezekiel 7 _ Luke 3
9/12 _ 2 Kings 18 _ Ezekiel 8 _ Luke 4
9/13 _ 2 Kings 19 _ Ezekiel 9 _ Luke 5

9/14 _ 2 Kings 20 _ Ezekiel 10 _ Luke 6
9/15 _ 2 Kings 21 _ Ezekiel 11 _ Luke 7
9/16 _ 2 Kings 22-23 _ Ezekiel 12 _ Luke 8
9/17 _ 2 Kings 24-25 _ Ezekiel 13 _ Luke 9
9/18 _ 1 Chronicles 1 _ Ezekiel 14 _ Luke 10
9/19 _ 1 Chronicles 2 _ Ezekiel 15 _ Luke 11
9/20 _ 1 Chronicles 3 _ Ezekiel 16 _ Luke 12
9/21 _ 1 Chronicles 4 _ Ezekiel 17 _ Luke 13-14
9/22 _ 1 Chronicles 5 _ Ezekiel 18 _ Luke 15
9/23 _ 1 Chronicles 6 _ Ezekiel 19 _ Luke 16
9/24 _ 1 Chronicles 7 _ Ezekiel 20 _ Luke 17
9/25 _ 1 Chronicles 8 _ Ezekiel 21 _ Luke 18
9/26 _ 1 Chronicles 9 _ Ezekiel 22 _ Luke 19
9/27 _ 1 Chronicles 10 _ Ezekiel 23 _ Luke 20
9/28 _ 1 Chronicles 11 _ Ezekiel 24 _ Luke 21
9/29 _ 1 Chronicles 12 _ Ezekiel 25 _ Luke 22
9/30 _ 1 Chronicles 13-14 _ Ezekiel 26 _ Luke 23

October

10/1 _ 1 Chronicles 15 _ Ezekiel 27 _ Luke 24
10/2 _ 1 Chronicles 16 _ Ezekiel 28 _ Galatians 1-2
10/3 _ 1 Chronicles 17 _ Ezekiel 29 _ Galatians 3-4
10/4 _ 1 Chronicles 18-19 _ Ezekiel 30 _ Galatians 5-6
10/5 _ 1 Chronicles 20-21 _ Ezekiel 31 _ Ephesians 1-2
10/6 _ 1 Chronicles 22 _ Ezekiel 32 _ Ephesians 3-4
10/7 _ 1 Chronicles 23 _ Ezekiel 33 _ Ephesians 5-6
10/8 _ 1 Chronicles 24-25 _ Ezekiel 34 _ Philippians 1-2
10/9 _ 1 Chronicles 26 _ Ezekiel 35 _ Philippians 3-4
10/10 _ 1 Chronicles 27 _ Ezekiel 36 _ John 1
10/11 _ 1 Chronicles 28 _ Ezekiel 37 _ John 2-3
10/12 _ 1 Chronicles 29 _ Ezekiel 38 _ John 4
10/13 _ 2 Chronicles 1-2 _ Ezekiel 39 _ John 5
10/14 _ 2 Chronicles 3-4 _ Ezekiel 40 _ John 6
10/15 _ 2 Chronicles 5-6 _ Ezekiel 41 _ John 7
10/16 _ 2 Chronicles 7 _ Ezekiel 42 _ John 8
10/17 _ 2 Chronicles 8 _ Ezekiel 43 _ John 9-10
10/18 _ 2 Chronicles 9 _ Ezekiel 44 _ John 11
10/19 _ 2 Chronicles 10-11 _ Ezekiel 45 _ John 12
10/20 _ 2 Chronicles 12-13 _ Ezekiel 46 _ John 13-14
10/21 _ 2 Chronicles 14-15 _ Ezekiel 47 _ John 15-16
10/22 _ 2 Chronicles 16-17 _ Ezekiel 48 _ John 17-18

10/23 _ 2 Chronicles 18-19 _ Daniel 1 _ John 19
10/24 _ 2 Chronicles 20 _ Daniel 2 _ John 20-21
10/25 _ 2 Chronicles 21-22 _ Daniel 3 _ Acts 1
10/26 _ 2 Chronicles 23 _ Daniel 4 _ Acts 2
10/27 _ 2 Chronicles 24 _ Daniel 5 _ Acts 3-4
10/28 _ 2 Chronicles 25 _ Daniel 6 _ Acts 5-6
10/29 _ 2 Chronicles 26-27 _ Daniel 7 _ Acts 7
10/30 _ 2 Chronicles 28 _ Daniel 8 _ Acts 8
10/31 _ 2 Chronicles 29 _ Daniel 9 _ Acts 9

November

11/1 _ 2 Chronicles 30 _ Daniel 10 _ Acts 10
11/2 _ 2 Chronicles 31 _ Daniel 11 _ Acts 11-12
11/3 _ 2 Chronicles 32 _ Daniel 12 _ Acts 13
11/4 _ 2 Chronicles 33 _ Hosea 1 _ Acts 14-15
11/5 _ 2 Chronicles 34 _ Hosea 2 _ Acts 16-17
11/6 _ 2 Chronicles 35 _ Hosea 3 _ Acts 18-19
11/7 _ 2 Chronicles 36 _ Hosea 4 _ Acts 20
11/8 _ Ezra 1-2 _ Hosea 5 _ Acts 21-22
11/9 _ Ezra 3-4 _ Hosea 6 _ Acts 23-24
11/10 _ Ezra 5-6 _ Hosea 7 _ Acts 25-26
11/11 _ Ezra 7 _ Hosea 8 _ Acts 27
11/12 _ Ezra 8 _ Hosea 9 _ Acts 28
11/13 _ Ezra 9 _ Hosea 10 _ Colossians 1
11/14 _ Ezra 10 _ Hosea 11 _ Colossians 2
11/15 _ Nehemiah 1-2 _ Hosea 12 _ Colossians 3-4
11/16 _ Nehemiah 3 _ Hosea 13 _ 1 Thessalonians 1-2
11/17 _ Nehemiah 4 _ Hosea 14 _ 1 Thessalonians 3-4
11/18 _ Nehemiah 5-6 _ Joel 1 _ 1 Thessalonians 5
11/19 _ Nehemiah 7 _ Joel 2 _ 2 Thessalonians 1-2
11/20 _ Nehemiah 8 _ Joel 3 _ 2 Thessalonians 3
11/21 _ Nehemiah 9 _ Amos 1 _ 1 Timothy 1-3
11/22 _ Nehemiah 10 _ Amos 2 _ 1 Timothy 4-5
11/23 _ Nehemiah 11 _ Amos 3 _ 1 Timothy 6
11/24 _ Nehemiah 12 _ Amos 4 _ 2 Timothy 1
11/25 _ Nehemiah 13 _ Amos 5 _ 2 Timothy 2
11/26 _ Esther 1 _ Amos 6 _ 2 Timothy 3-4
11/27 _ Esther 2 _ Amos 7 _ Titus 1-3
11/28 _ Esther 3-4 _ Amos 8 _ Philemon 1
11/29 _ Esther 5-6 _ Amos 9 _ Hebrews 1-2
11/30 _ Esther 7-8 _ Obadiah 1 _ Hebrews 3-5

December

12/1 _ Esther 9-10 _ Jonah 1 _ Hebrews 6-7
12/2 _ Job 1-2 _ Jonah 2-3 _ Hebrews 8-9
12/3 _ Job 3-4 _ Jonah 4 _ Hebrews 10
12/4 _ Job 5 _ Micah 1 _ Hebrews 11
12/5 _ Job 6-7 _ Micah 2 _ Hebrews 12
12/6 _ Job 8 _ Micah 3-4 _ Hebrews 13
12/7 _ Job 9 _ Micah 5 _ James 1
12/8 _ Job 10 _ Micah 6 _ James 2
12/9 _ Job 11 _ Micah 7 _ James 3-4
12/10 _ Job 12 _ Nahum 1-2 _ James 5
12/11 _ Job 13 _ Nahum 3 _ 1 Peter 1
12/12 _ Job 14 _ Habakkuk 1 _ 1 Peter 2
12/13 _ Job 15 _ Habakkuk 2 _ 1 Peter 3-5
12/14 _ Job 16-17 _ Habakkuk 3 _ 2 Peter 1-2
12/15 _ Job 18-19 _ Zephaniah 1 _ 2 Peter 3
12/16 _ Job 20 _ Zephaniah 2 _ 1 John 1-2
12/17 _ Job 21 _ Zephaniah 3 _ 1 John 3-4
12/18 _ Job 22 _ Haggai 1-2 _ 1 John 5
12/19 _ Job 23-24 _ Zechariah 1 _ 2 John- 3 John
12/20 _ Job 25-27 _ Zechariah 2-3 _ Jude 1
12/21 _ Job 28 _ Zechariah 4-5 _ Revelation 1-2
12/22 _ Job 29-30 _ Zechariah 6-7 _ Revelation 3-4
12/23 _ Job 31-32 _ Zechariah 8 _ Revelation 5-6
12/24 _ Job 33 _ Zechariah 9 _ Revelation 7-9
12/25 _ Job 34 _ Zechariah 10 _ Revelation 10-11
12/26 _ Job 35-36 _ Zechariah 11 _ Revelation 12-13
12/27 _ Job 37 _ Zechariah 12 _ Revelation 14
12/28 _ Job 38 _ Zechariah 13-14 _ Revelation 15-16
12/29 _ Job 39 _ Malachi 1 _ Revelation 17-18
12/30 _ Job 40 _ Malachi 2 _ Revelation 19-20
12/31 _ Job 41-42 _ Malachi 3-4 _ Revelation 21-22